From the introduction by Max Frankel

"THIS IMPORTANT BOOK WILL COMMAND ATTENTION OVER MANY YEARS ON MANY LEVELS . . . A THROBBING DOCUMENT THAT TEACHES MANY LESSONS IN HOW TO PREVENT, MINIMIZE OR CONTAIN SUCH RECKLESS OUTBURSTS OF POLITICAL AND SOCIAL PASSION."

Here, in response to the widespread interest in a crucial episode in American history, Bantam Books is making the Walker Report available to readers across the nation and throughout the world less than a week after its official release to the press.

This edition contains the complete text of the Report, and all its supplementary material, exactly as it was submitted to the National Commission on the Causes and Prevention of Violence. It includes the extremely obscene language which was considered essential to the accuracy and effectiveness of the Report and was so significantly a part of the confrontation between demonstrators and police. It also reproduces the full photographic narrative, which gives the Report an unforgettable reality.

RIGHTS IN CONFLICT

The Violent Confrontation of Demonstrators and Police in the Parks and Streets of Chicago During the Week of the Democratic National Convention of 1968

A Report Submitted by Daniel Walker,
Director of the Chicago
Study Team, to the National Commission on
the Causes and Prevention of Violence

Special Introduction by Max Frankel of
The New York Times

BANTAM BOOKS
NEW YORK • TORONTO • LONDON

*This book is available in a cloth edition
from E. P. Dutton & Co., Inc., 201 Park Avenue South,
New York, N. Y. 10003*

RIGHTS IN CONFLICT
A Bantam Book / published December 1968

Published simultaneously in the United States and Canada

Bantam Books are published by Bantam Books, Inc., a subsidiary of Grosset & Dunlap, Inc. Its trade-mark, consisting of the words "Bantam Books" and the portrayal of a bantam, is registered in the United States Patent Office and in other countries. Marca Registrada. Bantam Books, Inc., 271 Madison Avenue, New York, N.Y. 10016.

PRINTED IN THE UNITED STATES OF AMERICA

INTRODUCTION

BY MAX FRANKEL

We are known for our violence, we Americans. The creative violence with which we haul down the good for what we fancy as better. The cruel violence with which we have treated red men, and black. The intoxicating violence of our music and art. The absurd violence of our comics and cartoons. The organized violence of our athletic and corporate games. The coarse violence of our speech, even our jokes.

And now we have come violently to disagree about the nature of our violence in Vietnam or Dallas or Watts or Hiroshima. We seek the primitive within ourselves and bemoan the failure of affluence to civilize. Our young deplore the violence of the old and are tempted to use violence against them. The old deplore the ferocity of the young and are tempted to use violence to suppress them.

Thus we came, already maimed, to 1968. The ugly war in Asia dragged on. The proud President in the White House gave up. The Commission on Civil Disorders spoke, nay cried, about the bitter heritage of our racism. Martin Luther King fell slain, and the rotten cores of a hundred cities burned. Robert Kennedy fell slain, and even his safe suburban enemies wept.

In the summer of our discontent, not even George Wallace's angry young men could turn up a roster of scapegoats to blame by name. We threatened Dr. Spock, the permissive baby doctor, with jail for his prescriptions of dissent. And we railed, in the name of law and order, against the guardians of the law on the Supreme Court. We tried suppression here and appeasement there, but still the hostilities and frustrations and ambitions of the deprived, whether rich or poor, propelled us from melee to mayhem.

We perpetrated hate even in the name of love. Preachers and teachers, politicians and policemen were struck dumb, or furious. Columbia University collapsed in chaos. So did the Sorbonne, as if to challenge the last premise of American superiority. We were not unique or alone.

As we buried Robert Kennedy beside John, President Johnson named yet another commission, "on the causes and prevention of violence." Some judges and congressmen, a Negro woman, a longshoreman philosopher, a Roman Catholic Archbishop, an unimpeachable name, Dr. Milton Eisenhower, Chairman.

Another commission for another crisis to be ignored by another President?

To select that President the Republicans assembled in lush Miami Beach, insulated by water from the upheavals in black Miami. The Democrats converged on grimy Chicago, boldly defying the threats of disruption, sabotage and assassination. They nominated their most familiar and least abrasive contenders, Richard M. Nixon and Hubert H. Humphrey, in a vain but understandable effort to soothe the nerves of the nation. Yet whereas the Republicans escaped with a dull and decorous rally, the Democrats staged a brawl surrounded in the parks and streets of Chicago by a convulsion. The new National Commission on the Causes and Prevention of Violence had found its first substantial assignment, for there, in Chicago, two fundamental American rights in conflict had posed an essential question about our current violence: how can we assure both a people's right to dissent and a community's right to protect its citizens and property.

Rights in Conflict was the result.

This important book will command attention over many years on many levels.

It is a graphic and comprehensive account of the violence in the parks and streets of Chicago during the Democratic National Convention—August 25 to 29, 1968—driving dispassionately toward the momentous conclusion that many policemen charged with preserving law and order in the nation's second largest city at a crucial moment in history responded to the misbehavior, obstruction, obscenity and occasional violence of bands of provocateurs midst crowds of peaceful dissenters with frequently unrestrained and indiscriminate violence of their own, in thought, word and deed.

It characterizes the gas, mace and club attacks by policemen on peaceful demonstrators, innocent bystanders, newsmen, photographers and Chicago residents as often gratuitous, ferocious, malicious and mindless, and finds that they amounted to "what can only be called a police riot."

Given the anxiety of the city, its leaders and political visitors and the "exceedingly provocative circumstances" that developed in and out of Convention Hall, the reports says, the loss of police control and discipline "can perhaps be understood, but not condoned." If no action is taken against most of the offenders and if no effort is made to understand the deeper conflicts here exposed, it warns, there will follow not only discouragement among the majority of responsible policemen but a further strain between the police and the community and between governors and dissenters, in Chicago and throughout the nation.

Running through this book, as through the Chicago streets in that fateful week, are the demonstrators—peaceful and violent, purposeful and confused, inflammatory and jocular, bitter and idealistic—alternately parading their grievances against flag, country, party and all established doctrines of order and decorum and defying the efforts to contain or disperse them, resorting to petty insult or outrageous taunt of the police but driven also to physical barricading, the throwing of rocks and other dangerous objects, the burning of trash cans and the spreading of foul-smelling chemicals.

Overwhelming these impressions, however, is the testimony of horrendous police action, the clubbing of innocent and injured citizens merely because they were dirty or long-haired or affluent and educated or for no reason at all, the gassing of orderly and unprotected knots of onlookers, and the abuse, verbal and physical, of the pettiest of violators and even of stray passersby and people minding their own business in their homes and neighborhoods.

Running through this book are cogent accounts of the accumulated grievances of the clever or merely desperate young men and women who seek to organize dissent somewhere between the established world of political conformity and the underworld of violent revolution, through the now-challenged devices of free speech and assembly to the deliberately provocative tactics of disobedience and violent confrontation.

And running through this book are the attitudes and convictions of policemen, loyal and erring, who typify so many of their fellow citizens in wishing to uphold the sanctity of flag, the certainty of law, the privacy of sex, the civility of manners and dress and who resent to the point of uncomprehending rage the irreverence and perhaps even ingratitude of so many of the most articulate and educated members of the coming generation.

Through this almost dispassionate chronicle of the Chicago turmoil we are being asked to reflect not only on the problems of public order in a flamboyant political season but also upon a profound conflict developing throughout American society. It is a conflict between the affluent and educated upper classes of American society who, together with the poorest classes, are demanding ever faster change and even wholesale upheaval, and the large body of middle-class Americans, newly prosperous or still striving, who fear the loss of what they have acquired or intend to achieve if the ways and priorities of life are to be seriously altered.

Though this volume deals almost entirely with what occurred outside the Democratic Convention, the crisis that it represents and the questions it provokes go to the heart of the issues that produced bedlam inside the Convention and inside the Democratic Party as well. The pressures for reform of the party, alternately formed around the candidacies of Robert Kennedy, Eugene McCarthy and George McGovern in 1968, will outlive most memories of these events, and it was no mere coincidence that inside the convention hall, as outside, Mayor Richard J. Daley of Chicago became the symbol of the uncomprehending old guard that are being pitied or despised by the rebels within the system and without.

Mayor Daley loves his native city and the orderly political processes that made him its leader and gave him charge of the defense of life and property there. When Negroes rioted in April, 1968, his policemen handled the situation efficiently and with restraint and some of the same men who prepared this report praised their performance. But the Mayor rebuked them, insisting in a statement that he later felt compelled to modify, that in times of trouble they should "shoot to kill arsonists and shoot to maim looters."

There, the Walker Report finds, began much of the trouble that culminated in the riot of the police themselves. And there, the men of the old order advertised the fears and exacerbated the anxieties that make them heroes to many and yet easy targets for provocation by others. The uncomprehending officials who succumbed to similar provocation at Columbia University are the kin of Mayor Daley, just as the police who were found to have broken discipline at Columbia are the kin of the Chicago forces. Particular though they are in this volume, the incidents and difficulties it describes are national, perhaps even universal, in import.

As the Walker Report asks at the outset, what happens when the undeniable rights of dissent and safety are brought—deliberately by some—into conflict? Its answer: "Convention week in Chicago is what happens, and the challenge it brings is plain: to keep *peaceful assembly* from becoming a contradiction in terms."

The provocative thoughts and conclusions in this book are formally ascribed to a single man—Daniel Walker. A prominent Chicago attorney and civic leader, the president of the prestigious but unofficial Chicago Crime Commission, a former naval officer, aide to Adlai E. Stevenson and currently Vice President and Counsel of Marcor, Inc. (the result of a recent merger between Montgomery Ward and the Container Corporation of America), Mr. Walker is the very essence of an establishmentarian using his influence and standing in the community to promote the traditional rights of both dissent and civic order.

This is a personal document, because The National Commission on Violence contracted with Mr. Walker for a study of the Chicago disorders and published his report without evaluation or substantive comment. Dr. Eisenhower, the Commission Chairman, merely said it was distributed promptly "because of the widespread interest in it," but before the thirteen-member Commission had fully reviewed it. Therefore, at least at the time of publication, he stipulated, "it carries neither the approval nor disapproval" of his group.

Other persons familiar with the work of the Commission said Mr. Walker's report reached the staff toward the end of November, 1968, and was recognized at once not only as a weighty and authoritative study but also as a controversial one that could not long be kept from the public even though the Commission might long debate its evaluation.

Similar reports on disorders in Miami and Cleveland in the summer of 1968, and many other commission studies, were still in preparation when the Walker Report arrived. For reasons that were never disclosed—but which appear to relate to fears at the commission that efforts might be made to suppress it by legal or political action—the report was rushed to as many Commission members as were available during the last week of November so that a "substantial majority," according to some sources, could authorize its publication.

But at least part of the Commission's haste and enthusiasm derives from a basic confidence in the judgment and credentials of Mr. Walker and from the knowledge that whatever the formalities, this is much more than a personal report.

Starting with the F.B.I.-trained staff of his Chicago Crime Commission—a distinguished citizens group that has devoted itself to fighting gangsterism and exposing the links between business interests and crime syndicates—Mr. Walker built a study team of 90 full-time and 121 part-time interviewers and researchers. Many lawyers and trained investigators were lent to him, at no cost, by prestigious Chicago law firms and banks. Together they took 1,410 statements from eyewitnesses, reviewed 2,017 others provided by the Federal Bureau of Investigation, and studied 180 hours of motion picture films, more than 12,000 still photographs and thousands of news accounts. They began work on September 27, 1968, and "only by disregarding clock and families," as Mr. Walker put it, completed the Report 53 days later, on November 18.

A striking and to many no-doubt shocking feature of the Report is its liberal and literal transcription of scores of obscene epithets used by the demonstrators and police alike to express their resentment and hostilities and, often, to provoke each other to violence. For many of the demonstrators, obscenity was said to have been the only weapon, and for many of the allegedly offending policemen, it was the most vivid evidence of their rage.

The Government Printing Office in Washington refused to publish a document containing so much outrageous language and thus the Commission could provide only a limited number of copies to the press. But Mr. Walker insisted, "with considerable reluctance," that the offensive language remain as a part of his record.

"Extremely obscene language was a contributing factor to the violence described in this Report," he wrote in a prefatory note, "and its frequency and intensity were such that to omit it would inevitably underestimate the effect it had."

Whatever the proprieties of disseminating these obscenities, it is difficult to argue with Mr. Walker's reluctant conclusion.

The picture of a girl raising her skirts and shouting filthy words at a policeman or of a policeman screaming the vilest words of which he is capable while swinging his club against defenseless and even injured persons is essential to an understanding of the ugliness of some of the provocation and the mindlessness of some of the responses unleashed in such confrontations.

Yet the ultimate value of the Walker Report is its demonstration that the violence of word and deed in Chicago was the product not only of momentary rage but also of the gradual conditioning of both the demonstrators and policemen. Some of each were plainly determined to cause trouble and sought a pretext for it. Many others, while planning no violence, clearly expected it.

We are left, therefore, with invaluable new material about the nature of some of our violence, but without any real explanation yet of its many causes. We have here a throbbing document that teaches many lessons in how to prevent, minimize or contain such reckless outbursts of political and social passion.

But it does not satisfy the yearning for simple analysis. Fundamentally, it provokes only further wonder about the violence in our streets, our policies and our hearts, about that apparently contagious spirit of destruction which so frequently erupts in the name of the very values by which we set out to find freedom and peace.

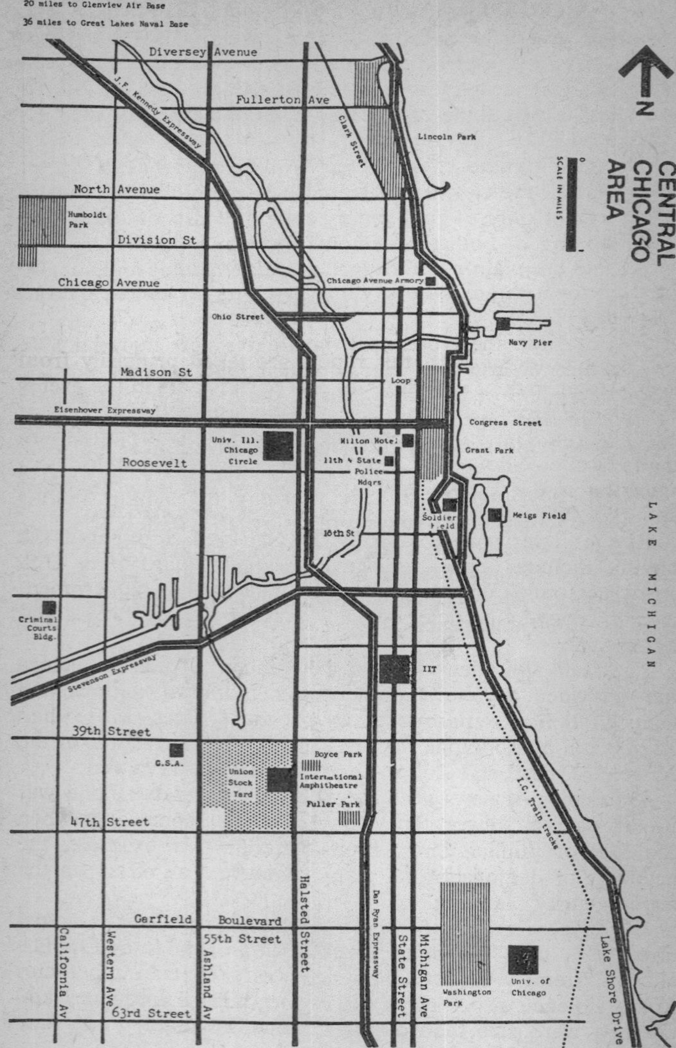
18 miles to O'Hare Field
20 miles to Glenview Air Base
36 miles to Great Lakes Naval Base
CENTRAL CHICAGO AREA
N
SCALE IN MILES
0
1
Diversey Avenue
Fullerton Ave
J.F. Kennedy Expressway
Clark Street
Lincoln Park
North Avenue
Humboldt Park
Division St
Chicago Avenue
Chicago Avenue Armory
Ohio Street
Navy Pier
Madison St
Loop
Eisenhower Expressway
Congress Street
Univ. Ill. Chicago Circle
Hilton Hotel
11th & State Police Hdqrs
Grant Park
Roosevelt
Soldier Field
Meigs Field
18th St
LAKE MICHIGAN
Criminal Courts Bldg.
Stevenson Expressway
IIT
39th Street
G.S.A.
Union Stock Yard
Boyce Park
International Amphitheatre
Fuller Park
I.C. Train tracks
47th Street
Halsted Street
Dan Ryan Expressway
Garfield Boulevard
55th Street
California Av
Western Ave
Ashland Av
State Street
Michigan Ave
Washington Park
Univ. of Chicago
Lake Shore Drive
63rd Street

ABOUT THE REPORT

The facts included in this report are taken primarily from 3,437 statements of eyewitnesses and participants in the events chronicled. Our staff took 1,410 of the statements; another 2,017 were taken by the Federal Bureau of Investigation and made available to us. A few others were provided by such agencies as the U.S. Attorney's office in Chicago. In total, about 20,000 pages of witness statements were reviewed.

Persons interviewed, both in Chicago and throughout the nation, included police officers, National Guardsmen, U.S. Army personnel, demonstrators and their leaders, government officials, convention delegates, news media representatives and bystanders.

The staff also viewed about 180 hours of motion picture film provided by television networks and local stations, the Chicago Police Department and private sources. More than 12,000 still photographs were examined. Official records of the National Guard and Police Department were reviewed.

Thousands of news accounts were examined but none was used as a fact source. They appear in the report only when the fact of publication is itself material—for example, the accounts of demonstrators' plans which had an effect on the city's security planning.

We have, with considerable reluctance, included the actual obscenities used by participants—demonstrators and police alike. Extremely obscene language was a contributing factor to the violence described in this report, and its frequency and intensity were such that to omit it would inevitably understate the effect it had.

The 212 persons in and outside of Chicago who made this report possible are listed at the end of the report. I am grateful to them all—and particularly to the dedicated Chicago staff. The real leaders were the Assistant Directors, Victor R. deGrazia and Harvey N. Johnson, Jr.; the Editorial Director, Ralph Caplan; and each of the Team Directors: James Barr, William T. Carney, Frank M. Covey, Jr., Verne H. Evans, Michael C. Johnson, James Keffler, John A. Koten, Gary Nelson, Hamilton Smith and Wesley S. Walton.

The Chicago staff started on September 27, 1968, and only by disregarding clock and families was it able to complete the report 53 days later.

Daniel Walker, Director
Chicago, Illinois
November 18, 1968

FOREWORD

The right to dissent is fundamental to democracy. But the expression of that right has become one of the most serious problems in contemporary democratic government. That dilemma was dramatized in Chicago during the Democratic National Convention of 1968—the dilemma of a city coping with the expression of dissent.

Unlike other recent big city riots, including those in Chicago itself, the events of convention week did not consist of looting and burning, followed by mass arrests. To a shocking extent they consisted of crowd-police battles in the parks as well as the streets. And the shock was intensified by the presence in the crowds (which included some anarchists and revolutionaries) of large numbers of innocent dissenting citizens.

The initial response, precipitated by dramatic television coverage, was a horrified condemnation of city and police. When demonstrators compared the Chicago police to the Soviet troops then occupying Prague, news commentators sympathetically relayed that comparison to the world. Not since Birmingham and Selma had there been so heated a mood of public outrage.

An immediate counterresponse, however, expressed the feeling that the demonstrators got what they deserved, and the thinking that the city had no alternative. Many observers thought that, in view of the provocation and the circumstances, police had performed admirably and with restraint.

The commentary far outlasted the convention. Major writers in some of the world's most respected periodicals denounced the city, the police, and the Democratic leaders. For its part, the City of Chicago issued "The Strategy of Confrontation," a paper detailing the threat to the city, itemizing provocations, describing a battery of bizarre weapons allegedly intended for use against law enforcement officers, and charging the American news media with biased coverage. The city also prepared a one-hour film shown nationally on television.

These conflicting responses, and the nature of the dilemma imposed upon Chicago, make this study necessary. Our purpose is to present the facts so that thoughtful readers can decide what lessons come out of them; for it is urgent that any such lessons be speedily incorporated into American public life. The *Chicago Tribune* began its special report on convention week with the line, "Not everyone wins." They might have added that there are circumstances in which *no one* wins, in which everyone loses. Such circumstances make up this report.

We have addressed ourselves to questions like the following. What were the objectives of the planned demonstrations, and who planned them? How did the city prepare itself? What types of people made up the crowds in the parks? Were physical and verbal attacks typical of demonstrator behavior? And did they precipitate police violence or follow it? Was the clubbing done by a few tired policemen goaded into "overreacting," or was there large-scale police brutality? Is there evidence that newsmen were singled out for assault? Was Chicago itself conducive to violence, or was it merely where the convention, and the cameras, happened to be?

We believe we have laid a factual foundation for meaningful answers to those questions.

Our charge was not to decide what ought to have been done, or to balance the rights and wrongs, or to recommend a course of action for the future. Having sought out the facts, we intend to let them speak for themselves. But we urge the reader, in assessing these facts, to bear in mind that the physical confrontations in Chicago will be repeated elsewhere until we learn to deal with the dilemma they represent.

In principle at least, most Americans acknowledge the right to dissent. And, in principle at least, most dissenters acknowledge the right of a city to protect its citizens and its property. But what happens when these undeniable rights are brought—deliberately by some—into conflict?

Convention week in Chicago is what happens, and the challenge it brings is plain: to keep *peaceful assembly* from becoming a contradiction in terms.

TABLE OF CONTENTS

MAPS

A SUMMARY

During the week of the Democratic National Convention, the Chicago police were the targets of mounting provocation by both word and act. It took the form of obscene epithets, and of rocks, sticks, bathroom tiles and even human feces hurled at police by demonstrators. Some of these acts had been planned; others were spontaneous or were themselves provoked by police action. Furthermore, the police had been put on edge by widely published threats of attempts to disrupt both the city and the Convention.

That was the nature of the provocation. The nature of the response was unrestrained and indiscriminate police violence on many occasions, particularly at night.

That violence was made all the more shocking by the fact that it was often inflicted upon persons who had broken no law, disobeyed no order, made no threat. These included peaceful demonstrators, onlookers, and large numbers of residents who were simply passing through, or happened to live in, the areas where confrontations were occurring.

Newsmen and photographers were singled out for assault, and their equipment deliberately damaged. Fundamental police training was ignored; and officers, when on the scene, were often unable to control their men. As one police officer put it: "What happened didn't have anything to do with police work."

The violence reached its culmination on Wednesday night.

A report prepared by an inspector from the Los Angeles Police Department, present as an official observer, while generally praising the police restraint he had observed in the parks during the week, said this about the events that night:

"There is no question but that many officers acted without restraint and exerted force beyond that necessary under the circumstances. The leadership at the point of conflict did little to prevent such conduct and the direct control of officers by first line supervisors was virtually non-existent."

He is referring to the police-crowd confrontation in front of the Conrad Hilton Hotel. Most Americans know about it, having seen the 17-minute sequence played and replayed on their television screens.

But most Americans do not know that the confrontation was followed by even more brutal incidents in the Loop side streets. Or that it had been preceded by comparable instances of indiscriminate police attacks on the North Side a few nights earlier when demonstrators were cleared from Lincoln Park and pushed into the streets and alleys of Old Town.

How did it start? With the emergence long before convention week of three factors which figured significantly in the outbreak of violence. These were: threats to the city; the city's response; and the conditioning of Chicago police to expect that violence against demonstrators, as against rioters, would be condoned by city officials.

The threats to the City were varied. Provocative and inflammatory statements, made in connection with activities planned for convention week, were published and widely disseminated. There were also intelligence reports from informants.

Some of this information was absurd, like the reported plan to contaminate the city's water supply with LSD. But some were serious; and both were strengthened by the authorities' lack of any mechanism for distinguishing one from the other.

The second factor—the city's response—matched, in numbers and logistics at least, the demonstrators' threats.

The city, fearful that the "leaders" would not be able to control their followers, attempted to discourage an inundation of demonstrators by not granting permits for marches and rallies and by making it quite clear that the "law" would be enforced.

Government—federal, state and local—moved to defend itself from the threats, both imaginary and real. The preparations were detailed and far ranging: from stationing firemen at each alarm box within a six block radius of the Amphitheatre to staging U.S. Army armored personnel carriers in Soldier Field under Secret Service control. Six thousand Regular Army troops in full field gear, equipped with rifles, flame throwers, and bazookas were airlifted to Chicago on Monday, August 26. About 6,000 Illinois National Guard troops had already been activated to assist the 12,000 member Chicago Police Force.

Of course, the Secret Service could never afford to ignore threats of assassination of Presidential candidates. Neither could the city, against the background of riots in 1967 and 1968, ignore the ever-present threat of ghetto riots, possibly sparked by large numbers of demonstrators, during convention week.

The third factor emerged in the city's position regarding the riots following the death of Dr. Martin Luther King and the April 27th peace march to the Civic Center in Chicago.

The police were generally credited with restraint in handling the first riots—but Mayor Daley rebuked the Superintendent of Police. While it was later modified, his widely disseminated "shoot to kill arsonists and shoot to maim looters" order undoubtedly had an effect.

The effect on police became apparent several weeks later, when they attacked demonstrators, bystanders and media representatives at a Civic Center peace march. There were published criticisms—but the city's response was to ignore the police violence.

That was the background. On August 18, 1968, the advance contingent of demonstrators arrived in Chicago and established their base, as planned, in Lincoln Park on the city's Near North Side. Throughout the week, they were joined by others—some from the Chicago area, some from states as far away as New York and California. On the weekend before the convention began, there were about 2,000 demonstrators in Lincoln Park; the crowd grew to about 10,000 by Wednesday.

There were, of course, the hippies—the long hair and love beads, the calculated unwashedness, the flagrant banners, the open lovemaking and disdain for the constraints of conventional society. In dramatic effect, both visual and vocal, these dominated a crowd whose members actually differed widely in physical appearance, in motivation, in political affiliation, in philosophy. The crowd included Yippies come to "do their thing," youngsters working for a political candidate, professional people with dissenting political views, anarchists and determined revolutionaries, motorcycle gangs, black activists, young thugs, police and secret service undercover agents. There were demonstrators waving the Viet Cong flag and the red flag of revolution and there were the simply curious who came to watch and, in many cases, became willing or unwilling participants.

To characterize the crowd, then, as entirely hippy-Yippie, entirely "New Left," entirely anarchist, or entirely youthful political dissenters is both wrong and dangerous. The stereotyping that did occur helps to explain the emotional reaction of both police and public during and after the violence that occurred.

Despite the presence of some revolutionaries, the vast majority of the demonstrators were intent on expressing by peaceful means their dissent either from society generally or from the administration's policies in Vietnam.

Most of those intending to join the major protest demonstrations scheduled during convention week did not plan to enter the Amphitheatre and disrupt the proceedings of the Democratic convention, did not plan aggressive acts of physical provocation against the authorities, and did not plan to use rallies of demonstrators to stage an assault against any person, institution, or place of business. But while it is clear that most of the protesters in Chicago had no intention of initiating violence, this is not to say that they did not expect it to develop.

It was the clearing of the demonstrators from Lincoln Park that led directly to the violence: symbolically, it expressed the city's opposition to the protesters; literally, it forced the protesters into confrontation with police in Old Town and the adjacent residential neighborhoods.

The Old Town area near Lincoln Park was a scene of police ferocity exceeding that shown on television on Wednesday night. From Sunday night through Tuesday night, incidents of intense and indiscriminate violence occurred in the streets after police had swept the park clear of demonstrators.

Demonstrators attacked too. And they posed difficult problems for police as they persisted in marching through the streets, blocking traffic and intersections. But it was the police who forced them out of the park and into the neighborhood.

And on the part of the police there was enough wild club swinging, enough cries of hatred, enough gratuitous beating to make the conclusion inescapable that individual policemen, and lots of them, committed violent acts far in excess of the requisite force for crowd dispersal or arrest. To read dispassionately the hundreds of statements describing at firsthand the events of Sunday and Monday nights is to become convinced of the presence of what can only be called a police riot.

Here is an eyewitness talking about Monday night:

> "The demonstrators were forced out onto Clark Street and once again a traffic jam developed. Cars were stopped, the horns began to honk, people couldn't move, people got gassed inside their cars, people got stoned inside their cars, police were the objects of stones, and taunts, mostly taunts. As you must understand, most of the taunting of the police was verbal. There were stones thrown of course, but for the most part it was verbal. But there were stones being thrown and of course the police were responding with tear gas and clubs and everytime they could get near enough to a demonstrator they hit him.
>
> "But again you had this police problem within—this really turned into a police problem. They pushed everybody out of the park, but this night there were a lot more people in the park than there had been during the previous night and Clark Street was just full of people and in addition now was full of gas because the police were using gas on a much larger scale this night. So the police were faced with the task, which took them about an hour or so, of hitting people over the head and gassing them enough to get them out of Clark Street, which they did."

But police action was not confined to the necessary force, even in clearing the park:

A young man and his girl friend were both grabbed by officers. He screamed, "We're going, we're going," but they threw him into the pond. The officers grabbed the girl, knocked her to the ground, dragged her along the embankment and hit her with their batons on her head, arms, back and legs. The boy tried to scramble up the embankment to her, but police shoved him back in the water at least twice. He finally got to her and tried to pull her in the water, away from the police. He was clubbed on the head five or six times. An officer shouted, "Let's get the fucking bastards!" but the boy pulled her in the water and the police left.

Like the incident described above, much of the violence witnessed in Old Town that night seems malicious or mindless:

> There were pedestrians. People who were not part of the demonstration were coming out of a tavern to see what the demonstration was . . . and the officers indiscriminately started beating everybody on the street who was not a policeman.

Another scene:

> There was a group of about six police officers that moved in and started beating two youths. When one of the officers pulled back his nightstick to swing, one of the youths grabbed it from behind and started beating on the officer. At this point about ten officers left everybody else and ran after this youth, who turned down Wells and ran to the left.
>
> But the officers went to the right, picked up another youth, assuming he was the one they were chasing, and took him into an empty lot and beat him. And when they got him to the ground, they just kicked him ten times—the wrong youth, the innocent youth who had been standing there.

A federal legal official relates an experience of Tuesday evening.

> I then walked one block north where I met a group of 12-15 policemen. I showed them my identification and they permitted me to walk with them. The police walked one block west. Numerous people were watching us from their windows and balconies. The police yelled profanities at them, taunting them to come down where the police would beat them up. The police stopped a number of people on the street demanding identification. They verbally abused each pedestrian and pushed one or two without hurting them. We walked back to Clark Street and began to walk north where the police stopped a number

> of people who appeared to be protesters, and ordered them out of the area in a very abusive way. One protester who was walking in the opposite direction was kneed in the groin by a policeman who was walking towards him. The boy fell to the ground and swore at the policeman who picked him up and threw him to the ground. We continued to walk toward the command post. A derelict who appeared to be very intoxicated, walked up to the policeman and mumbled something that was incoherent. The policeman pulled from his belt a tin container and sprayed its contents into the eyes of the derelict, who stumbled around and fell on his face.

It was on these nights that the police violence against media representatives reached its peak. Much of it was plainly deliberate. A newsman was pulled aside on Monday by a detective acquaintance of his who said: "The word is being passed to get newsmen." Individual newsmen were warned, "You take my picture tonight and I'm going to get you." Cries of "get the camera" preceded individual attacks on photographers.

A newspaper photographer describes Old Town on Monday at about 9:00 P.M.:

> When the people arrived at the intersection of Wells and Division, they were not standing in the streets. Suddenly a column of policemen ran out from the alley. They were reinforcements. They were under control but there seemed to be no direction. One man was yelling, 'Get them up on the sidewalks, turn them around.' Very suddenly the police charged the people on the sidewalks and began beating their heads. A line of cameramen was 'trapped' along with the crowd along the sidewalks, and the police went down the line chopping away at the cameras.

A network cameraman reports that on the same night:

> I just saw this guy coming at me with his nightstick and I had the camera up. The tip of his stick hit me right in the mouth, then I put my tongue up there and I noticed that my tooth was gone. I turned around then to try to

leave and then this cop came up behind me with his stick and he jabbed me in the back.

All of a sudden these cops jumped out of the police cars and started just beating the hell out of people. And before anything else happened to me, I saw a man holding a Bell & Howell camera with big wide letters on it, saying 'CBS.' He apparently had been hit by a cop. And cops were standing around and there was blood streaming down his face. Another policeman was running after me and saying, 'Get the fuck out of here.' And I heard another guy scream, 'Get their fucking cameras.' And the next thing I know I was being hit on the head, and I think on the back, and I was just forced down on the ground at the corner of Division and Wells.

If the intent was to discourage coverage, it was successful in at least one case. A photographer from a news magazine says that finally, "I just stopped shooting, because every time you push the flash, they look at you and they are screaming about, 'Get the fucking photographers and get the film.' "

There is some explanation for the media-directed violence. Camera crews on at least two occasions did stage violence and fake injuries. Demonstrators did sometimes step up their activities for the benefit of TV cameras. Newsmen and photographers' blinding lights did get in the way of police clearing streets, sweeping the park and dispersing demonstrators. Newsmen did, on occasion, disobey legitimate police orders to "move" or "clear the streets." News reporting of events did seem to the police to be anti-Chicago and anti-police.

But was the response appropriate to the provocation?

Out of 300 newsmen assigned to cover the parks and streets of Chicago during convention week, more than 60 (about 20%) were involved in incidents resulting in injury to themselves, damage to their equipment, or their arrest. Sixty-three newsmen were physically attacked by police; in 13 of these instances, photographic or recording equipment was intentionally damaged.

The violence did not end with either demonstrators or newsmen on the North Side on Sunday, Monday and Tuesday. It continued in Grant Park on Wednesday. It occurred on Michigan Avenue in front of the Conrad Hilton Hotel, as already described. A high-ranking Chicago police commander admits that on that occasion the police "got out of control." This same commander appears in one of the most vivid scenes of the entire week, trying desperately to keep individual policemen from beating demonstrators as he screams, "For Christ's sake. stop it!"

Thereafter, the violence continued on Michigan Avenue and on the side streets running into Chicago's Loop. A federal official describes how it began:

> "I heard a 10-1 call [policeman in trouble] on either my radio or one of the other hand sets carried by men with me and then heard 'Car 100—sweep.' With a roar of motors, squads, vans and three-wheelers came from east, west and north into the block north of Jackson. The crowd scattered. A big group ran west on Jackson, with a group of blue shirted policemen in pursuit, beating at them with clubs. Some of the crowd would jump into doorways and the police would rout them out. The action was very tough. In my judgment, unnecessarily so. The police were hitting with a vengeance and quite obviously with relish. . . ."

What followed was a club-swinging melee. Police ranged the streets striking anyone they could catch. To be sure, demonstrators threw things at policemen and at police cars; but the weight of violence was overwhelmingly on the side of the police. A few examples will give the flavor of that night in Chicago:

"At the corner of Congress Plaza and Michigan," states a doctor, "was gathered a group of people, numbering between thirty and forty. They were trapped against a railing [along a ramp leading down from Michigan Avenue to an underground parking garage] by several policemen on motorcycles. The police charged the people on motorcycles and struck about a dozen of them, knocking several of them down. About twenty standing there jumped over the railing. On the other side of the railing was a three-to-four-foot drop. None of the people who were struck by the motorcycles appeared to be seriously injured. However, several of them were limping as if they had been run over on their feet."

A UPI reporter witnessed these attacks, too. He relates in his statement that one officer, "with a smile on his face and a fanatical look in his eyes, was standing on a three-wheel cycle, shouting, 'Wahoo, wahoo,' and trying to run down people on the sidewalk." The reporter says he was chased thirty feet by the cycle.

A priest who was in the crowd says he saw a "boy, about fourteen or fifteen, white, standing on top of an automobile yelling something which was unidentifiable. Suddenly a policeman pulled him down from the car and beat him to the ground by striking him three or four times with a nightstick. Other police joined in . . . and they eventually shoved him to a police van.

"A well-dressed woman saw this incident and spoke angrily to a nearby police captain. As she spoke, another policeman came up from behind her and sprayed something in her face with an aerosol can. He then clubbed her to the ground. He and two other policemen then dragged her along the ground to the same paddy wagon and threw her in."

"I ran west on Jackson," a witness states. "West of Wabash, a line of police stretching across both sidewalks and the street charged after a small group I was in. Many people were clubbed and maced as they ran. Some weren't demonstrators at all, but were just pedestrians who didn't know how to react to the charging officers yelling 'Police!' "

"A wave of police charged down Jackson," another witness relates. "Fleeing demonstrators were beaten indiscriminately and a temporary, makeshift first aid station was set up on the corner of State and Jackson. Two men lay in pools of blood, their heads severely cut by clubs. A minister moved amongst the crowd, quieting them, brushing aside curious onlookers, and finally asked a policeman to call an ambulance, which he agreed to do. . . ."

An Assistant U.S. Attorney later reported that "the demonstrators were running as fast as they could but were unable to get out of the way because of the crowds in front of them. I observed the police striking numerous individuals, perhaps 20 to 30. I saw three fall down and then overrun by the police. I observed two demonstrators who had multiple cuts on their heads. We assisted one who was in shock into a passer-by's car."

Police violence was a fact of convention week. Were the policemen who committed it a minority? It appears certain that they were—but one which has imposed some of the consequences of its actions on the majority, and certainly on their commanders. There has been no public condemnation of these violators of sound police procedures and common decency by either their commanding officers or city officials. Nor (at the time this Report is being completed—almost three months after the convention) has any disciplinary action been taken against most of them. That some policemen lost control of themselves under exceedingly provocative circumstances can perhaps be understood; but not condoned. If no action is taken against them, the effect can only be to discourage the majority of policemen who acted responsibly, and further weaken the bond between police and community.

Although the crowds were finally dispelled on the nights of violence in Chicago, the problems they represent have not been. Surely this is not the last time that a violent dissenting group will clash head-on with those whose duty it is to enforce the law. And the next time the whole world will still be watching.

THE GATHERING FORCES: A PRELUDE TO CONVENTION WEEK

The events examined in this report cannot be understood apart from the social context and the city in which they occurred.

Near the center of the city, the Chicago River flows west out of Lake Michigan and, in about a mile, forks into a north branch and a south branch. Beyond the fork is the West Side, now largely populated by Negroes and Spanish Americans. Just south of the river is the Loop, a downtown area of banks and businesses, theaters and restaurants, and the seats of government of both Chicago and Cook County. Also in the Loop are most of the hotels which house the 1,300,000 visitors who come each year. The largest of these hotels, the Conrad Hilton, faces Grant Park, which lies between Michigan Avenue and the lake.

Downtown Chicago has relatively few permanent residents. Half of the city's population lives on the sprawling South Side, where a "Black Belt" of Negroes extends for almost ten miles, bound on the east by Lake Michigan and on the west by white ethnic neighborhoods. As in other American urban centers, the Negroes are concentrated into a few overcrowded sections. On the North Side thousands of Negroes live in uneasy proximity to bohemians and affluent whites.

Racial tensions have been high in Chicago in recent years. Riots broke out in 1966 and again in April, 1968, after Dr. Martin Luther King's assassination. Arson and looting were widespread during the April, 1968, riots. The police had, however, benefited from the findings of the President's National Commission on Civil Disorders and from the experience of police departments in coping with previous riots in Chicago and other major cities. The Mayor's Chicago Riot Study Committee, appointed after the April disturbances, cited the restraint exercised by the Chicago Police Department as a major factor in preventing the riots from becoming even more violent and widespread. Shortly after the April riots, however, Mayor Richard J. Daley held a press conference in which he seemed to criticize the Police Department for precisely that restraint, asserting that the police should shoot to kill arsonists and shoot to maim looters.

While the Mayor later modified his statement in conformance with restrictions imposed by Illinois law on police use of deadly force, his initial remark was widely reported both in Chicago and throughout the nation. Undoubtedly it had some effect on the attitude of Chicago policemen towards their role in riots and other disorders.

On April 27, 1968, several Chicago peace organizations held a demonstration march in the Loop to protest the war in Vietnam. There was controversy concerning the permit for this march, which was made up of some 6,500 persons and ended in a confrontation with the police at the Civic Center. Eyewitnesses maintain that the police used excessive force in dispersing these demonstrators at the Civic Center and that police officers clubbed several bystanders. Whatever the truth with respect to specific incidents, it is quite clear that the police used direct physical force to dispel the demonstrators. Their tactics on that occasion were severely criticized in the report of a citizens' committee headed by Dr. Edward J. Sparling, president emeritus of Roosevelt University.

These recent and local circumstances reflected the gathering national forces propelling public dissent. While it is not the purpose of this report to analyze those forces, we must recognize that they impinged significantly upon convention week in Chicago.

Among those national forces were the civil rights movement, the peace movement, the changing role of universities, the changing emphasis of organized religion, the growth of an affluent middle class, the ubiquity of television, the stresses of urbanization, and the failure of federal, state and city governments to find solutions to social problems fast enough to satisfy aspirations raised by the solutions they *have* found. But the issue most immediately relevant to convention week in Chicago was the war in Vietnam.

Following the Montgomery, Alabama, bus boycott of 1955, the Reverend Martin Luther King, Jr. emerged as a leader in the cause of both civil rights and nonviolence. There was nothing new about boycotts or sit-ins or the fusion of civil rights and pacifism. But for the first time a nonviolent confrontation was widely publicized enough to become a rallying point for mass dissent and for what could loosely be called a "movement."

The civil rights protests of the fifties were in some respects like the Chicago confrontation of 1968. They were heterogenous; they resulted in violence; they involved students and clergy; they depended on novel strategies for outmaneuvering the authorities; they were given wide television coverage; and they were blamed by the authorities on "outside agitators."

In the sixties, Negroes demanded, and took, control of their own movement. White students found other points of rebellion right on campus, in the machine-like impersonality of the large university, with its emphasis on research rather than instruction—research that, moreover, was often tied to the war in Vietnam. In a general way the issue was one of student participation in their own affairs. But while some students wanted a place in the system, other wanted to replace the system.

Still others—students, nonstudents, ex-students—equally alienated from the system, turned their backs on it and became "hippies."

Many students came to distrust a society that, in their eyes, took refuge in liquor but forbade marijuana, that preached individualism but sought security in large corporations, that talked peace but dropped napalm, and that nurtured, they believed, a climate favorable for the recent assassinations of the most prominent civil rights leader and a presidential candidate. Enjoying an unprecedented sexual freedom (partly because of the steady liberalization of mores and partly because of the easy availability of effective contraceptive devices), they challenged the way society talked about sex. Thus, at Berkeley the demand for free speech included the right of obscene speech. Others seized obscenity as an offensive weapon, one that they brought to Chicago.

To ignore society was to simultaneously challenge it—with communal living, with drugs, with rhetoric, with music, exemplified by Bob Dylan's lyrical warning that "The Times They Are a-Changin'."

Conventional behavior and traditional values were under

attack at every level. They always have been. But never before had a generation been in so strong a position to launch an attack on the society they were inheriting.

One reason was affluence, which meant free time and unprecedented mobility.

Another reason was education and experience in protest techniques, not all of them nonviolent.

But perhaps the most influential contributing factor to the strength of dissent was the existence of communications media of all kinds. There is no question that the protesters in Chicago, as elsewhere, "played to the cameras" or that they often did it very effectively and, this, too, had been learned in earlier protests. What "the whole world was watching," after all, was not a confrontation but the picture of a confrontation, to some extent directed by a generation that had grown up with television and learned to use it.

It was also a generation facing the draft. And the issue of war in Vietnam brought large groups of young people to Chicago to express dissent. They were joined by citizens of all ages.

On October 8, 1967, it was announced that the Democratic National Convention would be held in Chicago. At the time, it seemed most likely that President Lyndon Johnson and Vice President Hubert Humphrey would be nominated to run again.

From the start there were misgivings about the location. McCormick Place, Chicago's giant lakefront conventionl hall, had been destroyed by fire. The Chicago Amphitheatre, the only appropriate substitute, was over five miles from the major hotels which would house the convention delegates. Moreover, the Amphitheatre was close to one of the city's ghettos and there had been ghetto violence across the country the previous summer.

As the convention week neared, new complications appeared and further misgivings were expressed. The April riots had shaken Chicago. A bitter telephone workers strike remained unsettled. Most of the city's taxi cabs were idled by strike and a public transit workers walkout added to the confusion anticipated. Plans for massive protest demonstrations had been disclosed and thousands of young dissidents, including hippies, black militants and motorcycle gangs from the West Coast were expected to converge on the city. In the meantime, assassination plots, sabotage and disruptive activities were rumored and extensive precautions unveiled in recourse.

But suggestions for relocating the convention were swept aside—the convention, scheduled for August 26 through August 29, would unfold in Chicago, where the nation's problems were waiting to greet the delegates, almost literally face to face.

By the eve of convention week, the political scenes had shifted dramatically. President Johnson announced on March 31, 1968, that he would not accept renomination. In the meantime, Senator Eugene McCarthy had won a significant primary vote in New Hampshire. McCarthy continued to rally significant support, especially among younger citizens, campaigning principally in opposition to the current administration's policy in Vietnam. Senator Robert Kennedy joined the race for the Democratic nomination and he, too, followed by Senator McGovern, vigorously challenged the Johnson-Humphrey administration's Vietnam policy. The antiwar movement had, in a sense, become politically legitimatized.

When Vice President Humphrey entered the race there was little question that the Democratic National Convention was to be the arena for a sharply contested debate on United States involvement in Vietnam. Chicago was to become the focal point for an abrupt confrontation of national policies, both within and without the framework of the Democratic Party.

While the various factions within the party were preparing for convention week, anti-war activists and dissident groups of various sorts were considering plans to stage demonstrations. Many of those expected to join these demonstrations were supporters of Senators McCarthy, Kennedy and McGovern. Others viewed the Democratic Party as unresponsive to the public will and inexorably connected with what they considered to be an inhuman war.

Among the dissidents planning to come in protest were violent revolutionaries, pro-Peking sympathizers, communists, anarchists, militant extremists, as well as pacifists, poor people's campaigners, civil rights workers and moderate left-wingers.

For those who had forsaken electoral politics, the convention offered a convenient occasion to rally supporters and to broadcast their disillusionment.

There were also hippies, and among them were hippies turned inside out: becoming concerned with their relationship with the "other society," they cast themselves in the role of self-styled revolutionaries. A few of the more deliberate and creative of these invented an acronym, YIPPIE! and a "non-organization" to go with it.

The tactics planned by radical dissenters reflect various attitudes, ranging from complete pacifism to hard-core militance. And their motives vary from individual to individual and association to association. In the main, though, the disruptive tactics, whether violent or not, were intended to expose the inhumanity, injustice, prejudice, hypocrisy or militaristic repression with which dissenters take issue. Disruptive tactics obviously impose a high cost upon society and its leaders and eventually, the dissidents argue, the price will become too great.

It is clear that the great majority of protesters in Chicago had no preconceived intention to initiate violence. This is not to say, however, that they did not expect it to develop.

Most of those who intended to join the major protest demonstrations scheduled during convention week did not plan to enter the Amphitheatre and disrupt the proceedings of the Democratic convention, did not plan aggressive acts of physical provocation against the authorities and did not plan to use rallies of demonstrators to stage an assault against any person, institution or place of business.

During the months preceding the convention, provocative and inflammatory statements, made in connection with activities planned for the forthcoming convention week, were published and widely disseminated through underground channels and by exposure in the general media. Numerous articles, speeches and disclosed conversations promised threatening acts of public disorder and terrorism which could not be responsibly dismissed. Those committed to such actions, however, appear to have been unable to combine a broadly based following nor a well-organized plan.

A Coalition for Protest

On April 15, 1967, at least 100,000 people gathered in New York City's Central Park and marched to the United Nations Plaza to protest the war in Vietnam. A parade permit had been issued by the city, and the demonstrators quietly occupied ten city blocks, listening to speeches by Dr. Martin

Luther King, Jr. and others. Nearly 150 separate organizations were represented in the demonstration, including student groups from various colleges; community organizations, mostly from the suburbs, adjoining New York City; women's affiliations like the Women Strike for Peace, whose members were mostly housewives, with children accompanying them; and one black organization which marched in from Harlem. The demonstration could be generally characterized as nonviolent and, in the main, nondisruptive. The general attitude of the marchers was serious but friendly; there was a large number of middle-aged people in attendance.

That demonstration had been organized by the Spring Mobilization Committee, formed in late 1966 by David Dellinger and the late A. J. Muste. These men had also helped coordinate a similar demonstration in San Francisco on the same day. The National Mobilization Committee to End the War in Vietnam, formed shortly after these two demonstrations, began its work with a list of the groups that had participated in the April 15 marches. Throughout its brief history the National Mobilization Committee has attempted to organize and inform through such "local" organizations.

One of the more prominent of such local organizations is the Fifth Avenue Anti-Vietnam Peace Parade Committee in New York. The administrator, Eric Weinberger, also a representative to National Mobilization's Administrative Committee, describes the uncertain composition of peace rallies:

> . . . the people come out, but we don't know who they are. The vast, vast majority of these people are on nobody's mailing list. They don't want to be on anybody's mailing list. They want to come out two, three times a year and make their feelings known.

The "motivations" of such unknown participants ranged from a general dissatisfaction with the war in Vietnam to their belief that the Democratic Party was unresponsive to urban problems. Some simply felt that electoral politics were irrelevant and that "direct action," as in demonstrations, was necessary to influence American policy makers.

As the 1968 elections moved closer, the pressure of such frustrations increased, especially in the eyes of National Mobilization organizers. One of their key position papers states:

People are being asked to spend their taxes and blood supporting a government in which, it becomes clearer day by day, they have little voice. The supreme insult will be the "choice" between two candidates supporting identical policies which are destroying our country's potential for decency. The fraudulence of this choice must be exposed and opposed by a movement of people determined to see their needs attended and their voices heard. (Davis-Hayden: Movement Campaign 1968: An Election Year Offensive)

While such a "movement" was designed to focus upon the more salient complaints of war protesters, draft resisters, black dissenters and disaffected leftists, there was a continuous effort to appeal to a broader-based constituency, unified by its opposition to the war.

The tendency to intensify militancy without organizing wide political support is self-defeating. But so is the tendency to draw away from militancy into milder and more conventional forms of protest. The problem is to build the broadest coalition which can give political support and interpretation to the militancy, as the government makes it clear that its only response to revolution abroad and resistance at home is violence and suppression. A movement must either reach for new support or be eroded away. . . .
We must continually show that the anti-war movement is increasing in militancy and numbers. We can show the establishment that deeper social conflict at home will result from the Vietnam crisis. We can accelerate the breakdown of confidence in the government and military by stressing that the decisions which led to the Vietnam war were rigged in the same way and by the same people who are rigging the conventions and elections in 1968. (Davis-Hayden, *op, cit.*)

Movement organizers wanted to launch an election year program that would combine a militant front in opposition to the war, to racism, to social injustices, to unresponsive and unrepresentative government. A program, moreover, which would coalesce independently active organizations, involve insurgent forces throughout the country, and coordinate a multilevel protest focused on the failure of government to deal with social and political crises. The Democratic National Convention promised to provide the occasion for a massive expression of united protest and an opportunity to solidify the "movement," to reach new people dissatisfied with the system, and to expose "increasingly repressive government machinery." The organizational effect would not be designed to represent anyone, but "to structure opportunities for communication and coordination."

There was hope that such a national coalition could mobilize and bring to Chicago "an assembly of people too large to be considered the lunatic fringe."

When planning among structural protest groups for Chicago began in early October, 1967, there were expectations that more than 100,000 demonstrators from across the country would be persuaded to come. President Johnson seemed the likely choice for the Democratic Party's nomination:

> There was really a sense among many people, Democrats, peace groups, student organizations and others that this was really going to be a Convention period and an election in which the central issue of Vietnam was going to be buried, and that the Democratic Convention which would most likely be renominating Johnson was the logical place to bring the concern of people who wanted peace in Vietnam to some kind of dramatic focus. (David Dellinger)

It was a matter, then, of deciding upon a program for organizing the massive turn-out which was expected.

The National Mobilization Committee to End the War in Vietnam and its predecessor had been successful in coordinating massive antiwar demonstrations in the past. One such demonstration was the Pentagon march on October 21, 1967. Working from a list of groups which had participated in the April demonstration, National Mobilization acted as the primary organizing force to rally somewhere in the neighborhood of 50,000 demonstrators. The demonstration resulted in disruption and violence. Some 2,000 demonstrators had pushed their way up the steps in front of the entrance to the Pentagon, where they physically confronted federal marshals and military policemen. Another 3,000 or so were able to step through police lines and rush another entrance—some entering the building. Before it was over, 600 or more had been arrested and many injured.

This type of confrontation, resulting in violence, was the same type that the authorities in Chicago expected to result from the demonstrations planned for the convention.

Chairman of National Mobilization is 52-year-old David Dellinger. He had become the senior member of the peace movement and his efforts contributed significantly to mobilizing for the Pentagon march.

Dellinger, a native of Wakefield, Massachusetts, graduated *magna cum laude* from Yale College in 1936, was elected to Phi Beta Kappa, and won the coveted Henry Fellowship for study in England. He served two prison terms during World War II for refusing to serve in the army although he could have received deferment as a student at Union Theological Seminary in New York. Between prison terms, he was married and now has five children. He has visited both Hanoi and Cuba twice and has organized a delegation of 41 members which met with North Vietnamese and National Liberation Front members in Bratislava, Czechoslovakia, in September of 1967. During November of 1967, Dellinger was one of 14 War Crime Tribunal members who met in Denmark to hear charges of war crimes against the American forces in Vietnam.

After the Pentagon demonstrations, Dellinger wrote:

> . . . the mixture of Gandhi and guerrilla was planned in advance. . . . At the very least there was bound to be a juxtaposition of Gandhi and guerrilla, given the presence of both schools of thought and the permissiveness of the coalition. But juxtaposition is not the same as creative synthesis, which was the goal of the Mobilization's direct-action committee and those members of the staff and officers who worked most closely with it. . . .
> We wanted something with far more teeth in it, a real confrontation instead of a legitimatized one . . . we refused to negotiate the terms of the civil disobedience or direct action at all. . . .
> . . . One of the lessons of the weekend was that it is indeed practical to forge a creative synthesis of Gandhi and guerrilla. . . .
> . . . The Mobilization had a maximum impact because it combined massive action with the cutting edge of re-

sistance. (*Liberation Magazine,* November, 1967)

Another writer, in the same issue of *Liberation,* which Dellinger edits, noted:

> The Pentagon siege can be treated as a tactical event to be analyzed and criticized as one possible model for future physical confrontations. This is a necessary process: there will be more occasions for physical confrontations and they ought to be much better planned than the Pentagon was. Can we do better at the Democratic National Convention in Chicago? . . .

National Mobilization officers began thinking about Chicago during the fall of 1967, and a meeting of the Administrative Committee was scheduled for December. Composed of representatives from various peace groups around the country, it is the perpetuating influence of National Mobilization.

According to National Mobilization delegates, all meetings of the Administrative Committee are essentially "open":

> The coalition has been built, in a counter reaction to the McCarthy days, on a purely nonexclusive basis. Anybody who is against the war, whether that is its full program or part of its program, is welcome to participate. (Eric Weinberger.)

As a result, within the coalition are groups ranging from pacifists to pro-Viet Cong, from revolutionaries to anarchists. While they are at odds on almost everything else, they are united in their opposition to the war. There are some 150 such groups involved in this loose coalition, but the association of affiliated groups is somewhat fluid, depending upon proposed events.

> . . . it may be that at some meetings . . . some people show up we've never seen before. We say, "Who are you?" And they say, "Well, we've come down from Boston," from the newly organized Boston Committee Against the War! Or the Boston Housewives Against the War. And if we ran a tight ship in the sense that it was a membership organization . . . then you might either say—well, question their credentials, or say, "Well, you can't vote." (David Dellinger)

The Administrative Committee elects its own officers, who represent different regions and are supposedly in touch with local groups participating in National Mobilization. The officers select a date and a tentative agenda. Each organization participates in deciding what action will be taken, and then decides for itself whether to take part in it. Also, according to David Dellinger, "We try to provide different levels of participation, so people may participate at one level but not at another."

As a result of such meetings, as well as the success of the demonstrations to which they led, the Administrative Committee began to become the focal point for discussion among the various antiwar factions.

On December 18, 1967, the Administrative Committee of National Mobilization held a meeting in New York City. Between 60 and 70 people were present.

> There was pretty loose talk at that point . . . I spoke about the consensus, there has to be some kind of feeling amongst a lot of different groups and a lot of different people, or else a thing like that (i.e. whether to demonstrate in Chicago) won't be decided on. And Chicago was kind of a natural thing. . . . But there were others who hadn't talked about it in their areas or in their groups, and so there was no decision made. It was decided that we should explore the possibilities and we should get together with other groups who hadn't attended that meeting, and discuss it. (Rennie Davis)

During the next several months preliminary planning was undertaken, and various dissident groups which had shown some interest in coming to Chicago worked out organizational positions. Toward February, National Mobilization considered opening a Chicago office at 407 South Dearborn Street in preparation for a multilateral action during the Democratic National Convention. Rennie Davis, a young community organizer working in Chicago, was selected as the Chicago coordinator and would work closely with another young activist, Tom Hayden.

Rennie Davis holds a political science degree from Oberlin College and a master's degree in labor and industrial relations from the University of Illinois. His father was an economic adviser to President Truman. In 1965, after one year of graduate study at Michigan, Davis went to New York, where he worked as a community organizer for SDS (Students for a Democratic Society). In the summer of 1967, he traveled to North Vietnam and joined the Mobilization Committee upon his return. He has had experience with community organizing in Chicago, where he helped to form JOIN (Jobs or Income Now), a project aimed at organizing Appalachian whites in the Uptown area, concentrating on housing and welfare problems. He was a planner at the Center for Radical Research and an organizer of the Resistance Inside the Army (RITA). Davis was a principal participant in the New Politics Convention in Chicago, where he gained a reputation for his theory of building local organizations as bases for militant political action.

Tom Hayden, also 28, was born in Michigan and in 1961 graduated from the University of Michigan, where he was editor of the *Michigan Daily* in his senior year. During the summer of 1961, Hayden worked on the summer project of the Student Non-Violent Coordinating Committee (SNCC) in Mississippi. In 1962 he went to Port Huron, Michigan, where he was a cofounder of the Students for a Democratic Society and authored the Port Huron Statement, as well as the SDS by-laws and constitution. He helped organize the Newark Community Project, a community union similar to JOIN. In 1965, he traveled to Hanoi with Herbert Aptheker and Staughton Lynd. In early July of 1968, he went to Paris for two weeks to consult with the North Vietnamese. He was reportedly active in the Columbia University rebellion during the spring of 1968.

On February 11, 1968, in Chicago, National Mobilization hosted a meeting of delegates from various black organizations, including representatives from SNCC, CORE (Congress of Racial Equality) and NRO (National Rights Organization). At the meeting, Rennie Davis and Carlos Russell, former head of the NCNP (National Conference on New Politics) Black Caucus attempted to explore the possibility of synthesizing a national structure of black organizations and predominantly white protest groups. National Mobilization spokesmen had for some time recognized the desirability of fusing the peace movement with support for "black liberation." It was determined that a major movement conference in late March might yield a commitment from black organizations, Mobilization affiliates, and from a broadly based composite of regional community groups and college students—a commitment to combine in a united front which then would be exhibited in Chicago.

The national conference was called for March 22 to 24 and was to be held near Lake Villa, in northern Illinois. Some 250 delegates were invited.

A number of position papers were drafted by interested parties in anticipation of this Lake Villa conference. Perhaps the most thorough and deliberate was one jointly prepared by Rennie Davis and Tom Hayden. This paper demonstrated a serious concern with the problems of involving disaffected youths and the Negro community in a national coalition.

> In the March 24th meeting, there was in some sense an effort to go beyond the old coalition that the Mobilization had established. We wanted at this particular meeting to reach more young people than had previously been involved in the planning of organizational activities. (Rennie Davis)

As to the Negro groups, a suggestion as to structure was made:

> . . . The black liberation and anti-war movements should consider parallel organizations that allow for communication and cooperation where political interests merge. . . .
> The conference participants might elect two coalition boards, representing different interests in the anti-war and black movements. These two boards, in our opinion, should be empowered to add membership, as new constituencies decide they wish to participate in the challenge coalition. (Davis-Hayden, *op. cit.*)

The paper also treated the challenge which a desire for local, decentralized action presented to the effective construction of a national coalition. Movement centers were proposed, and local planning encouraged. Focusing on convention related activities, decentralized demonstrations would be combined with a massive assembly of all protest groups joining in a "funeral march" to the International Amphitheatre as President Johnson was re-nominated.

Here are some further excerpts from the Davis-Hayden paper:

> Such a march could be led by retired generals, admirals and Vietnam veterans. The funeral procession might be organized by constituencies: blacks followed by clergy followed by women followed by farmers and faculty and workers and resistors and so on. This funeral would speak for those who say that the elections represent no choice and a complete breakdown of democracy. . . .
>
> What we want to create is a greater consciousness that organizations of protest, resistance, and independent politics, under the control of the actual people with grievances, are more important than casting a vote or working for the "better" of two conventional candidates.
>
> We must be arguing that the Democratic Party and the limits of the electoral system itself are what we oppose . . . our strategy is to build political organizations of our own rather than to "reform" the Democratic Party.
>
> Any national demonstration in Chicago should come out of a program that has stressed local organizing during the spring and summer and can support community base-building in the fall.
>
> The summer would be capped by three days of sustained, organized protests at the Democratic National Convention, clogging the streets of Chicago with people demanding peace, justice and self-determination for all people. The Chicago challenge must convey a broad but concrete critique of the Democratic Party and its failure to meet the crisis of our cities and the war. It must say to the world that Johnson represents wealth, the military and the politically corrupt of America, not ordinary people. It must attempt to delegitimate the Democratic Party while building support for an independent people's movement during the 1968 elections.
>
> The campaign should not plan violence and disruption against the Democratic National Convention. It should be nonviolent and legal.

The Lake Villa meeting was an attempt to make the Mobilization offices more genuinely representative of their constituencies. The meeting was long and tedious, with little emphasis on Chicago planning and much discussion of the "movement" as a whole and the manner in which black groups and local community student organizations might become more involved in the coalition.

During the conference, a number of dissident organizations had declared, or implied, that they would have no interest in joining a massive demonstration in Chicago. One of these groups was the SDS.

Nor did a strong alliance with black organizations ever develop. Shortly after the Lake Villa meeting, prospects for the demonstration of a united black-white front in Chicago disintegrated. The change of direction may, perhaps, have been related to the assassination of Dr. Martin Luther King, Jr., and the ugly aftermath of riots, including the use of Guardsmen and federal troops to quell disturbances. There were blacks, however, who did participate in demonstrations during convention week, but the organizations they belonged to did not, as such, directly become parties to the protest coalition envisioned by promoters of the Lake Villa Conference.

Following the March 22 to 24 conference, David Dellinger spoke to the press and made a much-repeated statement: "We are not going to storm the convention with tanks or mace. But we are going to storm the hearts and minds of the American people."

The Administrative Committee of National Mobilization, which had decided to postpone the formal adoption of a position on Chicago, met in Washington, D.C. The elation regarding numbers and militancy which had been expressed in late 1967 was waning. According to Rennie Davis, "The feeling was that the meeting in March had not been successful in creating new organization." A decision on Chicago was again postponed. (It would not come until the Administrative Committee met again on July 20.) In the meantime, a parade of tumultuous national events had begun to unfold; they had the effect of further dissipating support for convention demonstrators.

President Johnson's withdrawal from candidacy for re-nomination, the reduced bombing of North Vietnam, and the opening of peace talks in Paris gave pause to the determination of many moderate antiwar groups.

Further blows to the Chicago programs were struck, according to National Mobilization organizers, by the emergence of Eugene McCarthy as a peace candidate, the riots following the assassination of Dr. Martin Luther King, Jr.,

Mayor Daley's public rebuke of his Superintendent of Police for failing to take stronger action during the April 5 disorders, and the violent dispersal of peace paraders on April 27 in Chicago.

These events prompted a growing skepticism about the efficacy of mass demonstrations, at least in Chicago, and the hope for reorganization and broadly based support in Chicago was never rejuvenated.

The assassination of Senator Kennedy in June and the entrance of Vice President Hubert Humphrey into the campaign, however, had the effect of somewhat revitalizing interest in convention-related demonstrations.

National Mobilization took the reigns of organization and in a July 20 meeting in Cleveland definitely committed themselves to making plans for Chicago a reality.

The Chicago coordinating office, financed by a reported $20,000, continued, now at a highly accelerated rate, to coordinate participants and to make a multitude of arrangements for activities during convention week. There were meetings and news conferences and promotional ventures. There were negotiations with city officials and contacts with hundreds of different organizations from coast to coast which might conceivably have a role to play in Chicago. There were long, hard hours devoted to preparing a program for activity during convention week.

Only a few of the groups which cooperated in one way or another with National Mobilization are:

(1) *Church Groups:* Several church groups were represented, including the Lutheran Action Committee and a number of local congregations, whose facilities were made available for housing. The American Friends Service Committee was only marginally involved in the planning, concentrating instead on the counseling of conscientious objectors.

(2) *The Chicago Peace Council:* Active in Chicago since 1966, this group of Chicago war objectors, many of them doctors and teachers, was responsible for the April 27 march to the Civic Center to protest the war, in conjunction with other similar demonstrations across the country. The Peace Council worked closely with the Chicago Mobilization office and played a major role in securing accommodations, and in making arrangements for legal and medical presence. Partly as the result of the Peace Council's concern with the violation of civil liberties during the April 27 demonstration, it cooper-

ated in establishing the Chicago Legal Defense Committee.

(3) *Legal Groups:* National Mobilization worked with two distinct groups. The first was the National Lawyers Guild, whose planning for legal assistance in Chicago apparently had begun with a New York City meeting in January, 1968, sponsored by the Guild. In attendance at the meeting were a number of lawyers who were active in various antiwar, civil rights, and leftist organizations. Several members of the National Mobilization Administrative Committee (including Tom Hayden) were also present. While the discussion centered around the need to organize the legal assistance apparatus for the Chicago protest, there were also discussions of the continuing needs of the movement for organized legal assistance.

At this meeting, held on January 26, 1968, according to minutes supplied by an informant, Tom Hayden stated:

> We should have people organized who can fight the police, people who are willing to get arrested. No question that there will be a lot of arrests. My thinking is not to leave the initiative to the police. We have to have isolated yet coordinated communications. We don't want to get into the trap of violence versus passive action.
>
> Another speaker at this meeting said, after listening to the planning discussions, "We have to have two hats—nice and violent."

The second group planning legal assistance was the Legal Defense Committee, organized by a group of Chicago attorneys following the April riots. The aftermath of those disorders had demonstrated that available legal counsel in Chicago was woefully inadequate during mass arrest situations.

The two groups, but primarily the Legal Defense Committee, cooperated to help National Mobilization recruit volunteer lawyers and law students for the many tasks needed. Two law students helped prepare and distribute arrest information. The information was also distributed through the flyers and mailings of the participating organizations and was printed in many of the various convention specials published by the underground press.

(4) *Medical Groups:* The "medical presence" during the demonstrations was primarily provided by a group of volunteers, drawn from all parts of the country, and organized, under the guidance of National Mobilization, by the joint effort

of the Medical Committee on Human Rights (MCHR) and the Student Health Organization (SHO).

MCHR is a national group of health professionals and laymen. Formed some time in the early sixties, it had its origin in the civil rights movement, and has been active since in mass demonstrations. The Student Health Organization, formed in California in 1965, has similar goals.

These groups were approached by National Mobilization during the spring of 1968 and the request for a medical presence in Chicago was considered at a combined MCHR-SHO meeting on July 9, 1968. It was decided at this meeting to provide that medical presence during convention week if it were needed.

Shortly afterward MCHR was asked by SHO members if they would help in obtaining sanitation facilities for Lincoln Park. A member for SHO, working with the Free City Survival Committee, had already approached the director of Medical Care of the Chicago Health Research Institute with a similar request, which was then passed on to the Board of Health. A letter from the Free City group to David Stahl of the Mayor's Office listing their health requirements was also given to the Chicago Board of Health.

Subsequently, MCHR personnel contacted and tried, not with much success, to involve various city and voluntary agencies in providing personnel, transportation and supplies. MCHR and SHO went ahead with their plans, setting up a planning subcommittee and putting out a nationwide call for volunteers.

Many of the members of MCHR and SHO share the antiwar and political attitudes and feelings of the demonstrators, and a number are members of groups that were planning demonstrations during convention week. Some of the SHO chapters were also active in planning for convention week demonstrations. MCHR and SHO were involved with the National Mobilization planning effort. However, members actually serving as volunteers during the demonstrations were told not to take part, but rather to maintain a "neutral posture."

MCHR and SHO put out a number of flyers and pamphlets describing their plans and activities. Several flyers were directed to the demonstrators, informing them of the services to be provided during the period between August 24 and August 30, and the precautions to take against injury. Another was directed to the volunteers, explaining their roles, the structure of the medical service effort, and the location of various hospitals; it also contained information to be used in case of arrest. A first aid handbook was also distributed.

About 400 health volunteers reportedly served in either stationary first aid stations—to which injured demonstrators, bystanders, and policemen were taken—or on mobile first aid teams. A 24-hour telephone alert service was also manned.

(5) *Cleveland Area Peace Action Committee and the Fifth Avenue Peace Anti-Vietnam Parade Committee:* These groups were regional coalitions of several antiwar groups. Both were represented on the Administrative Committee and, in terms of numbers "mobilized" from outside the Chicago area, they probably contributed the best organizational force to Mobilization.

(6) *Radical Student Groups:* Prominent student groups included SDS (Students for a Democratic Society) and various draft resistance organizations, such as CADRE (a draft resistance group), which operated on a local level. Many of these groups, including SDS, opened movement centers but otherwise chose not to be officially identified with the major antiwar demonstration planned by National Mobilization.

Students for a Democratic Society is a radical left organization conceived in 1961. Its national headquarters are in Chicago. It claims to have 40,000 national and local SDS activists in more than 300 chapters, colleges and universities throughout the country. In its early years it supported reformed Democratic electoral campaigns. Since the 1964 presidential campaign, however, it has taken a much more radical stand.

The SDS decision not to join the Mobilization demonstrations was motivated in part by a fear that Chicago police might use such involvement as a pretext for closing their Chicago offices. Furthermore, it meant to continue with the traditional approach of local, continuous action, rather than sporadic national involvement. In Chicago its main objective was the quiet recruitment of disillusioned McCarthy supporters. The organization was largely committed to the organization of university campuses (especially at Columbia) and probably lacked the manpower to contribute much to Mobilization planning in any event.

The SDS publication, *New Left Notes,* on August 19 published a guide to the convention, giving addresses of five movement centers in the city, and with respect to planning stated: "Hang loose and maintain contact mobility."

(7) *Women's Peace Groups:* Women Strike for Peace had been influential in both the United Nations and Pentagon peace marches. Organized to bring "housewives" in the movement, it apparently had little influence in the Chicago planning. Local organizations such as North Shore Women for Peace and Women Mobilized for Change were active during convention week.

(8) *Militant Extremist Groups:* Youth Against the War and Fascism and the Revolutionary Contingent are among a number of small especially militant organizations. Representatives of the two named were reportedly present in Chicago during convention week.

(9) *The Communist Party, the Progressive Labor Party and the Young Socialist Party:* The Communist Party and other "Communist front" organizations had representatives at almost all Mobilization meetings but none of them had much direct influence during either the planning period or the convention week insofar as Mobilization's program was concerned. The Progressive Labor Party was also present, but it, too, played a small role. The Young Socialist Party actually tried to discourage demonstrators from coming to Chicago, since they felt this would be viewed as support for McCarthy. They were represented in Chicago during convention week, however.

(10) *The Youth International Party:* The "Yippies" were not formally represented at most Mobilization meetings although the leaders of both groups were friendly and often discussed preparation for Chicago and collaborative activities. Mobilization officers, however, occasionally expressed concern over the lack of conviction and seriousness on the part of the Yippies.

> I think that my reaction to the Festival of Life . . . was to feel that it would be projected at the time of the convention and that it was *very important* that that not come to be too important in the public mind or in the movement's mind. (Rennie Davis)

Movement centers were planned to accommodate many of these groups and others as well. Each movement center was to have a special purpose and there was the possibility that several of the "local" groups would come to Chicago and live at the center of their choice, thereby transporting their own "organization" from one city to the other. It was hoped that the surrounding community and other Chicago visitors would engage in an educational dialogue at many of these centers. Certain movement centers were expected to engage in decentralized protests. "We expect many, many activities, multiform and multilevel, and the thing was not to dictate to people, to avoid offending people with an excessive amount of centralism," says Eric Weinberger.

The operation of movement centers may have been envisioned as a tactical response to the tight security measures taken by the city. It may well have been thought that the movement center program would offer protection for dissidents if they could somehow be "absorbed" by the community, yet still maintain their own separate identity and organization.

While preparing for a wide variety of independent, decentralized activities by diverse protest groups, National Mobilization had hopes of bringing a massive assembly together for a march on the Amphitheatre. The Democratic National Convention was to be placed before the "cutting edge of resistance."

It was thought that an "open hearing" held near the Amphitheatre might provide sufficient symbolic contrast to the proceedings within the convention itself. There was some discussion of civil disobedience after the speeches for the "open hearing." "We meant," one of the organizers explains "to go to Chicago and stage . . . non-violent civil disobedient confrontational actions."

Such an act of "resistance" might have taken the form of an attempt to "turn the delegates back" as they left the Amphitheatre after selecting their candidate. At such time, members of the movement might subject themselves to arrest, as at the Pentagon. But there is little evidence that this plan was adopted on a broadly based organization level.

There had been discussion about the employment of disruptive tactics in Chicago throughout the prelude to convention week. National Mobilization generally introduced discussion of a disruptive approach at its meetings, but, at least after February, they claim that disruptive tactics were never "officially" considered as appropriate for Chicago.

Rennie Davis recalls:

Our clear decision that it was not valid to disrupt the convention was based on the fact that we realized that if we transferred our attention from the Pentagon to the Convention there would be a shift in the kind of institution that we were confronting. . . . And whereas there is a pretty unanimous agreement that the Pentagon is *per se* an evil institution and therefore we felt quite prepared to call for disruption of the Pentagon, for shutting it down, the Convention itself was not an evil institution *per se*. . . .

Despite these protestations, there were continued references in the publicity to disruptive tactics and this type of talk undoubtedly influenced Chicago's preparatory measures.

At the Lake Villa meeting, for example, there was discussion of tactics. It was reported that "sentiment among the delegates ranged from ignoring the convention to "closing" it (*New York Times,* March 24, 1968). Davis, however, was quoted as saying:

I think we can do better than attempting to prevent the Convention from taking place, as some have suggested, by closing down the city on the first day of pre-Convention activity. . . . The delegates should be allowed to come to Chicago, so long as they give their support to a policy of ending racism and the war. I favor letting the delegates meet in the International Amphitheatre and making our demands and the actions banning those demands escalate in militancy as the Convention proceeds. . . .

"It's a moral impact we're trying to have," said Dave Dellinger, "not that we think we're going to bring down . . . the war by physical means." But while National Mobilization spokesmen professed a nonviolent credo with respect to Chicago, Dellinger hastened to add: "We are flexible enough to permit each to act in his own style and we will support all of our associated groups." (*Guardian,* August 17, 1968)

Eric Weinberger observes that:

The large mass of peace movement constituency feels that it is adequate to attend a rally, have some speeches, perhaps have a parade, as a way of letting their numbers be counted, and the smaller but very significant part of the peace movement feels that its acts are an essential part of the protest. To show how deep it goes, to show that these are not lightly held beliefs, such people are actually willing to go to jail and suffer.

Mobilization as a whole adopted a multi-level policy that those groups whose members wouldn't take part in civil disobedience nevertheless recognized its existence as a factor. Those groups who felt that confrontation was necessary nevertheless recognized the value of having large numbers of people present who would not choose to take part.

Mobilization had hoped that those "large numbers" would be supplied by young McCarthy supporters who would join the demonstrators after they realized that the Democratic Party would not adopt a peace plank and that the nomination would go to Hubert Humphrey. Such a contingency, it was believed, would lend legitimacy to the demonstration.

Davis says:

We felt very much that the McCarthy movement represented large numbers of people trying to take the effort of peace into an electoral activity. . . . It is very important that the movement not be splintered and ruptured in Chicago, that they see that, particularly if McCarthy were defeated . . . there is a necessity for ongoing work and for peace issues, that the Mobilization and other peace forces represent a framework in which they can continue to carry the spear of their concerns beyond electoral politics, so in that sense we were very concerned about relating to and involving McCarthy's force.

Some realized that the use of disruptive tactics on a large-scale basis would either be absolutely futile or self-defeating in view of the security precautions which had been mounted in the Amphitheatre area. Others felt it would be unnecessary—"the convention will disrupt itself," said Davis, ". . . security would become insecure . . . the overkill policy will devour itself."

Tom Hayden elaborated:

Consider the dilemmas facing those administering the regressive apparatus. . . . They cannot distinguish "straight" radicals from newspapermen or observers from delegates to the convention. They cannot distinguish rumors about demonstrations from the real thing. . . .

. . . There is a point beyond which the security system turns into its opposite, eclipsing the democratic image and threatening the security of the convention itself. The threat of disorder, like all fantasies in the establishment mind, can create total paranoia . . . at a minimum, this process will further erode the surface image of pseudo-democratic politics; at a maximum, it can lead to a closing of the convention—or a shortening of its agenda—for security reasons. (*Ramparts* Wall Poster, August 25, 1968)

Davis claims that he would have known of any plans to disrupt the convention because "disrupting a convention requires that people come prepared with the organization to implement their preparations." But his contact with other protest groups may not actually have been that thorough. For example, it came to his attention at one point that a group in Cleveland had printed a button which read: "Stop the Convention!" Davis describes a July meeting he had with this group:

. . . I went through the point very carefully . . . I said we wanted to put a permanent end to the kind of politics that is represented by the Democratic Convention—politics which ignore democratic processes and primaries . . . and popular sentiment against the war . . . I then went through a whole argument as to why we should be in Chicago with a strong presence and what we would do. . . . And then we had a long discussion . . . and it was quite clear at the end of that meeting that there was no opposition to my interpretation of their slogans—interpreting it to mean end of this kind of politics in America without a literal interpretation to disrupt the convention.

After National Mobilization concluded on July 20 that they would push forward with their plans for Chicago, more determined promotional efforts were undertaken, but they were hardly satisfactory in terms of mobilizing significant support. Eric Weinberger describes the problem:

> There was basically no work to get people to come to Chicago until a month beforehand, which was a failure on our part. But because of the incredible division of opinions within the peace movement, there was no way to agree: "What are we going to do? When are we going to do it? Who's going to be in charge of it?" or anything like that until about a month before. That's when the leaflets started coming out. They never did come out in sufficient quantity.

Another difficulty was Mobilization's inability to contact students and explain the movement centers which were being set up. While the Student Mobilization Committee had successfully organized a student strike on April 26, the organization was no longer active and the students were difficult to contact because they were on summer vacation. Moreover, decentralization made it difficult for Mobilization leaders to keep track of the actions planned by the various groups. The Chicago office never was able to establish a central focus for those who were to participate in the movement centers.

While the need for a demonstration in Chicago was widely publicized, apparently no specific date for the main protest had been set by the beginning of August. As early as December, one loosely affiliated group the (NCNP) had published a full-page advertisement in the *New York Times* urging demonstrators to descend upon Chicago, but no one was told how or when. Even the letter issued by Mobilization to its supporters on July 31 failed to specify anything beyond the request that participants appear in Chicago in the week of August 24 to 29.

By plan or force of circumstance, National Mobilization seemed to rely heavily on local efforts to promote Chicago activity. One such "local" group was the Fifth Avenue Anti-Vietnam Peace Parade Committee in New York City. In contrast to Chicago, an officer claims, the Parade Committee had issued one million leaflets to advertise the April 27 march in New York City alone. However, Weinberger says.

> . . . the first move we made in New York which mentioned Chicago in a public way at all was at the August 3 annual Hiroshima Day Commemoration Demonstration . . . and at that demonstration the chairman referred to

Chicago. Chartered bus tickets were available to go out to Chicago, and he sold practically none.

Weinberger adds that the Parade Committee had sent more than 200 buses to the Pentagon rally. With reference to the Chicago effort, prospects were much lower.

> I had reserved 10 buses and had told the bus company, "We may need two or three times that many," and eventually sent five. So the bus ticket sales were going badly, and my estimates were continually decreasing, but it wasn't until Monday night when the huge crowd that was supposed to show up to buy tickets didn't . . . that I realized that ten or 15 thousand was all were were going to get.

Even that estimate was wildly over-optimistic; the Parade Committee was able to mobilize "maybe 750 people that came in car pools . . . plus an estimated 250 people who responded to our call but took private transportation," and only five bus loads.

National Mobilization officers held several meetings in early August, highlighted by an August 4 gathering of some 50 people in Highland Park, Illinois. Thirty-two of the participants were from the Chicago area, representing such groups as the Chicago Peace Council, the Coalition for an Open Convention, the Student Health Organization and Vets for Peace. There were nine people from New York City, four from Wisconsin and five from other parts of the country. Approximately 25 distinct antiwar organizations were represented.

Dellinger chaired the meeting, emphasizing that the purpose of the demonstration was not disruption but to "demonstrate on the central issue"—racism and the war in Vietnam. This statement was apparently motivated by a continuing concern, even at this time, among some of the more "conservative" members of the Mobilization hierarchy that other members might be favoring disruptive tactics. It was explained that the demonstrators hoped to develop a "positive relationship" with the delegates. The movement center program was outlined and it was disclosed that at least 25 were expected to open on August 24.

Rennie Davis then presented the "scenario" for convention

week demonstrations, which would include picketing to be arranged in front of the Hilton on Sunday, August 25, an anti-birthday party for President Johnson on Tuesday, August 27, and independent actions originating in the movement centers. The central emphasis, however, was on the march to the Amphitheatre scheduled for August 28, when the marchers were to "hold a vigil, picket, create theatre and rally for as long as the convention lasts." One veteran of the Washington march suggested that volunteers be urged to disobey any curfew, in order to force the police into a mass arrest situation. Ostensibly, the position was not adopted by the National Mobilization. In a direct repetition of the Pentagon strategy, there was to be a teach-in with the troops, "stressing that our differences are not with them." On Thursday, August 29, more decentralized actions were scheduled.

After a long discussion, it was decided that the Mobilization would not be officially represented at the rally scheduled for Monday by the Coalition for an Open Convention. But marshals were to be provided, if requested by the COC.

New officers were appointed to provide communication to and between the movement centers, to edit the *Ramparts Daily*, to train marshals, to negotiate with the city for permits, and to coordinate the legal and medical concerns. Since it was felt that permits for the march would eventually be granted, the bulk of the discussion was centered upon such practical arrangements as housing and publicity. Responsibility for these arrangements was either assigned to individual officers or left to the "organic nuclei" of the movement centers.

With reference to the black community, it was reported that the opinions of Lincoln Lynch, Cleveland Robinson, John Wilson and Ralph Abernathy had been solicited, while informal contact with several black organizations was being maintained. However, it was admitted that attempts to contact the Blackstone Rangers and other Chicago groups were meeting with little success.

In terms of finance, Davis outlined a program for parties and mailings to raise money. Ten thousand dollars was needed immediately for sound and communications equipment. A total of $24,000 was needed by August 18. When sources of loans were discussed, it was announced that the Cleveland Area Peace Action had pledged a $1,000 loan.

Shortly after the meeting, about 50,000 flyers, complete with the schedule of events approved at the meeting, were issued by National Mobilization.

Final National Mobilization preparations according to the general outline discussed at this meeting would continue during the few remaining weeks.

A Festival of Life

While plans were being made by antiwar and other dissident groups for activities in Chicago during convention week, preparations were under way within the hippie communities in New York, Chicago, on the West Coast and elsewhere for a massive convocation. The vision was one of a carnival-like party in one of Chicago's lakefront parks, a festive counter-convention offering entertainment, discussion forums, information exchanges, workshops in problems facing dissenting youth and other attractions of interest to the nation's subculture dropouts. The festival was seen as continuing day and night throughout convention week, and the prospect excited hippies across the country. For those who were already coming, the festival was an added attraction; for others, it was to be a demonstration in itself—the demonstration of an alternative "life style," the surfacing of an underground culture, "a renaissance of youth," as they called it.

Long-haired, political activists who had participated in the Pentagon march on October 21, 1967, viewed that demonstration as a turning point, "a new kind of experience in which creativity was unleashed." "People were devising their own schemes," Abbie Hoffman, one of the flamboyant spokesmen for the "underground" movement, recalls.

"Hippie-types" had joined the more formalized protest groups and had added a new dimension which they considered to be satirical. Their statements, while objectionable to many, made good newspaper print. "We saw a chance of developing a real populous involvement among the people within the revolution," Abbie Hoffman said. "Revolution for the hell of it!" "Theatre in the streets!"

This theatrical concept was a primary ingredient of their approach. The audience would be the American public, the means of communication would be the mass media, manipulated to create distorted images of themselves. The stage would be the streets and the message would be a demonstration of disrespect, irreverence and ridicule. It is an approach most graphically described in Abbie Hoffman's words:

> You got a TV set? That's a jungle. You think that gives a shit about words, lineal concepts? We get on that tube . . . we get information out, and our information is heavy, and it sticks, and it's exciting, it's alive. . . . *(New York Free Press, October 3-9, 1968)*

These active hippies, many of them with backgrounds in the creative arts, journalism and the theater, meant to put creativity into protest demonstrations, with an emphasis on individual participation. Hoffman describes how:

> People will be attempting to use guerrilla theater techniques, people will be attempting to use satire, people will be attempting to talk to other people and people will be passing out newspapers, and some will be stoned and some will be fucking on the grass, and people will do whatever they want to do. There is no reason why people come to demonstrations . . . no single cause. It's multifaceted and it's generally a feeling of disgust with what's going on in this country, in every area conceivable that's controlled by the power. . . .
>
> I use guerilla theatre as a medium for creating what I call blank space. Blank space is where you use media so that the observer, the audience becomes a participant, becomes involved.

These activists styled themselves as revolutionaries, promoting a movement within their own dropout community aimed at demonstrating to the "other society" that they were serious about the way of life they had chosen; and that they wanted the freedom to follow their own ways—free love, free traffic in drugs, free music and art, free stores and all.

Again, Abbie Hoffman:

> You see in the whole hippie movement the possibility that people in this country, young white kids, can make their own revolution around their own dreams, their own visions, their own needs. We're already living in the future, we're living 30 years ahead, and, you see, we like it; you see, we like it so much that we're willing to die to defend

it and that's where it's at and that's why we're gonna win. . . .

There's no doubts about it. We're going to wreck this fuckin' society. If we don't, this society is going to wreck itself anyway so, we might as well have some fun doin' it.

Hippies were talking about fighting, "by any means necessary," against repression of their concept of life.

Shortly after Chicago was announced as the convention city, hippie activists began thinking about how to channel the new outward-looking energy within their community into a demonstration directed against President Johnson's administration and what was expected to be this convention in Chicago.

One of these activists, Jerry Rubin, invited others to come to Chicago as early as November.

In the apartment of Abbie Hoffman, on New York's lower East Side, a small group got together to discuss specific plans for organizing massive participation of the hippie community. The date was New Year's Eve, or *Christmas* Eve. There is disagreement among those present, including Hoffman, Rubin and writer Paul Krassner.

Hoffman describes the scene:

There we were, all stoned, rolling around the floor . . . yippie! . . . Somebody says oink and that's it, pig, it's a natural, man, we gotta win. . . . Let's try success, I mean, when we went to the Pentagon we were going to get it to rise 300 feet in the air . . . so we said how about doing one that will win.

And so, YIPPIE was born, the Youth International Party. What about if we create a myth, program it into the media, you know . . . when that myth goes in, its always connected to Chicago August 25 . . . come and do your thing, excitement, bullshit, everything, anything . . . commitment, engagement, Democrats, pigs, the whole thing. All you do is change the H in Hippie to a Y for Yippie, and you got it . . . you can study the media and you say well, the H is switching, now they're talking about Yippies. New phenomena, a new thing on the American scene. . . . Why? That's our question. Our slogan is why? You know as long as we can make up a story about it that's exciting, full of shit, mystical, magical, you have to accuse us of going to Chicago to perform magic.

The idea was to get people involved and the expectations were high. President Johnson had become the personified object of hippie discontent. The Festival of Life was conceived as a contrast to what they called the "Convention of Death" to be held at the Amphitheatre. The Festival of Life, featuring 30 or 40 popular rock groups, would be the drawing card for perhaps hundreds of thousands of young people around the country. They viewed it as a massive demonstration of an alternative life style, and recognized that it would undoubtedly require major security precautions on the part of the city. But, they say, this was part of their plan—the Democratic National Convention re-nominating President Johnson under military guard—an achievement for the "Politics of Absurdity."

The "Politics of Absurdity" is represented by *"Be Realistic, Demand the Impossible,"* a Yippie flyer prepared for convention week and distributed in Lincoln Park. Its demands include the ludicrous, the outrageous, and the routine.

> An immediate end to the War in Vietnam . . . the abolition of the military draft. . . . An end to the cultural and economic domination of minority groups. . . . The legalization of marijuana and all other psychedelic drugs. . . . A prison system based on the concept of rehabilitation rather than punishment. . . . The total disarmament of all the people beginning with the police. . . . The abolition of Money. . . . A conservation program geared towards preserving our natural resources and committed to the elimination of pollution of our crowded cities . . . free birth control information and devices but also abortions when desired . . . student power to determine his course of study. . . . The open and free use of the media. . . . An end to all censorship. . . . We believe that people should fuck all the time, anytime, whomever they wish . . . a national referendum system conducted via television or a telephone voting system. . . . A program that encourages and promotes the arts. . . .

Was all of this simply a put-on, or was there a serious political motive? Said Jerry Rubin, "I think we succeeded in making the Pentagon look ridiculous—forcing troops carrying bayonets to "protect" it from unarmed, hairy, young people. Our strategy for Chicago was more or less the same."

Rubin, 30, is a former Cincinnati newspaper reporter, now

active in the pro-Maoist Progressive Labor Party in California. He had participated in organizing the Pentagon march in October, which ended in violence, and was involved in various violent demonstrations in Berkeley, California. He is also reported to have been one of the sponsors of the April, 1967 peace demonstration in New York.

The objectives of Yippie were explained by Hoffman:

> 1. The blending of pot and politics grass leaves movement—a cross-fertilization of the hippie and New Left philosophy. 2. A connecting link that would tie as much as the underground as was willing into some gigantic national get-together. 3. The development of a model for an alternative society. 4. The need to make some statement, especially in revolutionary action-theater terms, about LBJ, the Democratic Party, electoral politics, and the state of the nation.
>
> —*Realist*, September, 1968.

Hoffman, 31, had been active in the Movement for some time. Once a psychologist, he left his job to participate in civil rights demonstrations in the South. Along with Rubin, he had more recently taken part in demonstrations in Berkeley, New York and at the Pentagon.

Paul Krassner describes Yippie as "a national disorganization whose sole purpose would be the Theatre of Disruption," explaining:

> . . . [It was] a gesture to show that they felt they had to protect the convention. We didn't know they were going to do the thing with the barbed wire, but they played their roles perfectly . . . our mere appearance there, thousands of freaky looking people is in itself a disruption . . .
>
> * * *
>
> For example, when they knew we were running a pig, they put an armed guard on the pig in the zoo. It just made them look ridiculous. We wanted to make them look ridiculous because we felt they were.

Krassner, 36, for ten years has published *The Realist*, a satirical underground magazine with a circulation of over 100,000. A close friend of Hoffman and Rubin, he has covered major demonstrations across the country for some time. This literature was always fanciful, confusing and belligerent, a blend of playfulness and militancy, whimsy and contempt. Half serious and half in jest, it is always calculated to excite reaction. It was consciously threatening and deliberately unpredictable.

By early January, plans for the Festival of Life had progressed rapidly, and underground newspapers carried articles promoting the event.

The following example is from the *New York Free Press:*

> We've got to get crazy. Craziest motherfuckers they ever seen in this country. Cause that's the only way we're gonna beat them. So fucking crazy that they can't understand it at ALL. They know something's up, something's going on down there, something's happening, some change coming on in this country, just like Dylan says, "There's something happening but you don't know what it is, do you, Mr. Jones?"
>
> We won't tell 'em what it is. What do you want to tell them for? Don't tell 'em shit. NEVER.
>
> . . . That's the problem you have when you focus in on an issue, when you make a demand. They can deal with a demand.
>
> We put a finger up their ass and tell them, "I ain't telling you what I want," then they got a problem.

The Festival of Life plan travelled rapidly throughout the hippie communities by word of mouth. Letters came into New York from various parts of the country, asking how to become a Yippie. The answer: "How do you become a Yippie? Say you're a Yippie, and you're a Yippie! Just say you're a Yippie leader and do your own thing!"

There was great enthusiasm and organizational activity during the early months of 1968, particularly in New York. Posters and flyers and buttons were distributed. A benefit was held and afterwards a Yippie office opened. Weekly meetings began and committees for entertainment, theater, press, food, housing and other preparations were set up.

When those who had taken an active role in organizing the Festival travelled and spoke to other groups, Chicago was mentioned. Folk and rock musical groups also promoted the Festival.

Sometime in February, Jerry Rubin made contact with a

Chicago hippie group centered around *The Seed,* a local underground newspaper, and solicited their help to promote the Festival and to make local arrangements.

Further plans were worked out during this period. There would be a giant music fair, a nude-in on the beach, workshops of various sorts, including draft resistance, use of LSD, underground newspapers and other matter uniquely of interest to the dropout community. There would be poetry sessions, information exchanges, political forums and a convention of underground intellectuals to discuss the direction of a new society. The protest march to the Amphitheatre, being planned by National Mobilization, was considered, but not scheduled as part of the proposed program for the Festival of Life. Each individual was left to "do his own thing."

In February, the New York Yippies staged their first event: a raid on the Stony Brook campus of the State University of New York, intended to satirize a previous dope raid by the police. It was disruptive and gave Yippies the publicity they sought.

By March, the Yippies had made contact with an impressive number of prominent radio personalities, poets, folk singers, theater people and somewhere between 20 to 40 rock groups, all tentatively committed to come to Chicago.

On March 21, the Yippies staged another event in New York, a nighttime party at Grand Central Station. Although there was little promotion, around 5,000 people showed up. The result was sustained disruption, a police confrontation, violence and more publicity for Yippies. There were more than 50 arrests and many injured.

On the following day Abbie Hoffman, Jerry Rubin, and Paul Krassner went to Chicago to attend the Lake Villa meeting of various New Left and black groups to discuss convention week plans. They had been invited by National Mobilization. The three Yippies announced that they were coming to Chicago and that they expected tens, maybe hundreds of thousands to join their Festival of Life.

Most of the participants in that conference had trouble communicating with the Yippie contingent. One of the Yippie spokesmen is reported to have said:

> America is dead, you all know it, and yet you're getting involved in a dance with a dead lady. The Democratic Party is going to foul you up. The only way you're going

to change America is to involve people with their emotions, not their minds. *Chicago Sun-Times,* March 25.

Abbie Hoffman commented on what he had to say at the meeting:

> We demanded such relevant things . . . (as) the abolition of pay toilets—that was one of our key items . . . they didn't understand what I was talking about I'm sure. They're the Left, they're into heavy words, words mean something—I'm into emotion. I'm into symbols and gestures and I don't have a program and I don't have an ideology and I'm not a part of the Left.

So while the "Left" continued to debate whether or not they were coming to Chicago and what they were going to do when they got there, the Yippie organizers took a positive attitude—they were coming, to be sure, with music and myth and with their threats to disrupt the city.

Before leaving Chicago, the three Yippies renewed personal contact with the *Seed* group. They worked up a permit application for the use of a Chicago park during the convention.

After President Johnson's announced withdrawal from the presidential campaign on March 31, 1968, there was a marked decline of interest in the Festival of Life. The New York Yippie spokesmen, after a period of several months of little organizational activity, actually decided to drop the idea of coming to Chicago. During this period, underground publications carried articles criticizing the Yippie plans, stressing local action as the proper focus. In the meantime, the softer side of the Yippie-hippie community pointed to the violent Grand Central Station incident, to the severe encounter of the April 27 peace marchers with the Chicago police and to the tough statements on police action being made by Mayor Daley. A violent confrontation with the Chicago police seemed likely if the Festival of Life were to take place, and many simply didn't want to travel hundreds of miles to join a tumultuous battle of police and demonstrators in a Chicago park. The more militant side of Yippie professed, however, that if some were "into violence, that was their thing," and it shouldn't concern anyone.

Planning for the Festival of Life, consequently, proceeded at a slower pace; persons that were still interested were referred to the Chicago *Seed* group or asked to work on it locally.

On the weekend of May 10, Abbie Hoffman flew to Chicago. He conferred with the *Seed* people. They talked about local preparations, and Hoffman encouraged the Chicagoans to plan weekly music festivals in the park to accustom local residents to the "long hair" community, thus preparing them for the August influx. It was also hoped that such "little" festivals would lessen the danger of disturbance by "greasers," lower middle-class white gangs about whom the Yippies were particularly apprehensive.

Following this meeting, the Chicago *Seed* group decided to abandon a public association with "Yippie." On April 25, a meeting of the group under the aegis of Yippie! had been raided by the Chicago police. Twenty-one were arrested. A subsequent benefit at the Electric Theatre was also raided, and again there were more arrests, this time about 30. Because of the reputation the New York Yippies were building for violence and disruption, and because productive negotiations for the August Festival under the auspices of Yippie were considered dubious, the Chicago group formed the Free City Survival Committee. It was this committee which would officially continue negotiations with the city through June, July and the first week of August and which would carry on with local preparations for the Festival of Life.

The Free City Survival Committee worked closely with the Chicago Commission on Youth Welfare, the Park District and the police. It also conducted weekly music festivals in Lincoln Park beginning in mid-May. Some of these occasions attracted more than 1,000 people.

For Yippie activists in New York and California, this late spring period offered activities, particularly at Columbia and Berkeley, that took priority over the Festival of Life. The rash of convention related underground literature, designed to develop the Yippie myth, to create mystery and excitement and thus expand enthusiasm for Chicago, had come and gone.

Then, after Senator Robert Kennedy's assassination and with schools closed for the summer recess, interest in the Festival of Life was suddenly revived. "People wanted to know when the hell we were going," Abbie Hoffman remembered, "and I would say, 'A week after Kennedy's assassination I became convinced that I was going to Chicago.' "

Preparations again accelerated, but expectations were never the same. Permit negotiations by the Chicago *Seed* group were making no visible progress, and rock bands were unwilling to commit themselves without a permit, without some assurance that the Festival of Life would not turn into a Grand Central Station riot. This presented serious problems to the Yippie organizers. They felt certain that a permit would be granted at the eleventh hour, but they couldn't wait until then if they were going to get firm commitments from entertainers. Without them, they would be unable to attract the tens of thousands they hoped for. Their plans were frustrated, and the Festival was in jeopardy. On the one hand, they kept assuring the rock groups that a permit would be granted; on the other, they promised the city officials that there would be tens of thousands of kids coming to Chicago for the Festival, so they had better issue a permit.

"At that time," Abbie Hoffman recalls, ". . . we were very unclear as to who was coming and who was not coming. . . . Many of the rock groups that had pledged themselves to come had either broken up and reformed, or were very difficult to locate. Those we did locate said, 'Yes, we're coming if there's a permit,' and we were reluctant to put out any kind of call to Chicago based upon the fact that rock groups were coming."

It was about this time that a split began to develop between the Chicago hippie group and the New York Yippies; between the cultural Yippies and the political activists, or "heavies," as they were called. "Cultural hippies wanted nothing to do with the Democratic convention," said Abe Peck, editor of the Chicago *Seed*, "but they dug the idea of people coming to Chicago and grooving there. The political Yippies, on the other hand, like Rubin, wanted to demonstrate." At a Free City Survival Committee meeting in June, a motion to cancel the entire Festival was made, but rejected.

In the meantime, there were reports of sizable security preparations undertaken in Chicago. Police action against demonstrators in New York had been stepped up, at least in the minds of many demonstrators. Moreover, "law and order" had become a political issue and demonstrators felt that it was directed towards them. In New York, Jerry Rubin was arrested. In Chicago, the group remembered the police "sweeps" in Old Town.

Earlier Yippie literature had talked about disruption of the convention, about burning Chicago and had made other wild and provocative threats. There were deliberate attempts to "play upon the American psyche," to "blow their minds," to "freak them out." But Yippie articles and conversations now took on a much more somber tune. It was realized that there was going to be violence in Chicago, at least on Wednesday night.

"You couldn't go to a demonstration without expecting violence," Abbie Hoffman said. "There is no such thing any more in this country; you've got to expect violence." Consequently, promotional literature and discussions always warned of violence and did not attempt to encourage participation in the Wednesday night march to the Amphitheatre. Hoffman says:

> When it gets to a thing like Wednesday—risking your life, as we felt it was into, we were not about to tell everybody there was one thing planned and this was it and this is what you had to do.

During the early part of August, the New York Yippie organizers came to Chicago to talk to the Chicago *Seed* people about the permit problem. The meeting between the *Seed* group and the New Yorkers then turned to a discussion of violence in Chicago. Hoffman recalls,

> In the original schedule [for Chicago], I wrote "Wednesday—police riot" and that spooked them, I mean they, these people were kids, you know, in Chicago. They did not have the experience that we had and they were not as tough. When they asked me what my personal predictions were for that day, I got into 20 or 30 killed, you know, 6,000 arrests. . . . There was no doubt in my mind that the demonstration was going to be at least as intense as the one at the Pentagon in October.

Apparently the Free City Survival Committee became apprehensive. Jerry Rubin sounded militant and aggressive. Moreover, he and his radical associates were strangers who could come to Chicago during convention week, and then leave again when it was all over. The Chicago people felt, on the other hand, that if violence did erupt, they would be held responsible and their life of hippie leisure would be suddenly snuffed.

When the *Seed* group became convinced that a permit for

Lincoln Park would not be forthcoming, they issued a statement urging people not to come to Chicago, warning youngsters that they had been misled if they were looking for fun and frivolity.

"Don't come to Chicago," the statement read, "if you expect a five-day festival of life, music and love. The word is out. Chicago may host a festival of blood." The New York Yippies were furious. Abbie Hoffman, Jerry Rubin and Paul Krassner flew to Chicago immediately. They had no intention of calling off the Festival, permit or not. A torrid meeting with the Free City group convinced a number of the Chicagoans to modify their position and join with the New York spokesmen in filing a substitute application for the August Festival.

Abraham Peck, editor of the *Seed,* told newsmen in a press conference that seekers of joy were being urged to stay home. Because of the apparent impasse in securing a park permit and the firm resolve of the New York Yippies and some of those in Chicago to continue with their plans for a Festival, he feared that "the chance for confrontation with repressive agencies had increased." He urged "those who remain uncommitted to change to avoid Chicago," but called upon "those who deem change necessary to lend their support by their presence in Chicago."

The New Yorkers had been influenced by the Chicago group's stand, however. Hoffman explains:

> They convinced us that we had to start talking about violence in Chicago and that it was gonna happen and that people oughta prepare for it and we oughta get a little more serious in our statements and eliminate a lot of the bullshit. We felt that the time was getting close and the kind of information that we had to get out and the kind of work that we had to do, had to be of a very concrete nature. You know, we had to start setting up medical centers and we had to prepare, we had to start telling kids about vaseline, about self-defense measures. We had to start working real hard on self-defense classes in the park and start building them up. We had to prepare for war. That requires a little different approach than preparing for a festival of life, although war is part of life, you know.

The New York group decided that Abbie Hoffman should stay in Chicago and carry on with local preparations. This was only about two weeks preceding convention week and there was no permit in the offing, few entertainers committed, no food, little organization and only the most speculative expectation about who was going to come and what was going to take place in Lincoln Park.

Coalition for an Open Convention

The Coalition for an Open Convention (COC) was formed in an attempt to unite various antiwar and anti-Humphrey factions within the Democratic Party after the assassination of Senator Robert Kennedy. The prime mover of the group was Allard K. Lowenstein, a 39-year-old lawyer and candidate for a seat in Congress on both the Democratic and Liberal tickets from New York's Fifth District on Long Island.

Lowenstein had been the chief organizer of the Coalition for a Democratic Alternative, which had sought to unite forces looking for a presidential candidate who would oppose the war in Vietnam. He had actively supported Senator Eugene McCarthy for the presidency.

An organizational meeting of COC was held at the Sherman House in Chicago on June 29, 1968, attracting Kennedy and McCarthy workers and college student groups. A caucus of students suggested a program for convention week, including mass rallies for the discussion of political issues and for the demonstration of antiwar, antiadministration sentiments. This suggestion was adopted by the group at large, and McCarthy's slogan "On to Chicago" was chosen as the name of the project. Clinton Deveaux was named "Chicago Coordinator" and Martin Slate "Project Coordinator." A rally at Soldier Field, Chicago's huge lakefront stadium, was scheduled for Sunday, August 25, as the main event. As many as 100,000 persons were expected.

But COC was never to stage this massive rally. Allard Lowenstein announced a cancellation of the program after Senator McCarthy's public statement urging his followers to avoid Chicago, and after an unsuccessful bid to obtain a permit for the use of Soldier Field.

McCarthy and His Supporters

A large part of the expected influx of demonstrators were those coming to show support for Senator McCarthy. Most of the workers in the McCarthy campaign were young people, many drawn into political activity for the first time and others, more jaded, giving the "system" one last try. They had worked hard for the Senator in the difficult primary campaigns, and many now wished to come to Chicago for the finish.

But, suddenly, their candidate announced that he wanted them to stay away. On August 12, McCarthy during a press conference appealed to his supporters to keep away from Chicago during convention week to avoid the possibility of unscheduled rallies leading to "unintended violence." He urged them to conduct rallies in their own communities rather than contribute to the tensions in Chicago. In addition, telegrams were sent to each of the many McCarthy campaign headquarters around the country to reinforce the request. It was reported that Senator McCarthy had been in contact with Mayor Daley, that he had learned of potential violent disruption and rumored assassination plots, including one in which he himself was a target.

National Mobilization, the Yippies, and COC had counted on the youthful McCarthy contingent to buttress their numbers and had hoped to win some converts.

Reactions were mixed. The co-chairman of the Pennsylvania Coalition for an Open Convention, for example, announced that his group would comply with Senator McCarthy's request and that they had cancelled plans to take 2,000 persons to Chicago for the mass rally on August 25. But while the overall effect was to decrease significantly the number of McCarthy people who would be coming for the Democratic convention, many were not dissuaded. Determined groups of McCarthyites boldly announced their intention to come in any event, and went ahead with their preparations.

Rennie Davis, on behalf of National Mobilization, continued to urge McCarthy supporters to come to Chicago and join the demonstrators. He stated at a press conference that planned demonstrations would be orderly and not disruptive. He interpreted McCarthy's statement as reflecting the Senator's need to separate himself from the demonstrations so that delegates would not feel his supporters were trying to coerce them.

The Black Community

One of the first public reactions to the announcement that the convention would be held in Chicago was a statement by Dick Gregory, a former comedian and a black civil rights activist. Gregory, who lives in Chicago, threatened to lead demonstrations that would make it impossible for the convention to be held. He continued to press this theme in statements throughout the winter and spring, and his remarks received extensive press coverage. Although Gregory was involved in an abortive march to the South Side on Thursday night, August 29, the massive disruptions by blacks which he had earlier promised never materialized.

National Mobilization organizers had for many months preceding the convention attempted to coalesce a united demonstration of white antiwar groups and black dissidents.

At the planning level, several leaders of the Black Caucus of the National Conference for New Politics, and representatives of other black organizations, national and local, moderate and militant, took part in an attempt to merge the antiwar and black movements. This united effort would combine whites and blacks in a paralleled organizational structure, consistent with the current black separatist philosophy. But the manifestation of a front of solidarity envisioned for Chicago never came to fruition. Ambitious expectations for a ponderous black demonstration of this new coalition evaporated some time between the Lake Villa meeting over the weekend of March 22 and convention week.

Many blacks felt that demonstrations like those planned for Chicago, focusing on the war in Vietnam, were traditionally conducted by whites and were remote from the problems which plagued the black man—problems which have to be dealt with by blacks themselves. Still others feared the heavy security forces which were expected to be amassed in Chicago and wanted to avoid what they thought could develop into a massacre of blacks.

A number of local black organizations, reportedly including The Woodlawn Organization, The Black Consortium and Operation Breadbasket urged Chicago blacks not to get involved in the demonstrations and to "stay cool." In an effort to keep peace in the ghettos, a number of city officials and cooperating black community leaders also worked to keep demonstrators from coming through such areas in the course of their proposed marches. Many black leaders expressed dismay at the prospect of a march through the ghetto which might bring troops with them—a grim reminder of the April riots.

The chief officer of the city's poverty program, himself a black, confidentially predicted a week prior to the convention that there would be no trouble in or from the black communities during the convention. He also said that about two weeks before the convention, police were stopping and searching people in the black community and that this had caused apprehension in the poverty centers because people were complaining about it. The disturbance caused by this stopping and searching did not reach the proportion of extreme hostility, he added.

One leader of a black community organization said that complaints of police brutality received by that organization increased dramatically in the week or so before the convention.

One of the militant black groups which seems to have aroused concern was the Black Panthers, originally a West Coast organization of black militants. Huey Newton, a Black Panther leader, had been indicted for murder of an Oakland police officer. In mid-July, a memo sent to various Panther chapters in New York, Atlanta, Cleveland and Oakland urged support for convention related activities. On Saturday, August 17, a group of Black Panthers was arrested near a Chicago church where Senator McCarthy was speaking—weapons and ammunition were found in their car.

During the weeks preceding the convention, Rennie Davis, the Chicago coordinator for National Mobilization, had been in contact with the Blackstone Rangers, a South Side gang of black youths. Davis tried to negotiate an agreement with the Blackstone Rangers to protect political peace workers from a racial clash in the ghetto. The deal never materialized. Blackstone Ranger people were also contacted by Abbie Hoffman and encouraged to join the Festival of Life in Lincoln Park. Very few blacks, as it turned out, appeared in Lincoln Park during convention week, except in connection with the "Free Huey Newton" rally on Tuesday night. As a matter of fact, some of the city's militant black leaders, encouraged by city officials and black civic leaders to leave the city during the convention week, and Ranger notables Jeff Fort and Edward Bey, had withdrawn to a farm in downstate Illinois. One leader said that the local police commander had suggested that it would be better if he were out of the city convention week. He did leave for the weekend but returned Monday, August 26, because it became apparent that there would not be any ghetto violence.

The Blackstone Rangers had been under investigation during the summer in connection with Congressional hearings on misuse of OEO funds. During the weeks preceding the convention, Chicago police had employed a measure in black communities called "preventive surveillance." The reported intention was to make it obvious to certain black activists that they were being closely watched by the police. In addition, many of these black activists were being interrogated by federal agents. Immediately prior to convention week, Jeff Fort, Edward Bey, and other Ranger "chiefs" had been called to testify before a grand jury investigation into assassination plots, allegedly originating with a group of Rangers.

PERMIT NEGOTIATIONS

The promoters for the various organizations planning to bring people to Chicago for convention week were faced with the necessity of obtaining permits for their activities. Clearance from such agencies as the Park District, the Department of Streets and Sanitation, the Police Department, and, indeed, the Mayor's office would be required. They would also need the city's cooperation in obtaining adequate sanitary provisions, health facilities and other accommodations.

As it developed, only three groups made formal application for the necessary permits and subsequently entered into discussions with local officials. In each instance, a lawsuit was ultimately filed. The three groups were the National Mobilization Committee to End the War in Vietnam (National Mobilization), The Youth International Party (Yippies), and the Coalition for an Open Convention (COC). There were, of course, numerous other requests for the use of Chicago's public facilities. For example, the McCarthy for President Organization had made an early inquiry about the availability of Soldier Field, the city's huge lakefront stadium. Each of the three organizations also requested the use of Soldier Field.

Soldier Field, however, had been reserved for the entire convention period by the Democratic National Committee and the Chicago Non-Partisan Committee, the host group formed to attempt to bring both political conventions to Chicago. The Park District's tentative (March 4) and final (June 13) schedules for Soldier Field showed the period from August 23 to August 28, inclusive, reserved for "President Johnson's birthday." President Johnson never did come to Chicago for the convention although there was continuing speculation that he might.

Representatives of the three demonstration groups knew from past experience that municipal authorities had often delayed granting massive demonstration permits until the very eve of the event. They were also aware of a high Park District official's reported remark in the spring of 1968 that its facilities would not be made available to "unpatriotic" groups. As convention week approached, leaders of the demonstration groups knew that the city was intent upon maintaining strict security measures and suspected that the withholding of permits could be part of an overall policy to discourage demonstrators from coming to Chicago. Nonetheless, the initial expectations of most of those involved in negotiations with the city were that the permits requested would be granted. Even after it became perfectly clear that permits would not be granted for sleeping in the park or for a march to the Amphitheatre, some thought that there would be an informal concession at the last minute.

City officials charged with the responsibility of considering the permit applications of National Mobilization did not discount the possibility of disruption. The Pentagon march and rally in October, 1967, had been sponsored by National Mobilization. A march to the South Side could cause serious unrest in the black ghettos, and city officials had been informed that federal authorities were very concerned about massive demonstrations in the Amphitheatre area.

City officials also felt that the leaders of the various groups planning to come to Chicago would not be able to control all persons responding to their invitations. They knew that the leadership for planning the Lincoln Park Festival of Life had been taken over by the New York Yippies. Jerry Rubin and Abbie Hoffman had impressed the city negotiators as militant and unpredictable. Their association with the Stony Brook raid and the Grand Central Station disturbance in New York had not gone unnoticed. Furthermore, they sought not only the daytime use of Lincoln Park, but had also requested sleeping privileges. A local ordinance, however, was construed to make an 11 p.m. curfew applicable, so that the permit applied for would be in violation of the law. Although this provision had been flexibly enforced in the past, the Yippie program for Lincoln Park was considered a far cry from previous, more conventional requests for park usage.

Finally, the city was aware that militant agitators would be among the crowd and that these persons would do their utmost to cause trouble.

All of these factors influenced the city in its negotiations with the various groups seeking permits.

National Mobilization Committee to End the War in Vietnam

National Mobilization sought use of a large number of facilities for holding its rallies and demonstrations. They initially requested two parade permits for August 28, 1968. The first was for a parade of 150,000 marchers from State Street and Wacker Drive, up State Street to Jackson Boulevard, and east to the Grant Park bandshell. The second was for a parade and assembly on Halsted Street from 39th to 47th Streets between 7 p.m. to midnight; the original estimate was 200,000 marchers.

In addition to these parade permits, National Mobilization sought ten parks for "meet-ins" with sound equipment, to be available throughout the week for any organization which might want to conduct an independent rally. Six park areas, including Lincoln Park, were also requested for sleeping.

Extensive negotiations were carried on by National Mobilization and the city concerning these initial requests. In addition to Rennie Davis, the negotiators for National Mobilization were two law students and later a lawyer. During the final stages, officers of National Mobilization also participated in the talks.

National Mobilization's first contact with the city was on June 16, 1968, when Al Baugher of the Chicago Commission on Youth Welfare met with Rennie Davis at a coffee shop near the National Mobilization office at 407 South Dearborn Street. Davis spelled out National Mobilization's interest in seeking permits for parades, rallies and sleeping in the parks. He mentioned the use of Garfield Park and Washington Park, among other large city parks, as possible sites. In reply, Al Baugher warned of the problems there would be in using these two parks in predominantly black neighborhoods, as well as the general difficulties the city would have in meeting such requests. Davis asked for meetings with city and Park District officials. Baugher returned to his office and proposed such a meeting in a memorandum sent to David Stahl, the Mayor's administrative officer.

National Mobilization also sought the intercession of Roger Wilkins, head of the Community Relations Division of the U.S. Department of Justice. Wilkins first sent one of his men to speak with Davis and later came to Chicago himself.

Davis asked Wilkins to assist him in obtaining demonstration sites and the use of Soldier Field the night of August 29 for an antiwar rally and a protest against the anticipated nomination of Hubert Humphrey.

In mid-July, Wilkins met with Mayor Daley, thinking that he might serve as a mediator between the demonstrators and the city, but the meeting was not productive. Subsequently, Wilkins introduced Rennie Davis to Thomas Foran, United States District Attorney, in Chicago. It was hoped that Foran might have some influence in bringing the city and the demonstrators to a mutually agreeable understanding. The demonstrators felt that both Wilkins and Foran understood their point of view, but neither was able to obtain any results.

Meanwhile, Mark Simons, one of the law students engaged by National Mobilization, undertook the task of obtaining permits and starting formal negotiations with the city. He attempted to arrange a meeting with David Stahl and Al Baugher for July 15 at the National Mobilization office but city officials did not appear. Between July 15 and July 25, Simons called Stahl's office several times, but received no response.

Stahl was apparently very upset about a TV interview in which Davis said that he was asking the Justice Department to conduct an investigation of the Chicago Police Department, on the grounds of possible police violence and disruption during convention week. He told Simons that he saw no point in meeting with someone who made statements like that.

However, Stahl agreed to a meeting with Davis and Simons on August 2.

In the meantime, Simons filed the two parade applications on July 29. He, another law student and a lawyer (Davis' negotiating team) then met with Thomas Barry, acting superintendent of the Park District, on July 31, and discussed National Mobilization's park usage requests. Barry asked for a written memorandum about the facilities requested. He indicated he would then contact National Mobilization before the next meeting of the Board of Park Commissioners on August

13. The memorandum was prepared and delivered the following day.

On August 2, 1968, David Stahl had a breakfast meeting with Davis and his negotiating staff at the Palmer House. Davis gave an outline of National Mobilization's plans for convention week, while Stahl listened, took some notes and said he would keep in touch with them.

At National Mobilization's August 4 meeting in Highland Park it was decided to alter the parade plans and seek a permit for one late afternoon march to the Amphitheatre rather than the two marches; and an amended parade application to the Department of Streets and Sanitation was filed two days later. The consensus of the Highland Park meeting was to press for a demonstration within eyesight of the Amphitheatre. Rennie Davis explains its significance:

> We wanted to have legal and undisrupted demonstrations, and we felt the real power of our coming to Chicago would be around those public hearings at the Amphitheatre, and that's really what we wanted to secure. . . . We felt that . . . there was an important political presence that needed to be made on the eve of the nomination, as we anticipated at that time Humphrey would be nominated. . . . [A]n antiwar presence outside the Amphitheatre. And that the political impact of that presence would be lost if we held a demonstration five miles from the Amphitheatre or held it in Detroit. I mean it was at the Amphitheatre where . . . that presence would be made and felt. (Rennie Davis)

Davis claimed that granting permits would be to the city's advantage because the demonstrators would thereby be able to conduct a well-planned march and rally. Otherwise, Davis argued, the demonstrators would be apt to divide, spread out through the city and move into the South Side without organization.

On August 5, 1968, Davis, along with David Dellinger, Robert Greenblatt, Sydney Peck (all officers of National Mobilization), and Simons met in the Old Colony Coffee Shop with two men from the Justice Department's Community Relations Division. These men were asked, as Roger Wilkins had been, to assist in negotiations with the city. They told the National Mobilization group that Mayor Daley had advised them the city's parks would not be available for sleeping. This was the first solid indication to National Mobilization that the city could be "uncooperative," although the lawyer on Davis' negotiating team had already for several days been urging them to bring suit for the permits. He believed that the city was engaged in a "power game" and was attempting to stall in order to see how many demonstrators would actually show up.

That same day, a letter was sent by National Mobilization to Police Superintendent Conlisk about parade security measures. Later in the month, Simons and several others had meetings with members of the Police Department to discuss the role of the marshals and National Mobilization's desire to lessen tension during the demonstrations by not having the police present in huge numbers. The first meeting with the police was on August 7; a second, on August 21, the day after there had been a marshal training session in Lincoln Park which had received considerable media attention; and a third on August 23, at which the schedule of activities was discussed and a detailed explanation of the marshals' function presented.

On August 10, 1968, Davis and his negotiating team met with Stahl at a coffeeshop near Monroe and Clark Streets. According to Davis, he made it clear that he felt the negotiations were dragging, that he didn't feel he was talking to someone who could make a decision, and that he wanted to meet with Mayor Daley.

Stahl reportedly replied that Mayor Daley does not make decisions concerning park or parade permits, indicating that these requests were handled by the Park District and Department of Streets, respectively. National Mobilization, however, indicated that they wanted the next scheduled meeting on August 12, 1968 to be a decision-making one, at which there could be real progress made. The National Mobilization leaders viewed the August 12 meeting as crucial. They expected one of three possible outcomes: agreement to their original proposals, outright rejection, or a dialogue about alternatives.

The August 12 meeting was attended by members of National Mobilization's Administrative Committee, who had come in from various parts of the country. Stahl and Baugher were joined by a city legal aide. No decisions were reached; the National Mobilization leaders were asked, however, whether they would still march if they did not receive a permit.

The National Mobilization group expressed their disappointment that the heads of the Police Department, Bureau of Streets and Sanitation and Park District were not there, as they had expected. The meeting accomplished little and another attempt to arrange a broader meeting failed.

On August 13, the negotiating team attended a meeting of the Park Commission, expecting the permits to be on the agenda. They were not. A commission member, responding to a reporter's question, stated that the permit applications were under advisement. On August 14, Rennie Davis sent a telegram to Mayor Daley, requesting an emergency meeting of city officials to deal with the permit requests.

In the meantime, National Mobilization spokesmen attempted to persuade the Democratic National Committee to intervene with the city. Unsuccessful in their attempt to present their case in a meeting forum, they confronted Democratic Party Chairman John M. Bailey at a press conference on Friday, August 16. Yippie representatives were also there. Bailey said he would speak with Mayor Daley but added that decisions had to come from the city, not from the party.

Another meeting of the National Mobilization hierarchy was held on August 18. Most of the out-of-town leaders had come to Chicago to stay on for the convention. There was considerable discussion about permits, and it was now generally assumed that no formal permits would be granted.

On August 19, National Mobilization filed suit in the United States District Court for the Northern District of Illinois. The case was assigned for hearing before District Judge William J. Lynch. In essence, the suit charged Mayor Daley and other city officials with conspiring to deny the antiwar group the right to assemble and with the denial of equal protection. The group said that it had applied on July 25 for parade and assembly permits from the Department of Streets and Sanitation to hold a demonstration August 28. The suit also stated that the organization requested sleeping quarters in public parks but had failed to receive a reply. The city moved that the suit be dismissed.

Filing the suit led to negotiations with the city during a discussion in Judge Lynch's chambers between Rennie Davis and Raymond Simon, city corporation counsel, on August 21. Present at the conference were National Mobilization attorneys.

After summarizing the original permit requests, Simon stated that the city would not consider at all a parade during nighttime, but would consider a daytime parade. He proposed alternate routes:

1) Assembling at the McCormick Place parking lot, north on the Outer Drive (one or two lanes only) to the Grant Park bandshell;
2) Assembling at Lake Shore Park, Chicago Avenue and the Outer Drive, south on the Outer Drive (one or two lanes only) to the Grant Park bandshell;
3) Assembling at Wacker Drive and Jackson Boulevard, east on Jackson to Columbus Drive to the Grant Park bandshell; and
4) Assembling at the Monroe Street parking lot (in Grant Park) marching south along Columbus Drive to the Grant Park bandshell.

Davis said that any one of the four proposals would be acceptable for the daytime demonstration on August 28, but indicated that National Mobilization also wanted a parade and rally at the Amphitheatre which would coincide with the nominations set for that evening.

Simon replied that state law prohibits parades during the hours of 4 p.m. to 7 p.m. but that the city would permit a rally at night, in some other area than that requested by Davis —Halsted Street from 39th Street to 45th Street. That area, he explained, was forbidden to all groups by the police and Secret Service for security reasons.

Davis then suggested that they rally either on the Amphitheatre lot or at a shopping center parking lot at 47th and Halsted Streets. Simon replied that the shopping center parking lot is private property but that the city might consider an assembly there if Davis could procure its use. As it turned out, the shopping center planned to stay open and would require use of its parking lot for customers. Simon said further that the Amphitheatre lot, also privately owned, was reserved for the Democratic National Committee. He aded that other areas of the city could be used for assembly, however, specifying Burnham Park on Northerly Island, Washington Park, Lincoln Park, Garfield Park or the Grant Park bandshell.

Davis insisted that the site for the evening assembly be within "eyeshot" of the Amphitheatre in order to provide a psychological impact. Unless they were in close proximity to the Amphitheatre, Davis said, the group might just as well "meet in Detroit."

Simon then asked Davis for a promise that demonstrators

would not sleep in the city parks. Davis said that he had secured housing for nearly 30,000, but replied that if there is no place for 70,000 people to sleep, they will sleep in parks:

> Practically, one cannot separate the issue of free speech and assembly from the issue where people will stay when they come to Chicago. If people come to Chicago with no place to go, and begin to sleep in parks, or wherever they can find a place to sleep, and then will be forced out of the park, that entirely breaks down our ability to provide organization, which leads to the kind of disruption that you and I both want to prevent, and the issue of peaceful assembly becomes shattered against a practical reality that people have no place to go and will be confronted by police, leading to disruption and possible violence all through the week of the convention.

At the suggestion of the court, both sides agreed to confer with their principals and return the following day, August 22, 1968. When the session was reconvened, Davis reported that his committee had rejected the city's offer for parades and insisted upon a parade and rally in proximity to the Amphitheatre. The city's position remained unchanged. Davis did, however, accept the city's offer of Grant Park for a rally on Wednesday afternoon. The city maintained that the 11 p.m. park curfew could not be avoided.

Following National Mobilization's rejection of the city's alternate march routes, Judge Lynch heard formal arguments on behalf of all parties. At the conclusion of the arguments, he took the matter under advisement. On August 23, 1968, Judge Lynch dismissed the complaint. The opinion stated:

> This court is unable to find that the Park District and City of Chicago have acted arbitrarily in declining to issue permits for the particular places and at the particular times sought by plaintiffs.

The decision made reference to the city's attempt to contact the owner of private property in the Amphitheatre area, and referred also to the various alternative march routes proposed by the city. The court concluded that:

> . . . the defendants have acted in a reasonable and nondiscriminatory manner so as to preserve the public safety

> and convenience without the deprivation of any First Amendment guarantees of speech and public assembly.

In reference to sleeping in the parks, the opinion stated:

> Such a use of the park is in violation of existing ordinances, and permits have never been granted for such a purpose in the past. This court believes that it indeed would be a novel interpretation to hold that the First and Fourteenth Amendments require a municipal government to provide a public park as sleeping accommodations for persons desiring to visit the city.

Immediately following the announcement of Judge Lynch's ruling, Rennie Davis, along with David Dellinger, Sydney Peck and others went to City Hall in an effort to see Mayor Daley. The Mayor was not in. Davis and Stahl met on the following Monday but the meeting was unproductive.

One permit was eventually granted; and that only for an afternoon rally at the Grant Park bandshell on Wednesday, August 28. The permit was issued by the Park District and delivered the evening of August 27. It was conditional, however—distribution of literature was prohibited, and a $100,000 to $300,000 public liability insurance policy and payment of Park District expenses were required. The policy was never obtained.

Yippie Group

The Youth International Party, or "Yippies," sought a permit for the use of park facilities to stage their Festival of Life, which had been announced in January, 1968.

Early in the year, George Peters, a self-styled "bad trip counselor" who had worked with the Chicago hippies, learned of the Yippie plans. Concerned about local arrangements for the Festival, he took it upon himself to contact the Chicago Park District. He inquired about the possible use of Grant Park for camping and was told to put this request in writing, which he did. On March 25, Peters sent a written request to the Park District, stating, however, that he was not affiliated with the Yippies.

The next day, Yippie representatives (a group of Chicago hippies later called the "Free City" group) met with David

Stahl, announced their intentions and presented a request for the use of Grant Park. A written request was also presented to the Park District which referred to a "need to sleep in the park."

No immediate response was made to either Peters' letter or the Yippie request. Soon thereafter, however, Al Baugher of the Chicago Commission on Youth Welfare was assigned the task of working with the Chicago hippies, and met with them almost weekly until the middle of August.

In late May, David Stahl met with the Free City group at the Chicago *Seed* office. It was agreed that lists of specific requests covering the general format and calendar of events for the Festival of Life would be submitted. Stahl indicated at this time that Grant Park would be impossible as a site for the Festival but that Lincoln Park might be made available.

Al Baugher stated that there would be a "good" chance of obtaining a permit and suggested a circus tent for Lincoln Park. Baugher later took the group on a tour of Soldier Field and Navy Pier, suggesting the possibility of these facilities being used for housing. The Edgewater Beach Hotel, closed in a bankruptcy proceeding, was also mentioned.

The Festival planners, however, did not feel that these sites would be in any way appropriate for their Festival. Consequently, Free City spokesmen, conferring with the New York Yippie promoters, pushed ahead for a park permit and for the suspension of curfew laws and regulations prohibiting persons from sleeping on the beaches. They also asked that arrests for narcotics violations be suspended.

The next meeting was held June 5. The Free City people had, for the first time, a list of suggested preparatory arrangements and specified their expectations for the Festival. David Stahl and Al Baugher represented the city. The chief result of this meeting was getting an official go-ahead for weekly Sunday afternoon rock concerts in Lincoln Park. With respect to the Festival, Stahl made only a short statement to the effect that there could be no illegal activities.

Immediately following the meeting, the Free City group prepared a long letter detailing their expectations for the August Festival, had it checked by a lawyer and delivered it to David Stahl's office on June 7, 1968.

A list of the city's criteria for the Festival of Life was later delivered to the Free City group. It was not on city letterhead nor was it signed, and it was in a plain envelope. However,

Stahl admitted authorship of the document at a subsequent meeting. It listed eight points:

1. Work out plans for self-policing of your groups in the areas they use.
2. Obey our laws.
   A. Curfew (state, city parks).
   B. Use of drugs.
   C. Indecent exposure.
   D. Obtain required permits.
   E. Use of sidewalks and streets.
   F. Disturbing the peace.
3. Advise the city of events you plan.
4. Develop alternative location for temporary housing during the convention. Grant Park may not be used.
5. Cooperate with the Board of Health on health standards.
6. Let us know your problems.
7. Let us know your counterparts in other cities.
8. Give us your best information on the number of arrivals each week.

Although permission had been granted for the Sunday rock concerts, and these events passed without major incident, some of the Festival promoters believed that the city was committed to a policy of stalling for the purpose of dissuading many potential participants from coming to Chicago. Subsequently, a city official recalled that the city was interested in discouraging a massive influx of demonstrators into the city during convention week. City officials claimed, however, that they were having great difficulty in understanding what specific plans the promoters had in mind for the August Festival.

There were further meetings with the city in June and July. At one of the July meetings, Stahl asked that a second written request be given to the Chicago Park District for the Festival of Life to be held in Lincoln Park. On July 15, the Free City group made formal application for Lincoln Park. This letter, a Park District official states, did not mention sleeping in the park.

The new request spoke of 25,000 people attending the Festival. Use of Soldier Field was also requested for August 30. The letter stated: "Our purpose in making this request is to stage a concluding rally. We feel that this would be the best way to encourage people to vacate the campsite prior to to the expiration of our permits (for Lincoln Park)." It should be noted that the June 13, 1968 Chicago Park District schedule for the use of Soldier Field showed August 30 as an open date.

On July 31, Thomas C. Barry, acting general superintendent of the Park District, asked by letter for a meeting to discuss the request.

In August, representatives of the Chicago Police Department, a high police official and a police sergeant assigned to the Chicago hippie area, met with the Free City group. The Free City group suggested that participants in the Festival of Life should be allowed to sleep in Lincoln Park during the Democratic convention. They proposed a plan whereby approximately 50 police officers and hippie marshals would cooperate to control the demonstrators and maintain order in Lincoln Park. Although the sergeant was responsive to the suggestion, his superior rejected the proposal, insisting that the law relating to closing the parks at 11 p.m. must be obeyed.

In early August, Jerry Rubin, Abbie Hoffman and Paul Krassner came to Chicago and conferred at length with the Chicago group. David Stahl was contacted and asked about some detailed preparations such as food and tents. No progress was made. In the meantime, a day-by-day list of events planned for convention week was prepared.

At an August 4 press conference in Chicago, Abbie Hoffman, using the name "Frankie Abbott," announced the Yippie plans for the Festival and stated they were going ahead with these plans even if the Chicago Park District refused them a permit. The New Yorkers did not stay in Chicago for a meeting scheduled for the next day with the Park District.

At the August 5 meeting, according to Thomas Barry, the Free City group asked that the Lincoln Park Zoo be closed during convention week and that the Park District keep persons who are not hippies out of the park during that period. They also mentioned sleeping in the park. Barry stated that he was unaware of the plans to sleep in Lincoln Park.

Following this meeting, the Free City Survival Committee issued a statement to the underground press and discouraged their readers from coming to Chicago for what they now called a "festival of blood." The New York Yippies returned to Chicago immediately when they heard about the statement.

That evening David Stahl talked with the New York Yippies. At the meeting, some of the Yippie group were hostile. They said that they understood the city's plan was to hold off granting a permit until the last minute to hold down attendance. But, they warned, people would come anyway. They predicted a "most dangerous social problem" and offered to drop the whole thing for $200,000.

One of the city officials involved in these negotiations stated later that his study of confidential reports on Rubin and Hoffman had convinced him that these men were true revolutionaries bent on the "disruption" of the Democratic convention.

While in Chicago, the New York Yippies had an angry meeting with the Free City group. Paul Krassner of New York explains what happened:

> . . . Out of that meeting came the decision that those people who didn't want to feel responsible for inviting people to a blood-bath that they would give up their application for a permit. We felt, of course, we understand their position; they were in Chicago, we would come from New York and elsewhere, I'd be in Chicago and leave and they would still be there and be subjected to harassment, which has been happening in Chicago. They have been subject to harassment. But we can understand those things. We had them withdraw their permit and we'd put in an application signed by both Chicago and New York people. You see, their thing had been applied for under the Free City Survival Committee, and they didn't want to endanger that . . . kind of a free community. So now under the name of YIPPIE!, Chicago and New York Yippies, we reapplied.

On August 8, the Free City group withdrew its permit application and simultaneously a new request was filed, signed by members of both the New York Yippies and the Free City group.

That afternoon Abbie Hoffman and the other major New York Yippies met formally with David Stahl and several assistant corporation counsel. The meeting was very short, less than ten minutes, with the lawyers discussing various technicalities. There were later meetings—for example, on August 10 Allen Ginsberg met with Stahl—but, in general, these were unimportant meetings, and nothing came of them.

A suit against the city to require the issuance of a permit for Lincoln Park was filed on August 19. Since the hearing on National Mobilization's case had been set before Judge Lynch, an emergency motion was made for a joint hearing of the Yippie case, and both were scheduled for August 22. On that day, the Yippies' lawyer appeared in the courtroom and simply witnessed the conference described earlier between Rennie Davis of National Mobilization and Ray Simon, city corporation counsel.

The following day, the Yippies decided to withdraw their suit, feeling that they had little chance of succeeding (the signs advising of an 11 p.m. curfew were already being increased in Lincoln Park) and knowing that a decision would be rendered in the National Mobilization suit treating the issue of sleeping in the park. Perhaps the foremost consideration was that the Yippies did not want a decision which might prohibit them from even holding a daytime Festival.

After Judge Lynch rendered his decision in the National Mobilization case, it became clear to the Yippies that no permit was going to be issued for the Festival of Life. Promoters of the event, however, went ahead with final arrangements, trusting that an informal concession would be made as thousands gathered in the park over the forthcoming weekend.

Coalition for an Open Convention (COC)

On July 12, Martin Slate, named rally coordinator for the "On to Chicago" project, made his first attempts to reach Thomas Barry, acting superintendent of the Chicago Park District, by phone. The result was a meeting with two staff members who explained the permit application procedure. Slate also met the man who supervised Soldier Field, who advised that the stadium had been reserved for five days by the Democratic National Committee.

On July 12, Slate sent a special delivery letter to Barry, advising him of COC's plans "for a series of rallies to be held during the period of August 25 to August 28." The letter stated that approximately "100,000 people" were expected and suggested "one of Chicago's largest parks, such as Grant or Washington, or Soldier Field." On July 15, Slate phoned Barry, whose secretary acknowledged receipt of the letter. She said the call would be returned.

Subsequently, until July 31, Slate claims that he made numerous calls to the Park District without receiving any response. Park District officials, on the other hand, state that they attempted to contact Clinton Deveaux, Chicago coordinator for the project, who they thought was authorized to discuss COC plans, but met with no success.

On July 25, Slate sent a registered letter to Governor Shapiro asking his assistance in obtaining a rally site. He also sent a letter to Thomas Barry requesting a reply to the July 13 letter. On the same day, another COC associate wrote to Vice President Humphrey.

Finally, as a result of the letter to Barry, a meeting was held on July 31. Arrangements for the use of the stadium facilities were discussed. No definite dates, however, were worked out. Slate also inquired as to what sleeping facilities the city could offer, but Barry advised Slate that there was an ordinance against sleeping in the parks.

The arrangements discussed at this meeting were quite involved. Leasing Soldier Field for a major program was generally done with professional promoters long in advance of the scheduled event. Parking, transportation and utility facilities would be carefully considered; ushers, concessioners, medical personnel and ambulance service would have to be engaged; staging and sound equipment would be required, liability insurance and rent would be worked out. These are only some of the matters which, as a rule, are provided for or which must be settled upon before a formal leasing agreement is drafted and executed by the city and the promoters. These matters were discussed only generally at this meeting and were never definitely dealt with. The COC rally promoters had not evidenced the organization, experience or inclination to meet the planning demands which such arrangements required.

On August 1, Slate wrote a letter to the Park District stating: "The replies from speakers we have invited indicate that Sunday, August 25th would be the most appropriate day . . . we would consider Monday or Tuesday as alternate dates." COC officials had agreed that the original series of rallies they had planned were too ambitious. Barry, not considering this letter as an application for permission to use the stadium on a definite date, did not reply.

On August 7, representatives of COC met David Stahl, knowing the position that Stahl had taken in negotiations with National Mobilization and the Yippie group. Stahl advised that the request was under consideration.

On August 8, there was a reply from Governor Shapiro referring COC to Mayor Daley. Slate then wrote to Mayor Daley and Barry, asking for a response to the permit request by August 10 so plans for the rally on August 25 could be announced by Allard Lowenstein, who had scheduled a press conference on that date.

On August 12 Clinton Deveaux wrote to Barry specifying: "Soldier Field on Sunday, August 25, 1968—late morning to late afternoon."

On August 13, Barry phoned Slate and said the Park District's Board had met and taken no action on the COC application. Slate asked the ACLU to file suit. Senator McCarthy, however, had already asked his followers to "stay home" and it appeared that Soldier Field would be too large for the number of people expected.

The suit was filed on August 14, petitioning the United States District Court for an injunction to force the Chicago Park District to grant permission to COC to use Soldier Field for a rally on August 25. The suit charged that the refusal of the Park District to issue the permit was "without explanation" and denied COC "rights to free speech and peaceably assembly." The matter was set for hearing on an emergency motion before Judge Lynch on August 16.

By agreement of the parties, the hearing was continued to August 19, and, in the meantime, the Park District filed a motion to dismiss. The Park District pointed out that it had designated four park areas where public assemblies could be held without permits. The areas were Burnham Park on Northerly Island, Garfield Park, Washington Park and Lincoln Park.

At the hearing on plaintiff's motion, Judge Lynch ruled that because the actions of the Park District in granting permits are "legislative functions," the court had no authority to issue an injunction requiring the district to grant a permit to plaintiffs. Judge Lynch, however, did not dismiss the complaint but continued the Park District's Motion to Dismiss to September 15.

COC organizers realized at this late date that any attempt to immediately pursue the matter further in the courts would be fruitless. A decision was made to cancel all plans for an August 25 rally.

There was no longer any "permit controversy," and there was no permit.

THE ELEVENTH HOUR

During the final weeks preceding the convention, there was a surge of activity focused primarily on preparations in Chicago for the planned demonstrations. Abbie Hoffman, advance man for the New York Yippie contingent, came to stay in Chicago and worked long hours to put the proposed Festival of Life together. The Chicago office of National Mobilization, headed by Rennie Davis (the Chicago coordinator) and staffed at times by as many as 25 workers, was busy coordinating the arrangements of participants in the scheduled demonstrations.

The Movement Centers

An integral part of National Mobilization's plans was the movement center concept. There had been a great deal of discussion within the ranks of the "New Left" as to how a broadly based coalition for major national demonstrations could be achieved, while at the same time accommodating the desires of numerous dissident groups who preferred to remain essentially autonomous. The movement center concept was thought to be a suitable compromise.

The efforts of National Mobilization, therefore, were directed towards drawing together dissident groups of widely diverse political and social leanings, of various sizes and geographical sites and involving them all in one major antiwar demonstration focused on the Democratic National Convention. Many of the groups solicited were for one reason or another simply not interested in exposing themselves to participation in such a demonstration. Some of these, however, took the position that their presence in Chicago during convention week was important. SDS (the radical students' group) and others recognized an opportunity to recruit disaffected Democrats, particularly Senator McCarthy's army of young supporters. The movement center would serve very well as a meeting place and repository of literature.

Many groups, although enthusiastic about participating in the major demonstration for Wednesday night, also wanted headquarters for independent operation. Such a center might be implemented as a gathering place, a forum for discussion and information exchange, a base for independent demonstrations—for example, sit-ins or protests at hotels, police stations, military establishments, draft boards, induction centers, other government offices and research institutions or businesses doing national defense-related work.

To accommodate these interests and to achieve the program for decentralized activity, 30 to 40 movement centers were planned, and National Mobilization people coordinated most of the arrangements. The centers were set up primarily in store fronts and church basements. Each movement center, it was planned, would direct the activities of its associates and send a delegate to National Mobilization meetings.

A number of meetings were held in the weeks just before the convention. Matters discussed included accommodations for demonstrators, legal defense, medic presence, parade routes, marshal training and the like. Detailed maps, floor plans of major hotels and the Amphitheatre and instructions would also be prepared for distribution so that demonstrators coming to Chicago would know where to be, when, and how to act.

National Mobilization Plans

National Mobilization worked out a schedule of events for convention week and published the following program:

> August 24: PEOPLE'S ASSEMBLY IN MOVEMENT CENTERS. We focus on an agency which the convention will overlook. Movement centers will open across Chicago for workshops on imperialism and the war, racism, organizing around the draft and within the armed forces, working class organizing electoral politics, university struggles. First issue of *Daily Ramparts* appears.

August 25: PEOPLE'S ASSEMBLY WELCOMES THE CONVENTION. Massive demonstrations at 2 p.m. at the Conrad-Hilton, Pick-Congress and the Palmer House to greet arriving delegates. Assemble on the sidewalks in front of the hotels. Keep a lane open next to the buildings for sidewalk traffic and keep moving.

Alternative plan: Assemble at southern end of Lincoln Park.

Other activities: Movement Centers continue. Yippie Festival of Life begins in Lincoln Park with music show.

August 27: JOHNSON'S BIRTHDAY. Masses of demonstrators arrive. Democrats hold big pageant celebrating Johnson, while Johnson himself calculates whether or not to come to the Convention from Washington. The Movement focuses on the real legacy of Johnson. A "Johnson Pavillion" will dramatize the issues through film exhibitions, theatre and photography. Guerrilla theatre groups everywhere. Yippies organize a meeting to chant that Johnson stay in office; dollar bills are burned. Church assembly sponsors actions demanding amnesty for resisters. Evening performance by prominent entertainers will focus on the "state of the union" under Johnson. Scores of direct actions at racist and military institutions.

August 28: THE NOMINATION. Mass march on the Convention to protest ratification of status quo, beginning downtown in the afternoon and marching to rally outside the International Amphitheatre.

Alternative plan: If we are not allowed to march, continue demonstrations in the Loop area.

August 29: THE END. Democrats nominate vice-president and give initial campaign speeches. Mobilization sponsors demonstrations at federal offices, war oriented universities, induction centers, etc., to underline determination to stay in the streets until the troops are brought home and domestic institutions are changed. Massive People's Assembly meets to discuss issues, directions and work that have been suggested by the week in Chicago.

Plans and tactics for smaller demonstrations were generally left to the particular group or composite of groups, and such actions were to be directed for the most part on the movement center level. The major Wednesday night demonstration, however, was always discussed in some detail by all representatives participating in the National Mobilization meetings. Tactics were discussed, and some advocated disruption of the convention. National Mobilization spokesmen, however, continued to encourage a nonviolent, nondisruptive demonstration and to take that as their official position. It is not certain, however, to what extent this overt posture influenced Mobilization's affiliates.

Several alternatives were urged for the march to the Amphitheatre. Some wanted to pass through the Loop, to draw the attention of the city to their cause. The commotion created would impose a certain cost on the city and, symbolically, on society. It might very well disrupt traffic and be inconvenient for the city and its residents, but there was a strong conviction that the Democratic convention should not be permitted to take place calmly, as if what the political system was achieving were perfectly acceptable to all. The demonstrators, rather, had to dramatically impress upon the delegates and the public their belief that dissent in this country is real, that it cannot be repressed or ignored, and that the convention, like the entire system of electoral politics, is unresponsive to it.

Some thought that the march should pass through the ghetto. Substantial efforts had been made throughout the past months to build a coalition of the war protest and the civil rights movement. The coalition had never materialized organizationally, but it was hoped that by marching through the ghetto, the antiwar group would pick up large support from the black community and thereby demonstrate a united movement against the establishment. But there was concern among some that a march through the ghetto might further alienate the black community and drive them away from the movement.

A good deal of concern was expressed about marching directly to the Amphitheatre from a downtown location, since that would mean passing through a primarily white working-class community and the possibility of trouble before even getting near the Amphitheatre.

The more conservative spokesmen at these meetings thought that the parade route to the convention would in all likelihood be dictated by police action or by an agreed arrangement with the city. So no specific route was chosen. The consensus was that any route would be acceptable as long as the demonstrators could get within eyeshot of the convention hall.

Reports on accommodations indicated that private homes,

churches, schools, fraternities, theaters and various other facilities would be available to house as many as 30,000 demonstrators, according to Davis. Before it became apparent that a permit to sleep in the parks would be denied, expectations were that most would sleep on the beaches and in the parks. The procurement of tents, toilet facilities and the like were discussed. As it developed, there were probably enough housing commitments to take care of all who actually came. However, since the turn-out was planned to be over 100,000, there was a great deal of concern about securing adequate housing. Some 50,000 letters had been sent to request accommodations.

In cooperation with various local groups and Yippie organizers, National Mobilization launched a fund-raising campaign to meet such expenses as offices, loudspeakers and bullhorns and other crowd control equipment and bail bond reserves. They meant to train photographers and to develop a communications system, including walkie talkies, to keep movement centers and people in the streets in continuous contact with Mobilization headquarters.

Other efforts were being made to facilitate communication. At least 50,000 special issues of the RAT, an underground publication, were circulated, advertising plans for convention week, and *Ramparts* Magazine was to publish a daily bulletin on the convention. Other underground publications regularly covered National Mobilization's plans and the Festival of Life. In addition, leaflets were distributed around the country, urging people to join the demonstrations. National Mobilization reportedly made a special effort to attract McCarthy supporters by passing out literature at major McCarthy rallies during the weeks preceding the convention.

Individual dissident groups were also preparing literature.

Participation was also encouraged by speeches made around the country. On August 20, for example, Tom Hayden, speaking to a crowd of 800 delegates of the National Student Association, urged a show of dissident strength in Chicago.

Festival of Life

In the meantime, Abbie Hoffman and other promoters of the Festival of Life, although not nearly as well organized as National Mobilization and its associates, were continuing negotiations for the park, securing entertainers and creating buttons, leaflets, posters and promotional articles for underground papers. There were attempts to provide all of the features they had promised for Lincoln Park—free food and dope, tables, sound equipment, pigs, band stands and balloons. They made maps to orient visitors to the city, particularly to locations where major demonstration events were to take place and where police, National Guard and television centers of concentration might be. A "VD clinic" was set up and attempts were made to install an "LSD—bad trip" booth in Lincoln Park.

Workshops were an important part of the Festival of Life plans. Workshops in draft-resistance, use of drugs, communal living, underground newspapers, free stores, survival and other matters of special interest to the hippie subculture had been promised, and last minute efforts were being made to keep the promise. Yippie organizers and Mobilization people worked together to get workshop leaders and literature.

An "Un-birthday Party for LBJ" at the Coliseum in Chicago was scheduled for Tuesday night of convention week and they needed entertainers. The Yippies, through Ed Sanders of the Fugs, a popular underground rock group, were in touch with other rock groups and National Mobilization turned to them for help. The Yippie group also joined with Mobilization in planning for the Coliseum, and as it turned out this was the only event the two groups jointly endorsed prior to convention week. The Yippie spokesmen would make no assurances that they would encourage others who might congregate in Lincoln Park to join Mobilization's march to the Amphitheatre.

Abbie Hoffman says that the Yippies did not state a position on the march until shortly before Wednesday, August 28:

> We had a press conference in Lincoln Park and we ran around the park and we found two kids who never had their faces on TV. We asked one kid, "Do you want to march on the Amphitheatre?" and he said yes. We said okey. Have you ever been on TV? He said no. What's your name? He said Tim Kelly. We said okay Tim. He said, "Do you want to know my reason?" I said no, tell it to the American public. We went around, asking "Is there anybody here who doesn't want to march—who thinks we ought to stay in the park." One kid says "I

do." We found out his name. The two of them went right up, and Tim Kelly got up and said I'm going to march on the Amphitheatre, and these are the reasons. . . . People who like that, cheered. Another kid got up and said I'm going to stay—stay in the park—people who like that, cheered. That's the way it happened. That's how we announced our plans to march on the Amphitheatre.

In what was described as a "Daring Expose—Top Secret Yippie Plans for Lincoln Park," a schedule of events for the Festival of Life was outlined, and is reproduced below:

August 20-August 24 (AM): Training in snake dancing, karate, non-violent self-defense. Information booth in Park.
August 24 (PM): Yippie Mayor R. Daley presents fireworks on Lake Michigan.
August 25 (AM): Welcoming of the Democratic delegates—downtown hotels (to be announced).
August 25 (PM): MUSIC FESTIVAL—Lincoln Park.
August 26 (AM): Workshop in drug problems, underground communications, how to live free, guerrilla theatre, self-defense, draft resistance, communes, etc. (Potential workshop leaders should call the Seed, 837 N. La Salle Street, 943-5282.)
Scenario sessions to plan small group activities.
August 26 (PM): Beach Party ON THE LAKE ACROSS from Lincoln Park (North Avenue Beach).
—folksinging, barbecues, swimming, lovemaking.
August 27 (dawn): Poetry, mantras, religious ceremony.
August 27 (AM): Workshops and Scenario sessions. Film showing and mixed media—Coliseum, 1513 S. Wabash.
August 27 (PM): Benefit concert—Coliseum. Rally and Nomination of Pigasus and LBJ birthday—Lincoln Park.
August 28 (dawn): Poetry and folk singing.
August 28 (AM): Yippie Olympics, Miss Yippie Contest, catch the candidate, pin the tail on the donkey, pin the rubber on the Pope, and other normal, healthy games.
August 28 (PM): Plans to be announced at a later date.
4 P.M.—Mobilization Rally scheduled for Grant Park.

March to the convention.
August 29-30: Events scheduled depend on Wednesday night. Return to park for sleeping.

Doctors, Lawyers and Marshals

Of particular interest to the Yippies were the arrangements which National Mobilization and its affiliates had made for a Legal Defense Committee, a bail bond reserve, medical presence during convention week, and the training of marshals.

By the third week of August, there was still no park permit, and warnings of strict and tough law enforcement had been widely publicized.

The demonstrators had planned accordingly. Bail bond funds were established and contributions solicited. A large number of sympathetic lawyers and law students had volunteered to work for the Legal Defense Committee. As previously described, the Medical Committee on Human Rights and the Student Health Organization were ready to provide medical assistance throughout the week. Both organizations had attended previous major civil rights and peace demonstrations across the country and were active in recruiting volunteers during the weeks preceding the convention. They planned to demand that city officials regard them as neutrals.

Arrangements were also made with Near North Side hospitals and clinics in preparation for the contingency of mass injuries. City and county health authorities also had responded to the prospect of violence during convention week, and gave special attention to alerting hospitals and other medical facilities in preparation for the event.

Out-of-towners were advised to learn first aid, to bring bail bond money with them and to contact the Legal Defense Committee when they came to town; they were instructed on what their rights were if arrested. Articles in underground publications urged expectant visitors to bring vaseline, helmets, heavy over-clothing, baking soda and other protective devices and medication.

Trained marshals had been effectively used before by National Mobilization to coordinate and police the activities of participants in massive demonstrations. The organization hoped to train thousands of marshals for the task of controlling the expected 100,000 demonstrators. When marshal training began, however, there were only 30 or 40 in attendance (apparently there were never more than 100 marshals active at any time during convention week, despite continuous recruiting efforts).

As convention week drew near, the media gave considerable coverage to the activities of both National Mobilization and the Yippie contingent. Spokesmen were always asked how many would come. They had no way of knowing, but the estimates, at least up until the last few days were very high. Mobilization people were hopefully looking back on the Pentagon march in Washington and the April Peace Rallies which had been massive. The Yippie promoters envisioned something like the "Be Out" in New York's Central Park, where tens of thousands came to witness a carnival of hippies in late spring of 1968. Thoughtful demonstration promoters knew, however, that such estimates were totally unrealistic.

There were many factors working to keep dissident groups away from Chicago, most of them described earlier in this report. Many had so completely given up on electoral politics that they were unconvinced that a demonstration focused on the Democratic National Convention would be meaningful. Others were dissuaded by the spectre of a violent clash with Chicago police and the National Guard. There had been warnings that Chicago would be a "blood bath" in late August. Moreover, neither Mobilization nor the Yippies had yet been able to obtain a permit. Finally, as noted earlier, Senator McCarthy had urged his followers to stay away from Chicago and Allard Lowenstein, following suit and also unable to secure a permit, called off the proposed COC rally in Soldier Field.

The Preconvention Publicity

Yippie spokesmen and authors of Yippie literature gave newsmen plenty to write about—outrageous designs to "turn the city upside down."

The general media published an elaborate array of potential threats to the city and to the delegates. There were reports of proposals to dynamite natural gas lines; to dump hallucinating drugs into the city's water system; to print forged credentials so that demonstrators could slip into the convention hall; to stage a mass stall-in of old jalopies on the expressways and thereby disrupt traffic; to take over gas stations, flood sewers with gasoline, then burn the city; to fornicate in the parks and on Lake Michigan's beaches; to release greased pigs throughout Chicago, at the Federal Building and at the Amphitheatre; to slash tires along the city's freeways and tie up traffic in all directions; to scatter razor sharp three-inch nails along the city's highways; to place underground agents in hotels, restaurants, and kitchens where food was prepared for delegates, and drug food and drink; to paint cars like independent taxicabs and forceably take delegates to Wisconsin or some other place far from the convention; to engage Yippie girls as "hookers" to attract delegates and dose their drinks with LSD; to bombard the Amphitheatre with mortars from several miles away; to jam communication lines from mobile units; to disrupt the operations of airport control towers, hotel elevators and railway switching yards; to gather 230 "hyper-potent" hippie males into a special battalion to seduce the wives, daughters and girlfriends of convention delegates; to assemble 100,000 people to burn draft cards with the fires spelling out: "Beat Army"; to turn on fire hydrants, set off false fire and police alarms, and string wire between trees in Grant Park and Lincoln Park to trip up three-wheeled vehicles of the Chicago police; to dress Yippies like Viet Cong and walk the streets shaking hands or passing out rice; to infiltrate the right wing with short haired Yippies and at the right moment exclaim: "You know, these Yippies have something to say!"; to have ten thousand nude bodies floating on Lake Michigan—the list could go on.

Much of the Chicago convention-related underground literature which found its way into general media and police files was amply sprinkled with obscene and vilifying references to the American way of life and its values. A typical Yippie flyer reads:

> . . . Who says that rich white Americans can tell the Chinese what is best? How dare you tell the poor that their poverty is deserved? Fuck nuns: laugh at professors: disobey your parents: burn your money: you know life is a dream and all of our institutions are man-made illusions effective because YOU take the dream for reality. . . . Break down the family, church, nation, city, economy: turn life into an art form, a theatre of the soul and a theatre of the future; the revolutionary is the only artist. . . . What's needed is a generation of people who are freaky, crazy, irrational, sexy, angry, irreligious, childish and

mad: people who burn draft cards, burn high school and college degrees: people who say: "To hell with your goals!"; people who lure the youth with music, pot and acid: people who re-define the normal; people who break with the status-role-title-consumer game; people who have nothing material to lose but their flesh. . . . The white youth of America have more in common with Indians plundered, than they do with their own parents. Burn their houses down, and you will be free.

Abbie Hoffman says of his publicity, "It was a freak show—and it was groovy."

In an interview, he expressed his philosophy this way:

We're cheerleaders. We encourage everything. A cheerleader doesn't say no. We say that . . . people got a bitch against this government, you know, or want to see a better system, they know what they're doing, you know, and they'll figure out a way of doing it, in the style that feels good to them. So if their style is to print up a leaflet, if their style is to carry a picket sign, if their style is going to stand in a vigil or fast or burn themselves or burn the President, or whatever it is. That's their thing.

* * *

Does gassing 20 city blocks disrupt a city? I'll tell you what urban guerrilla warfare is about. Urban guerrilla warfare is a psychological attempt to trick the enemy into developing a policy of over-kill. . . . It's when you have a machine, when you have an opposition built on machines, you know, and built on massive show of force, you know, fighting against people who believe in their cause and are prepared to die and prepared to take tremendous risk—you will have that, you will have developed that policy of over-kill on the part of the aggressor, on the part of those people in power and what they do is you see then, is start to gobble themselves up.

* * *

We wanted to fuck up their image on TV. I fight through the jungle of TV, you see . . . it's all in terms of disrupting the image, the image of a democratic society being run very peacefully and orderly and everything is according to business.

There were other types of publicity concerning the convention—some of which had gone back to the time when it was first announced that it would be held in Chicago. The importance of this publicity lies in the fact that it played a part in conditioning authorities and demonstrators alike as to what to expect in Chicago; it undoubtedly influenced the security measures planned by the city.

Following are some selected samples:

From an article in the November, 1967, issue of *Liberation:*

. . . when we attempt to block the Pentagon with our bodies, or interfere with an induction center or a napalm plant or a campus recruiting booth, we are saying something very special. . . . We believe that, confronted with such a direct challenge from evergrowing numbers (though a minority) of Americans, the majority will decide to stop . . . even if these challenges are carried on with the greatest toughness and energy—like the Pentagon siege, and more—they are still basically a tactic of persuasion. They are built on the assumption that it is legitimate to be arrested if one violates what seems to be the law. . . . We may find that we meet each other again in Chicago . . . at the Democratic National Convention, because the tactical situation will be good. . . . If there are 100,000 people on the streets, prepared to do civil disobedience, what should their demands be?

A greeting from Jerry Rubin, reported in *The Village Voice,* November 16, 1967:

See you next August in Chicago at the Democratic National Convention. Bring pot, fake delegate's cards, smoke bombs, costumes, crud to throw and all kinds of interesting props, also football helmets.

In late 1967, Dick Gregory is reported to have notified President Johnson that unless racial conditions were improved in Chicago, he would lead demonstrations "which would make it possible for the Democratic party to hold its Convention here only over my dead body." (*Chicago Tribune,* December 31, 1968)

The *Chicago Tribune,* December 31, 1967, reported the following:

A plan to disrupt the Democratic National Convention in Chicago next August was ascribed to Communist influence yesterday by Alice Widener, . . . a specialist on subversive activities. In an interview, Mrs. Widener said she attended a meeting of the New York chapter of the National Conference for New Politics . . . one unidentified speaker at the New York meeting declared that, "We'll stop the Convention if we have to burn down the hall."

In a January, 1968 article, Jerry Rubin wrote:

The Yippies are out there blocking traffic, throwing blood, burning money, tying up government telephone wires, milling in, fucking up the draft, throwing live snakes into Dow Chemical executive cocktail parties.

The *Chicago Daily News,* January 6, 1968, reported that James Rollins, National Co-Chairman of NCNP, said he might summon a million demonstrators to march and picket at the convention. "We might even have to disrupt the convention," he is reported to have said.

In a National Mobilization Committee document dated February, 1968, Rennie Davis is quoted:

I would like to see us be able to carry our incredible action even against Chicago's blanket injunction bill prohibiting all demonstration, even against the two U.S. Army regiments that will be protecting the Convention. Also to release the real power of our many forces in a new and significant way at the time that Johnson is nominated, turning delegates back into the Amphitheatre as they attempt to leave. . . .

In the February 3, 1968 issue of the *Guardian,* an article discussed tactics for Chicago:

What will happen at the Democratic National Convention to be held in Chicago next August? . . .

. . . [one] position calls for massive demonstrations probably involving disruption tactics, during the 10 days that the Convention will be held.

Finally, there are those who say that Chicago should be

completely disrupted and the Convention not even allowed to take place.

The . . . strategy of a massive confrontation appears to be gaining most support. . . . Some want an almost chaotic confrontation. . . .

New Left Notes said in its March 4, 1968, issue:

> To envision non-violent demonstrations at the Convention is to indulge in unpleasant fantising. It should be clear to anyone who has been following developments in Chicago that a non-violent demonstration would be impossible.

The June 20th issue of the *Village Voice* carried an article which said:

> If the Central Committee gives us Humphrey anyway, then . . . We can leave the country, we can drift into quietism and tend our private gardens, or we can disrupt, disrupt, disrupt.

In the July-August issue of *Liberation,* a letter from National Mobilization was reproduced. It read, in part, as follows:

> In part, the purpose of the Chicago action will be to reassert the politics of street actions. . . . Tom insists that violence, which is rapidly becoming a national pastime, is the responsibility of those making war and not listening to peaceful protests. He adds that in Chicago "we will physically protect our people and are already working on chemical deterrents."

A *UPI* press release of August 13, 1968 reported:

> Their (National Mobilization's) battle plan is to raise cain outside the convention hall. As their Chicago coordinator, Rennie Davis, warns, a storming of the convention hall itself is "obviously not out of the question."

During the second week of August, the Chicago *Seed* published the following statement of the Free City Survival Committee:

The word is out. Many people are into confrontation. The Man is into confrontation. Nobody takes the Amphitheatre. Cars and buildings will burn. Chicago may host a Festival of Blood. . . .
There will be ample opportunity to disrupt the Democratic Creep-Follies. There are many reasons to disrupt the Death Gala. If you feel compelled to cavort, then this is action city. There is no reason to wear flowers for masks. If you want to go up against the wall, then come."

The statement was picked up by underground papers around the country.

One preconvention flyer, of unidentified origin, spelled out the schedule for Tuesday and Wednesday as follows:

> TUESDAY, AUGUST 27:
> Harass the delegates. . . .
> WEDNESDAY, AUGUST 28:
> . . . We can be sure that the rally would be surrounded and contained by the Guard and the cops. This would mean that once the demonstration started people could neither enter nor leave the area. . . . There are a couple of contingency plans dealing with the problem of getting all of the people participating in this rally to the amphitheatre en masse. A mass march through the loop. . . . This would effectively tie up traffic in the loop and make our numbers seen and felt in a most effective way. . . .
> The other form of demonstration will be unofficial and not sponsored by the Mobilization Committee. The strategy of these actions would be that of employing mobile street tactics. The delegates will be entering the Amphitheatre via the parking lot. . . . The mobile demonstration (50, 100, 150 people in each group) would be involved in general disruption and more specifically in disrupting the delegates as they attempt to enter into the parking lot. . . .

This, then, was the publicity from the demonstrators' side. There was also the city's side—and much publicity was given to the massive security precautions taken by the city to prepare itself for the expected inundation of demonstrators.

Those Who Arrived

The massive security precautions and the well-publicized portrayal of a firm stand by law enforcement agencies, along with the lack of permits, dissuaded many potential demonstrators from making the trip to Chicago. According to the best estimates there were probably around 5,000, maybe fewer, who came from out of town to participate in the major demonstration on Wednesday night. They represented many regions of the country, with the largest contingents coming from New York, New Jersey, New England, Cleveland and California. Most were in their lower twenties, although many, seasoned protesters, were older. Some came in chartered buses and car pools; others by plane, train, bus, family car, or even by hitchhiking. The demonstrators carried a host of organizational tags with them, but could be chiefly categorized as responding to National Mobilization's bid for a peace demonstration, the Movement Center programs, or the Yippies' Festival of Life. Many, particularly the older order of protest participants, planned to come to Chicago for Wednesday only.

Hippie types, some of whom wanted only to participate in the experience of the subcultural Festival, joined the Chicago underground community in Lincoln Park. The Chicago hippie community was accustomed to spending many afternoons in Lincoln Park, particularly over the weekends. The out-of-towners came with knapsacks, bed rolls, and pot, sometimes barefoot, shabbily dressed and destitute. Most were of college age or in their twenties, some older, and some of high school age.

Among Chicago's visitors were communists, anarchists, peace advocates, revolutionaries, New Leftists, bizarre flower folk, draft resistors, radical militants, professional agitators, moderate but discontented liberals, disaffected straights, housewives opposed to the war, black power militants—all with their own motivations and objectives.

Among the organizations represented in Chicago were the following:

1. People Against Racism;
2. Students for a Democratic Society;
3. CADRE;
4. Concerned Citizens;
5. Clergy and Laymen Concerned;
6. New University Conference;

7. Resistance;
8. Radical Organizing Committee;
9. Committee of Returned Volunteers;
10. Women for Peace;
11. Vets for Peace;
12. Women Mobilized for Change;
13. Revolutionary Contingent;
14. Dow Action Committee;
15. Chicago Peace Council;
16. Fifth Avenue Anti-Vietnam Peace Parade Committee;
17. Communist Party;
18. Socialist Worker Party;
19. Progressive Labor Party;
20. Young Socialist Party;
21. Youth Against War and Fascism;
22. Youth for a New America;
23. American Friends Service Committee;
24. Cleveland Area Peace Action Committee.

As demonstrators arrived, they would check into the National Mobilization office, or the movement centers, or Lincoln Park. They would pick up literature and consider the events ahead.

The hippies, most independent and not at all leadership-oriented, were disorganized. But through movement centers, the action of others could be directed. National Mobilization was also capable of organizing and directing demonstrators through communication with movement centers and directly by leaflets. Moreover, they had trained marshals and loudspeakers. Rennie Davis recalls:

> Mobilization had organization. Only mobilization had organization. . . . We have marshals whom we can use in the event that we can be present at a demonstration—surface marshals, marshals who have a network of communication. They can exercise leadership in a street situation.
>
> * * *
>
> We had . . . organization in Chicago . . . but it was not effective because our purpose was to have non-violent demonstrations and the situation did not allow that, so as a result, the people basically reacted out of the given situation—reacted as any crowd would react.
>
> We don't think people at any one moment were sure of what the next moment was going to bring. Each moment

was in response to a particular situation.

Although Senator McCarthy had admonished his followers to stay away from Chicago, many came anyway. Certainly among the crowd in Grant Park on Wednesday and Thursday were a sizeable group of McCarthy youths who probably had only the vaguest notion of getting involved in the convention demonstration, at least not until the apparent defeat of their candidate and his peace plank. However, although National Mobilization people had for many months preceding the convention attempted to coalesce a united demonstration of white antiwar groups and black dissidents, relatively few blacks were seen among the demonstrators during convention week.

Through the weeks preceding the convention, Rennie Davis, the Chicago coordinator for National Mobilization, had been in contact with the Blackstone Rangers, a south side gang of black youths. Blackstone Ranger people were also contacted by Abbie Hoffman and encouraged to join the Festival of Life in Lincoln Park. Very few blacks, as it turned out, appeared in Lincoln Park during convention week, except in connection with the Free Huey Newton Rally on Tuesday night.

Two other groups, present during convention week, congregating for the most part in Lincoln Park, were motorcycle gangs and "greasers," working-class youths primarily from the Chicago area. It was one of the motorcycle gangs, the Headhunters, which Officer Robert Pierson, the Cook County State's Attorney's special investigator, first infiltrated. Pierson eventually gained the confidence of Jerry Rubin, a Yippie spokesman, and reported regularly to the police whatever he learned from Rubin and his friends.

As it became apparent that original estimates of expected visitors to Chicago would be sorely disappointed, National Mobilization and Yippie organizers talked to each other concerning initial support, to demonstrate some show of solidarity. Each urged their own constituencies to avoid arrest or other mishap prior to the planned demonstrations. Numbers were becoming a paramount consideration.

The climate in Chicago on the eve of the Democratic convention was both figuratively and literally hot. The city had been enveloped in a late August heat wave, and some supposed this to be an ominous signal for trouble in the ghettos. There was a general consensus that Chicago would be incredibly fortunate to avoid violence.

HOW THE CITY PREPARED

Even under normal circumstances, a national political convention demands extensive security preparations. In order to protect officials, delegates and their families, extraordinary precautions must be taken at the convention site, at the hotels and along the routes that provide access to them.

But the circumstances in 1968 were not normal.

As we have documented in the previous chapter, the announcement that the convention would be held in Chicago was almost immediately followed by the prospect of mass demonstrations involving hundreds of thousands of people and threatened disruption of the city, ghetto riots and assassinations. The problem was enlarged by the possibility that the President himself would appear at the convention, a possibility that was never entirely ruled out.

The following pages describe the security measures taken by the Chicago Police Department and other law enforcement agencies, by the National Guard and by other governmental bodies.

Overall Security Planning

In January, 1968, a Convention Planning Committee was set up by the Police Department to organize police planning and to coordinate the preparations of city, state and federal agencies. Included on the committee were representatives of the Police Department, Secret Service, Military Intelligence, the Mayor's Office, the Fire Department and other governmental agencies. The committee met every two weeks through May and weekly thereafter until mid-August.

The committee concentrated upon the Amphitheatre and Loop areas, and transportation between them, with lesser attention being given to other parts of the city except as they specifically related to those areas.

Throughout its deliberations the Planning Committee concerned itself with a large variety of security measures—such as identification for security personnel, access to the Amphitheatre, traffic and transportation problems, dispelling of anxieties among Amphitheatre area residents which might be created by "rumors or overzealous press reports," arrangements for media representatives, utilization of plainclothes policemen on the floor of the Amphitheatre and procedure in case of mass arrests or mass injuries.

Throughout the planning and the convention week the Police Department worked closely with the National Guard, Secret Service, Democratic National Committee and other agencies. It is clear that many decisions were not made solely by the city officials. Some were made on a group basis. Thus, while the mission of the Secret Service was specifically protection of the President, the candidates, and their families, it gave an opinion, when asked, on security matters not directly related to protection of its principals. For example, when asked about its opinion on enforcement of existing laws and ordinances, such as those relating to park usage and street marches, the Secret Service strongly encouraged strict enforcement.

In addition to the Planning Committee meetings, periodic command staff meetings were held during the summer. These were concerned primarily with police planning; the only nonpolice agency in attendance was the Secret Service. Information concerning the possible types and locations of demonstrations was divulged and plans were discussed.

Early in August, the results of the Planning Committee action were turned over to the men who were assigned operational commands for the convention week. Implementation and continuing development of the plans they received was accomplished by the operational commanders with the assistance of members of the Planning Committee.

Intelligence Information

The city regularly received information concerning activities planned or threatened for the convention week which, if implemented, could have a direct impact on not only the convention but on the city itself. This information—which came from a variety of federal and local governmental agencies—was disseminated after evaluation to persons concerned with security measures at the decision-making level.

Some of the information was available to the mass media, and they gave extensive coverage to it. We have already described some of the published plans and threats.

Similar information came from confidential sources. Examples are:

1. Reports that black power groups were allegedly meeting to discuss the convention and the assassination of leading political figures.
2. Unnamed black militant groups in the East were reported to have discussed renting apartments near the Amphitheatre for use as sniping posts.
3. An organization was reportedly organized to secure weapons and explosives and to plan a revolution to coincide with the convention.
4. A report that the National Mobilization Committee intended to prevent Vice President Humphrey from utilizing surface transportation to reach the convention.
5. An allegation from militant white racists to the effect that black militants intended to invade white Chicago neighborhoods and "lay siege" to the city.
6. Reports that black gangs were allegedly accumulating weapons to attack police precinct stations in order to draw police forces away from the convention.
7. Reports that black nationalists in California were alleged to have devised a plot to assassinate certain prominent Negroes in Chicago in order to create disruption throughout the city.
8. Reports that weapons had been sent to Chicago to be used to assassinate one of the presidential candidates.
9. Reports that various organizations planned to put LSD into the Chicago water supply.

An unidentified document in police intelligence files describes in detail the Chicago Avenue Armory and the surrounding neighborhood, and suggests where materials could be obtained to obstruct movement of personnel out of the armory. It also suggests escape routes:

> . . . 750 of us could easily block all doors symbolically, also possible provocation: detour Lake Shore Drive traffic into immediate neighborhood with wooden horses, etc., then stop cars with other wooden horses, then saturate with people, then let air out of tires of more and more cars until tanks, etc., in armory can't get out. A few cars sacrificed for most direct blocking of garage doors. Aluminum door could be bent out of operation. Could NWU [Northwestern University] form a sanctuary? Source of cadre?
> Lots of fire hydrants for further confusion, first aid for gas attacks. Construction site(s) would provide barricade materials. Apartment houses and hotels provide many blind alleys, which connect, for possible escape through confusion . . .

The Intelligence Division sought information from police departments in other cities around the country to ascertain and estimate the number and propensities of militant activists in those cities who might come to Chicago during the convention week. This effort began during the early summer and continued through the convention.

Some of the intelligence reports contained information of a type not unlike that described in the August 6, 1968 issue of *Saga* magazine, detailing the alleged plans of more than 85 known groups and organizations. Tactics described in the articles included: putting ground glass into food served in downtown restaurants, disrupting communications and electrical service and fire bombing buildings. Guerrilla warfare of the type prevalent in Vietnam was referred to as a possibility.

Intelligence authorities recognized that material of the type described above, as well as the published threats related earlier, could not all be taken seriously. They realized that the published and nonpublished plans and threats were comprised of both fact and fiction. But since their responsibility takes in the protection of the entire public, they could not take the risk of underestimating any intelligence, however absurd it might seem to a private citizen. There were attempts made to verify information received, and the authorities concluded that there was enough fact to require intensive security precautions. The Secret Service, of course, never can afford to ignore threats of assassination of presidential candidates.

The Intelligence Division of the Chicago Police Department believed prior to the convention that most of the demonstrating groups would be politically motivated white groups, rather than black civil rights groups. They found no evidence of high-level coordination, cooperation or liaison between the two categories and formed the impression that they would not join in creating disorder at the convention. However, against the background of violence in 1967 and 1968, the city felt that it could not ignore the ever-present threat of ghetto riots being sparked by demonstrator activity during the convention week.

In determining the security precautions needed to cope with large numbers of demonstrators, the intelligence agencies apparently made little effort to distinguish between the philosophies and intents of various groups. They were concerned not with whether a group advocated violence or adhered to nonviolent tenets, but with the dangers inherent in large crowds of demonstrators, regardless of whether all members espouse violence. They believed that even an orderly crowd of peaceful demonstrators could easily develop into a mob and could be led by a few determined agitators of violent action.

Organization and Planning of the Chicago Police Department

The Chicago Police Department is under the command of the Superintendent of Police, who reports directly to Mayor Daley. Under the Superintendent are three Deputy Superintendents in charge of Field Services, Staff Services and Inspectional Services. There are a total of about 12,000 men in the Police Department. About 10,000 of these are in the Bureau of Field Services, which was the division most directly involved in the convention activities.

Under the Deputy Superintendent in charge of Field Services are five divisions: the Patrol Division, the Detective Division, and the Traffic Division, each headed by a Chief; the Community Service Division, headed by a Deputy Chief; and the Youth Division, headed by a Director.

In the field there are six areas, divided into 20 police districts. Each area is headed by a Deputy Chief, and each district by a District Commander. Within the districts, patrolmen are divided into companies of four platoons, each containing four squads of eight men. Squads are commanded by sergeants. There are special detective units in each area headquarters; these report directly to the Deputy Chief in charge of the Detective Division. The Task Force Commander reports to the Chief of the Patrol Division.

Five special security functions were designated for the convention week: Amphitheatre exterior, Amphitheatre interior, Reserve Forces, Loop and Traffic (including Grant Park) and Lincoln Park, the latter two continuing under the command of their respective area commanders.

The entire police force was placed on 12-hour shifts for the convention week. This in effect increased usable man hours by 50 per cent. Thus, two-thirds of the force was able to continue all normal duties while the other one-third was available for special assignment. The additional men from some districts were assigned to specific locations, such as the Amphitheatre, the Loop area, or Lincoln Park.

The remaining men were divided into company-size units under the overall command of a Deputy Superintendent and were held at various district stations as reserve forces, with buses assigned and available to transport them anywhere in the city as needed. This was in accordance with the standard Department policy of assigning only as many potrolmen as it is anticipated are necessary with a reserve always available but not conspicuously located. During the first few days of the convention, Police Academy instructors were sent to the district stations, where the reserve companies of patrolmen were being housed, and conducted drill sessions in crowd control.

Insofar as possible, assignments were made so that the men would work under the sergeants who commanded them in their normal operations.

During convention week, all police on crowd control duty wore helmets. Some patrolmen purchased face shields for their helmets. Each policeman carried a nightstick (baton), service revolver and a can of mace.

In addition to the reserve companies and the patrolmen assigned to special areas, the Task Force was available for duty.

The Task Force

The Task Force is a division of the Police Department which always operates from cars and is normally assigned specific missions. During the convention the Task Force duties were to patrol designated areas and to act as a front-line reserve force capable of making immediate entry into troubled areas and maintaining order until other emergency forces arrived in relief. In planning for the convention week the Task Force Commander attended the Command Staff meetings.

Following the April riots, 170 detectives were assigned to the Task Force and worked the 10 a.m. to 6 p.m. shift as a body, thus leaving the remainder of the force to work the night shift. During the convention, when the entire Department was placed on 12-hour shifts, the plan was to have the detectives work from midnight until noon and the remainder work from noon until midnight. This became impossible, however, because many of the disorders occurred in the late evening and continued into the early morning hours, thus forcing postponements of the change overs. During the convention, four men, rather than the usual two, were assigned to each car; this was true of both day and night shifts. Walkie talkies were issued to all Task Force lieutenants and sergeants in order to maintain communications when the men left their vehicles to carry out a mission.

Task Force personnel are normally equipped with helmet, service revolver, baton, mace, and one shotgun per car. For the convention, gas masks and tear gas were issued to the Task Force. Regular police units had no shotguns or gas. The U.S. Army loaned to the police a large gas disperser which was mounted on a Department of Sanitation truck. (It was used on only one occasion, Tuesday night in Lincoln Park.)

The Task Force is composed of seven distinct sections. Six of them (Marine, Canine, Chicago Transit Authority, Helicopters, Evidence Technicians, and Detail Unit) were assigned to the tasks they would normally perform in time of threatened disturbances. The Tactical Unit Section had been used in the past for direct action against disturbances and was therefore designated as the front-line emergency force for the convention. It was directed to concentrate 100 men in each of three areas (Lincoln Park, Loop and the Amphitheatre) while maintaining, to the extent possible, a surveillance force for the rest of the city.

The plan was to design patrol routes which were tightly concentrated at the center of each area and became progressively dispersed as the distance from the centers increased.

The Task Force Commander felt that such a plan would permit the relatively strong central forces to answer emergencies within an area while the zones they vacated were being covered by men entering from the outlying routes. The plan worked well on the several occasions when Task Force personnel were ordered to supplement police escorting marches or quelling disorders. The procedure was to send the nearest Task Force cruisers to the designated trouble area in order to render immediate support. As soon as emergency forces arrived, the Task Force returned to its pre-assigned routes and resumed patrolling until further orders were received.

Nine cars from the Task Force unit assigned to the Loop patrolled the Dan Ryan Expressway during the hours that people were travelling to or from the Amphitheatre. They were used to mark the route and to keep traffic moving; during other hours they moved along predesignated patrol routes in the south Loop area.

The Police Department helicopter was used during convention week for surveillance of routes to the Amphitheatre and for traffic survey. On August 29, it was used to view rooftops in the vicinity of 16th Street and Michigan Avenue, and later in the vicinity of 18th Street and Michigan Avenue, due to reports of snipers (none of which was verified). U.S. Army helicopters were used by the Secret Service to support its mission of protecting the presidential candidates.

Use of Gas Masks

Five hundred gas masks had been on order for the Police Department since the beginning of the year. They had not been ordered with the convention specifically in mind, but they arrived approximately one week before it began. In one week the Police Academy's instructors, therefore, trained the entire police force in the use of these gas masks.

Narcotics Control

Reports to the Narcotics Division indicated that large quantities of drugs would be brought to Chicago during the convention. Fields of marijuana were said to have been planted specifically for the convention, and it was expected that drugs would be withheld from the market elsewhere in the country in the belief that they would bring higher prices in Chicago that week.

Nevertheless, of the Division's 56-man staff, only one four-man team dealt with drug-related problems during the week. The others were largely assigned to the Patrol Division and to other law enforcement areas.

(During the convention week, five or six raids netting perhaps 200 pounds of narcotics in all, were conducted by the Narcotics Division. The bulk of the narcotics consisted of benzedrine, LSD, marijuana, DNT and COP, with little or no "hard stuff" such as heroin.)

Amphitheatre Security

While the Chicago Police Department implemented most security measures at the Amphitheatre, the Secret Service had overall control of the convention site security. The Amphitheatre area was divided into two basic sections of responsibility: exterior security and interior security, each under the command of a deputy chief of police.

The deputy chief in charge of exterior security believed that the depth of the security measures recommended to him by the Planning Committee could not, as a practical matter, be reached. He also thought that, with the restrictions imposed by narrow streets and abundant police security, there would be few disturbances around the Amphitheatre.

On the basis of information garnered from the media and from various meetings, however, he concurred in the Police Department's decision to prepare for the possibility of large numbers of demonstrators. With this in mind, he worked with the Secret Service in determining the manpower needed at various points: 530 men used in exterior security during convention hours and 130 during nonconvention hours. A special 100-man exterior Amphitheatre reserve, located at Graham Elementary School, was available in addition to the reserve forces at the district stations. The deputy chief was provided with ten squad cars, two or three motorcycles, three vans and 25 walkie talkies.

For exterior security an outer and an inner perimeter were created, with different requirements for entry. During the hours the convention was active, the outer perimeter was bounded by the alley east of Halsted Street, 47th Street on

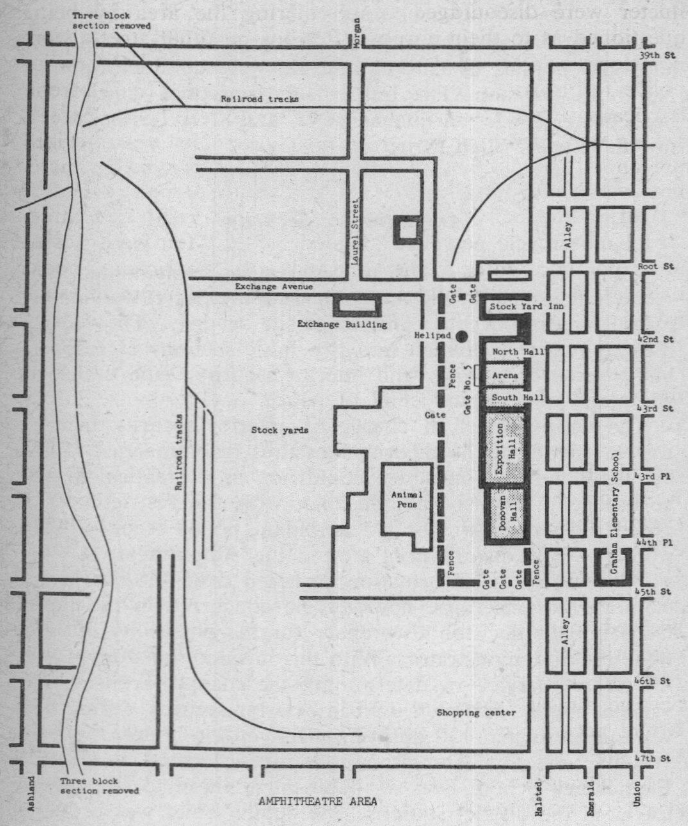

Three block section removed
Morgan
39th St
Railroad tracks
Laurel Street
Alley
Root St
Exchange Avenue
Gate
Gate
Stock Yard Inn
Exchange Building
Helipad
42nd St
North Hall
Arena
Fence
Gate No. 5
South Hall
43rd St
Gate
Stock yards
Railroad tracks
Exposition Hall
Graham Elementary School
43rd Pl
Animal Pens
Donovan Hall
44th Pl
Fence
Gate
Gate
Gate
Fence
45th St
Alley
46th St
Shopping center
47th St
Ashland
Three block section removed
AMPHITHEATRE AREA
Halsted
Emerald
Union

the south, 39th Street on the north, and Ashland Avenue on the west. During nonconvention hours, the east boundary moved from the alley east of Halsted Street to the west side of Halsted Street itself.

Persons travelling on through streets within this outer perimeter were discouraged from entering the area by being questioned as to their purpose. Persons on other streets were not stopped, although it was hoped that the strong show of police force would discourage entry. As a further deterrent, barricades were erected on Halsted at 39th and 47th Streets during convention hours to prevent access by unauthorized personnel; people with legitimate reasons for being there, however, were permitted to move relatively freely.

During the convention hours one cruiser and one three-wheel motorcycle patrolled Halsted Street. Men were posted at all points of entry to the area and at the barricades. Lookouts carrying walkie talkies but no additional equipment (such as rifles) were posted on the roofs of the Amphitheatre and the Exchange Building, and in a flat at Halsted and 43rd Street.

All manhole covers within several blocks of the Amphitheatre were either sealed or periodically checked by police stationed nearby.

The inner perimeter was bounded on the east by the alley one-block east of Halsted, on the north by Exchange and Root, on the south by 45th Street, and on the west by a cyclone fence topped with barbed wire. The fence was erected early in August, at the request of the Democratic National Committee, to enclose the Amphitheatre parking lot.

All were stopped at the inner perimeter and no one was allowed to enter without a pass or a legitimate reason. All deliveries had to enter at the 39th Street and Morgan gate. Prior to delivery, a letter had to be submitted to the Secret Service. Once a deliveryman was admitted, no police officer would accompany him to the place of delivery and back to the gate.

No changes were made in the exterior security plans as a result of occurrences during the convention; security posts remained the same and entrances through the perimeter were not changed throughout the week.

Security inside the Amphitheatre is usually handled by ushers, but for political conventions is handled through the combined efforts of the police and the Secret Service. A total of 472 men, divided into two shifts, were assigned to interior security; also available was a 50-man reserve force in Donovan Hall.

Three or four men were assigned to the Amphitheatre catwalk, high across one wall of the arena, in order to keep people off and to observe the convention. Eight to ten men were assigned to the carport. Four men were stationed in the passageway between the Amphitheatre and the Stock Yard Inn, where many of the delegates were staying and political meetings were held. There was also a detail stationed at the Inn itself. About ten men were assigned to assist the Secret Service control of admissions at Gate 5. That gate, which was located at the west side of the Amphitheatre, was the only entrance available to delegates and visitors. All other entrances, including the side entrances used by employees and suppliers, were under the primary surveillance of the police.

A plainclothes policewoman was stationed at each ladies' washroom and two uniformed police were posted at the entrance of each TV studio because of rumors that these facilities would be taken over by dissidents if they managed to enter the Amphitheatre.

The presidential candidates were under the surveillance of both the Secret Service and the Chicago police. One police lieutenant and one Secret Service agent were in charge of the Command Post, which was shared with the Fire Department and located in a trailer in Donovan Hall. It was equipped with a radio tuned to the emergency frequency, commercial telephones and walkie talkie communication with all posts. The Secret Service Command Post around the corner had a closed circuit TV system through which all areas in the convention hall could be observed at once.

The deputy chief of detectives supervised approximately 60 plainclothes detectives who provided security for the delegates' portion of the convention floor. They operated under the direction of the Secret Service, as is usual in a situation of this type. Some security employees from the Andy Frain company were designated as assistants to the sergeant-at-arms and were responsible for determining the validity of delegates' credentials. Uniformed police in the Amphitheatre were not to enter the convention floor unless called in by the detectives.

The mission of the detectives on the convention floor was to maintain an unobtrusive presence and to be ready and available to answer any request for assistance by the Secret Service or the sergeant-at-arms. Even if a physical outbreak were to occur, the detectives were ordered not to intrude unless the situation was such that the Secret Service and the sergeant-at-arms could not handle it. The men were strategically located throughout the floor and were anonymous except for the red convention insignia which identified them to security personnel.

Except for the number of personnel involved, preparations made by the Secret Service, not only at the Amphitheatre but throughout the city, were typical of those made when one of the persons they are assigned to protect is present or expected to be present. The largest complement of Secret Service agents ever detailed for a national political convention was on hand for two reasons: more such persons, including the President, were expected than ever before; and threats and reports of assassinations had been received.

Loop Security

While the Planning Committee had determined that special arrangements should be made for security in the Loop, determination of the specific measures to be taken was left to the deputy chief whose responsibility included the Loop and Grant Park. The four sources of manpower available to him were: 195 uniformed men and 50 plainclothes detectives placed under his command for the entire week, 100 men from the Task Force ordered to patrol the Loop, emergency companies of approximately 200 men each held in reserve at various district stations and the National Guard in the event that police strength proved to be inadequate.

The deputy chief's plan was to use the uniformed men primarily for security at the Conrad Hilton Hotel, which was the convention headquarters and his primary command post. Men were assigned to provide security at other Loop hotels, two of which (the Palmer House and the Sherman House) were used as secondary command posts. The men were to restrict themselves to the security of their assigned hotels, leaving demonstrations or disturbances to the area's Task Force personnel and the emergency reserve forces.

The 50 plainclothes detectives assigned to the deputy chief's command were divided among the three command posts. They all had assigned duties at the three hotels and none remained in reserve. The primary command post had some additional personnel not found at the others; among these were 14 youth officers and 8 policewomen, for possible arrests of juveniles or women; and representatives from the Secret Service and the Chicago Fire Department.

One of the missions of the forces at the Hilton Hotel was the preservation of order as candidates arrived or left, at which times the Secret Service had overall authority. At its request, on three or four different occasions during the week, 30 or 40 patrolmen were assigned to clear the streets and direct traffic immediately in front of the hotel entrance.

The effectiveness of the reserve police forces was enhanced by the module system of communications, a recently developed radio which has been supplied in quantity to the United States Army. Its range is short compared to that of a walkie talkie, but it is extremely compact and ideally suited for law enforcement agencies faced with civil disturbances. Through the efforts of the Police Planning Division, it was loaned to the Chicago Police Department specifically for the convention. The units were first issued to the police detail at Lincoln Park. The supply was limited, however, and the remaining units were used only when emergencies developed, particularly in Grant Park.

Lincoln Park

Lincoln Park, because it was to be the demonstrators' "headquarters," received special attention. A deputy chief of police is responsible for Area 6, which is comprised of Districts 18, 19 and 20. This area includes Lincoln Park and many of the streets adjacent to the west, north and south. As noted earlier, 100 Task Force men were concentrated in this area.

On August 18, the deputy chief informally requested that the Intelligence Division undertake surveillance activities in Lincoln Park. Thereafter and throughout the convention week, there were police undercover agents among the demonstrators. At the same time arrangements were made to set up a command headquarters at the Cultural Arts Center in the park and on August 24 the police detail which was to remain there throughout the week moved into Lincoln Park.

Because the entire police force had been assigned to 12-hour shifts, two shifts could be assigned the normal work load of three, leaving an entire shift of policemen available for additional duties. The third shift from Area 6 was specifically assigned to Lincoln Park and was split in such a manner that two-thirds of the men were on duty from 4 p.m. to midnight.

The main functions of the police detail in the park were to be loose surveillance of the crowds and enforcement of closing hours. The normal summer vehicle assignment in Lincoln Park of one squad car and three three-wheel motorcycles was increased to four squadrols, ten three-wheel motorcycles, and four unmarked patrol cars. Every night during the summer the Beach and Park Detail had been clearing the park. Due to the increased number of persons in the park, eight additional patrolmen and a sergeant on three-wheel motorcycles, who usually patroled only the beach area, assisted in clearing the park from August 18 through August 24.

Prior to the convention, the policemen in Area 6 were told by the deputy chief to stay within reach of each other for their own security and for effectiveness. They were warned that they would probably be exposed to a great deal of taunting and baiting by the demonstrators. They were instructed to avoid arresting people in borderline cases and to consult with their senior officers if there was any doubt. If there were an insufficient number of policemen to carry off an arrest properly, they were told that the arrest should be avoided.

The deputy chief also spoke of the need for professional conduct at all times and stressed that their duty as policemen was to preserve law and order and to protect lives and property. He said the convention security would, in his opinion, be successful if there were no arrests, disorders, or incidents of violence.

Police Training

All policemen initially spend 14 weeks in the Police Academy, including two weeks of field training in the streets and district stations of the city. They are issued weekly training bulletins on particular aspects of police work. Every year, each patrolman on the force returns to the Police Academy for an additional five-day training session. Members of the Task Force, the special unit available for deployment anywhere in the city, receive yet another day of training every year. Seventeen hours of crowd control training are given initially; thereafter, all policemen receive three hours at the annual training session and the Task Force members another 13.

Police training emphasizes that the object of an arrest is a conviction in court. "The basic rule of the Department with regard to arrested persons is that they are to be booked, charged, and made eligible for bond in that order; and that these processes are to be completed without unnecessary or unreasonable delays. . . . Great care is to be exercised by all personnel concerned with the processing of arrested persons to insure that they are not being held for unnecessary or unreasonable periods of time before being made eligible for bond." (TB, Vol. IX, No. 8.)

The average policeman's equipment includes a service revolver, baton (nightstick), helmet, handcuffs and can of chemical mace. He is taught that weapons are to be used in self-defense, to subdue a violent prisoner, or to prevent a person from doing bodily harm to the officer or to another person and that the service revolver is to be used only in the most extreme situations. (TB, Vol. VII, No. 19.)

According to police orders, the baton and chemical mace can only be used when the officer reasonably believes such use is necessary "to make the arrest, . . . to defend himself or another while making the arrest . . . or to prevent the escape of a person already arrested." (TB, Vol. VII, No. 19.) The police officer is cautioned against swinging his baton as a club, poking a person with it, or attempting to use it to knock a gun from his opponent's hand and is ordered never to strike a person on the head with the baton. (TB, Vol. VII, No. 19.)

Police are instructed to use mace "only when absolutely necessary" in order "to subdue an unarmed attacker or a violently resisting suspect." (TB, Vol. IX, No. 11.) In order to insure that mace is used with discretion, an officer must complete a Firearms Use Report whenever it is used.

The police training bulletins stress repeatedly that force must be used with caution, particularly in crowd-handling situations. One bulletin states that the policeman "can be almost certain that the object of his force will say 'police brutality,' even though such use of force was justified." (TB, Vol. IX, No. 2.)

Police training covers the role of a police officer in preserving order at peaceful gatherings, preventing disorder in tense situations and restoring order when mob action takes place. As a cadet and as a member of the force, he is instructed in the psychology of certain types of crowds and the best means of dealing with these crowds. He is taught that in every type of crowd there are likely to be some persons who are potential trouble makers and that the manner in which the policeman deals with these persons determines to a great degree what direction the rest of the crowd takes.

The police officer is instructed to show no emotion and to remain impartial to everything except the law and the rights of all people. He is warned to be wary of his actions so that he does not precipitate disorder. If it can be determined that one person or small group of persons is creating tension and contributing to unrest, he is taught that they should be taken into custody and removed from the scene.

When a crowd becomes disorderly, a policeman is supposed to summon assistance available under the Police Department's special emergency plan. Under this plan, the police are trained to arrest anyone violating a law, disperse the crowd and prevent it from reassembling. Peaceful methods of dealing with participants in a tension situation or mob action are emphasized in preference to force. When the crowd does disperse, whether it be of its free choice or not, the police are instructed to allow avenues of escape so that the tension will dissipate quickly.

If the crowd becomes disorderly and resists the police, the supervising officer is authorized to use riot control formations, chemical agents or, in extreme situations, to order fire by selected marksmen at specified targets. Three basic riot control formations are used in dispersing, holding and moving disorderly crowds and unarmed mobs: the wedge for breaking up, splitting, or striking into a crowd; the diagonal for moving crowds away from walls or buildings or to turn a crowd down a street or into an open area; and the skirmish line as a holding formation to block entrance to a street or other area or to drive a crowd out of a specific area.

Riot control formations are a last resort, used only when all other attempts at solving the problem have been exhausted. The Police Department is opposed to force if it is not a necessity and continually reminds "all officers regarding the special precautions to be taken against the excessive use of force." (TB, Vol. VIII, No. 30) "Physical handling of a rioter is not the best recourse so it usually should be the last. Punishment is a function of the courts. An avenue of escape should always be left open. The primary purpose of a riot formation is to disperse the unruly mob, not to take them into custody." (TB, Vol. VIII, No. 15)

Where mass arrests are required the policeman is instructed not to make them randomly since "Mass arrests made by many police in a helter-skelter manner will serve absolutely no purpose as far as maintaining law and order is concerned. However, arrests made in an orderly and well-planned manner indicate a trained force prepared for such emergencies and will help convey to the demonstrators and to the rest of the city that they are dealing with a superior force." (TB, Vol. VII, No. 38)

National Guard

The Illinois National Guard Emergency Operations Headquarters (EOH) was created at the Chicago Avenue Armory to direct guard assistance in case of civil disaster or disturbance anywhere in the state. Brigadier General Richard T. Dunn, commander of the EOH, first became involved in convention security measures at a meeting held with Mayor Daley, at the latter's request on June 19, 1968. In answer to the Mayor's questions as to what security assistance the National Guard might be able to provide during the convention, General Dunn suggested three options:

1. Plan in advance to call a predetermined number of guardsmen to state active duty during the convention.
2. Schedule the weekly training assemblies of the National Guard units in a staggered manner in such locations that one unit would be immediately available for call on any night during the convention week.
3. Do nothing in advance and request assistance from Guard only if needed.

The Mayor thought it was still too early to decide that the National Guard should be called to active duty, but he did not dismiss the possibility of a call-up at a later date should information from the Secret Service and other sources indicate its advisability.

Following this conference, EOH began work on a plan to effectuate the second of the three options. This plan, which came to be known as "Demcon," was explained to Mayor Daley in a letter from the General dated July 17. According to this plan, on August 24 and 25, one battalion (800 men) and one military company (300 men) would be on duty in a training status from 8 a.m. to 5 p.m. or later, if necessary. From Monday through Thursday, August 26 to 29, one battalion would be on duty in a training status each evening, with about one-fourth of the Guardsmen being located at Boyce Park and the rest at Fuller Park, both of which are readily accessible to the Amphitheatre. During all this time the appropriate command and staff elements would be available in the same vicinity. The following Saturday and Sunday, one battalion would be training at the Chicago Avenue Armory.

In sending a copy of this letter to the Chicago Police Superintendent, the General noted that the Demcon plan was the greatest force the Guard could provide without being activated, and stated:

> As far as I am concerned, I would rather have them (Guardsmen) readily available on duty than to encounter difficulties and wish that we had done so. The decision in this regard, however, rests with the Mayor and the Governor.

On August 2, General Dunn met with Governor Shapiro, who, following the General's explanation of Demcon, approved the plan in substance. They then discussed the manner of communications to be used by them in case activation of the Guard was required.

On the morning of Thursday, August 8, the U.S. 5th Army held a conference at its headquarters at Fort Sheridan, Illinois. At the conference were representatives of the 5th Army, the U.S. III Army Corps from Fort Hood, the Secret Service, the Chicago Police Department, the Illinois National Guard and, at the request of the U.S. 5th Army, a representative of the Indiana National Guard. Representatives of the various organizations explained their plans for convention week and details were ironed out. During the meeting, the representatives of the Secret Service distributed a written intelligence summary reporting the plans of the demonstrators for the convention week.

According to General Dunn, the National Guard's plans and, to the best of his knowledge, the security plans of other agencies, had been up to this time directed toward insuring adequate security for the Amphitheatre and for the downtown hotel areas, with the greater emphasis being placed on protection of the Amphitheatre area. At the August 8 conference, General Dunn learned that the Secret Service wanted more emphasis placed on the hotels and the downtown area.

With the exception of the representative from the Indiana National Guard, those present at the morning meeting met that afternoon with Mayor Daley and presented their plans. That evening, the General met with his staff and conducted a similar briefing.

Six days later, on August 14, General Dunn was asked by the Department of Defense to come to Washington, D.C. He complied and met with the Undersecretary of the Army in charge of all matters pertaining to civil disturbances, the Director of Civil Disturbance Planning and Operations for the Army, members of both of their staffs and the Secret Service. This meeting followed a conference between the Undersecretary and the Civil Disturbance Director on August 14 and an intelligence briefing given to both of them by the Assistant Chief of Staff for Intelligence of the Army on August 15.

At the meeting on August 16, the General was asked to describe, and was then questioned closely about, Demcon, the plan which provided for some National Guard security protection without activating the Guard. There appeared to be some concern as to whether or not federal troops should be used. Federal troops could not be used until the National Guard had been activated. No decision was made as to Guard activation while General Dunn was present.

After that meeting, General Dunn flew to Springfield, Illinois, then drove to his home in Bloomington. While he was en route from Springfield to Bloomington, Governor Shapiro's office called General Dunn's home requesting that the General return to Springfield the next day to meet with the Governor.

At noon on Saturday, August 17, General Dunn returned to Springfield and met with the Governor, two assistants, the Governor's legal advisor, the Director of the Department of Finance, and the Illinois Adjutant General. After informing those present that the decision had been made to call the Illinois National Guard to state active duty during the convention week, the Governor solicited their advice as to the timing and manner in which the activation and operations could be accomplished most effectively. Final plans were made, but it was agreed that the decision to activate would remain secret until August 20, when the Governor would make a public announcement.

General Dunn discussed the activation with the State Adjutant General and members of both generals' staffs later that afternoon, and, the following day, with the Commanding General of the Brigade which was to be activated.

At 1:30 on Monday afternoon, August 19, General Dunn met in Chicago with top officials of the Chicago Police Department to review and discuss troop strength, division of responsibility, and the operating procedures to be followed by the Police Department and the National Guard. Following that meeting, representatives of the U.S. 5th Army, U.S. Army III Corps, the Secret Service and the National Guard met with representatives of the Chicago Police, Fire and other departments. Representatives of the Chicago Police Department briefed those present on the security plans for the convention week but did not disclose the decision to activate the National Guard.

After that meeting, General Dunn, 5th Army Chief of Staff Lt. General Michaelis, 5th Army Deputy Commander Major General Chiles, Superintendent of Police Conlisk and Fire Commissioner Quinn met with Mayor Daley. All present approved the recommendation of General Dunn that the civil authorities handle the situation and call upon the Guard only if needed. In addition it was agreed that EOH would request use of Soldier Field but that the Guard units would actually operate out of the armories and adjacent parks. Only U.S. Army Armored Personnel Carriers would be located at Soldier Field, thus reserving it and making it available for U.S. Army and Guard troops if needed. Additional U.S. Army Armored Personnel Carriers were to be located at the General Services Administration offices.

The next morning, Mayor Daley called General Dunn to make sure that the Guard would automatically request the use of Soldier Field following the Governor's announcement of its activation, and was assured that the request would include Soldier Field, Humboldt Park and Washington Park. The Mayor reported that he had notified the president of the Park District to expect such a request.

At 2 p.m., Governor Shapiro publicly announced that National Guard troops would be called to active duty during the convention week. When the decision to call the Guard to state active duty was made, the Demcon plan was rejected.

Instead, OPlan 1-68 (Chicago), the already existing general plan for activation of Guard forces to assist in Chicago in case of any emergency or civil disturbance, was put into effect. This plan was not specially prepared with the Democratic convention in mind.

After the announcement that National Guard forces would be activated, General Dunn continued making plans and coordinating them with the Police Department. In addition, he had regular and continuous contact with Lt. General Michaelis, who had been appointed Commander of Task Force III, the name used to identify the federal force which would have been committed if needed. If the Guard troops had not been able to control the situation, and if one more battalion had been activated anywhere in the state, federal assistance could have been obtained. Had this occurred, the Guard troops would have been federalized and the entire force, Guard and U.S. Army, would have been under the command of General Michaelis. This explains the closeness with which General Michaelis followed the planning and activity. On August 26, approximately 6,000 Army troops, all trained for riot control, were air lifted from Ft. Hood, Ft. Sill and Ft. Carson to Glenview Naval Air Station, 20 miles northwest of the Loop, and to Great Lakes Naval Training Station, 37 miles north of the Loop, in anticipation of the possible need for federal assistance. They were equipped with full field gear, including rifles, flame throwers and bazookas.

On the morning of Friday, August 23, approximately 5,000 guardsmen were mobilized under EOH Command for duty in Chicago. The troops remained at the armories until called upon. These guardsmen were part of the 33rd Brigade and constituted five battalions and three supplementary companies. The companies were each divided into four or six platoons, each platoon consisting of four squads made up of approximately ten enlisted men supervised by a sergeant.

National Guard Training

Civil disturbance training for Illinois Army National Guard troops began at the direction of the Illinois Adjutant General during 1965 and 1966 and was increased in 1967. According to a survey made following the Detroit and New Jersey riots, the Illinois Guard, with 34 hours per year, had received more civil disturbance training than the Guard of any other state.

Following those riots, the Department of the Army outlined a plan requiring that both the regular army and the National Guard administer a certain number of hours of civil disturbance training per year. In accordance with that plan, the Illinois National Guard administered 16 hours of training by September 1, 1967, and thereafter exceeded the yearly supplementary requirements; 44 hours of training were given at summer field training in 1968, much of it on the Guard's own initiative. Each Illinois Guardsman had received by convention week a total of 64 hours in riot and emergency training.

The Guard is conceived of as a supplemental rather than as a primary force. Its role in civil disturbances is that of providing assistance to civil authorities, and even then it functions as a restraining, rather than as an aggressive force. This is important, because the Guard's training stresses the nature of its use for a holding action rather than arrest and confinement action.

Certain principles of control guide the training of Guardsmen. The formation of crowds is to be prevented if possible and, if they do form, they are to be dispersed as quickly as possible. Leaders of militant groups are to be apprehended when they excite their followers against Guardsmen. The men are trained not to allow any advance or attack upon them, since once begun it may be difficult to control. Two of the principles of control are similar to those used in the training of the Chicago policemen: no more force than necessary is to be used in performing riot control, and avenues of escape should be provided for militant crowds.

Decisions are made by a leader for his entire group. The Guard's function as a powerful containing force has a definite effect on the individual Guardsman's reaction to harassment. Less abuse is dealt the Guard because insults are taken by the Guard team, which is always together. This is in contrast to city police, who frequently act alone or in small groups and can be singled out as objects of scorn.

The training of Guardsmen is directed toward teaching proper individual attitudes and individual skills to be used as part of a unit. Course work familiarizes them with such agitator techniques as the use of extensive propaganda, a forceful harangue by a fiery speaker, the appearance of an irritating individual and the use of an emotion-provoking rumor. The

Guardsmen are taught to ignore the taunts of agitators and not to allow personal feelings to interfere with the execution of their mission; they are told to expect objects to be thrown at them, to avoid them, and never to throw them back.

The importance of creating a favorable impression on the civilian community through proper carriage, dress and personal conduct is emphasized, but the Guardsman is made to realize that his actions may have to be taken in the face of popular disfavor. The importance of following leadership decisions and of strict adherence to prescribed standards of conduct and fair treatment of civilians is continually stressed.

Training is given in the proper use of gas dispensers, with emphasis upon the different kinds of gases, the factors of wind and weather upon their dispersal and the nature of their toxic effect.

In addition to the training he receives on attitude and behavior, the Guardsman is taught to operate as part of a unit in the formations most practical for controlling rioters. The advantages of riot control formations as against large crowds and the disadvantages as against small or rampant crowds are covered.

There are four basic riot control formations taught to the Guardsmen. The first is the line, which is used to push or drive crowds straight back, across an open area, up a city street, or to hold and deny access. The second riot control formation is the echelon, which may be pictured as a "V" with the open end facing the crowd; it is used in either open or built-up areas to turn the crowd. The wedge is the third formation and is used to penetrate and split crowds. The last formation is the diamond, which may be used either when entering a crowd or when all-around security is required.

These formations are frequently used as a "show of force." There are times, for example, when troops make a surprise, formidable appearance as a unified force, or when troops fix bayonets on order or march in column formation a reasonably safe distance from the mob and within plain view of it. Bayonets are fixed only on order. (During convention week, General Dunn specified that bayonets were not to be used unless so ordered by the field commander.)

The Guardsmen are cautioned that special care is to be taken in their actions when the riotous elements are intermingled with innocent civilians. They are taught that the use of necessary force to accomplish a military mission does not make an otherwise lawful act by military personnel illegal, but that reckless or malicious use of force may subject military personnel to civil or criminal liability, or both.

The persistent problem of the extent to which a Guardsman could protect himself in case of direct attack was covered in two memoranda issued during the summer of 1968. They provided that deadly weapons could be used if an attack was clearly made with the intent to injure a Guardsman or the people assigned to him for protection, and that arrest was to be made only if a city police officer was not available and it was the clearly indicated action to be taken.

Other Government Agencies

The Police Department in Chicago was the law enforcement agency most deeply involved in security preparations, but Cook County and Illinois state law enforcement agencies also took some precautions.

Sheriff and State Police

The Sheriff's office conducted advance planning to insure that they would be able to respond if the need should arise; this was due in part to rumors that the demonstrators might conduct diversionary activities in areas outside of Chicago. A special command post was set up at the Bedford Park Station and a representative was assigned to the National Guard command post in the Chicago Avenue Armory. The Sheriff's Task Force was placed on 12-hour shifts from August 23 to 30, and all days off were cancelled. Evictions which would ordinarily have been conducted were suspended in the ghettos during convention week to avoid the possibility of setting off disturbances.

The State Police increased Governor Shapiro's personal guard protection during the two weeks he was in Chicago. Additional men were posted at his hotel room and accompanied him wherever he went. The other precaution exercised by the State Police was that of intensifying normal surveillance for anything unusual on tollroads and expressways.

Personnel of the State Fire Marshal and the State Arson Investigation Squad were placed on alert and all leaves were cancelled during the convention because of rumors that diversionary fires might be set in the suburbs to prevent suburban firemen from going to the aid of the Chicago Fire Department.

Another reason for the alert was the report that a pamphlet distributed by a "militant group" contained specifications for a new incendiary bomb with a 15-minute delayed ignition (none of the incendiary bombs were seen in Chicago).

Fire security in the Amphitheatre area was a responsibility of the Chicago Fire Department. Immediately after the announcement that the convention would be held in Chicago, the Fire Department began extensive planning. On several occasions, Commissioner Quinn and other top fire department officials met with representatives of the Police Department and Secret Service to discuss fire safety precautions for the convention.

The Fire Prevention Bureau spent considerable time inside the Amphitheatre from November, 1967, to August, 1968. Floor plans were obtained and studied; members of the Bureau surveyed the Amphitheatre for possible fire hazards, gas shut-off valves, exit ways, etc.; all Amphitheatre fire boxes were equipped with new hoses and hand-operated extinguishers were installed.

In order to prevent unauthorized access into the Amphitheatre, all ventilators were covered with metal screens. One hundred and ninety-three men from the Bureau, previously cleared by the Secret Service, were deployed throughout the Amphitheatre complex by the Fire Department. Each Amphitheatre door was manned by a Fire Prevention Bureau man and a Frain security guard; the remaining 68 men in the Bureau were stationed at the major hotels.

Three chemical fire wagons and two ambulances were located inside the Amphitheatre, which had been set up with sufficiently wide aisles to allow for their possible use. Seven light wagons were provided for illumination of the entire Amphitheatre area, including the helicopter pad, in case the regular lighting was disrupted. The Fire Department's "communications wagon," equipped with a closed circuit TV camera having a zoom lens capable of picking up a license plate at three blocks, was stationed at the Amphitheatre and had communication contact with all important locations including the major delegate hotels and all key city agencies. Fire Department equipment from distant stations was moved closer to the Amphitheatre.

There was a fireman assigned for the entire week to each alarm box located within a six-block radius of the Amphitheatre. The two Fire Department helicopters with ground control units circled the Amphitheatre and the downtown area watching the movement of the crowds. In addition, a 24-hour watch around the Amphitheatre area was kept by the Fire Prevention Bureau.

Medical Preparations

Medical arrangements made by the city consisted of three plans: a recently developed city-wide disaster emergency program coordinated by the Chicago Hospital Council; a disaster plan designed specifically for the Amphitheatre; and ordinary first aid facilities at the Amphitheatre.

In February, 1968, the Subcommittee on Handling of Mass Casualties of the Chicago Hospital Council recommended that member hospitals join a coordinated program to deal with the hospitalization of persons injured in catastrophes. The program included a special communications system to provide for the maximum utilization of emergency facilities. It was not developed with the Democratic convention specifically in mind, but that even served as a deadline for the installation and possible testing of the system. This communications network was available to police and fire authorities at the time of the convention but was never utilized.

Prior to the convention, the Police Department contacted hospitals within easy access of the Stockyards area to determine what services would be available for the treatment of mass casualties. The Chicago Hospital Council distributed to ambulance services and to the Police and Fire Departments:

1. Maps showing special routes to hospitals from the Amphitheatre.
2. Lists of hospitals near the Amphitheatre with listings of distances, routes, capacities and special services.
3. Special communications numbers.

The Chicago Health Commissioner arranged for two first

aid stations at the Amphitheatre, each manned by teams of doctors and nurses. Two ambulances were available for transportation to hospitals. The Salvation Army and the American Red Cross had their services ready for any emergency which might occur. Space was planned in the convention hall for conversion to a temporary morgue, a temporary shelter and an emergency coordination unit in the event of a major disaster.

In addition, all injured policemen were treated at one hospital, the location of which was kept confidential to avoid possible action against it by the demonstrators.

Arrest and Court Procedures

The April riots in Chicago following the assassination of Dr. King established that mass arrest procedures were inadequate and needed reconsideration. The convention became a deadline for the completion of general emergency planning in this area.

On August 21, a comprehensive order was issued by the Chief Judge of the Circuit Court to cover mass arrest procedures. To implement this order, the State's Attorney's office issued directives for processing large numbers of people through courts. While the County Jail was planned as the primary area of detention, additional space, such as the hangars at Midway Airport, was also designated to be available during the convention.

On the weekend prior to the convention, the Cook County Public Defender's Office increased the number of its defenders on alert. On his own initiative, the Presiding Judge of the Municipal Court increased the number of alerted judges to ten, and all the supporting court personnel on alert were similarly increased.

As a supplement to the general procedures designated for mass arrest situations, certain additional action was initiated specifically for the convention. For example, an agreement was reached that if both a city and a state charge were drawn against a defendant, only one of the charges would be pursued, so that both an Assistant State's Attorney and a man from the Corporation Counsel's office would not be required. At the bond hearings, the Presiding Judge allowed volunteer attorneys to make special appearances for the hearings only and, following the arrests and bonding, allowed out-of-town defendants to appear by counsel at their first hearings to set a date for trial without the necessity of attending in person.

Andy Frain Security

A supplementary force to the Police Department for security measures at the Amphitheatre was supplied by private organizations. The Democratic National Committee retained Frain Security Services, Incorporated to furnish security 24 hours a day to people passing into or out of the Amphitheatre itself or certain areas within it. There were also a number of "floating" agents to handle pilferage and to relieve the agents at regular posts.

The Democratic National Committee also retained Andy Frain, Inc. to handle tickets at entrances, to usher and to keep the aisles clear during the hours when people were present. A complex ticketing system, which entailed issuing a new ticket each day to each person entitled to attend the convention, was prepared by the Democratic National Committee. Tickets were required for entrance on the delegate buses, for admission to the Amphitheatre itself and for access to the convention floor. The Frain ushers handled tickets at the various points where they were used.

The coverage by the Frain company during the convention was basically the same as for any other similar type of convention. Frain security personnel were concerned with fire precautions as well as with crowd control and theft. None of them was armed in any way.

Transportation

Transportation for the delegates to the Amphitheatre was a crucial consideration in security planning. It was complicated by the city-wide taxi strike and the partial bus tie up resulting from the Concerned Transit Workers strike. It was feared that one goal of the militant groups might be to disrupt the movement of delegates, press representatives and other important groups of people.

Professional transportation people were loaned to the Democratic National Committee by private concerns to work on this problem. They worked with the Chicago Police Department, the Bureau of Streets and Sanitation, and the Secret Service in coordinating all the transportation arrangements and in planning the routes the delegates would utilize in going to and from the Amphitheatre.

Many of the delegates and visitors arrived in Chicago at O'Hare International Airport, 18 miles northwest of the Loop. On August 6, airport security measures were discussed by a representative of the Chicago Department of Aviation, officials of the Police Department, managers of all airlines based at O'Hare Airport and a representative of the Democratic National Committee. The Department of Aviation issued a memorandum cautioning airline personnel to watch out for unauthorized persons, equipment or material, to keep all doors and cabinets, vehicles and carts securely locked and to report anything unusual. As an additional security measure, and to avoid overcrowding of the public terminal, the chartered planes used by delegates arriving at O'Hare were instructed to use the military runway rather than runways used by commercial airplanes. The delegates were met by a convention welcoming committee and, except for the candidates, were delivered to their downtown hotels via chartered buses under no unusual or special security.

O'Hare Airport has a Chicago police detail assigned on a full-time basis. All their leaves, time off and vacations were cancelled, as they were for the entire Chicago Police Department. Since they worked longer shifts every day for two weeks no additional men were deemed to be needed.

One hundred and sixty buses and a number of private cars were hired to shuttle the delegates between their hotels and the Amphitheatre. When a delegation was ready to go to the Amphitheatre from the Loop, it would contact the communication center which had been established by the Traffic Operations Division of the Police Department; and buses with proper credentials would be sent from the bus assembly point at Soldier Field.

A group of not more than four buses, led and followed by two of the 70 police squad cars assigned as security for those groups, travelled one of the five alternate preplanned routes to the Amphitheatre. The specific route to be taken was known only by the lead squad car; bus drivers were not informed in advance.

All routes to the Amphitheatre were protected by barricades closing off cross streets and controlled by specially installed hand-operated switches on the traffic lights to insure that no delays or traffic jams occurred. A helicopter, in constant communication with the police station, was used to observe the buses on their routes to the Amphitheatre and back again to the hotels.

On arriving at the Amphitheatre, each of these small groups of buses and their police escorts parked facing north in the south half of the lot west of the hall so that the passengers could walk straight into the hall, moving only between the buses and the building. The north end of the lot was used for a heliport and for VIP cars. After each convention session, the delegates were returned to their hotels in a similar manner.

Park District

The General Superintendent of the Chicago Park District informally requested assistance in protecting the Park District's equipment prior to and during the convention week.

In Lincoln and Grant Parks, additional signs showing the closing time as 11 p.m. were put up and damaged signs were repaired or replaced. All toilet facilities were inspected and extra wastebaskets were set out. During convention week, a 24-hour clean-up detail was on duty in the downtown area and Near North Side parks.

Protection of Water Supply

The city took special precautions to protect its water system after being notified by federal narcotics agents that the city water supply might be poisoned or contaminated with LSD. The Police Department obtained diagrams of all Chicago water facilities. The water department officials were aware that no real threat existed, because of the massive amounts of poison that would be required. Nonetheless, to safeguard the facilities, the Police Department increased its guard on the two main water processing plants, including the intake tunnels, and the 11 pumping stations. Elements of the Canine Section of the Task Force were assigned to the filtration plants, as had been done during potentially disruptive conditions in the past.

At the Amphitheatre, water department engineers were assigned to round-the-clock duty. Instruments attached to incoming pipes allowed the city to keep check on the chemical content of the water. Plumbers continually inspected the plumbing at the convention hall.

Civil Defense Corps

In preparation for the convention, the Director of the Civil Defense Corps attended many meetings with members of the Police Department, the Fire Department and Administrators of Chicago hospitals. During convention week all volunteers were informed of the need to make themselves available at all times, and the Civil Defense searchlight vehicles were stationed at the Amphitheatre.

Sanitary District

The Metropolitan Sanitary District was warned by the Mayor's Office that sabotage might be planned against the three main sewage treatment plants. The Superintendent of the Sanitary District thought the plants were too vulnerable to protect completely since a bomb timed to explode when it floated into a plant could conceivably be dropped into a sewer. He also felt that the normal security precautions were sufficiently comprehensive to ward off the danger of sabotage. He did provide his security guards with emergency telephone numbers.

Federal Communications Commission

Police informants reported that demonstrators would attempt to break down police communications during the convention. The Police Department, therefore, asked the Federal Communications Commission to take appropriate security measures but were assured by the engineer in charge that normal precautions and repair crews would be sufficient to deal with any anticipated problems.

At the request of CBS, the FCC prepared a list of communications equipment used in the Amphitheatre in order to help isolate problem areas and to determine whether a breakdown in one system would affect any other. Although certain problems and breakdowns were anticipated, they were normal media problems which might occur at any convention of this type and no additional security measures were taken.

The Department of Public Works

The Commissioner of the Chicago Department of Public Works, after receiving a call from the Police Department informing him that many demonstrators would be arriving by expressways, called the construction companies working on or near the expressways and suggested that they take steps to protect their equipment.

Other Security Measures

During the April, 1968, riots on the West Side, the Police Department had suggested to officials of the Port of Chicago that, if it were anticipated the riots were heading for the Loop area, all bridges across the Chicago River could be raised to seal off an area comprising the Loop and the area south to about 22nd Street. The Deputy Port Director and his Supervisor considered this plan for convention week but concluded that rioting was not sufficiently probable to prepare for further implementation of such measures.

Several proposed plans for use of the Exhibition Hall at Navy Pier and its facilities were examined by both the Police Department and the Fire Department, but no plans were ever made final. (Suggested plans included use of the hall as an additional detention area if the jails were to become overcrowded, as a storage area for stolen goods in the event of arrested looters, and as temporary living quarters for firemen and policemen who might be kept on reserve for emergency duty.)

Representatives of the Federal Aviation Administration, the Chicago Police and Fire Department, the Secret Service and the National Guard met twice prior to the convention. Pursuant to those meetings, the FAA imposed a restricted area prohibiting aircraft operations below 2,500 feet mean sea level within an area bounded by the Eisenhower Expressway on the north, Lake Michigan on the east, Western Avenue on the west and Garfield Boulevard (5500 South) on the south.

It was in effect from midnight, August 25, 1968, to midnight, August 30, 1968, and was monitored by visual observation.

Thus, plans had been made, personnel had been trained and assigned. The city was ready for the demonstrators and for any emergency that might occur.

LINCOLN PARK: THE VIOLENCE BEGINS

Lincoln Park is situated on an 11,085-acre strip of land between Chicago's Lake Shore Drive and Old Town. Normally, the park is a haven for zoo fanciers, strollers, picnickers and bicyclists. But beginning August 18, habitués were joined by the first contingent of the demonstrators expected in Chicago. Among the early arrivals were Yippies and National Mobilization leaders. The Yippies established their headquarters at the southern end of the park.

The area is a natural gathering spot. A main North Side intersection—the Eugenie Triangle of Clark, LaSalle and Eugenie Streets—defines the southwestern tip of the park and feeds people in and out of the facility. Immediately west along Wells Street lies Old Town, normally active and bustling with activities of youth. High-rise buildings, converted brownstones, hippie shops and expensive boutiques all contribute to the composite that in Old Town is normalcy. Stockton Drive speeds visitors from Lake Shore Drive and points north to the southwestern half of this area of the park. And within the area itself, asphalt-covered sidewalks and bridle paths link up three baseball diamonds, a fieldhouse, a concession stand and statues of Grant and Garibaldi.

Throughout the summer, Chicago-based Yippies had conducted a series of Sunday "be-ins" near the fieldhouse. The rock bands which performed at them drew praise from devotees but scorn from some Old Town residents offended by the noise. This split typified a more general division in the Old Town community regarding the desirability of the Yippies and their proposed Festival of Life, or "invasion," depending upon the position espoused. Both *ad hoc* and existing civic groups lined up for and against the Yippies and their program.

Not knowing what to expect in Lincoln Park or elsewhere (but preparing for the worst), the Chicago Police Department assigned undercover officers to observe and photograph any suspicious looking persons in the park.

August 18 to August 23

Beginning August 18, National Mobilization members were present to recruit and train marshals for various convention week demonstrations. That afternoon about 25 persons, including Rennie Davis and Tom Hayden, gathered near the park fieldhouse and discussed the recruiting procedures, the ideals of nonviolent demonstrations, relations with police and the legal rights of demonstrators. Three seasoned protest leaders from Los Angeles demonstrated techniques to be used in the event of a confrontation with police.

Of particular interest to police and, as the week rolled by, to the news media, was instruction in the "washoi," a maneuver borrowed from the Japanese student demonstrations. The "washoi," explained a representative from the Detroit-based People Against Racism (PAR), is a device for moving a group out of a riotous situation without injury. Marchers line up, ten to 20 persons wide and as many deep as possible, linking arms and grabbing each others' waists. Depending on their expertise, the marchers can move forward, backward, or sideways in unison. When properly executed, the maneuver resembles the movement of a snake.

A nurse outlined plans for emergency medical centers to be established in the area during convention week. She said that the centers, organized by the Medical Committee For Human Rights, would also provide teams of "medics" to treat those who might be injured.

Listening to and observing all this were undercover police and representatives of Chicago's Commission on Youth Welfare. Police were "tailing" Jerry Rubin and Abbie Hoffman. At a "be-in" that afternoon, these crowd watchers spotted several members of the "Headhunters," a motorcycle gang from Posen, Illinois, numbering 75 to 100 members.

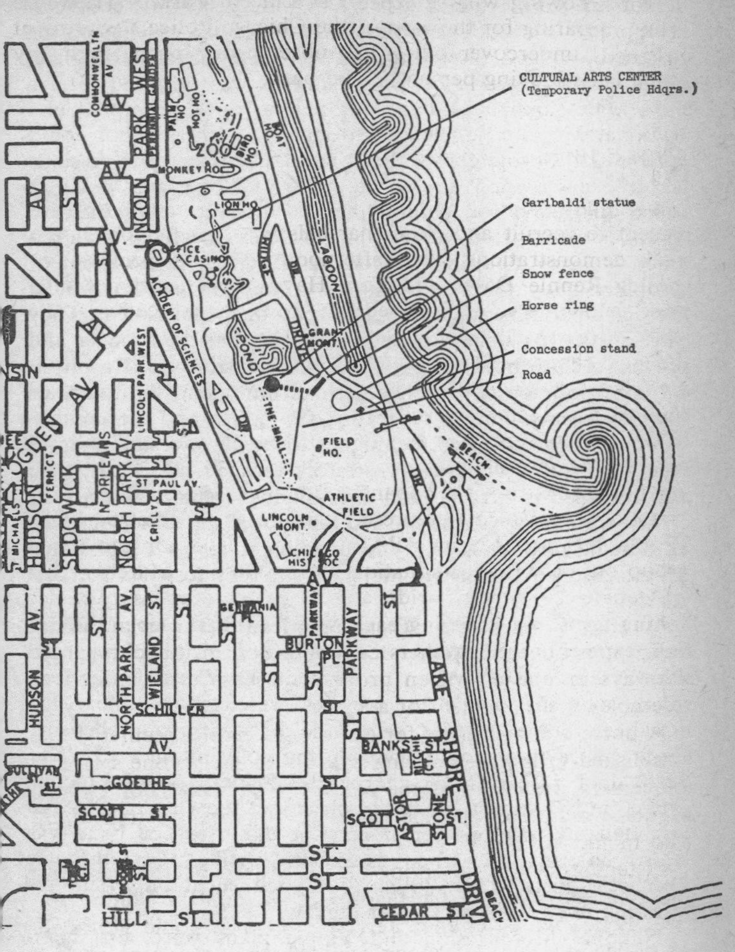
CULTURAL ARTS CENTER
(Temporary Police Hdqrs.)
Garibaldi statue
Barricade
Snow fence
Horse ring
Concession stand
Road
ZOO
MONKEY HO
LION HO
BIRD HO
BOAT HO
CASINO
LAGOON
POND
THE MALL
FIELD HO.
ATHLETIC FIELD
LINCOLN MONT.
GRANT MONT.
CHICAGO HIST SOC
BEACH
ACADEMY OF SCIENCES
COMMONWEALTH AV
LINCOLN PARK WEST
NORTH PARK AV.
ST PAUL AV.
SEDGWICK
HUDSON
OGDEN
N ORLEANS
CRILLY CT.
FERN CT.
GERMANIA PL.
BURTON PL.
PARKWAY
WIELAND ST.
SCHILLER
BANKS ST.
ASTOR
STONE
SCOTT ST.
GOETHE
SULLIVAN ST.
LAKE SHORE DRIVE
CEDAR ST.
HILL ST.

On August 19 and 20, National Mobilization conducted washoi practice sessions just west of the Lincoln Park fieldhouse. The Yippies and others who attempted to execute the maneuver lacked discipline and the necessary conditioning, but a covey of television news cameras was on hand to give them wide publicity. (The poor performance prompted one National Mobilization leader to state that the washoi could not be used during convention week.) Other practice sessions featured instruction in karate, judo, kicking and using a rolled magazine for defense against assault. According to Mobilization representatives, the marshals' meetings were devoted in large measure to detailing activities in the event of disorder. They were told that their function was to protect the demonstrators and attempt to keep them nonviolent. They were instructed to try to keep order within their ranks and prevent a clash between police and demonstrators. If a physical confrontation with police seemed imminent, the marshals were to form a cordon separating the police and the demonstrators. They practiced techniques to break and stall charges into their ranks while demonstrators escaped. Marshals were also schooled in first aid and in individual rights under arrest.

The training sessions revealed that not all of those recruited as marshals could accept the nonviolent tenets of National Mobilization. At least two marshals say they resigned for that reason.

As the Yippies and others practiced the washoi, police helicopters hovered overhead. Mobilization members regarded their presence as a form of harassment. They had similar feelings about the police motorcycles which moved near the marchers. Some Yippies were also becoming apprehensive about where they would sleep during convention week. The Festival of Life called for around-the-clock use of Lincoln Park, but by August 20, it was clear that the City of Chicago was unlikely to grant permission for this use. The issue was settled on August 23 when, as earlier described, United States District Court Judge William J. Lynch ruled on a suit requesting use of the park after curfew.

National Mobilization and Yippie plans were also hampered when the administrators of McCormick Theological Seminary, near Lincoln Park, denied the use of seminary grounds for sleeping purposes, though a number of North Side churches had promised the use of their facilities. (The Seminary did agree to permit the grounds to be used as a medical aid station by the Medical Committee For Human Rights.) Despite these setbacks, as the weekend approached, there were many Yippies who believed that city officials would look the other way at curfew hour and permit them to remain overnight in Lincoln Park.

Another setback to the Yippie plans occurred when some of the rock band groups which were supposed to appear Sunday, August 25, for a Newport-type "be-in" to kick off the Festival of Life, decided to cancel their performances. Nevertheless, the Yippies went ahead. They mimeographed a program outlining the week's planned activities. Following Sunday's music would be Monday morning workshops and an afternoon party at the North Avenue beach. And at dawn, Tuesday, August 27, a religious ceremony was planned. More workshops were to follow in the morning, and that night, an "un-birthday party" for President Johnson was scheduled at the Chicago Coliseum.

Poetry and folk singing were set for dawn Wednesday, August 28, with the "Yippie Olympics" and a "Miss Yippie Contest" planned for later that morning. The schedule concluded with a call for Yippie participation in a 4 p.m. National Mobilization rally at Grant Park on Wednesday, August 28. The remainder of the week's activities were in doubt, pending developments in Grant Park.

One incident which contributed to the week's uncertainty and the demonstrators' edginess was the August 22 killing of a 17-year-old American Indian, Jerome Johnson. Johnson, from Sioux Falls, South Dakota, was shot to death by police at North Avenue and Wells Street, just a few blocks southwest of the park. Police detectives said they fired their guns when the fleeing youth, identified as a Yippie, fired a .32 caliber revolver at them. The shooting caused one of the marshal trainers to say:

> We don't want to go overboard in ascribing malevolent intentions to the police, but obviously things are going to be getting very rough here. We've got to be prepared.

On Friday, August 23, several hundred persons were reported in the park. National Mobilization leaders and representatives of SDS (Students For A Democratic Society) were discussing first aid precautions, the availability of legal aid in the event of mass arrests and precautions against tear gas. Legal aid was to be provided through the Legal Defense Committee, made up of volunteer lawyers and law students.

The same day, Jerry Rubin caused a stir when he and several followers released a pig named "Pigasus" in the Chicago Civic Center Plaza. They said Pigasus was their candidate for president and that his platform was garbage: "Who knows more about that than a pig?" "If our president gets out of line," they vowed, "we'll eat him." Pigasus was confiscated by the police and locked up at the Chicago Humane Society. Six persons were arrested.

Saturday, August 24

On Saturday morning, August 24, the temporary police command post in Lincoln Park swung into operation, with a deputy chief briefing his men on strategy and tactics in dealing with the demonstrators in Lincoln Park.

About 300 to 400 persons gathered early Saturday afternoon in Lincoln Park, some of them out of curiosity (the Yippies and their planned Festival had been much publicized) and some to participate actively. Most congregated on a tree-filled knoll, north and west of the park fieldhouse. The knoll runs north and south through the southern end of the park. The crowd included a large number of out-of-towners, but many others were residents of the area.

National Mobilization marshals also met, separately from the main group, to plan supervision of Sunday's scheduled demonstration in front of the Conrad Hilton Hotel. It was decided that they would meet at noon Sunday at the Hilton, at which time marshals would receive identifying armbands of black cloth. After the meeting broke up, the marshals and others participated in a washoi which they said was for "spirit and morale."

Bongo drum and guitar music emanated from several clusters of young people gathered among the trees. Occasionally, some arose to dance. A few uniformed policemen mixed with the crowd, moving casually in groups of three and four. Plainclothes men moved singly or in pairs. The scene seemed cordial, with police often chatting with the crowd. One resident heard a young boy ask an officer what his riot helmet was for. "It's to carry popcorn," the policeman said.

But not all were friendly. Upon his arrival at Lincoln Park Saturday morning, a college student inquired of a policeman where the Yippies were. The policeman replied: "Over there; you can smell them."

There were reports from police undercover agents that persons in the park had purchased oven cleaner and ammonia to be used as weapons against the police. (This report was investigated by the police intelligence unit and the findings appear in the Supplement.) Upon hearing these reports, individual policemen naturally became apprehensive. Matters were not helped when the Yippies released a pig in the park and one of them yelled: "Kill the blue-shirted pigs and release humans, mother fuckers." The Yippies released the pig despite a warning from police that the action would violate a city law against unleashed animals in a park. The Yippie who released the pig was arrested. (Six persons had been arrested Friday for turning a pig loose at the Civic Center Plaza.)

At approximately 3 p.m. on Saturday, groups of eight to ten were practicing the washoi and various karate exercises. Police helicopters again hovered above these people, who in turn yelled and waved their arms to the pilots. By 5 p.m., the crowd had grown to more than 2,000 persons. The Yippies set up several tables amid the crowd. One was identified as a "Communication Center," where persons picked up leaflets explaining the Festival of Life and identifying emergency housing accommodations to be used if the park curfew were enforced. A medical aid station, "The Hospital," was also designated. Other tables were labeled "Free Food" and "Free Clothes."

On Saturday evening, most of the people in Lincoln Park clustered in two groups around bonfires. One group was singing. The other was listening to a flute and bongo performance. Small knots of persons sat around in the darkness. A sizeable number seemed to be "straight," middleclass people attracted to the park out of curiosity.

Across the street from the park, at "The Theatre," a group of 25 persons, including Abbie Hoffman, Jerry Rubin, Allen Ginsberg, Ed Sanders (of the "Fugs") and Paul Krassner were discussing a city decision refusing the use of Lincoln Park sound amplifying equipment as well as access to electrical outlets in the park fieldhouse. The group decided to borrow amplifiers brought to Chicago by out-of-town Yippies and to plug them into outlets at the park concession stand, just east of the fieldhouse. It was also decided that a flatbed truck, to be used as a stage for the rock bands, would be rented by Sunday afternoon. Ginsberg said he would telephone Mayor Daley's deputy, David Stahl, to inform him of the alternative plans.

At the same meeting, those present said that when the police ordered them to leave the park they would do so. Statements to this effect were drafted by Ginsberg, Sanders, Hoffman, Rubin and Krassner.

Ginsberg wrote:

> City police insist they'll bust anybody sleeping in Lincoln Park after 11 p.m. Help! All the Yippies wanted to sleep together safely under the sky and have a good time talking about God Politics.
>
> So far the park seems safe Sanctuary all day time for Yippie Life Convention. Police still forbid amplifier system for American Rock Music and apocalyptic Yippie harangues. Fantastic! That means everybody will have to make it together, grass roots communion without Authoritarian commands except from the city police. Almost human OM is possible.
>
> Unless 5,000 youngsters fall asleep at 11 p.m. in Lincoln Park and the police don't bother waking them up, peaceful, happy Yippie Pilgrims can find beds together, organized by kindly Mobilization to End the War. Also consult Free Housing Concession table.

Said Rubin and Hoffman in a joint statement:

> We are a revolutionary new community and we must protect our community. Chicago is a police state and we must protect ourselves. The cops want to turn our parks into graveyards. But we, not they, will decide when the battle begins.
>
> The cops have said they will beat and arrest us if we try to sleep in the parks which belong to the people. We are not going into their jails and we aren't going to shed our

blood. We're too important for that. We've got too much work to do.
If the cops try to kick us out of the park we have sleeping places. We're not going to make it that easy for them to get us. We'll sleep where we can, because we've got a lot to do when we're awake. Leave the park in small groups and do what is necessary—make them pay for kicking us out of the park but let's win!
P.S. When and if it becomes necessary to abandon the park, flares will light the best escape routes.

Ed Sanders' statement read as follows:

Gentlemen, joy, nooky, circle groups, laughing, dancing, sharing, grass, magic, meditation, music, theatre, and weirdo mutant-jissomed chromosome-damaged ape chortles have always been my concern for Lincoln Park.
Yours for the power of the lob-throb.

And Paul Krassner wrote:

Sleeping in Lincoln Park after 11 p.m. isn't as important as living our revolution there the rest of the day (the park opens at 6 a.m.). Mass arrests in response to civil disobedience would not outrage an American public which for so long has allowed money that could feed starving Mississippi children dead to be spent burying Vietnamese children alive.
We win this round, Mayor Daley. Up your law-and-order.

The statements were typed on a single sheet and mimeographed for distribution in Lincoln Park on Sunday. With the sheet was another which listed "crash centrals," area churches and hippie gathering places where emergency housing information could be obtained. These crash centrals were organized by National Mobilization, with the assistance of the North Side Cooperative Ministry.

By 10 p.m. Saturday, a crowd of about 600 persons gathered just northwest of the fieldhouse in a low, flat area known as the "mall." A number of them were sitting in a circle, staring at a large candle. Others were simply milling around, watching the crowd. After the candle burned out, they built a large bonfire. The Yippies claimed they were burning money and draft cards in the fire.

A few newsmen were circulating in the crowd, interviewing people, one of whom declared that police violence could not be permitted. He called the police "pigs" and "fascists." Several persons were carrying signs bearing the same epithets. The police were stationed primarily on the park perimeter and only occasionally would one or two walk through the crowd.

At about 10:30 p.m., a group of youths threw several full trash baskets onto the bonfire. A plainclothes police sergeant arrested one of them, but as he did so, a second one attempted to hit him in the face. The youth missed, but as his arm followed through, he struck a city legal aide in the face. Both youths were arrested.

The Curfew Hour

Almost simultaneously, police announced that the curfew hour was approaching and that the park would soon be cleared. Most of the people around the bonfire joined poet Allen Ginsberg in a move out of the park. Ginsberg was chanting "om," a sound which he says dissipates tension. "A thousand bodies vibrating om can immobolize an entire downtown Chicago Street full of scared humans, uniformed or naked," Ginsberg has stated. About 200 persons, however, remained in the park, grouped in a meadow north of LaSalle Drive, east of Stockton Drive and west of the fieldhouse.

At about 11 p.m. three lines of police, totalling not more than 60 men, formed north of the fieldhouse, facing the crowd, to commence clearing the park. The first line consisted of three-wheel motorcycles from the beach patrol unit. The second two lines were men on foot. The motorcycles moved slowly, herding the crowd west toward Clark Street. Occasionally, someone would yell "pigs" or other epithets at the police. Some stragglers were shoved by police but not hurt.

Police had been patrolling the park all summer. Until the week prior to convention, a single squad car had moved through at 11 p.m. On August 18, the beach patrol had begun a nightly curfew clearing operation. In accordance with the city's decision, the deputy chief of police in charge of the

Lincoln Park area ordered the park cleared each night during the convention week. He voiced the belief that if the curfew ordinance were not enforced, Yippies and others would take it as a sign of weakness:

> You can't give in to these people. You can't be selective about the laws you obey, otherwise there's a breakdown of law and order.

Once the park had been cleared, police formed a line along the eastern sidewalk of Clark Street, which is immediately adjacent to the west side of Lincoln Park. Most of the 200-odd persons pushed from the park stood on the west side of the street, jeering police. Some yelled: "Red Rover, Red Rover, send Daley right over." Police were generally quiet. Several newsmen who had been behind police lines were ordered out of the park.

Then the police swept across Clark, moving people north along the west sidewalk. The crowd gave way quickly and there was little or no confrontation with the police.

An exception was *Chicago Daily News* reporter Lawrence Green, who, as he moved north, was met by a single policeman with a raised baton. Green held out his press card and yelled: "Press! Press! Press!" The officer yelled: "Fuck your press credentials!" He struck him on the back with a baton as Green crouched by a parked car. Green says, however, that the blow was not administered with full force and he ran north out of the area.

Meanwhile, the crowd dispersed rather quickly, but regrouped and began running south on Wells, the main street of Old Town. As they moved, they began to chant: "Peace now! Peace now! Peace now!" and "Stop the Democratic convention!" Some motorists honked their horns. At first, police did not react in numbers. But as the crowd reached North Avenue, an "officer needs help" order was received at police headquarters.

When police reinforcements arrived, they found the intersection blocked. People were in the street and creating a traffic jam. One contingent of policemen managed to move the crowd east on North Avenue simply by walking toward them. Ultimately, the entire crowd was dispersed, but not before several police cars were stoned. Eleven persons were arrested and charged with disorderly conduct—ignoring police orders to disperse. Thus ended the first police-crowd confrontation.

Sunday, August 25

On Sunday morning, Lincoln Park was quiet; several hundred persons were present and there were no organized activities. At approximately 1:30 p.m., someone with a bullhorn announced:

> We're going to picket the major hotels where the delegates are staying, confront the warmakers and let them know that we are here and that this is only the advance guard. Follow the sound! Follow the sound! At two o'clock the first action will take place in front of the Sherman House. Follow the sound and we'll march downtown in our usual disorderly fashion.

The marchers left the park at approximately 1:30 p.m., accompanied by police. Most were wearing multicolored hippie garb and had long hair and beards. Some wore Yippie buttons. All were shouting antiwar slogans.

As they marched south on Clark Street, they entered part of Skid Row, attracting drunks and derelicts from flop-houses and 35-cent-a-shot saloons. The derelicts heckled them. "Why don't you take a bath?" a grimy spectator yelled. An old man waved and said, "Hey, I'm a hippie!" Grabbing the arm of an old woman, he led her in an impromptu dance on the sidewalk across the street from the march.

A car crossed an intersection, pulling a float with the banner, AGRICULTURE SUPPORTS HUMPHREY, and the crowd booed and oinked.

But the march was peaceful. *De facto* leaders took charge on occasion, instructing people to stop at red lights. The police did not harass or intimidate the group in any way, nor did the marchers create a disturbance.

Once they reached the Loop and discovered that their voices resonated off the buildings, they began chanting: "Hey, hey, LBJ, How many kids did you kill today?" "Dump the Hump!" and "End the War."

Their route—apparently improvised—took them past the Palmer House, where they stopped and shouted "Free Huey!" —a reference to Black Panther leader Huey Newton, then on trial for murder. When a policeman with a bullhorn ordered them to keep moving, they did, and took up the earlier chant, substituting "Richard J." for "LBJ."

At the corner of Jackson and Wabash they met a line of police who ordered them across the street. The group complied, as they had before, and finally, at about 3 p.m., filtered across Michigan Avenue, over the bridge and into Grant Park. After the downtown demonstrations, a large group returned to Lincoln Park.

By midafternoon, the skies were turning overcast and it was rather chilly. Nevertheless, some 3,000 to 5,000 persons gathered around the park horse ring near the concession stand, to listen to rock music.

The crowd was substantially young people: Yippies and hippies from Chicago and many other places throughout the country; Chicago teenagers in conventional dress; young professional people living on the Near North Side; some blue-collar workers; some motorcycle gang members in their heavy leather jackets; a few blacks, ranging from West and South Side teenagers to older militants from California. A man seated in the middle of the crowd was nude.

There were also older people, a significant number of them from the surrounding, middle-class community. Some families had also strayed over from the nearby Lincoln Park Zoo.

A police undercover agent described the crowd this way:

> About 50-75 were bikers, i.e., motorcyclists with leather jackets, etc., about 250 were leaders and their marshals who generally had the same political and tactical beliefs. Finally the vast majority were innocent people; or at least people whose political viewpoints were more concerned with anti-war protest, etc., than with violence or revolution.

As the week progressed, the age of the crowd increased as so-called "straights" joined it. But one witness says, "The crowd—even on Sunday—was never as young as people tended to believe. The average age must have been at least twenty-one."

There were also some extremists present. While SDS had few representatives in Lincoln Park, they did have posters like this one displayed on Sunday:

> Some of us will be into trying to show our feelings about the Convention by marching outside of the Amphitheatre

with picket signs. And a lot of us, besides these things, will be into not letting the fucking system work. . . . So far a lot of things have already gone down. Somebody threw a Molotov cocktail into an induction center. It broke the window and started a small fire.

A lot of people have painted things with spray cans on different buildings, store windows, viaducts, and the like. One of the grooviest of these painting things involved the CIA . . . painting "CIA Sucks" on the door.

People are talking about other things like letting animals loose in the delegates' hotels, things with smoke-bombs and butyric acid, and all kinds of other shit.

If we get into enough things, they don't have to be that big, we can close down and uptight the whole town, as far as the people who run the System are concerned.

When you seize a town a campus, get hold of the power stations, the water, the transportation, forget to negotiate, forget how to negotiate, . . . you are not demonstrating: you are fighting a war, fight to win, . . . take what you need, it's free because it's yours.

Since the musicians were performing without a stage, few persons could see them. After about half an hour, no one could hear them either. At the request of the concession stand owner, a policeman ordered the musicians' amplifiers unplugged from the concession stand electrical outlets. Shortly thereafter the Lincoln Park supervisor for the Chicago Park District interceded and okayed use of the outlets.

Near 4 p.m., a Chicago newsman assigned to cover the afternoon activities overheard Abbie Hoffman tell seven colleagues that "if the pigs come into the park tonight we are not going to stay. But we don't want to get trapped or forced into any mass arrest situation. Everybody knows what the police are planning." Hoffman asked that the seven remain together throughout the evening to assist persons in leaving the park.

Toward 5 p.m., additional persons began to arrive and the deputy chief, concerned about the size of the crowd and reports that it would resist curfew enforcement, considered closing the park and discussed it with a city legal official. He was advised that there was no legal basis for such action at that time.

At approximately 5:18 p.m., a large, flatbed truck was driven up to the southeast section of the park, near the band site. It was halted by a squad of ten policemen. Flying from the top of the truck was a Yippie flag, red letters spelling out "Yippie" against a purple background. A large sign draped over one side of the truck read: "Trip With Pigasus." The driver wanted to use the truck bed as a stage for the musicians. Police orders were to refuse passage to all vehicles except a van which had already delivered the amplifiers. The deputy chief states that he and Abbie Hoffman had agreed to this limitation at a noon meeting in the park. Hoffman, however, says that he understood that the vehicle to be admitted was the flatbed truck.

The police and Hoffman discussed use of the flatbed truck for about a half hour. As they did, a group of newsmen surged around them and the vehicle. The sergeant in charge of the police unit objected to the microphones poked in his face and ordered the newsmen to leave. They refused to do so. Meantime, some of the crowd had surrounded the truck. The sergeant said that one person offered a policeman a sandwich filled with excrement. Some 60 to 70 persons boarded the vehicle, jamming its bed, hanging over the wooden side railing, perching from the top of the cab and straddling the hood. A member of the "Headhunters" was on top of the cab.

The police sergeant, Hoffman and the truck driver agreed to a compromise: the truck would not be permitted in the band area, but it could be parked nearby. As the driver tried to turn the vehicle to move to the approved area, the crowd grew angry, moved closer and some persons began to taunt the police. "Who's fuckin' your wife this afternoon, pig?" They thought that the police had refused admittance to the truck.

One man stood in front of the truck and yelled: "Don't let the truck out!" The man was arrested and taken to a paddy wagon some 50 feet away. Meantime, a long-haired, young man blocked the path of the wagon. He was yelling to the crowd: "Sit in front of the paddy wagon!" Also he urged the crowd to "Get in close!" and "Get their guns!" When two plainclothes men moved to arrest the young man, the crowd yelled: "Let him alone!" "Let him alone!" The youth struggled vigorously and persons in the crowd tried to intervene. The plainclothes men, grasping the youth, were escorted by a group of uniformed police away from the truck.

The officers intended to get the man away from the crowd and then release him. A large section of the crowd followed and some of them screamed: "Kill the pigs!" "Fuck the pigs!" "Gestapo pigs!"

As the police moved, the youth screamed that he was bleeding and tried to escape. A heckler was seized by uniformed police and moved away also. As the officers reached the top of the north-south knoll, they broke into a run. But the crowd started to run also. The police appeared shaken by the aggressiveness of the crowd, some of whom yelled: "Pig, pig, fascist pig!" "Pigs eat shit! Pigs eat shit!" and "Kill the pig, flush him out, bring him in!" a cry from *Lord of the Flies,* one of the novels most popular on college and high school campuses in recent years.

As the officers ran toward Stockton Drive, which cuts through the western edge of the park, they were joined by 75 additional men from the park command post. These men formed a double line along a sidewalk just east of the Drive.

The first young man arrested was put into a waiting patrol car, parked about 20 feet behind the police line, and taken away. The police put the second man into a paddy wagon, also parked behind the police lines. As they did, an 18-year-old girl, who said she was the man's girlfriend, demanded to be let inside with him.

As the police tried to restrain her, she twisted and screamed, ripping at an officer's clothing. Finally, three policemen picked up the girl, and tossed her toward the open door of the wagon. But they missed their mark and the girl hit the back of the vehicle. The officers picked her up and threw her again. This time she landed inside. One of the three policemen moved, with his baton raised, toward a national magazine reporter standing by the wagon. When he saw the reporter's credentials, he lowered the baton and said: "You can tell them in your damn magazine that she was swinging, too."

Suddenly, those people who had been engaged in a face-off with police, surged into the police lines. The officers thought that they were being surrounded and called for help. Police then clubbed wide gaps in the crowd, permitting the entry of additional police from the park command post. The persons who had been harassing the police withdrew a few yards, but did not retreat. A second line of police was formed to the north, partially surrounding these people who the police believed were agitating for a confrontation.

The vast majority of people, however, were still some 40 yards east, at the top of a knoll running south of the Garibaldi statue. They had followed the action out of curiosity, but had stopped short when police reinforcements had arrived.

At least 25 policemen in these lines had removed their nameplates. Some had removed their badges as well. When an 18-year-old boy asked one of the officers why his nameplate was missing, the officer replied: "It's none of your business." Asked the same question, another officer said he had lost his plate. A police sergeant stated later that he had authorized his men to remove their badges and nameplates after a person in the crowd had ripped off one officer's badge and attempted to stab him with it.

As nightfall approached, the crowd was quiet. Some 3,000 persons gathered around several bonfires started in park trash baskets. Dead tree branches, papers and twigs fed the fires.

One of the witnesses describes the scene this way:

> It was just before nightfall, and they didn't have any plan. It was supposed to have been a festival of life, but I didn't see any happy people. Everybody I walked past looked depressed and aimless. There was no action, and it was starting to get quite cold. Although there were a lot of police in the park too, it was a very dead scene. But when it got dark, then things started to speed up.

There was more playing of bongo drums and singing. Leaflets were being distributed by both National Mobilization and the North Side Cooperative Ministry, indicating places of shelter other than the park. Again the crowd in the park was heterogeneous and clustered in three groups. One of these was located just south of the South Pond. The other two were near Stockton Drive. When one of these grew increasingly tense, the other group, led by Allen Ginsberg, who was conducting a "mystical" Hindu ceremony, merged with it. Ginsberg's group formed a circle. According to one observer, a CBS camera crew "barged into the mystic circle, disturbing the 'worshippers' and inciting a 12-year-old boy to give the cameraman a not-so-mystical sign with his middle finger." The spectators laughed. Then a white youth did a headstand behind the camera crew, resting his feet on the soundman's shoulders. This time even the worshippers laughed.

At about 8:30 p.m., a fire department truck arrived to extinguish several trash fires in the vicinity of the fieldhouse. When the firemen used hand-held fire extinguishers they were jeered by bystanders. A policeman who had snuffed out a blaze was pelted on the right shoulder with a bottle. At about the same time, police announced over a bullhorn that curfew was at 11 p.m. and that it would be enforced by clearing the park.

Police Against the Wall

While most people in the park were engaging in peaceful activities, there was a confrontation at the fieldhouse, where eight to 12 policemen were standing with their backs to the wall. Under the fieldhouse lights they made an ideal target for some 15 demonstrators, who formed a semicircle in front of them and jeered: "Mother fuckers!" "Shitheads!" "Pigs!"

The police had not initiated the barrage of abuse, and they were not responding to it in any way. As the crowd, attracted by the lights, kept growing, the abuse mounted. But the police stood impassively and said nothing. At first the demonstrators had kept a distance of about 20 feet, but as their numbers increased they moved in, and soon the police were clearly trapped. Someone on the roof threw a lighted cigarette at one of them. It landed on his bare right arm, but he didn't flinch. Others threw rocks.

This went on for about half an hour, the crowd still jeering and taunting, the police silent. Two squads of reinforcements arrived and took positions between the first line of police and the wall, but the crowd, which had grown to 150, continued to move in slowly.

Suddenly the police charged. There was a word of warning—"All right, get out of the way!"—but the crowd had no chance to get out of the way. The charge was fierce, with police hitting everyone they could reach. The crowd fell back, and was charged again at once. One witness says there were at least three charges.

A VISTA volunteer said he was hit in the stomach and back by police. He stated that the policemen who then arrested him did not wear badges or nameplates.

A volunteer medic from Northwestern University's medical school described the scene:

> When someone would fall, three or four cops would start beating him. One kid was beaten so badly he couldn't get up. He was bleeding profusely from the head. The kids scattered to the street as the police moved about 200 yards and then regrouped around the building. A couple of dozen Yippies were clubbed. I treated five myself.

The witness saw another medic, wearing a white coat, struck by an officer. When he yelled: "I'm a medic," the officer said, "Excuse me," and hit him again.

During this melee, a number of policemen removed their nameplates and badges. When a Chicago attorney asked one officer why he had removed his plate, the officer said: "See my sergeant." When asked the same question, a city legal aide said: "It's up to police."

While this incident was occurring, Yippie leader Abbie Hoffman was endeavoring to negotiate with a police commander about clearing the park. Hoffman said: "We're gonna stay here till eleven o'clock at night, and at eleven o'clock at night, we're going to test our legal right to be in this park and sleep here." When the commander said that anyone who stayed in the park after 11 p.m. would be arrested, Hoffman replied, "Groovy." That ended the negotiations.

Final Warning

At approximately 10:30 p.m., the U.S. Attorney, a legal official of the city and the deputy chief of police drafted a text of the evening's curfew announcement. The announcement read: "This is a final warning. The park is closed; all persons now in the park, including representatives of the news media, are in violation of the law and subject to arrest. The police have information that there are persons in the park who intend to injure police officers. The police will take what steps are necessary to avoid injuring anyone. This is a final warning; you are in violation of the law. Move out, NOW!"

When the announcement was completed, a police traffic safety education car moved through the park, an officer inside reading the announcement over a loudspeaker. The message was also broadcast via boathouse loud-speakers and police bull-horns.

Confusion followed. Some urged avoidance of conflict, others urged active resistance to the curfew. Two other recommendations were dispersal in small groups and street demonstrations.

A few persons climbed trees, and, using megaphones, urged a quick exit. One such person said: "We came here to show the country's political corruption. It's silly to abort our efforts and risk getting busted tonight."

A Yippie exclaimed: "We are here to defend freedom. You people who want to say in the park, stay in the park. People who want to leave, leave. People who want to grope, grope. But for those of you who want to stay don't panic if a motorcycle comes near you."

In the middle of a large group, one youth suddenly got up and yelled, referring to the Mobilization marshals, "Fuck the marshals! Down with the leaders!" Someone else was giving instructions to a crowd of demonstrators who did not wish to receive them. "Daley gives orders," someone yelled, "don't give us orders, you fascist." There were other objections in the same vein, and one witness says he was afraid that violence would break out within the demonstrating group itself.

Despite the conflicting advice, most persons left the park at about 11 p.m. Near Stockton Drive, in the light of TV cameras, a tall 14-year-old boy climbed on the shoulders of a friend and both the boy and a Chicago actor, standing alongside, began to chant: "Stay in the park! Parks belong to the people!" The boy waved a Viet Cong flag and the chant was picked up by others. Confusion resulted. Many persons ran back into the park toward the fieldhouse. Mobilization marshals were yelling: "This is suicide! Suicide!" They urged people to flee the park and told them they could sleep on the grounds of the McCormick Theological Seminary, apparently unaware that seminary officials had already denied such use.

As the marshals bellowed their announcements through a microphone, Yippies shouted them down as "authoritarian." Some Yippies even attempted to take the microphone away.

After several minutes of milling, the same 14-year-old youth again climbed onto the shoulders of another person and shouted: "Follow me! To the streets! To the streets! The streets belong to the people!" He was joined by several black youths who yelled: "Let's go to the streets."

Several three-wheel police motorcycles began zig-zagging among the people, prodding them along. Officers on foot and dressed in plain clothes, with riot helmets and batons, were telling people to "get out of the park or be arrested."

With the 14-year-old boy and the blacks leading the way, an estimated 600 persons surged out of the park into the intersection of LaSalle Drive, LaSalle Street, Clark and Eugenie—the Eugenie Triangle. But an estimated 200 to 300 persons stopped on the eastern edge of Stockton Drive and decided to move no further. Police motorcyclists moved back from Stockton Drive into the park. Reporters mixed with those at Stockton Drive, attempting to interview them.

The group which had flowed into the Triangle began to move south on LaSalle Street. An observer who moved with them described the scene:

> Hundreds of young men and women, some in beards and beads with painted faces, some long-haired and sandaled, and some in the latest turtleneck sweater fashion, followed whoever was ahead of them in a pell-mell run south, toward the loop, 18 blocks away.
>
> Chanting was loud but indiscriminate: "Humphrey go," "Ho, Ho, Ho Chi Minh," "The street is free. The street is ours" and "Free Huey."
>
> With two young men holding North Vietnamese flags in the front ranks, the black-long mass of people raced raggedly down both sides of Clark Street, hopping over hydrants and auto fenders, dodging telephone poles and running into each other.

As they moved, the crowd demanded that motorists honk their horns in support. When a motorist complied, the crowd cheered.

As the people approached North Avenue and LaSalle, they numbered between 1,500 and 2,000. They were met by a line of 20 policemen who were blocking their path west on North Avenue. The sidewalks, however, were left open. The officers moved into the intersection with their nightsticks out and ordered the crowd to get off the street and stay on the sidewalks. People were running in all directions but there was no physical contact.

One official state observer said the police appeared relaxed.

He even saw some officers giving persons in the crowd the sign of peace (a V).

At this point, reinforcements arrived—25 detectives in squad cars plus several more squads of uniformed police. The police line then retreated west on North and some people followed. At Wells, the officers turned and chased the crowd eastward. When the police stopped and then retreated, a group followed them again. The police about-faced and swept the street again.

Approximately 50 feet east of the Wells-North intersection, a man stood in the street with his arms folded across his chest. An officer pushed him and he fell to the ground. A second policeman kicked him and told him to move along. People on the sidewalks began screaming: "Police brutality!" Finally, at about midnight, the crowd dispersed. Many persons returned to Lincoln Park. Some ran in, shouting: "Welcome to the Che Guevara National Park!" Police did not try to stop the return.

Trouble on the Michigan Avenue Bridge

A large group started marching south along LaSalle Street. They did not return to Lincoln Park.

When they approached an intersection that was blocked by police, they would simply turn and move down another street. They finally wound their way onto Michigan Avenue and proceeded south on Michigan Avenue toward the downtown area. They marched south down the center of the Avenue, occupying the entire width of the street, which is 80 feet from curb to curb. Vehicular traffic in both directions was unable to pass. As one photographer who was covering the march said: "The whole march consisted of flooding the sidewalk from one side of whatever street we were going on [Michigan Avenue] to the other side."

As the marchers proceeded south on the Avenue, some were shouting, "Peace now!" "The streets belong to the people!" and others were chanting "Ho, Ho, Ho Chi Minh!" Some of the demonstrators were observed tipping over trash cans which lined Michigan Avenue. These containers were for the most part being uprighted by marshals at the rear of the line. However, the strewn contents of the containers did remain in the street. Other marchers were observed damaging some parked automobiles.

A young man and his girlfriend were driving north on Michigan Avenue in a Volkswagen. At about Michigan and Ontario Street they noticed a crowd of people, stretched across Michigan Avenue, marching south. Since the two young people were directly in line of the march and could not get through the crowd, they decided to stay in the middle of the street and wait until the marchers moved passed them. As the people approached the car, they were shouting "Ho, Ho, Ho Chi Minh." One of the marchers, and then about five others, climbed over the Volkswagen—a foot on the front hood, another on the roof, then the rear deck, the rear bumper and off. Other demonstrators were shouting: "Don't hurt the cars." Nevertheless, another demonstrator kicked in the windshield of the vehicle and others started kicking the doors and rocking the car.

The couple got out of the car and ran over to a squadrol which had been following the march. The girlfriend asked the officer what he was going to do about the broken windshield. The policeman said that he couldn't do a thing, that if he did it would be called police brutality.

At that same intersection, some of the marchers kicked the rear door and the left rear fender of an auto driven by a Chicago television news director. Others in the group beat their fists upon his car.

As the marchers came to the intersection of Ohio and Wabash, they forced a driver to stop his car. The driver got out and told the group to move on. While one of the demonstrators waved a Viet Cong flag in his face, others threw rocks at his car and kicked it. He got back inside his car and drove away.

A reporter who was covering the march said: "Wherever a cop car stopped at an intersection, the group would detour and go a block around instead of producing a confrontation."

There were apparently no policemen walking with the marchers.

As they approached the Michigan Avenue bridge over the Chicago River, the marchers saw about 15 policemen stationed at the south end of the bridge, backed up by police wagons. The marchers stopped in the street at the north end of the bridge, and some members of the press were on the sidewalk.

A police commander said with a bullhorn: "You cannot proceed with this unlawful march." However, a few of the marchers proceeded onto the bridge. The commanding officer then announced: "You have 30 seconds to clear the bridge." A newsman heard the commanding officer order, "If you don't get out, we're going to use gas."

Several persons, including reporters, continued across the bridge. A couple of police officers chased them back across the bridge with batons swinging. One reporter said he proceeded to cross the bridge, believing that the order to clear was meant only for the demonstrators and not for press. He admitted that he was not wearing any visible press identification. A police officer came up to him and hit him several blows on the head with a baton, telling him to get off the bridge.

The reporter yelled, "I'm with the press," and tried to get his official press card out of his shirt pocket. The commanding officer pulled the police officer off the reporter and instructed the officer to return to the south end of the bridge. The commander refused to give the reporter the policeman's name. The reporter relates that he is willing to give the officer the benefit of the doubt, since he was not attired in business clothing, had on collegiate attire, was marching with the demonstrators, and was not displaying any press identification. He said the officer could have mistaken him for a demonstrator.

At this point, the police moved slowly north across the bridge, but several of them broke ranks and charged toward the demonstrators. A helmeted press photographer, wearing an armband containing his press card and carrying two cameras, took a picture of a policeman chasing a man. While doing so, he was clubbed by a policeman on the left jaw and shoulder and his camera was broken.

The press and demonstrators retreated and the police formed a new line across the bridge. The bridge gates then dropped. One observer states, "The police had closed off the bridge at both ends, keeping the demonstrators off one end and the curious off at the other end. When it looked as if the people were going to cross the bridge, the warning lights would go on, the gates go down, and the bridge raised slightly, which effectively cleared the bridge."

Police officials had called for the Task Force and reserve units, which arrived in buses and squad cars. Some of these men were stationed at the stairwells leading to the lower level of Michigan Avenue to prevent the demonstrators from filtering down there. The remainder faced the demonstrators on the north side of the bridge. Shortly thereafter, the demonstrators dispersed and returned to Lincoln Park and the Old Town area. At Rush and Walton, several of them smashed plate glass windows in a liquor store. Others smashed some car windows and broke car aerials.

Clearing of Lincoln Park

At least a thousand persons had regrouped in the park despite repeated curfew warnings and the deputy chief began a major clearing operation. One hundred and twenty officers from the 18th, 19th and 20th Districts moved in a skirmish line, west from Cannon Drive. With them were 255 officers on loan from the 2nd, 3rd, 11th, 12th and 13th Districts. Intermingled were another 83 men from the Task Force. About half of these were armed with shotguns and carried canisters of tear gas.

Two Assistant U.S. Attorneys had been talking with several groups of police prior to the clearing. One said that the police were in a "state of excited anger." He recalls some police stating that "they wanted to bust the heads of the demonstrators."

Unknown to the deputy chief as the police clearing operation began, the police beach patrol motorcycle units again had moved westward, ahead of his lines. The cycles were about 50 feet apart. The skirmish lines moved at a walk, but the deputy chief kept urging his men to walk slower. A district commander was in charge of the (south) flank and the deputy chief the right (north). The district commander was using a bullhorn to urge those still in the park to leave, but the deputy chief did not have his bullhorn and was getting hoarse trying to shout instructions to his officers.

The beach patrol unit continued to move ahead of the police lines. Just east of Stockton Drive, they began encountering persons who refused to obey the command to leave the park. They yelled at and harassed the police. A police official yelled that they had 30 seconds to move. When some of them still stood their ground, the motorcycles charged and foot patrolmen, batons swinging, chased people up the slope to the Drive.

The motorcycles stopped at the bottom of the slope. The bulk of the crowd had now moved to the top of the slope, between a sidewalk and the Drive. Others were standing in Stockton Drive and the parking lot immediately west. The beach patrol then retreated and the first of the deputy chief's lines of men replaced them, forming a line to face the crowd. More announcements were issued to clear the park.

News photographers moved through the crowd taking

photographs. As they did so, according to police, their strobe lights blinded police officers, who simultaneously were pelted with several rocks and bottles. People at the front of the crowd were yelling: "Hell no, we won't go!" and "The parks belong to the people!" and "The streets belong to the people!" Officers were called "Oinks," "Pigs," "Mother fuckers," "Pig fuckers," "Fascists," and "Shitheads." The front ranks of the crowd moved closer to police, and in the words of a veteran reporter, "sought out a confrontation with the police."

At the same time 50 policemen began moving a crowd of 100 to 150 persons out of the Eugenie Triangle intersection. Newsmen were the first asked to leave. When they appeared reluctant, they were pushed and finally hit with batons. Several persons were put into squadrols.

Traffic was stalled and more cars continued to drive into the Triangle, exacerbating the situation. A police lieutenant shouted through a bullhorn that everyone must move, but his voice was barely audible. A man was walking down the line of cars in the Triangle, urging people to honk their horns —an apparent effort to increase the noise level even further.

Moments after the lieutenant's announcement, at 12:19 a.m., a second skirmish line of police moved quickly to the bottom of the slope leading to the Drive. Suddenly, a wedge of eight to ten men broke from this line and charged the crowd, flailing with nightsticks.

The crowd scrambled up to the summit of the ridge and into the first parking lot west of the northbound lane of Stockton Drive. The lot was jammed with cars and people were crawling over vehicles and squeezing between them to escape.

Some police were yelling: "Get out of the park, you mother fuckers!" "You bastards!" The people ran, some shrieking: "Pigs, fuck pigs, oink, oink, oink, pigs, pigs."

The people fled as far as the west parking lot, immediately adjacent to Clark Street. When they turned around they saw the police had not followed them as far as they had expected. The crowd suddenly moved back toward the police. One observer describes the advance:

> The thing about this crowd was that since it thrived on confrontation it behaved in a way much different than any other crowd I've ever seen. During racial riots, the police would break up the crowd and the crowd would

> stay broken up. It might regroup in another place but rarely would it head back for direct confrontation with its assailants.
>
> This was a most unusual crowd. This time . . . the police would break peoples' heads but the crowd would not run away. What it would do would . . . regroup and surge back to the police and yell more epithets, as much as saying: "Do it again."

The people began whistling and a rhythmic clapping. The police line charged again, driving the crowd into Clark Street, and this time some people were hurt. A 33-year-old Chicago school teacher was knocked to the ground by a baton blow to the back of his head. Hit between the shoulders, his girl-friend crumpled to the ground and curled up in a tight ball as six officers beat her repeatedly with batons.

"Arrest me, I'm breaking the law!" screamed the teacher. But he got no response. After kicking him and the girl several times, the police moved on. The teacher required five stitches at Augustana Hospital to close a head wound.

Some demonstrators resisted actively, fighting hand-to-hand with police. The majority of officers used their batons only to hit the backs of legs to get the crowd to leave the park. But other police met cries of "Leave us alone, pigs" with much more severe clubbing. A Chicago reporter was knocked to the ground and beaten as he protested that he was a newsman. He said none of the policemen who struck him was wearing nameplates. In the parking lot between Clark and Stockton Drive, a police official twice restrained officers from striking news photographers with their batons during the push into Clark Street. The official yelled at one of the men: "Don't leave the line!" and "Get back!" In the other case, the official raised his own baton in an attempt to stop an officer from hitting a photographer.

Task Force officers lobbed canisters of tear gas. When the canisters exploded, the crowd ran in Clark Street. Many poured into the Eugenie Triangle at about the time that police stationed there were managing to disperse the previous crowd north on Clark. As police drove the people into Clark Street, some officers were yelling: "Kill the commies!" and "Get the bastards!" Superior officers were yelling at their men to "stay in line and obey the orders of your sergeants."

A University of California criminologist, in Chicago to

study convention security procedures, was struck in the back with the barrel of a shotgun after he had been chased away by police from a fallen boy. The criminologist said that the boy had been struck repeatedly by several policemen who passed him.

In one instance, as an officer, his baton raised, was moving toward a television photographer, a lightman in the photographer's crew focused an extremely hot Fresnel light within inches of the policeman's nose. The officer backed away from the heat.

On Stockton Drive, about one-quarter block north of La Salle Drive, an Assistant U.S. Attorney saw policemen kick and punch a young man, about 24 years old, using what the attorney calls "excessive and unnecessary force." He says, "One particularly aggressive policeman was restrained by fellow officers from further assaulting the subject. After the subject was patted down for weapons, he was hurled into the rear of the van to the accompanying blows of at least one police officer."

By now, the Eugenie Triangle and the Old Town Triangle (the intersection of Clark, Wells, and Lincoln), were jammed with people and cars. "The streets belong to the people!" some yelled. Car horns were honked in approval. The flavor of the scene around the Eugenie Triangle is caught in a reporter's on-the-spot notes:

> Eugenie down to the end of the triangle, I guess where Lincoln Avenue begins, is jammed with people. Cars have been brought to a stop. The street is full of cars, and where there aren't cars there are people. They are surging through the streets and the police are coming out of Lincoln Park toward them. The people are yelling in the streets, they are trying to form a line at the edge of the park so the police won't push them into the street. Others have already been pushed into the street, and the cry is going up, "The streets belong to the people!"
>
> Some of the drivers are honking their horns and there is an incredible cacophony. You can't hear yourself think. The police are coming out of the park. Their faces are contorted with rage and so are the faces in the crowd. . . . They're in Clark Street and it's a mess and now the nastiness really begins. The crowd is picking up rocks and throwing them at the police.

Two squads of the district commander's men were sent to a point just north of the Eugenie Triangle to clear Clark Street. The squads moved north on Clark in a skirmish line, but allowed many people to stream by them, southward along the unblocked west sidewalk.

Other police formed a line extending from the Eugenie Triangle past Lincoln Avenue along the east side of Clark Street. Some people started throwing rocks. One man standing on the divider strip in the middle of Clark, near Menomonee, threw a bottle at an officer in the line. Four other officers dashed into the strip, knocked the man down and arrested him. More rocks were thrown, some hitting other policemen. Some in the crowd shouted: "Kill the pigs!" "Fuck the pigs!" "Your wife sucks cock!" and "Pigs, pigs, pigs!" More bottles were smashed in the middle of Clark Street.

At the northern end of the police line, the deputy chief's men moved across Clark Street and formed another line along the western curb. People were jammed up along an eight-foot wide sidewalk between police and porches abutting Clark Street. Because of the size of the crowd, north-south movement was severely restricted. With an announcement—inaudible to many—to clear the sidewalk, the northern end of the police line broke off and began moving people south. This element of the crowd gave ground as rapidly as the congested conditions permitted, staying at least ten feet in front of the oncoming police. These persons offered no resistance, threw no objects and yelled no epithets.

However, suddenly, in the 1700 block, 12 to 20 policemen broke from the skirmish line and attacked the retreating people with their batons. Other police joined them from the line at the curb. People fell to the sidewalk under the police blows. An official state observer saw police pin persons to the sidewalk and beat them about the head and neck. The sidewalk clearing operation disintegrated into wholesale confusion.

Watching the melee from their patio porch directly above the sidewalk were two residents and a friend, free-lance photographer Howard Berliant of Milwaukee. Berliant was snapping pictures of the action when a group of people, including several neighbors, dashed into the entrance of the building. They were being chased by police.

As the police chased the people into the building, they noticed Berliant taking pictures of them. "Get the man with the camera!" one policeman yelled. Most of those fleeing the police ran up to the porch where the two residents and Berliant had been standing. The latter ran into the vestibule of the building. The police followed and clubbed Berliant on the head, an incident which is more fully described in the police-press section of this report.

Police followed another group of persons who had sought a similar vestibule and hit one member of the group, a University of Illinois graduate student, on the head with a baton. As the student raised his hand to feel his head, he was hit again and two fingers were broken. Other officers ran up the exterior staircase of an apartment building and used their shotguns to force downstairs six or seven persons who had sought refuge there.

About this time, *Newsweek* reporters John Culhane and Monroe Anderson were clubbed; this incident, too, is described in detail in the section on media violence.

The crowd surged up and down Clark Street. More tear gas canisters exploded, sending people on the run, grabbing handkerchiefs and choking for air. *Philadelphia Bulletin* reporter Claude Lewis jotted down notes as police jabbed a young, blond-haired girl in the stomach near Menomonee and Clark. Despite her screams, police continued to hit her until she fell to the pavement.

When the officers spotted Lewis, one said: "Hey, you dirty bastard, give me that goddamn notebook." An officer then grabbed the notebook with his left hand and hit Lewis on the head with a baton. Both this incident and another occurring about the same time and involving James Davis of *Life*, are described in the police-press chapter.

The crowd dispersed via sidestreets, police pursuing one group east on Wisconsin. Two or three officers caught a girl in the group from behind and, according to an observer, clubbed her, knocked her to the ground and kicked her. The observer heard one officer yell: "We fucked one of the mother fuckers!"

Moments later a free-lance photographer was snapping pictures of the girl when police warned him: "Take your fucking camera and get the fuck out of here!" Before he did so, he was knocked to the ground and kicked.

Many persons ended up in emergency housing set up in churches and in such impromptu areas as a courtyard just north of The Theatre at 1848 North Wells Street. Gradually, the crowd dispersed and the violence ended.

Monday, August 26

At about 5:15 a.m., Monday, the Federal Bureau of Investigation received reports that demonstrators were planning such harassment tactics as turning on fire hydrants, calling out police and fire department units on false alarms, and stringing wire between trees in Lincoln Park to stop three-wheel police motorcycles. The FBI stated that it was uncertain when these tactics were to go into effect. The Bureau also reported that the wife of Eldridge Cleaver, a member of the Black Panthers of California, was in Chicago and would address the demonstrators some time on Monday.

At approximately 11 a.m. Monday, ministers in the Lincoln Park area came together for a regularly scheduled meeting at St. Paul's Church, 655 West Fullerton. The group included most of the ministers of the North Side Cooperative Ministry as well as others in the area. The meeting became the center for a discussion of police tactics Sunday night in Lincoln Park.

A staff member of the Chicago Presbytery said that during the Sunday night clearance of the park, police had been guilty of using excessive force. He said that he believed the clergy would have to act Monday night to avoid what he called further danger to the community. He proposed that those clergymen present enter the park Monday evening in teams to act as observers of the expected clearance and to act as a buffer between police and those in the park.

The clergy agreed to the proposal, although there was some disagreement on where the buffer ought to be established—in the park or at Clark Street. The ministers finally decided that at approximately 10:45 p.m., just before curfew, they would regroup on the west side of Clark Street and, at this point, each minister would decide whether he wished to return to the park—in violation of the curfew—or remain on Clark Street and stand between the police and the people as both groups emerged from the park.

At 11 a.m., the Yippies staged a press conference in the park to announce that they had sent a telegram to United Nations Secretary-General U Thant, charging that law and order had broken down in Chicago and demanding an "impartial observer."

"Mayor Richard J. Daley counts the votes here. We want someone to count Mayor Daley," said a Yippie from Berkeley, California. "Part of the freedom to demonstrate is a place to sleep. We don't think that the park belongs to Mayor Daley. We think it belongs to us. By us, I mean the American people. The violence was initiated by police. We didn't come to Chicago to initiate violence. We're going to stay in Chicago; if we have to fight to stay in Chicago, we're going to fight."

Looking forward to Monday night, the Yippie said, "If we have to move out of the park, we'll move out of the park for tactical reasons and we'll tie up Chicago."

The North Side Cooperative Ministry held an afternoon press conference at which they charged that Chicago had been turned into a "police state." A Chicago minister related his experiences Sunday night on Clark Street and said that earlier in the day a policeman who was a member of his parish had telephoned him to say he was leaving the parish because of the minister's involvement with those in the park. At the press conference, which was held at the Bethlehem United Church of Christ, 2746 North Magnolia, the clergymen announced that Near North Side churches would provide lodging for the protesters if police continued the ban on sleeping in Lincoln Park.

At about 2:25 p.m., Tom Hayden and Wolfe Lowenthal were arrested on a Lincoln Park baseball diamond as they were discussing plans for a parade from the park to the Conrad Hilton. The charges were obstructing police, resisting arrest and disorderly conduct (allegedly letting the air out of a police car tire Sunday night).

American Broadcasting Company news correspondent Jim Burns said that as his ABC crew tried to film the arrests, a policeman whacked soundman Walter James in the back with a nightstick and smashed a $900 lens belonging to cameraman Charles Pharris.

Within minutes a group of 400 to 500 persons left Lincoln Park to protest the arrests. They headed for Central Police Headquarters at approximately 2:30 p.m. (Note: this march ultimately proceeds to Logan Statue.)

This group, led by Rennie Davis, with a speaker system carried on his head, marched on Dearborn toward the Loop with Viet Cong and red flags waving. They obeyed traffic signals, moved quickly and kept to the sidewalks. By 2:45 p.m. they were at Dearborn and Oak.

Once the marchers reached the Chicago River, the police commander for the Central District took over the direction of their progress. He saw that there were no police cars paralleling the march—thus preventing traffic jams. The marchers complied with orders and kept half the sidewalk clear; however, members of the press covering the story filled up the remaining sidewalk area. Once the marchers arrived at police headquarters, they staged a short protest demonstration and moved on.

Two city legal aides who accompanied the march remember no incidents of disorder other than three arrests made en route.

One of those arrested was a man who had been in the street at Elm and Dearborn, urging marchers not to listen to police, to get into the streets and tie up traffic. The arresting officer told him to get off the street and back onto the sidewalk. When he refused, he was arrested. (The man has a police record ranging from vagrancy to assault.)

MARCHES AND MELEES

On Monday afternoon, the action shifts to Grant Park. The park lies roughly between Michigan Avenue and Lake Michigan just east of Chicago's Loop. It is normally a gathering place not only for visitors but for Loop workers. Although the park appears quite long, its scale is optically deceiving; what appear as long distances on a map can be walked in surprisingly short time. The park is a vital transportation hub of the city. It contains one enormous ground-level parking lot and other vast parking garages underground. One major traffic artery—Lake Shore Drive—flows parallel to it on the east. Another—a divided street within the park called Congress Plaza—is the origin of a thoroughfare that farther west becomes the Eisenhower Expressway. In a deep man-made ravine that slices north-south through the park run two commuter railroads, two national passenger railroads and a major freight network.

Struggle at the Logan Statue

Grant Park's first significant clash between demonstrators and police occurred late Monday afternoon, August 26, at the equestrian statue of Civil War Major General Jonathan Logan, which caps a knoll in the park at 9th Street just south of, and across Michigan Avenue from, the Conrad Hilton Hotel. It began with a march to police headquarters led by a khaki-clad young woman riding on the shoulders of a tall Negro and carrying a red flag to protest the arrest of Tom Hayden and Wolfe Lowenthal. The young woman was later arrested at Balbo and Michigan, and police records show nine previous arrests for various offenses. An estimated 300 to 400 returning marchers were approaching the Hilton on the sidewalks at about 5 p.m. As they passed policemen on duty in the area, some chanted in question-and-answer style: "What do we want?" "Revolution!" "When do we want it?" "Now!"

Joined by other demonstrators, the marchers paraded around the Logan Statue, and a number of them climbed on it. Logan and his horse were then draped with some of the Viet Cong and red flags that had been carried on the march to police headquarters. Cries directed at the police, included: "Pigs!" "Fuckers!" and "Ho, Ho, Ho Chi Minh." Some marchers carried signs reading, "Police are pigs."

Just what happened next is open to dispute. One witness claims that after the demonstrators had surrounded the statue for five or ten minutes "approximately 12 police . . . pressed themselves through the crowd and attempted to pull the kids off." According to another witness, the bulk of the crowd had already moved on voluntarily toward the Conrad Hilton Hotel, just across Michigan Avenue from the south end of the park, before the police made any move. Then, he claims, "Some police officers (a reserve squad called in from one of the holding areas) walked up the hill to the statue. A few people then started to come back from the crowd that was heading toward the Hilton. More cops came in. More people came back. Suddenly people started to rush back and the cops started to run to the statue."

A police officer states that when the crowd moved toward the Hilton, a skirmish line was formed by the police north of the statue and a sweep was begun northward. When this happened, he said, the crowd swore at the police and threw a brick and an empty, rusty one-gallon can at the officer in charge.

"Some kids on the statue," the first witness remembers, "were kicking the policemen in the face." She believes ten minutes passed before police removed the last demonstrator—"a boy with a red flag . . . kicking and very violent." The policeman who later arrested the boy stated that he was kicked in the shoulder and groin.

Films of the incident, from several sources, show the youth climbing higher on the statue while police are chasing away other demonstrators. He also tries to evade the police as they reach up to pull him down. He is flagless, astride General Logan's shoulders, both his arms raised in a double "V" sign chanting, "Peace, peace."

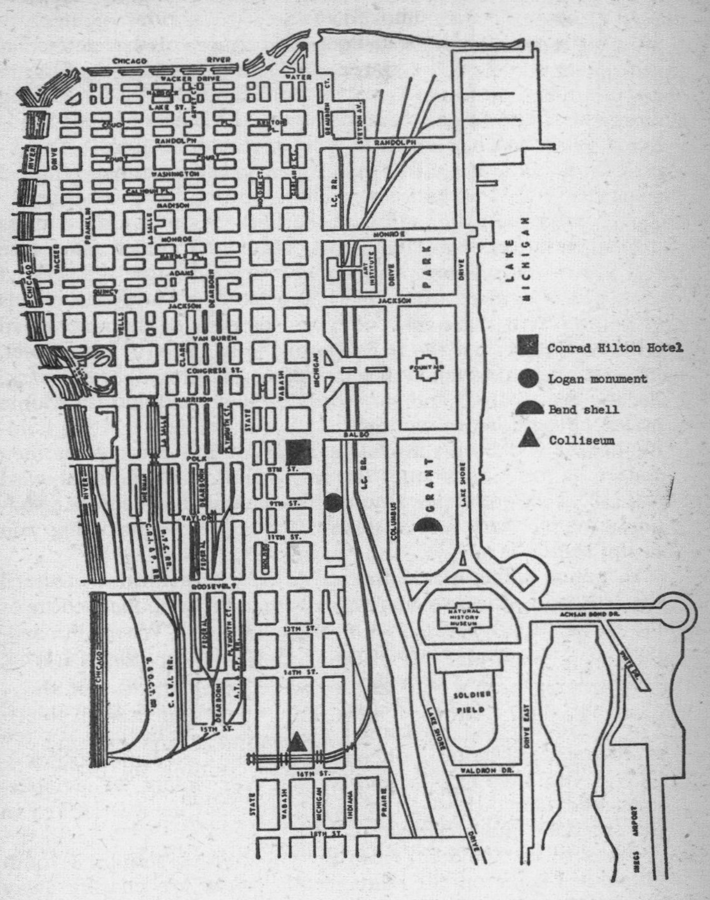
CHICAGO
RIVER
WACKER DRIVE
LAKE ST.
RANDOLPH
WASHINGTON
MADISON
MONROE
ADAMS
QUINCY
JACKSON
VAN BUREN
CONGRESS ST.
HARRISON
POLK
8TH ST.
9TH ST.
TAYLOR
11TH ST.
ROOSEVELT
13TH ST.
14TH ST.
15TH ST.
16TH ST.
18TH ST.
FRANKLIN
WACKER
DRIVE
WELLS
LA SALLE
CLARK
DEARBORN
FEDERAL
SHERMAN
PLYMOUTH CT.
STATE
WABASH
MICHIGAN
INDIANA
PRAIRIE
C. & W.I. RR.
WATER
BEAUBIEN CT.
STETSON AV.
I.C. RR.
ART INSTITUTE
PARK
FOUNTAIN
BALBO
GRANT
COLUMBUS
LAKE SHORE
LAKE SHORE DRIVE
LAKE MICHIGAN
NATURAL HISTORY MUSEUM
SOLDIER FIELD
WALDRON DR.
DRIVE EAST
AIRPORT
Conrad Hilton Hotel
Logan monument
Band shell
Colliseum

One of the officers who removed the boy stated in a report that the youth was carrying a Viet Cong flag; that he was shouting, "Fuck you and fuck this couutry"; that he was given two warnings to descend or face arrest before the officers moved in; and that the officer was kicked in the right shoulder. A total of five police officers later filed injury reports related to this incident. The boy suffered a broken arm and some films show him being hit in the groin by a policeman.

With the statue free of demonstrators, the police cleared the area. A photographer states that he saw a policeman beat a girl of 16 or 17 and another policeman join the action. When they realized they were being photographed, he states, they tried unsuccessfully to confiscate the film.

Immediately following the arrest of the youth on the statue, the U.S. Attorney reports, "a man was seen sitting on the grass with his back against a tree. He had a bandage in his lap and was talking with three men who had camera equipment. He then leaned back, put the bandage to the left side of his forehead and the cameraman began taking pictures. They were asked for their names and for whom they worked and they all scurried off without answering."

In their flight from the statue, many of the demonstrators passed a police lieutenant who was standing at the foot of the knoll. Two girls ran at him, the lieutenant reports, and shouted "You dirty son-of-a-bitch." One of them swung a chain at him, but missed. It fell at his feet.

The Logan statue incident involved only a small part of the demonstrators in the park. Others chanted and listened to speeches by Dave Dellinger and other protesters. People in the crowd were chanting: "Fuck you, Daley! Fuck you, LBJ!" Rocks, cherry bombs and bottles were being thrown at the police. The U.S. Attorney adds that "the vilest conceivable language was used by both men and women" and that there were "many incidents of demonstrators spitting on police." By 5:35 p.m., according to the Joint Command Monitor Log, "approximately 1,000 demonstrators" were in this crowd.

Aside from a log entry that police were "trying to move demonstrators into Grant Park" at 5:40 p.m. there is no evidence of additional police action, and by 6:50 p.m. the hotel area across from the park was reported "clear." The delegates had left for the Amphitheater and most of the demonstrators were on their way back to Lincoln Park.

Monday Night, August 26—Lincoln Park

Early Monday evening, in Lincoln Park, trash basket and bonfires abounded in the open area between the eastern slope leading up to Stockton Drive and the wooded area just north and west of the fieldhouse. Clustered around the fires were the same amalgamations of people that had been in the park on prior evenings. But the mood was predominantly peaceful. "There was a spirit of communion and good feeling," says one witness. TV cameramen appeared here and there, and whenever their lights illuminated the scene some demonstrators would start performing.

Two men wearing helmets waved black flags of anarchy and another man thrust a red flag in front of the cameras. The light from the bonfires also revealed a Viet Cong flag. When strobe lights focused for a moment on an American flag, a few bystanders cried: "Burn it! Burn it!" The fires were being fed not only with litter, but tree branches, most of them dead. One small group, however, had dismantled a picnic table and was using it for fuel. A teenage girl, wearing a patch over her left eye, said she had been beaten the night before by the police. "Those cops don't realize that I didn't want violence, but now that I've been clubbed I can't wait to get my hands on them."

At about 8:10 p.m., a contingent of young men wearing motorcycle jackets, German helmets and knee boots tossed a firecracker into a bonfire. Mobilization marshals moved through the area, urging people not to light fires in wooden trash containers.

Outside the park, a member of a group passing a police vehicle parked at 2041 Lincoln Park West suddenly squirted a biting fluid into the eyes of a policeman. He was later treated at Henrotin Hospital.

At 8:23 p.m., the U.S. Secret Service reported that Thomas Hayden had been released from jail on a $1,000 bond, pending a September 18 court appearance. Wolfe Lowenthal was also released on $1,000 bond.

At this time there were about 300 to 400 people in the park. Abbie Hoffman told a group: "We're not here to fight anybody. If we are told to leave, then leave." But another man with short hair and windbreaker jacket, shouted: "We gotta kill all the cops!" Allen Ginsberg was again "oming."

From 9 p.m. on, the Old Town area was chaotic. Groups

ranging in size from 150 to 2,000 streamed up and down the streets, some of them orderly but others walking on roofs of cars and throwing bottles and rocks. The police tactic was to prevent unruly groups from entering the downtown area and orders were given to Task Force units to stop such groups at the Chicago River. Four police vans were moved to Wacker and Michigan to handle any arrestees.

The U.S. Attorney's log is filled with emergency calls, crowd intelligence information and unconfirmed reports of violence. One unconfirmed report was a Secret Service call that blacks and whites were fighting at North and Wells. Another series of interagency calls began with an unconfirmed report by the Secret Service at 10 p.m. that the Illinois National Guard was coming to State and Madison, that windows were being broken and that there was looting. At 10:06 p.m. the Secret Service broadcast the unconfirmed report that the Guard was setting up advance command posts. At 10:07 p.m. the Chicago Police Department reported that they had made no call for assistance by the Guard, and at 10:09 p.m. the Secret Service radioed, "All rumors of looting and of participation by Illinois Guard still unconfirmed." At 10:15 p.m. the First District Police reported the Guard "not on the street," and 26 minutes after the first report, another was received: "National Guard Major stated that troops were not aiding CPD. Rumor started by CPD referring to their own men as troops."

As the groups surged through the area, police dispersed them with swinging clubs and epithets were hurled back and forth.

March South on Clark

At about 9 p.m., the first large evening march moved out of Lincoln Park, heading south on Clark Street. Reports of the size of this group ranged from 200, by a city legal aide, to police estimates of "1,500 hippies." The group moved out of the park through the underpass at La Salle Drive, with the announced intention of marching to the Sherman Hotel, headquarters of the Illinois delegation, "to protest to the Head Pig." An officer reports that he and 16 other policemen, including 12 men from the Area 6 Task Force, gathered at Clark and Schiller, blocking this intersection with police vehicles. The officers formed a line and walked north toward the marchers, turning them back to Lincoln Park. One arrest was made for aggravated battery and resisting arrest. An observer, a city legal aide, indicated that the group was turned around by the police because it had become disorderly.

An attorney with a Loop bank who was driving his motorcycle to his garage, describes his unintentional involvement in the dispersal of the crowd:

> The demonstrators had, because of their numbers, stopped all north-moving traffic, including myself. Since it was obvious I could not proceed north, I turned south, hoping to return my motorcycle to my garage on Burton Street. After I had turned south, the demonstrators suddenly began to run north on Clark Street, and soon I and several other motor vehicles which faced south on Clark Street began to move again. After moving several yards, I encountered a line of police moving north on Clark Street. The police shouted something at me, and I asked them to speak louder since I could not hear them clearly because of my motorcycle helmet. The policeman nearest me yelled at me to turn my motorcycle around; another yelled at me to get it off the street. As I began to turn around, one policeman shoved me hard enough to almost knock me off my motorcycle, and prevented me from turning around. Almost immediately another policeman smashed his nightstick against my motorcycle, denting the headlight rim. Still another policeman swung his nightstick at my head, but checked his swing when he realized that my helmet would make his swing ineffective. He then struck me in the chest with his nightstick causing a bruise that was still painful after two weeks. While all this was going on, all the police around me were yelling and waving their nightsticks, apparently to disperse the few demonstrators that were left in the area.
>
> I was shocked and surprised to have been attacked by the police, since I feel it was obvious that I was not part of any demonstration going on. I was wearing a green sweater and dark slacks. I was carrying a passenger on the back of my motorcycle. My passenger was also wearing a sweater and slacks. I was not shouting or carrying any signs. I was the first motor vehicle in a line of cars that had been held up by the demonstrators, but at the

time of attack, the demonstrators had, for the most part, fled some distance north from my position.

I was also shocked by the uncontrolled behavior of the police (some giving orders to me that were contradictory to orders given just a moment before by another officer), and also by the lack of judgment they showed. I was nearly knocked off my motorcycle while the engine was running; had I been knocked off, the motorcycle would have certainly run into a parked car and possibly over one of the officers themselves. Also, it was difficult to see why the police deemed the situation so critical; I saw no demonstrator-police contact at the time I was attacked; the demonstrators were well north at that time.

At 9:26 p.m. an Assistant U.S. Attorney reported that 1,000 demonstrators were moving west on Eugenie. This march continued one block beyond Wells, where it turned south on North Park. It moved at a fast pace to Schiller, then turned east to Wells and proceeded down Wells to Division. Many of the participants had just returned to the Park from the Clark Street dispersal.

By about 9:35 p.m. the group heading south on Wells had become unruly. They were marching in the middle of the street, yelling and chanting. A few bottles and rocks were thrown and some windows were broken along Wells. At 9:37 p.m. the group turned east on Division. A number of trash cans were thrown into the street. Shortly thereafter, the Chicago Police Department began to move the crowd back toward Wells.

A man and a woman, walking on LaSalle Street parallel to the march, said they saw 15 to 20 policemen with swinging clubs charge west into the marchers at Division Street. The pair crossed Division behind the police charge and then went up an alley toward Wells. They approached six policemen in the alley, one of whom asked the man where he had come from. The man, his voice breaking, twice said: "The street." A policeman grabbed him by the shirt, slammed him against the wall, and said: "Then why is your heart beating so fast?" Then, the man says, "he took his club, hit me once in the groin, hit me in the face with his fist once. I went down and covered my head with my hands and they ordered me to get out of there. As I turned to go I was hit several times on the body by him and several other policemen."

Within the brief span of ten to 15 minutes, the following media personnel were the victims of police action while attempting to report and photograph the clearing: Delos Hall, cameraman for CBS; Marv Kupfer, *Newsweek* correspondent; Bob Black, photographer for the *Chicago Sun-Times;* Jeff Lowenthal, *Newsweek* photographer; James Stricklin, cameraman for NBC; and Brian Boyer, reporter for the *Chicago Sun-Times*. The incidents are described in the police-press chapter.

Arrest reports from the Police Department show that some 46 persons were arrested in the immediate area of Wells and Division. The arrests were made when the crowd was confronted by police attempting to clear the street, and most of those arrested were charged with disorderly conduct.

Five police officers reported injuries at this intersection. Most of them suffered abrasions, contusions and sprains. One officer was struck by a 2-by-4, his helmet was smashed and a knuckle on the first finger of his left hand broken.

At approximately this same time, eight to ten blacks, ages 16 to 17, were arguing inside the Fire House Restaurant at 1539 North Wells. They broke the plate glass window and ran south on Wells.

The Exercise of "Collar Power"

Meanwhile, approximately 70 clergymen intending to act as a buffer that evening, had gathered at the Church of the Three Crosses, located just north of the park at 1900 North Sedgwick. They decided to move through the park in teams of three and five. They were dressed in clerical garb and wore armbands consisting of strips of white sheeting with black crosses. One of their leaders termed the clergy's role as the exercise of "collar power." At approximately 9:30 p.m., they went south on Clark to LaSalle Street, where they mingled for a short time with a small group, and then moved into the park proper.

Each clergyman carried a list of places where people could spend the night or receive emergency medical or legal assistance. Groups of medical volunteers for the Medical Committee For Human Rights were already in the park, dressed in white coats and equipped with stretchers and medical supplies.

The clergymen agreed to return to the west side of Clark Street at 10:45 p.m., where they would wait for a possible confrontation. If one occurred, they were to spread themselves four feet apart, close to the action, so that policemen would know they were present. Any clergymen who wished to return to the park would be permitted to do so.

The Chicago Police Department had received word that between 700 and 1,000 demonstrators would resist curfew enforcement. Department intelligence indicated that these people planned to split up into groups of 100. Other reports indicated that they were armed with sharpened bamboo spears, razor blades, a shotgun and bathroom tiles, and that "Headhunters" and Blackstone Rangers (a black South Side street gang) were in the park and intended to fight for it. Officials had met earlier to discuss clearance procedures and agreed that a police skirmish line would move slowly and that adequate warnings would be given to people in the park.

At about 10.45 p.m., some 45 of the clergymen who had been patrolling the park did reconnoiter on the west side of Clark Street. The majority decided to re-enter the park. At 11 p.m., a single squad car circled the perimeter of the park, its loud-speaker announcing that the curfew hour had arrived. Several hundred people did leave the park. But hundreds more remained, as police made no immediate attempt to disperse them. Three bus loads of officers simply waited near the police command post, some five blocks north of the crowd.

When a reporter approached the police to inquire about their strategy, none of the commanders would speak to him. He was puzzled. "Chicago police are never secretive with reporters in a circumstance like this," he says. The reporter was able to get rank-and-file policemen to talk, however. He says they were genial and not "up tight." He adds, however, that not one of the patrolmen he saw was wearing a nameplate or badge.

As the curfew hour passed, a VISTA volunteer walked south along a sidewalk east of the Garibaldi statue. Acting as an observer in the park for the American Friends Service Committee, he saw several young men moving six picnic tables to an area immediately east and somewhat south of the statue. He said the young men told him they were going to set up a temporary blockade in the event police tried to drive motorcycles or police cars toward the crowd.

A PICTORIAL REVIEW OF WHAT HAPPENED AND WHEN

The 1968 Democratic National Convention began in Chicago on Monday, August 26. This report deals not with the convention itself, but with the violent events in the city's parks and streets while it was going on. Here is a chronological review of those events.

The Week of August 19

An advance contingent of protestors arrived at Lincoln Park, which was used as a staging area. This week was a planning period, given over to strategy meetings, recruitment and training of marshals, development of various protest techniques, and a quest for publicity.

Abbie Hoffman and Allen Ginsberg, relaxed and content, pose in Lincoln Park.

A speaker outlines plans for the week's demonstrations.

© Time Inc. (Fred DeVan; Life)

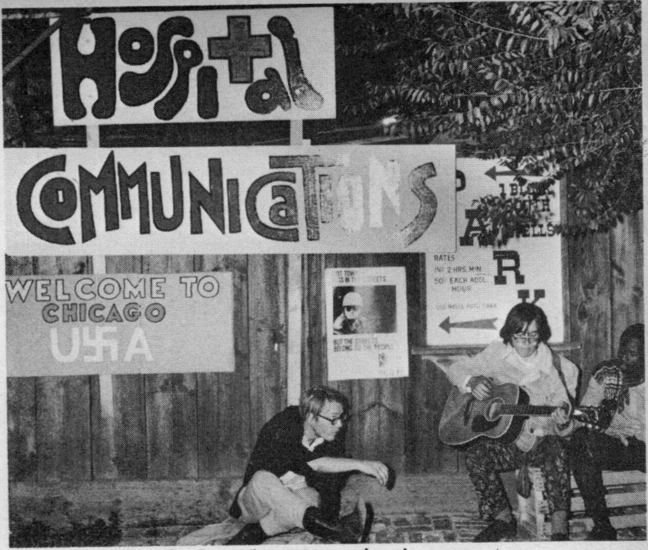

A medical and communications center is set up across the street from Lincoln Park.

© Time Inc. (Michael Mauney; Life)

Dissidents practice maneuvers to be used against police lines.

© Time Inc. (Bill Rogers; Life)

News media cover training session in how to use a rolled-up magazine as a weapon.

(Chicago Sun-Times)

Local youngsters call time out to watch athletic demonstrators work out.

(AP Wirephoto)

Yippies nominate a pig named Pigasus as their presidential candidate.

(AP Wirephoto)

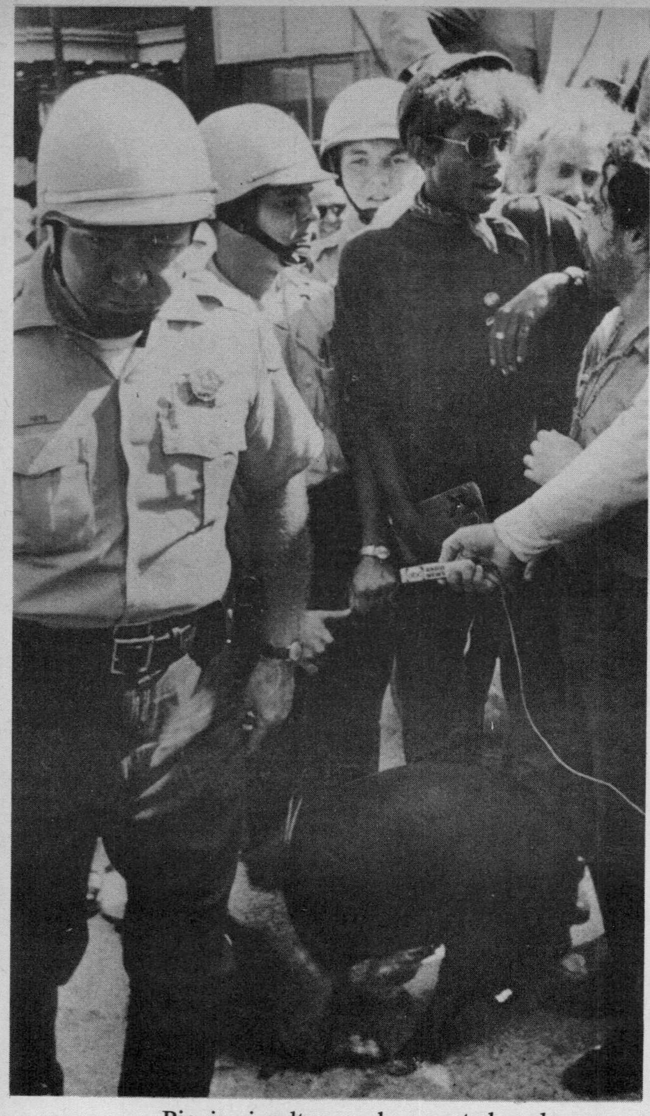

Pig is simultaneously arrested and interviewed at Chicago Civic Center.

Saturday, August 24

In the morning and afternoon, there was little activity in Lincoln Park. Peaceful police patrols watched demonstrators assemble. In the evening, the crowd learned that the park would be swept clear. At night it was swept clear and demonstrators were split into small groups and peacefully dispersed by police.

(J. P. Loarie)

Demonstrators gather and settle down in Lincoln Park.

(AP Wirephoto)

Women peace pickets march in front of Conrad Hilton Hotel.

(J. P. Loarie)

By Saturday evening, the crowd had grown to about 800 and has been told that the park will be cleared that night.

(New York Daily News)

After the clearing of Lincoln Park, demonstrators move into Old Town.

Sunday, August 25

Again the morning was quiet, and in the afternoon there were marches to Loop hotels. That evening the first demonstrator-police confrontation occurred. The crowd at night numbered about 5,000. It was not disorderly, but tension was rising. Chaos developed both in the park and on Clark Street, as dissidents were moved out. Some marched south towards the Loop and were confronted by police at the Michigan Avenue bridge. Others were in Old Town, where violence was frequent and intense.

(J. P. Loarie)

Sunday morning was quiet, with about 300 people gathered.

© Time Inc. (Jerry Brimacombe; Life)

There were a number of peaceful marches between Lincoln Park and Loop hotels.

(J. P. Loarie)

(J. P. Loarie)

By about 5:30 p.m., the crowd had swelled to between 3,000 and 5,000. Rock music groups entertained them. . . .

and they watched some demonstrators "doing their thing."

(Chicago Sun-Times)

While the bands were playing, the first demonstrator arrest of the week was made.

There were few disorders at this time. © *Time Inc. (Time)*

© Time Inc. (Time)

At about 11:15 p.m., after police announce that the park is closed, demonstrators set a bonfire in a trash basket.

Some of the crowd marches from Lincoln Park toward the Loop.

(Chicago Tribune)

(Chicago Sun-Times)

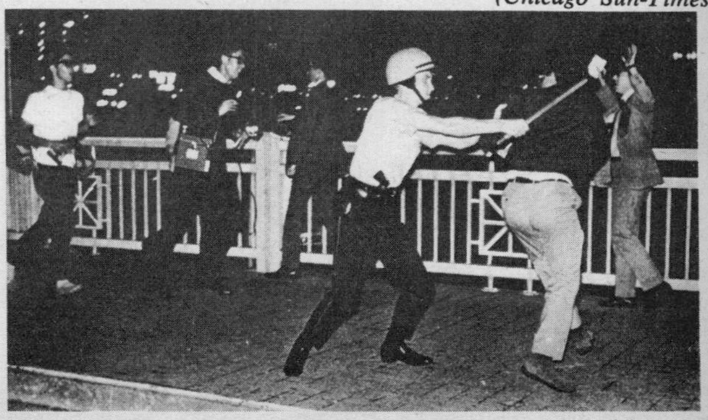

Marchers are stopped at Michigan Avenue bridge.

(Washington Post Company)

After midnight police begin a final sweep of Lincoln Park.

(Thomas England)

(Lester Sloan, Newsweek)

Demonstrators are swept out of the park and across Clark Street, into crowds of spectators. . . .

and removed from apartment house steps. *(AP Wirephoto)*

(AP Wirephoto)

© Time Inc. (Time)

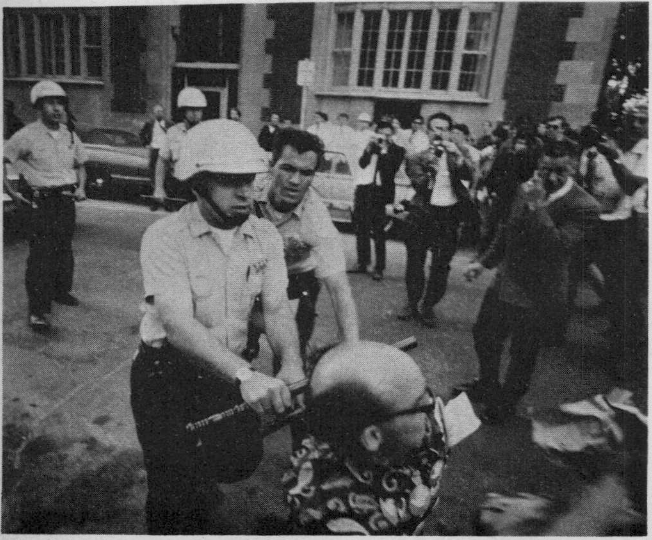

There are frequent isolated incidents of violence throughout the night, as police clear the streets of Old Town. . . .

(Chicago Sun-Times)

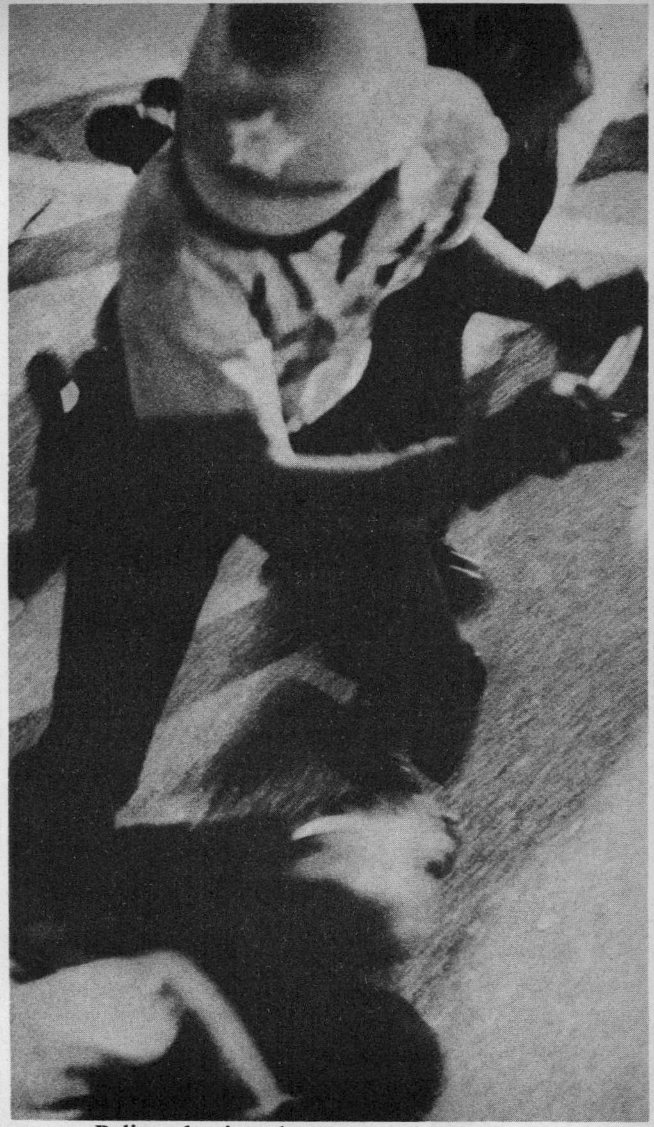

Police clearing the streets of Old Town.

(Chicago Sun-Times)

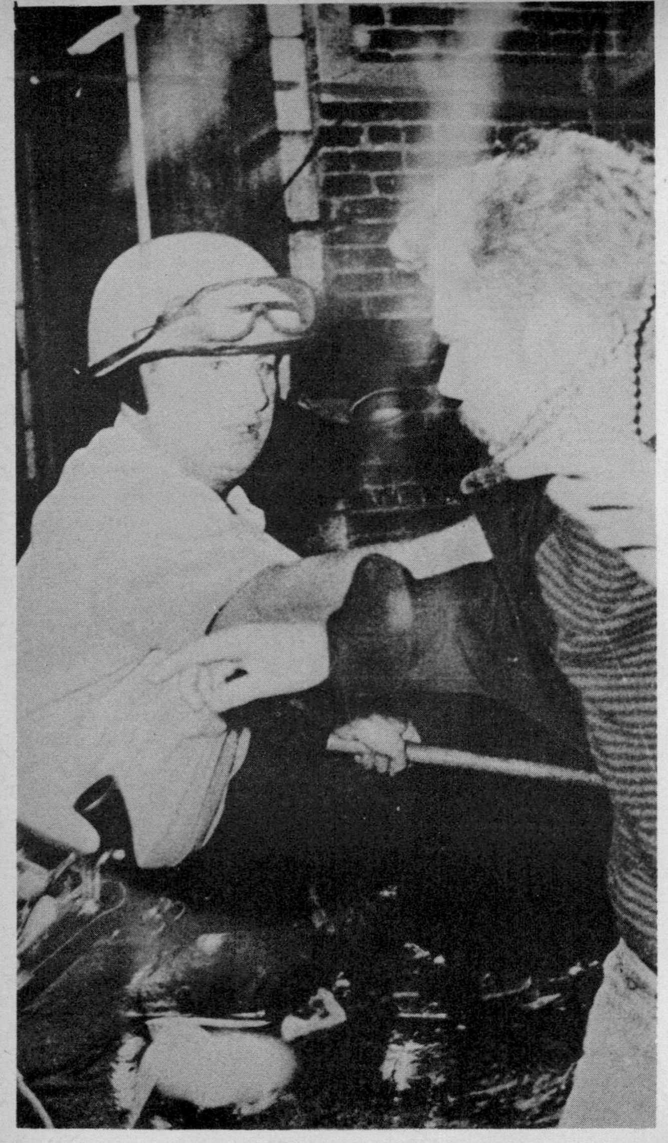

Monday, August 26

Not much happened in the morning, but in the afternoon there were protest marches to the Loop, Grant Park, and elsewhere, and demonstrations at the Logan Statue in Grant Park and in front of the Conrad Hilton Hotel. Demonstrators in Lincoln Park that night constructed an impromptu barricade, but the police swept the park at midnight, forcing the crowd into Old Town. Incidents of violence there exceeded those of the previous night both in number and in ferocity.

(Chicago Tribune)

On Monday morning, the park was once again quiet, and the scene normal. One abnormal element was the infiltration into the Yippie leadership by Chicago policeman Robert L. Pierson, wearing dark glasses.

Mathematicians march to Amphitheatre to protest war in Vietnam. *(AP Wirephoto)*

Aroused dissidents march to police headquarters, protesting the arrest of SDS leader Tom Hayden.

(AP Wirephoto)

(*New York Daily News*)

Crowd moves east from police headquarters, spies statue of General Logan, and captures it.

After demonstrators begin to move north to Conrad Hilton Hotel, a police skirmish line forms between statue and crowd. (*Chicago's American*)

A police officer restrains another as statue is cleared of demonstrators . . .

(Chicago's American)

. . . with one exception.

(*New York Daily News*)

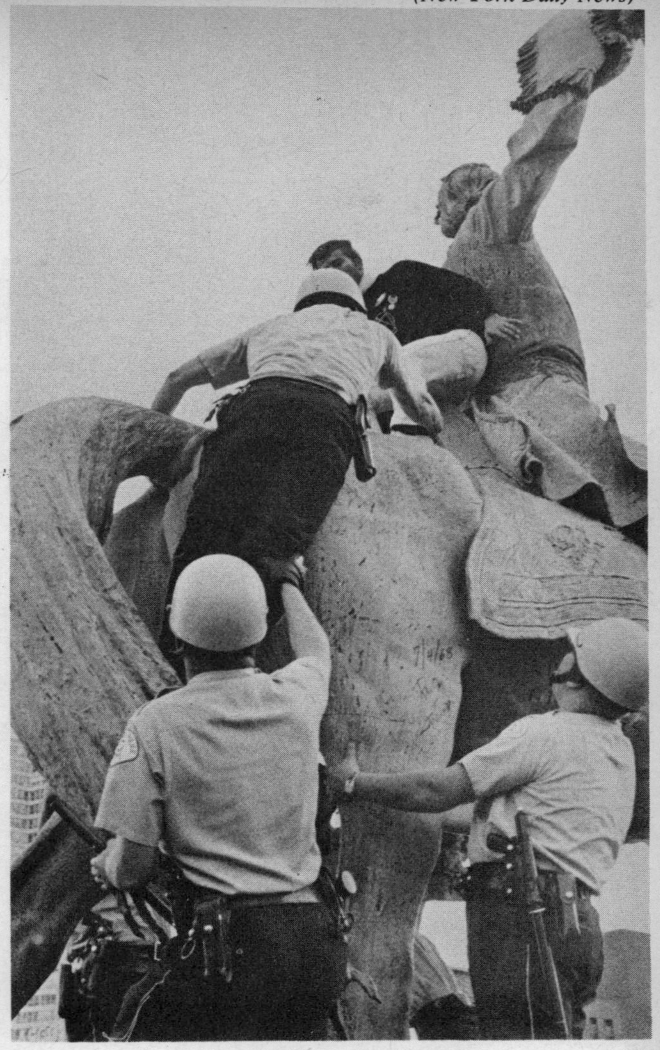

Police finally pull down lone demonstrator, breaking his arm in the process.

(Joshua Moorehead)

Police push both cyclist and cycle into the Lincoln Park Lagoon.

(Chicago Tribune)

Demonstrators construct a barricade with materials at hand.

(Chicago Sun-Times)

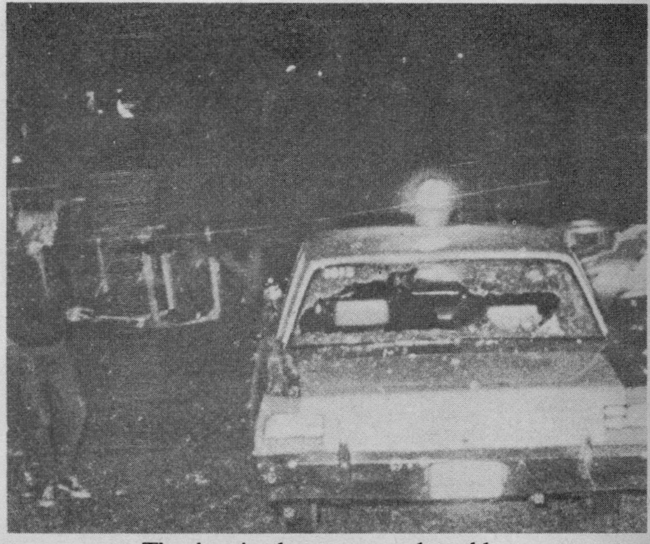

The barricade proves vulnerable.

(Charles Krejcsi, Chicago Daily News)

Heavily armed, and equipped with gas masks, police sweep Lincoln Park at midnight.

(Charles Krejcsi, Chicago Daily News)

(Charles Krejcsi, Chicago Daily News)

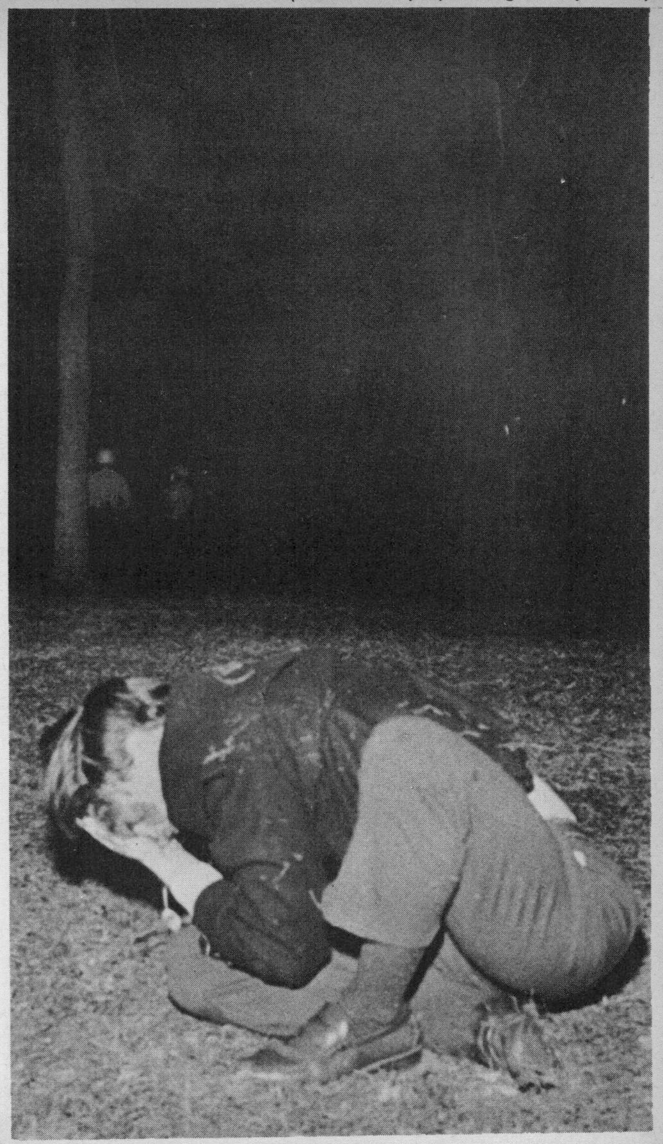

(AP Wirephoto)

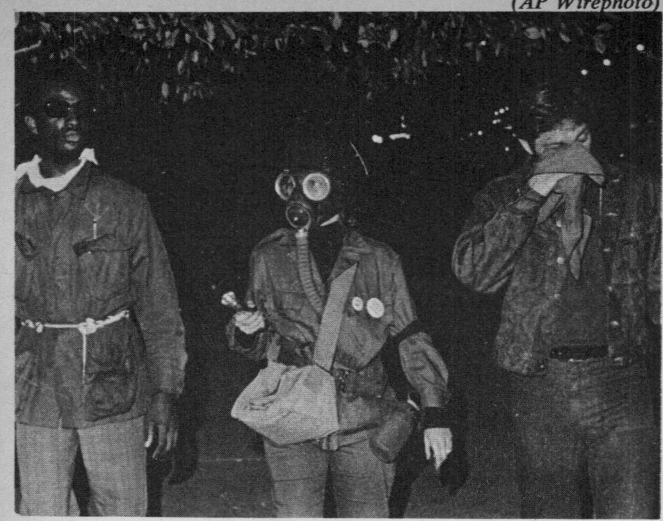

Not all demonstrators are unprepared.

Paul E. Sequeira, Chicago Daily News

Violence, exceeding even that of Sunday night, breaks out again in Old Town.

(Chicago's American)

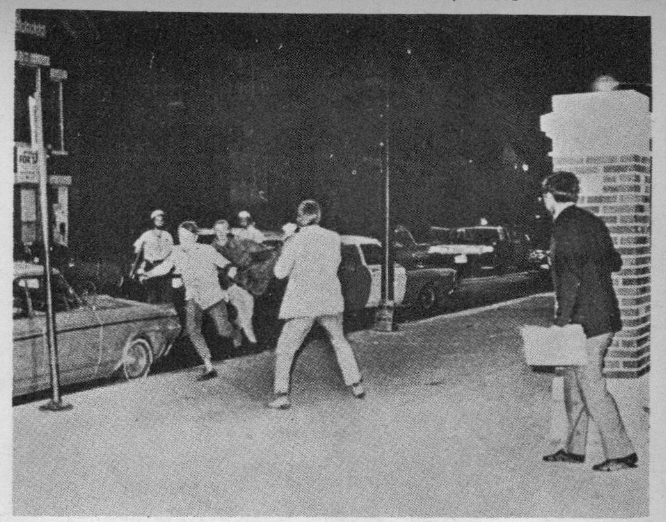

(AP Wirephoto)

© *Time Inc. (Time)*

© *Time Inc. (Time)*

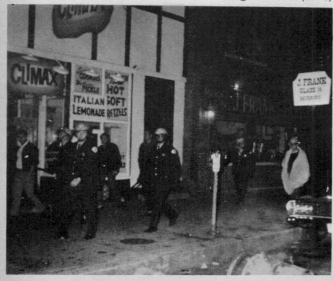

Tuesday, August 27

Another morning of quiet; another afternoon of marches, speeches, demonstrations. In the evening there was a peaceful march in support of striking transit workers and at night an "unbirthday party" for President Johnson was held. Lincoln Park was cleared at midnight and the action in Old Town was violent. In Grant Park, the National Guard relieved police. People were allowed to stay there all night.

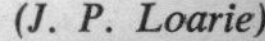

(J. P. Loarie)

Quiet morning in Park.

Paul E. Sequeira, Chicago Daily News

Threats in front of the Conrad Hilton . . .

taunts in front of the Sheraton Blackstone.

© Time Inc. (Life)

The crowd in Grant Park across from the Conrad Hilton Hotel grows in numbers and militancy as the evening progresses. *(Milwaukee Journal)*

A group of clergymen install an improvised wooden cross in Lincoln Park.

(Chicago Sun-Times)

Across from the Hilton.

(Washington Post Company)

At 3 a.m., the bone-weary police are relieved by the Illinois National Guard.

(Washington Post Company)

© Time Inc. (U. Merritt, Life)

In Lincoln Park, the mixture as before:

(Thomas England)

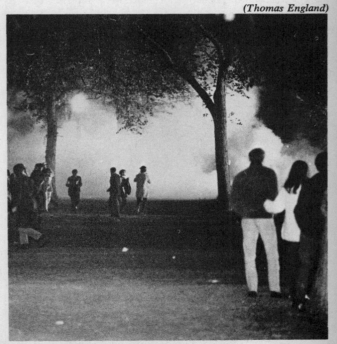

the park is swept . . .

(Associated Press)

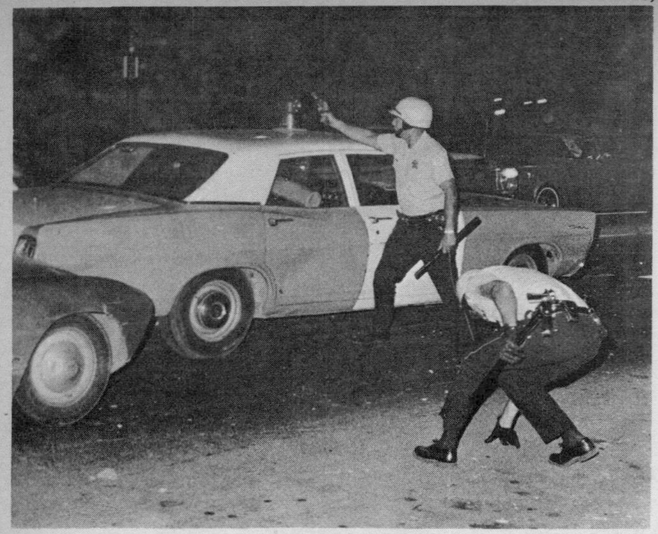

followed by chaos and violence in the streets nearby.

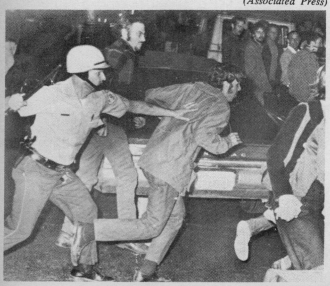

(Associated Press)

Wednesday, August 28

The crowd shifted from Lincoln Park to Grant Park where, in the morning, police relieved National Guardsmen. That afternoon a flag lowering incident, before a crowd of 10,000, lead to an unrestrained police charge. Later, angry speeches inspired a march towards the Amphitheatre, against police orders. The night was climaxed by a massive and violent confrontation in front of the Hilton and by incidents of violence in the Loop side streets off Michigan Avenue.

(Chicago's American)

In front of the Conrad Hilton Hotel, the demonstrators who remained spend early morning hours in talk or sleep.

(Chicago's American)

© Time Inc. (Life)

By mid-afternoon, the demonstrators had moved to the bandshell and their numbers had swelled to 10,000.

There were numerous speeches, but the crowd had no central focus.

(Associated Press)

French author Jean Genet speaks as poet Allan Ginsberg looks on.

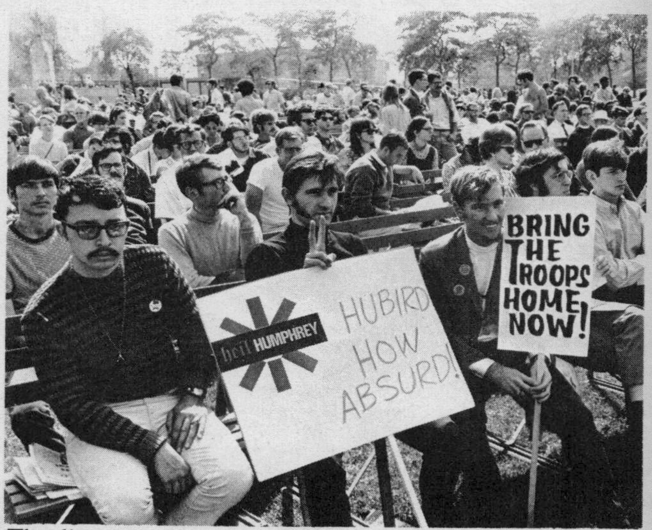

The listeners were not uniformly rapt.

(*Chicago Tribune*)

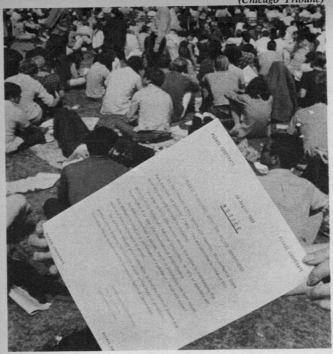

Police distributed a notice that no march or parade would be permitted.

(*UPI*)

To enforce this order, police, supplemented by National Guard, ring the park on three sides. A National Guard command post was also set up on the roof of the Field Museum, at right.

(Chicago Sun-Times)

A little after 3:30 p.m., a helmeted demonstrator lowers the American flag near the bandshell to halfmast.

© *Time Inc. (Life)*

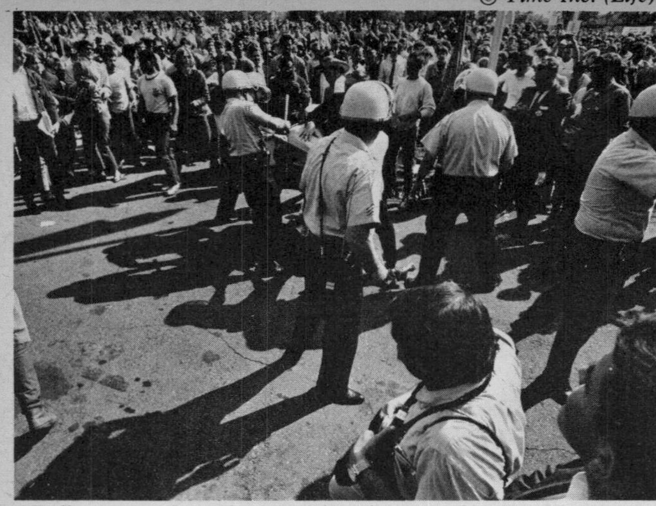

Police move into the crowd and arrest the demonstrator.

© *Time Inc. (Life)*

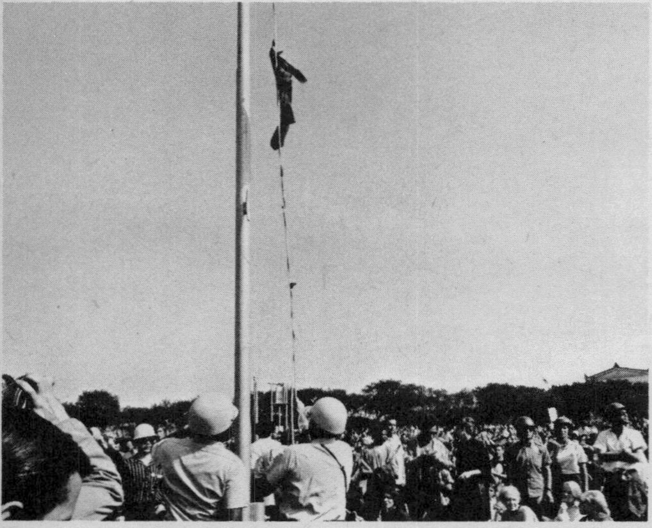

After police left, about six other demonstrators removed the flag entirely and raised a red rag in its stead, which police then removed.

Following this sortie, the crowd pelted police with various objects.

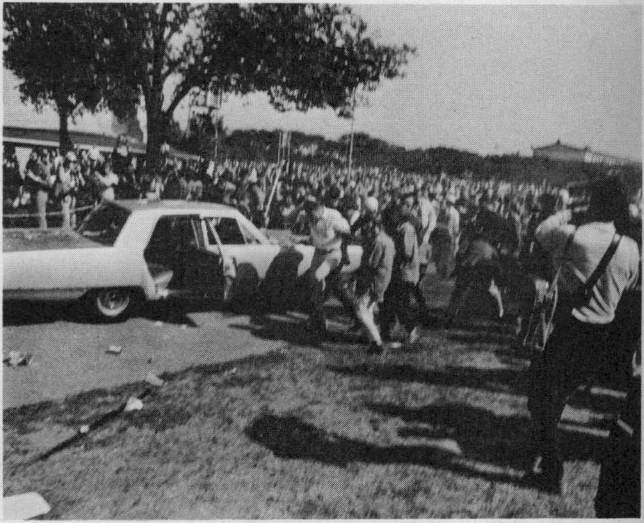

© *Time Inc. (Time)*

Police responded with a smoke bomb, which someone then threw back into the police lines.

A line of demonstrator marshals, including girls, formed along the edge of the crowd . . .

and faced the oncoming police line.

(Chicago Daily News)

As the police line reached the edge of the crowd, it broke . . .

(Associated Press)

and individual officers proceeded into the benches.

(Chicago Daily News)

Members of the crowd are clubbed . . .

(Chicago Tribune)

and maced.

© *Time Inc. (Life)*

(New York Daily News)

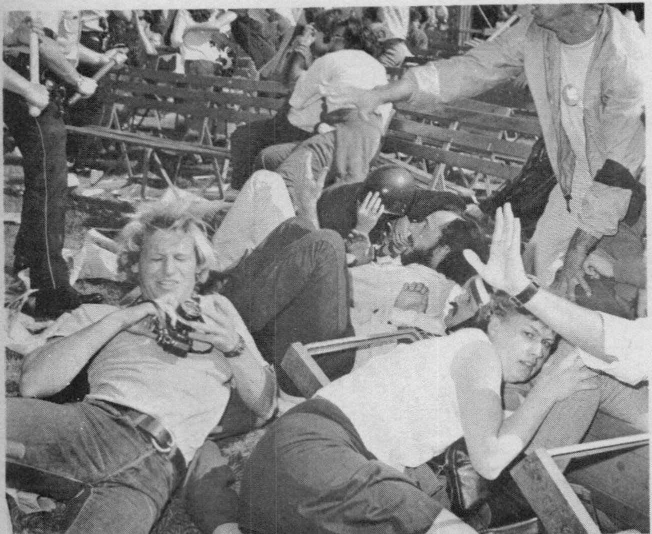

After the charge was over.

(Associated Press)

© Time Inc. (Life)

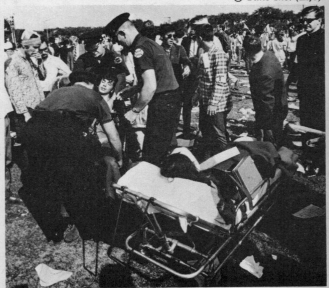

The injured are removed by a Chicago Fire Department ambulance . . .

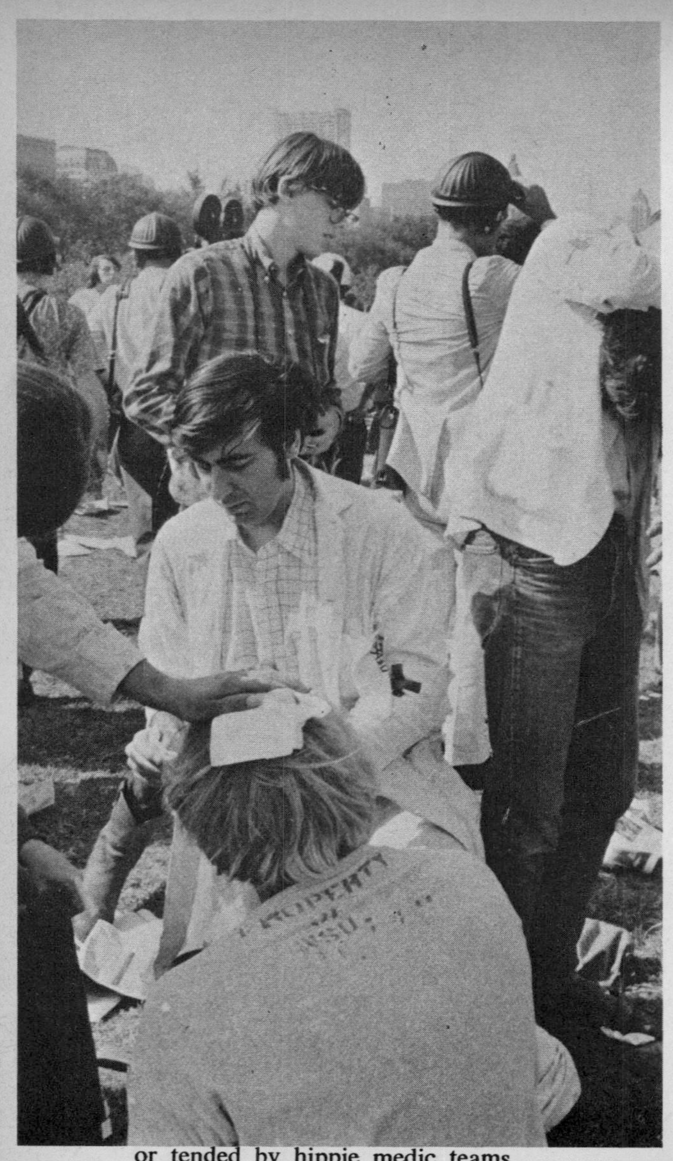

or tended by hippie medic teams.

© Time Inc. (Life)

© Time Inc. (Life)

About 5 p.m., the line of march formed up and moved north to Columbus and Balbo, where it was blocked by police and National Guard units. *(UPI)*

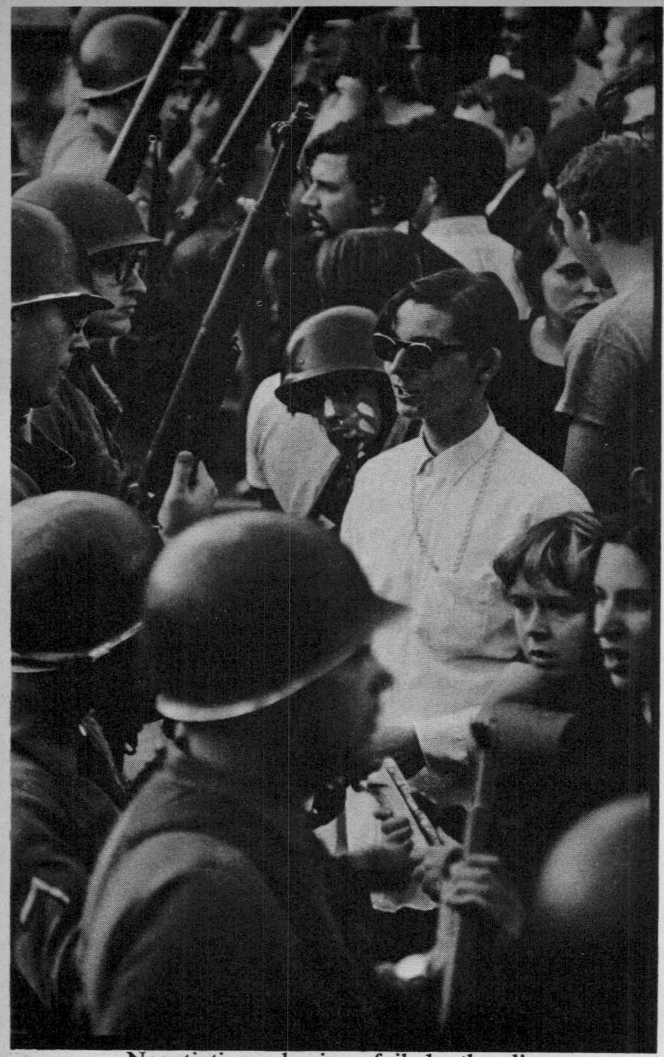

Negotiations having failed, the line of march dispersed. As demonstrators attempted to move towards the Conrad Hilton Hotel area, they found their passage blocked by National Guardsmen at Balbo Drive and Columbus Plaza bridge.

(UPI)

At Balbo, they were also met by two .30 caliber machine guns.

© Time Inc. (Life)

At Congress, demonstrators were faced by Guardsmen with fixed bayonets and gas.

The Jackson Boulevard bridge, however, was unguarded. The scattered demonstrators funnelled across this bridge and met the Poor People's Campaign mule train.

The mule train served as a magnet to draw the disorganized demonstrators together

(UPI)

As the mule train moved south on Michigan Avenue . . .

the crowd grew in numbers and engulfed it.

The mule train cleared the police lines on Michigan Avenue in front of the Conrad Hilton Hotel. Demonstrators filled the intersection.

(New York Daily News)

(New York Daily News)

A police platoon moves east on Balbo, reaches the center of the intersection and confronts sitting demonstrators.
The arrest process begins. (New York Daily News)

Police sweep the intersection clear of demonstrators, forcing them south and southeast.

Onlookers and demonstrators, fleeing the sweep of the intersection, are herded together by the police lines at the Hilton entrance and the west side of Michigan Avenue.

(New York Daily News)

(*New York Daily News*)

Police continue to mace the crowd trapped in front of the window.

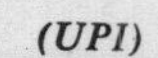
(*UPI*)

Under the heavy press of the crowd, the window of the Hilton's Haymarket Lounge broke and people fell and stepped through it.

© *Time Inc. (Life)*

Violent action at the intersection . . .

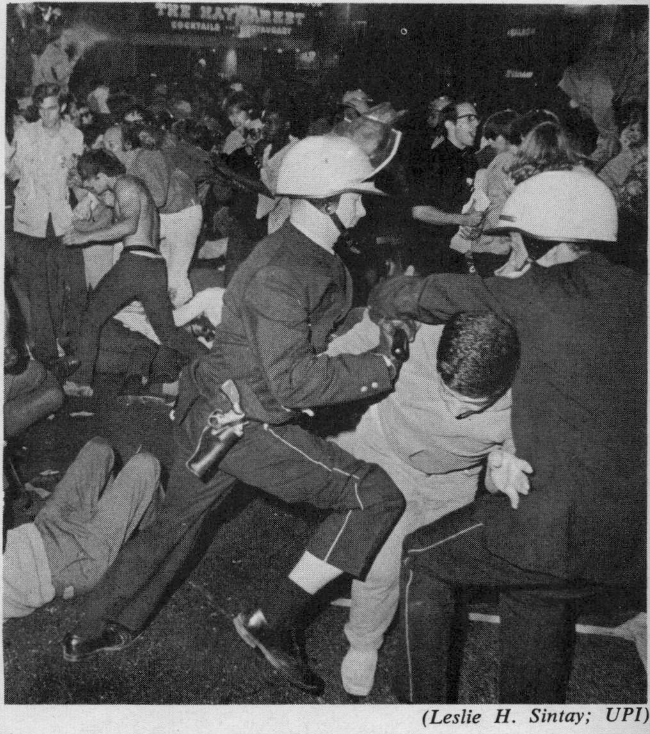

(Leslie H. Sintay; UPI)

© *Time Inc. (Life)*

© *Time Inc. (Jerry Brimacombe; Life)*

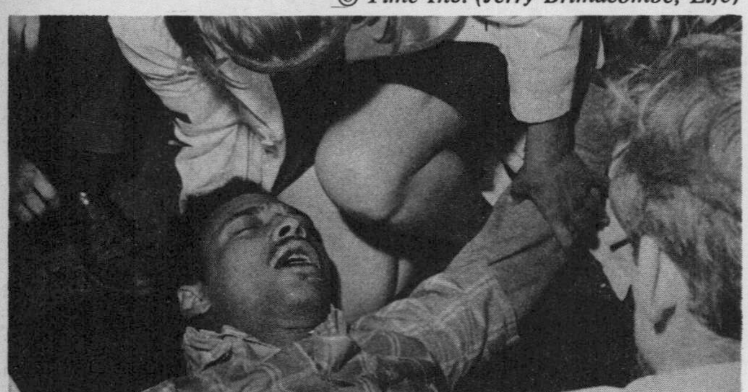

© *Time Inc. (Jerry Brimacombe; Life)*

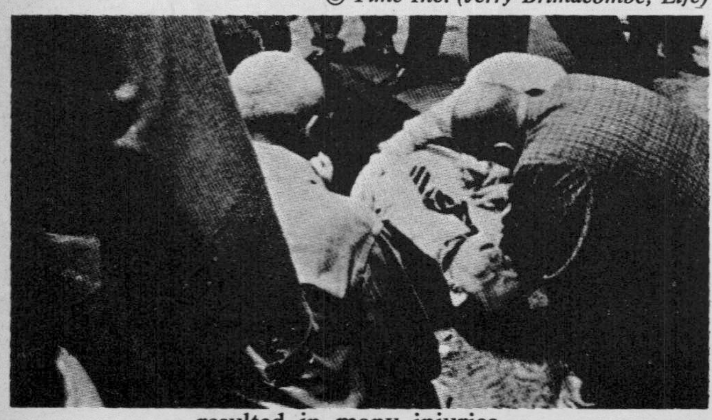

resulted in many injuries.

(UPI)

After clearing the intersection, police, now backed up by hastily called National Guard units, moved north on Michigan Avenue.

(UPI)

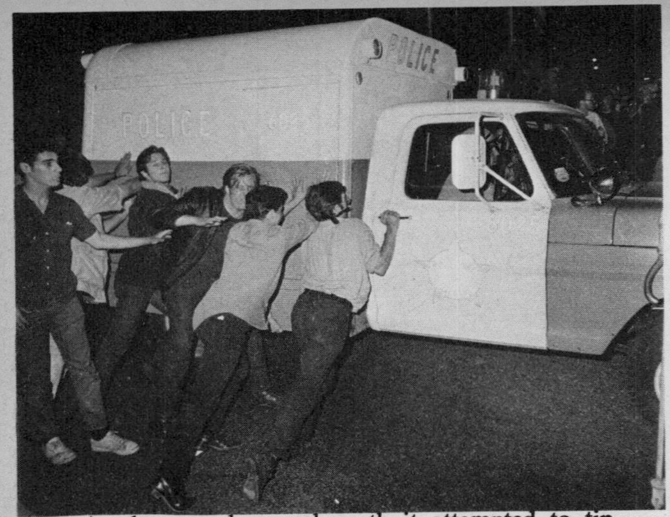

As the crowd moved north it attempted to tip over a squadrol near Jackson and Michigan . . .

and set numerous fires. (UPI)

Paul E. Sequeira, Chicago Daily News

Police stand by and watch a man dressed in Army clothes assault demonstrators.

(Chicago Sun-Times)

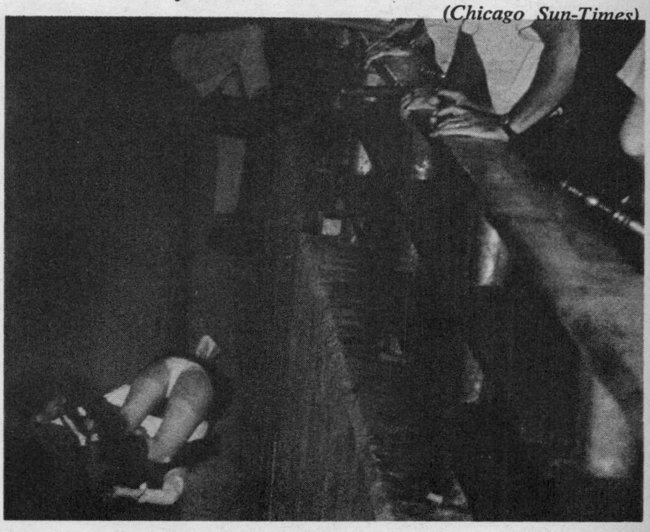

At Jackson and Michigan, the police pushed a woman over the railing onto the ramp leading from the underground garage.

(Washington Post Company)

(Chicago's American)

The action then moves to the side streets.

During the course of the evening, the police are met by:

Paul E. Sequeira, Chicago Daily News

prayers,

taunts.

and rocks. *(Chicago's American)*

(*Chicago's American*)

The National Guard takes up a line on the east side of Michigan Avenue.

(*New York Daily News*)

The line of Guardsmen was backed by machine guns and jeeps equipped with cages on top and barbed wire frames in front.

(Lester Sloan, Newsweek)

Obscenity was not confined to shouting.

© Time Inc. (Life)

An American flag appears . . . (later to be flown upside down) and draft cards were sporadically burned.

(*Chicago Sun-Times*)

In Old Town, as on previous nights, there were isolated incidents of violence.

(*Chicago Sun-Times*)

Thursday, August 29

Early in the morning, convention delegates conducted a candlelight march to Grant Park. The delegates tried further marches in the afternoon but were stopped. Later, Senator McCarthy addressed the crowd back in Lincoln Park, after which Dick Gregory attempted to lead a march by inviting the entire crowd to his home. They were stopped at 18th and Michigan, where Gregory and others chose to be arrested. Most of the demonstrators remained in the park all night.

(Chicago Tribune)

A number of convention delegates, led by senatorial candidate Paul O'Dwyer, conducted a candlelight march to Grant Park to express solidarity with demonstrators.

(UPI) © *Time Inc. (Life)*

(UPI)

In the morning, National Guardsmen lined the curb in front of Grant Park . . .

(J. Thomas Pugh, Peoria Journal Star)

as angry dissidents shouted over their heads.

© Time Inc. (Life)

In the park, directly across from the Hilton, the crowd heard speeches by delegates and other celebrities, like poet Robert Lowell, above.

Demonstrators and some *(Chicago Sun-Times)* delegates marching towards the Amphitheatre . . .

. . . are stopped at 16th and State by both National Guardsmen and police.

© *Time Inc. (Life)*

The crowd returned to Grant Park . . .

© *Time Inc. (Life)*

and heard more speeches, including remarks by Senator Eugene McCarthy, shown here with Dick Gregory standing by.

At about 6:30 p.m., Dick Gregory invited the entire crowd to come home with him, to determine freedom of movement on the streets of Chicago. The walk, or march, got as far as 18th and Michigan Avenue, where it was stopped by the National Guard.

(Chicago Sun-Times)

(Chicago Sun-Times)

The National Guard uses rifle butts to force the Gregory marchers back.

(Chicago Sun-Times)

(Chicago Sun-Times)

Dissidents, pushed back by jeeps and sprayed with tear gas return to Grant Park, where some bathe their faces in a fountain.

(AP Wirephoto)

Paul E. Sequeira, Chicago Daily News

Some demonstrators hang Mayor Daley in effigy.

© Time Inc. (Life)

National Guard forces contain the demonstrators in Grant Park.

Friday, August 30

In the morning several hundred demonstrators were in the park, and by noon they were almost one thousand. A police detail still guarded the Hilton, but there was no violent action . . .

(New York Daily News)

no action of any kind

(Chicago Police Department)

THE NEWS MEDIA AND THE POLICE

One of the most controversial aspects of convention week was the coverage by, and treatment of, representatives of the news media. City officials have charged the media with biased reporting, and with effecting news as well as affecting it. Media representatives have charged the Chicago police with physical attacks specifically directed to reporters and photographers; and with harassment intended to prevent full and accurate coverage of what was going on.

There were numerous instances of violent clashes between police and newsmen. Some of these are shown overleaf.

© Time Inc. (Life)

American Broadcasting Company
television truck incites demonstrators to gesture.

(Barton Silverman; New York Times)

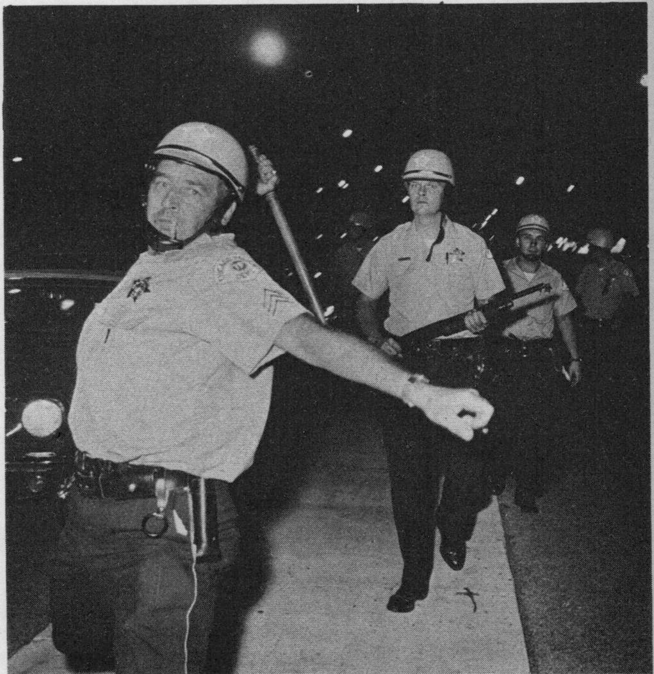

Police sergeant swings at photographer
Barton Silverman of the *New York Times*.

(P. Michael O'Sullivan)

Some demonstrators line sidewalk while police and reporter approach each other.

(P. Michael O'Sullivan)

Police force demonstrators off bridge as news photographer's flashbulb goes off.

(Duane Hall) (Chicago Sun-Times)

Newsmen try to move in closer to cover the events.

(Duane Hall) (Chicago Sun-Times)

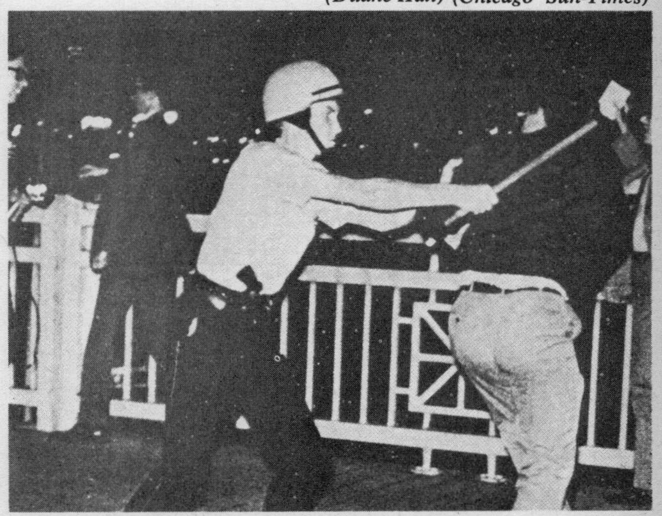

Reporter James Peipert is clubbed. Later . . .

(P. Michael O'Sullivan)

The photographer receives the same treatment.

(P. Michael O'Sullivan)

Photographer retreating

(Newsweek)

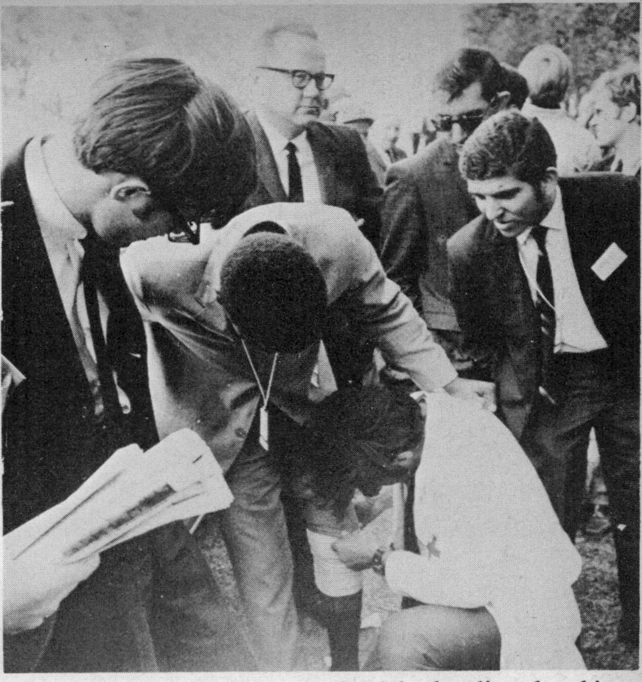

Don Johnson, his press credentials dangling, has his nightstick-injured knee bandaged by a medic.

Police officer asks for and gets film from photographer.

(Joshua Moorehead)

(Chicago's American)

Photographer Steve Northrup retrieves his smashed equipment.

Police harassing and threatening young people in Corvette observed by a reporter . . .

Paul E. Sequeira, Chicago Daily News

Paul E. Sequeira

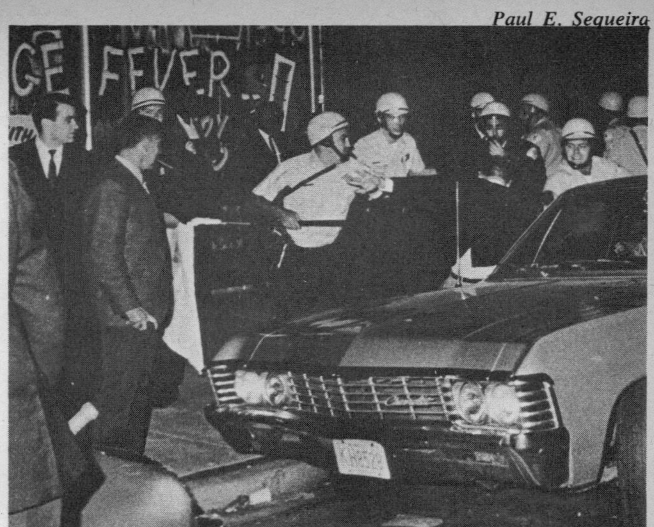

who yelled at police to stop it. They then turned on him.

(Frank Hanes, Chicago's American)

Teenagers in car, watch, horrified, as police continue attack on . . .

(Richard Fegley)

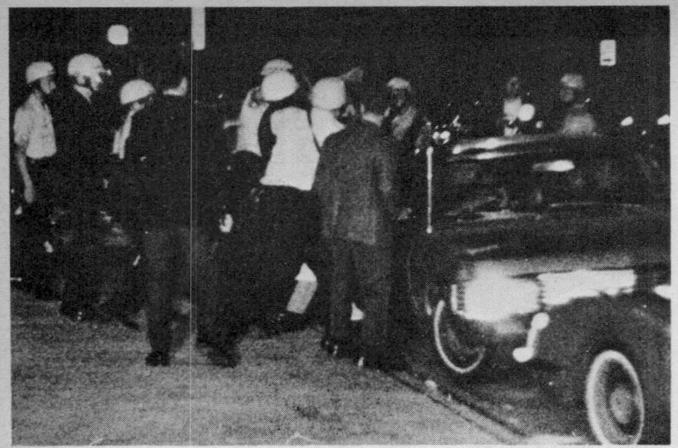

Paul E. Sequeira, Chicago Daily News

the reporter, who is finally taken away for medical treatment.

(AP Wirephoto)

NBC newsman John Evans with bandaged head (he was struck by a policeman and his equipment smashed), interviews photographer Dan Morrill, whose own head was bloodied during crowd dispersal.

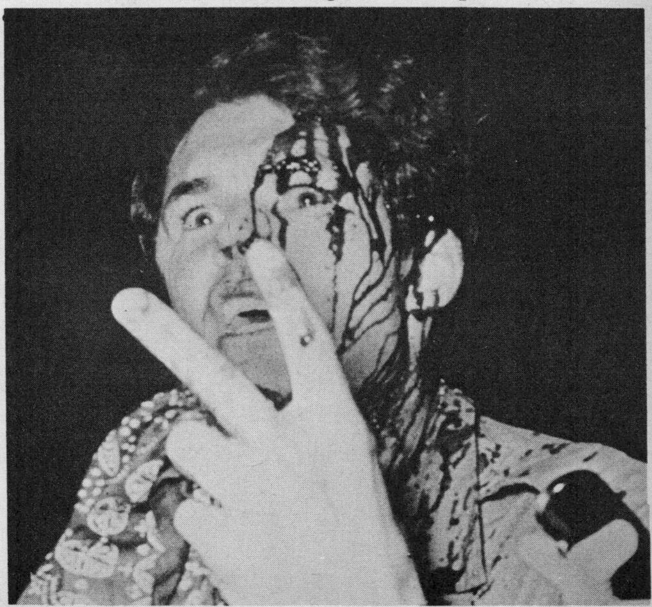

(Chicago's American)

Police lieutenant maces woman in photograph taken by Paul E. Sequeria, who was himself maced immediately afterwards by the same officer.

Paul E. Sequeira, Chicago Daily News

Photographer David Nystrom, in white, stands with other photographers in police-approved area, However, when Nystrom took pictures of those arrested, he was arrested, too.

(Fred W. McDarrah, for the Village Voice)

New York Times photographer Barton Silverman is dragged away and arrested after assault by police.

The tables were placed in a cluster, right side up, and close enough together so that a motorcycle could not pass between them. The men told the observer they did not intend the tables as a barricade but only as a means of slowing down the anticipated police skirmish line. The observer then helped carry the tables. Elsewhere, self-styled "Lincoln Parkers" were lining up wastebaskets and picnic tables along pathways to prevent police vehicles from approaching them without ample warning.

Suddenly, someone in the group got the idea of turning the tables over and forming a barricade. As he translated his idea into action, a large group of people moved toward the area to assist him. They dismantled the blockade and created a barricade stretching northwest from the snow fence which lies just at the foot of the bridle path up to the Grant statue. Helpers scoured the park for tables and trash baskets.

The barricade was about 35 yards long and in the shape of an arc running to a point adjacent to the Garibaldi statue. Its strongest point was at the center, where there was a five-foot high steel trash bin, but its strength tapered off on either side to scattered tables and trash baskets. Approximately 200 persons gathered immediately behind the center, but most people stood in what grew to be a crowd of about 1,000 some distance (perhaps ten yards) behind, forming a kind of bell-shaped curve. A number were standing on the slope leading up to the Garibaldi statue.

Several flags flew from atop the barricade—two Viet Cong flags, a black flag of anarchy and a red flag of revolution. Some of the people climbed atop the barricade and chanted: "Hell no, we won't go!" "Kill the pigs!" and "Fuck the pigs!" Those at the barricade told reporters they intended to stay in the park all night—even if the police used tear gas.

Behind the barricade, trash baskets were overturned and their contents set afire. Strobe and television floodlights focused on the crowd and on poet Allen Ginsberg, who squatted on the ground and began the now familiar "om." Shortly after 11 p.m., the deputy chief of police inspected the scene and determined that the people immediately behind the barricade were becoming more hostile and the total crowd was increasing in number. Private cars which had been parked along

Cannon Drive were stoned as they drove from the park, past the crowd.

The deputy chief decided he needed tear gas. He placed an immediate call for Area 6 Task Force units. Eighty men, supplied with tear gas and shotguns, began assembling at Cannon Drive and Fullerton, at the northeastern edge of the park. By 11:50 p.m., these Task Force units joined 160 district officers at a point along Cannon Drive, about 100 feet northeast of the barricade.

As the police began assembling, those behind the barricade threw bottles, stones and bathroom tiles at the officers. A police district commander ordered his men to retire from the west side of Cannon Drive to the east side to avoid the missiles.

A panel truck pulled up and two policemen passed out riot guns and shotguns to about 20 to 30 policemen. Gas masks were distributed to many district police, but there were not enough available for all. All Task Force officers had masks. At about 11:15 p.m., a traffic safety car equipped with a loudspeaker was driven near the barricade and police made the following announcement.

> Anyone remaining in the park from now on is in violation of the law. Please leave the park. This includes the news media. The park is now closed.

A reporter was terrified. "I thought—and I said to someone —'this is it, man. They're after us tonight.' " The response to the park clearance order from the crowd was "Sieg heil, schwein!" and "Hell no, we won't go!" Plainclothes police moved among the crowd and apprehended several persons alleged to have thrown rocks and bottles at police.

At 11:45 p.m., the traffic safety car again appeared in front of the barricade and repeated the announcement. This time those at the barricade responded by throwing rocks at the car. At midnight with some 2,000 to 3,000 persons in the park and more continuing to arrive from points south, the deputy chief decided to clear the park in 15 minutes.

On Cannon Drive, the Task Force lined up ahead of a line of district police and a group of newsmen. People at the barricade were thumping on a large trash bin and urging police to "come and get us!" Many were wearing helmets.

Ready to move out with the police skirmish line were two fire department light trucks. They were intended to spotlight people as the police moved against them.

Several police cars were also parked, facing the barricade,

with their lights on. At this point, three young men climbed lamp posts along the barricade. They taunted police. A young couple ran from behind the barricade and danced a Highland fling for the officers. Then they darted behind their redoubt.

Those on the lamp posts and atop the barricade urged others to join them in chanting, and taunting police. Below them, marshals moved among the people, urging them to walk—not run—out of the park when the police charged. The police lines were extended north and south to points where they clearly outflanked the barricade.

At about 12:20 a.m., a single squad car approached the people behind the barricade. The two officers in the car had encountered a traffic jam at the Eugenie Triangle en route to a call at Wisconsin and Lincoln Avenues. They detoured through the park to reach their destination and proceeded north along a sidewalk leading up to the Garibaldi statue. The deputy chief leading the police in the park knew nothing about the car until he saw it approaching the barricade. The vehicle's lights were turned off and it was travelling between ten and 20 miles per hour.

As the car approached, people began to scream: "Get the police car! Get the police car!" When the officer driving the car spotted the crowd, he pulled the car to a halt short of the barricade. People screamed, "Get the police car! Get the police car!"

The driver threw the car into reverse and backed up about ten feet. He turned the car west, parallel to the barricade. As he started the car forward, again, however, the crowd swarmed about it, throwing rocks, bottles and sticks. A bottle smashed the windshield on the driver's side.

There are accounts of an 18- or 19-year-old girl screaming hysterically as she was momentarily trapped between the right side of the car and the barricade. The crowd yelled: "Kill the cops!" They stoned the car with more rocks and bottles. From behind the police lines, a magazine reporter heard an officer scream: "They've got the squad, kill them!" Another yelled: "There's a squad car trapped!"

Approximately 50 Task Force officers broke ranks and moved rapidly toward the squad. They were ordered back by the Task Force commander. The car finally lurched forward, its lights now on and siren wailing, zig-zagging through the crowd. Reaction in both camps was instantaneous.

Those at the barricade felt police were trying to run them

down or breach their redoubt. From behind the police lines, an observer heard an officer yell: "If we back down here, the whole town goes up tonight!"

Several more Task Force officers moved toward the barricade with tear gas canisters in their hands, but backed off. The crowd threw rocks. One officer stumbled to the ground, producing a cheer from the people at the barricade.

Said one sergeant in a later statement: "It was the toughest thing I had to do as a policeman to order my men not to go to the assistance of police officers in trouble."

A Task Force officer was struck in the side by a rock. He left the line to pursue the man he thought had thrown it. When he grabbed the man, whom he described as a hippie, three others tried to intervene. In the scuffle, the officer sprained his right wrist and was smashed in the chest with a stick. He finally released the man he had cornered.

At 12:27 a.m. the clearing of the park began when several Task Force officers lobbed four canisters of tear gas and four smoke bombs toward the crowd. (The smoke bombs were intended to disorient people.) As the canisters exploded, the entire Task Force line moved toward the barricade. A barrage of bricks and bottles greeted them. According to some persons in the crowd, as the police charged around and through the barricade, they were chanting: "Kill, kill, kill!"

Following the police were several newsmen. One canister of gas exploded near them and one reporter, who had turned to watch, was doused in the face with an immobilizing spray. Momentarily frozen in his tracks, the reporter was then struck hard in the ribs with a blunt object. He fell to the ground and was dragged across the grass by the shoulders. He was finally dropped and someone started kicking him. When he looked up, he saw light reflecting off several helmets. A police officer leaned over him and said: "I'm sorry buddy."

The news editor of a national magazine was following the Task Force and district police. He feels that the amount of gas used was not excessive. The gas was drifting westward, however, along the people's route of escape. Suddenly, the editor states, "All hell broke loose."

About 25 persons had broken north from the barricade, down the slope from the Garibaldi statue, toward the South Pond. Task Force police at the northern end of the line charged after them. "Kill the mother fuckers!" yelled the officers. "Into the pond, into the pond, get the mother fuckers into the pond!"

The editor says he saw at least six people thrown into the pond by the police.

A young man and his girlfriend were both grabbed by officers. He screamed, "We're going, we're going," but they threw him into the pond. The officers grabbed the girl, knocked her to the ground, dragged her along the embankment and hit her with their batons on her head, arms, back and legs. The boy tried to scramble up the embankment to her, but police shoved him back in the water at least twice. He finally got to her and tried to pull her in the water, away from the police. He was clubbed on the head five or six times. An officer shouted, "Let's get the fucking bastards!" but the boy pulled her in the water and the police left. The girl required seven stitches in her head. Two ministers attempting to act as a buffer at the pond were shoved away. One of them was struck in the back. Both of them were ordered to "run you bastards, run."

Meanwhile the police commanders were having difficulty watching their lines. The terrain near the statue is uneven and despite the fire department light trucks much of the area remained dark.

Back near the barricade, two students at the McCormick Theological Seminary, who were on the scene to protect demonstrators, had attempted to calm the people as the gas canisters exploded. They had cautioned people to walk, not run, toward Clark Street. But as the police advanced, many had run anyway.

The two seminarians had themselves fallen behind the retreating people while restraining a rock thrower. They found themselves almost alone between police and the crowd. As they walked to catch up with the crowd, one turned to glance at the police line. As he did, he was smashed over the right eye by a gun butt. The second heard him cry "Help me!" At the same moment, he, too, was struck on the back and arm and knocked to the ground. He saw three officers standing over his friend. One officer came down hard with a gun butt, smashing the seminarian in the face. Another jabbed the second seminarian, yelling: "Get up! Get up! Get out of here fast, run, run!" He did. His companion lay on the ground. Another man who observed the beating shouted: "You killed a priest, you dirty god damned mother fuckers killed a priest!" Police commanders arrived on the scene and ordered the first seminarian taken in a police van to Henrotin Hospital. He had sustained multiple lacerations of the head and a skull fracture.

He had also lost part of the vision in his right eye and remained in the hospital for 12 days.

Cyclist in the Pond

Meanwhile, a 23-year-old area resident was bicycling through the park on his way home. He entered the park at LaSalle and Clark Streets and headed down Stockton Drive, toward the South Pond. This route, he thought, was the shortest one home. He said that although he knew people were in the park at this time and that they were in violation of the curfew, he did not stop and did not see any police officers when he entered.

He left Stockton Drive at a point just southwest of the pond and followed a paved path around the south end of the pond and then turned north on the bridle path which leads up to the Grant statue. He said it was dark and difficult to see.

Suddenly he was surrounded by what seemed to be eight policemen who had appeared from behind bushes along the path. "Where are you going?" they asked, and he responded: "I'm going home." Then one of the officers yelled: "Let's search him." The police pulled a hair brush, book of matches and a pen from his white parka. The next thing he knew he was pushed, still astride his bike, into the pond by the officers. Although stunned, he recovered and pulled himself out of the three-foot deep water. The officers had gone.

By 12:30 a.m., most of the people were near Clark Street, fleeing the gas. Many were experiencing a burning sensation in their eyes.

At Stockton Drive, police with batons were attempting to subdue a boy. As a news photographer photographed the scene, he was struck in the back with a shotgun. Knocked down, he was then searched by two officers for his film. This incident is described in the police-press chapter.

By 12:38 a.m., police declared the park empty. But the Eugenie and Old Town Triangles were jammed with people, many of them angered by the tear gas. Several youths who had carried long poles from the park attempted to smash traffic lights at the Eugenie Triangle, but were restrained by clergymen. Four or five bottles were thrown at police cars moving through the intersection. At 12:45 p.m., the Police Department received a call for assistance at the Eugenie intersection.

Task Force police who had swept the park had formed a

picket line on the east side of Clark Street. The crowd attacked them both physically and verbally. As a squad car passed the divider strip in Clark, one person in a group of about 15 standing there threw gravel through the open window of the car. Another person spat on the car. People on the west side of the street were yelling: "Pigs, Oink, Oink!"

The Task Force did not move into the street immediately; instead they waited for district officers to catch up to their line. Task Force superior officers had difficulty maintaining contact with all the men in the line, which stretched about two blocks. A Task Force lieutenant estimated the crowd at 1,500 persons.

Clearing of Clark Street

One observer describes the clearing of Clark Street in these words:

> The demonstrators were forced out onto Clark Street and once again a traffic jam developed. Cars were stopped, the horns began to honk, people couldn't move, people got gassed inside their cars, people got stoned inside their cars, police were the objects of stones, and taunts, mostly taunts. As you must understand, most of the taunting of the police was verbal. There were stones thrown of course, but for the most part it was verbal. But there were stones being thrown and of course the police were responding with tear gas and clubs and everytime they could get near enough to a demonstrator they hit him.
>
> But again you had this police problem within—this really turned into a police problem. They pushed everybody out of the park, but this night there were a lot more people in the park than there had been during the previous night and Clark Street was just full of people and in addition now was full of gas because the police were using gas on a much larger scale this night. So the police were faced with the task, which took them about an hour or so, of hitting people over the head and gassing them enough to get them out of Clark, which they did.

At this point, Task Force officers initiated a series of sallies into Clark Street to apprehend apparent rock and bottle throwers and highly vocal demonstrators. After each sally the officers returned to the police lines.

Later, a young couple was halted by police who used their batons on the man, leaving him sprawling against a mail box. The girl ran into the middle of the street and shouted: "Why do you do that?" Four officers moved off the east curb, grabbed the girl by her arms and legs, and dragged her toward a squadrol, behind the police line. A free-lance photographer, covering the clearance for a magazine, snapped pictures of the scene, but as he did, police pulled his strobe unit away from him, ripped off his battery pack and struck him in the arms and abdomen.

By this time, a police line was pushing a crowd estimated at about 1,000 persons north from their position blocking the Eugenie Triangle. At the same time, further north, another line of police was pushing people south.

As the first line of police passed the southwestern tip of the park, they yelled to a Chicago attorney, his wife and five or six others standing behind a park bench, telling them they had better get moving. The attorney and his wife hesitated. Then a group of officers broke from the line toward them. As they did, the attorney and his wife started to walk south toward the Chicago Historical Society building in Lincoln Park. The officer who had warned them was joined by seven or eight others who started to run toward them. They shouted: "Run!"

They ran about 20 or 30 yards, turned around and stopped. The attorney said to his wife: "Slow down, they're not following us." But then he heard his wife say, "Damn you." She had been struck on the back and head by an officer with a baton. The attorney was also hit.

At approximately the same time, according to a resident of the area, seven police officers, carrying what looked like knives or other sharp weapons, slashed the tires of cars parked in a parking lot, just opposite Lincoln Avenue and Clark Street, between Clark and Stockton Drive. He says he also saw police break the windows of several cars.

The editor of a Chicago community newspaper came to the same parking lot at 5 a.m. with a friend from California to retrieve a Volkswagen camper owned by the latter. They discovered the tires slashed and the windows bashed in. A guitar and luggage had also been damaged.

An Assistant U.S. Attorney says that on Monday night he

observed three police officers standing next to a vehicle on Stockton Drive, about one-half block north of North Avenue. "The three officers appeared to be joking as they moved away from the loudly hissing rear tire of the vehicle," said the attorney. "It appeared that the officers had either slashed or released the air from the tire." He says he saw several other vehicles in the area with one or more deflated tires.

The people were pushed, shoved, gassed and clubbed until they reached Wells Street and North Avenue. At this intersection Mayor Carl Stokes of Cleveland was walking through the crowds, talking to people, trying to calm them down. Some of the crowd argued with him. He left the area shortly thereafter.

A Chicago Transit Authority bus stopped to unload passengers at Lincoln Avenue and Clark. One of them was struck by policemen swinging batons. The man asked two ministers: "Why did they hit me? I'm just returning from work."

Another minister spotted a boy lying on the west sidewalk of Clark Street, at the foot of a line of police who were blocking foot traffic. The minister asked a sergeant for permission to aid the boy, who was bleeding. The sergeant agreed and a medic was summoned. When he had finished treating the boy, the medic and the minister walked by the police line. As they did, an officer yelled: "You sons-of-bitches, you big fakes. Give us a target."

Chaos

As the crowd fled, chaos and confusion traveled with them. An NBC truck stationed on Wisconsin Street was stoned, a squad car attacked, properly identified media personnel were beaten and some with cameras were attacked, and their cameras smashed or film destroyed. There were reports of shots fired and windows broken. Police moved everywhere in pursuit of the demonstrators, charging up streets, walks and into hallways. Many were not wearing identification.

The crowd called them "Pigs," and some of the police, brandishing their nightsticks, yelled back: "Give us targets. Come on, do something." Bottles were thrown, and the police charged the crowd up to Eugenie, pressing the demonstrators out from Eugenie onto Wells. Shouts of "Let's get the fuckers" were heard from the police.

Police lines had also formed on Wells and on Schiller, and the crowd was forced back to Burton where they were pinched off by the line of officers moving south on Wells from the Old Town Triangle. They tried to move east down LaSalle where they encountered yet another line of advancing police. Discovering that lines of escape were blocked, many demonstrators panicked and began to run in all directions. Officers leaped from unmarked cars and struck demonstrators with their nightsticks.

This scene was so chaotic that even residents attempting to assist the police were roughly handled. A doctor driving home that night saw "hippies" dumping trash cans onto the street and throwing objects at parked cars. When attempting to bring this to the attention of a policeman, he was met with, "Listen you god damn mother fucker, get this fucking car out of here." He tried again to explain his concern, but was interrupted with, "Listen, you son-of-a-bitch, didn't you hear me the first time?" The policeman then struck the man's car with his nightstick, causing a sizeable dent. The doctor gave up his attempt to assist and drove home immediately.

Violence raged through the early morning hours and was not limited to police actions. Groups of all types, including "locals," stoned police cars, broke windows and street lights, and shouted epithets at the police. One police officer was driving his squad car on Clark Street when his car door was pierced by a weapon which may have been a pickaxe. The officer suffered abrasions to his left forearm.

A young man got off a CTA bus near the Lincoln Hotel and walked north. A police officer walked up to him and hit him with his elbow in the chest and stomach. The young man, about 30 years old, folded over but did not fall. The officer walked away.

As a crowd of demonstrators moved past one observer, he noticed a young man being moved along by a policeman holding him by the upper arm. The young man was wearing identification badges or credentials around his neck. "This isn't a police state!" he said. Two or three other policemen joined the first, pushed the young man into a doorway and began hitting him. Immediately two persons with cameras began to move into the area yelling: "Police brutality." The observer said that two or three other policemen turned after the men with the cameras and began beating one of them.

By 1 a.m., police had cleared the Eugenie Triangle. At

about that time a *Chicago Daily News* reporter became involved in an incident with the police.

The tape of the Police Department radio log discloses the following conversation at 1:29 a.m. on Tuesday morning:

> Police Operator: "1814, get a wagon over at 1436. We've got an injured hippie."
> Voice: "1436 North Wells?"
> Operator: "North Wells."
> In quick sequence, there are the following remarks from five other police cars:
> "That's no emergency."
> "Let him take a bus."
> ""Kick the fucker."
> "Knock his teeth out."
> "Throw him in a wastepaper basket."

The Medical Committee For Human Rights and the Student Health Organization, an assisting group of medics, reported that they had treated 24 persons for injuries Monday night, almost all lacerations. They said three others had also been maced.

Most police had been on duty over 15 hours. All told, 15 policemen were reportedly treated for injuries Monday.

By 2 a.m., there was little activity left to observe on the streets. Several people had watched the action from the roof above an apartment building. Their presence, however, had inspired reports of snipers. Two policemen came to the door of the residence to investigate. "There's a sniper on your roof!" the officers exclaimed. They demanded to search the apartment. Other officers were searching the other apartments in the building. A dog began to bark and one of the officers pointed a gun at it. "Get this dog back or the dog will die." Quite distraught, another officer asked simply: "Why do you call us pigs?"

Tuesday, August 27—Morning and Afternoon

There were a number of marches on Tuesday, August 27. The first of these were to the Polish Consulate at 1525 North Astor to protest Poland's participation in the invasion of Czechoslovakia. A small group arrived about 11:30 a.m. and were, according to the Chicago Police Department, "not Lincoln Park hippies." They began to leave at 11:55 a.m. A second group of about 75 left Lincoln Park about 12:15 p.m. They arrived at the Consulate about 12:30 p.m. and within half an hour were returning to the park. There were no incidents or arrests in connection with either demonstration.

Between 11 a.m. and 2 p.m., approximately 50 Lincoln Park area clergymen were joined by a number of community residents at an emergency meeting at the Church of the Three Crosses, 1900 North Sedgwick. They agreed to form an *ad hoc* group, the Lincoln Park Emergency Citizens Committee, and drafted a statement asking police to lift the ban against sleeping on the grounds of Lincoln Park.

The statement argued that the demonstrators did not constitute a threat to the Old Town community and that "the best interests of the community would be served by the withdrawal of massive police forces from Lincoln Park and the surrounding community."

The committee decided that a delegation would meet with commanders of the 18th, 19th and 20th Police Districts in an attempt to get them to suspend enforcement of the curfew. The clergy present decided that rather than attempting to act as a buffer between police and park visitors, they would stage their own protest against the police on Tuesday evening. They announced that a prayer vigil would be staged from 11 p.m. Tuesday, until 4 p.m. Wednesday.

The vigil was to be an act of personal witness to what the clergymen believed had been unjust police treatment of persons in the park by police. The clergymen realized also that the vigil would constitute an act of civil disobedience; it would be in violation of the curfew ordinance.

Early that afternoon in the park, an Assistant U.S. Attorney observed less than 1,000 persons sitting in small, scattered groups. About 100 to 150 persons, he said, were practicing the washoi.

At 4 p.m., an Emergency Citizens Committee delegation of about 25 persons met with the 18th District Police Commander in the police command post at Lincoln Park. Spokesman for the group was a North Side attorney.

The delegation asked the commander to suspend the curfew ordinance, decrease the size of the police force in the park and community, and stop what the delegates called acts of police brutality. The attorney told the commander that police enforcement of the curfew was a "clear violation of the will of the people." He said, "massive police force will only destroy peace in the community."

The commander replied that the police were not interested in confrontation with people, arrests, or any physical contact. The director of the North Side Cooperative Ministry, NSCM, said that "by pushing these young people from the park, the police create a larger law enforcement problem than they have if they let the youths remain in the park."

The commander said he had no authority to suspend the curfew. He agreed, however, to relay the citizens' request to Superintendent James B. Conlisk, Jr. He refused to comment, however, on whether he would recommend to Conlisk that the curfew be lifted or if there was any possibility it would be lifted. The delegation said it would return for more information that evening, prior to curfew hour.

The delegation claimed that park curfews had seldom been enforced, nor even posted, except for a 2 a.m. curfew on the beach. The executive director of the Illinois Community Arts Foundation, said that he had lived in the area 18 years and had not seen anything to match the previous night's activity:

> I was "sticked" (struck with a baton), at Armitage and Lincoln, four blocks from the park. The police, it seems to me, are the disruptive force in our community.

The NSCM told the commander that police had called clergymen in the park the night before "fakes, bastards and SOB's." Before leaving, the delegation informed the commander of their intention to stage a vigil in the park Tuesday night. When the commander told them that this was an act of civil disobedience, they said they realized that.

An instructor at the McCormick Theological Seminary, explained the clergymen's position:

> If they [the police] want to gas us, people of Chicago will realize that it isn't just kids, but respectable people flipping in. We're going to celebrate freedom and peace for this community, for Chicago, for Vietnam.

After this delegation of citizens departed, the commander met with several others, representing various viewpoints. The

Old Town Triangle Association, for one, complained of rowdiness in the area between Menomonee on the south, Lincoln Park on the west and Lincoln Avenue on the north. The Association requested that police keep this section of Lincoln Avenue and adjacent streets clear of "park visitors" Tuesday night.

During the afternoon in the park, entertainer Sonny, of the Sonny and Cher singing team, argued that governmental bodies "will listen to reason" and said he was working with Cleveland Mayor Carl Stokes to bring before the Democratic Party Platform Committee a motion to increase participation in government by youth. Jerry Rubin also spoke to a crowd in the park, proposing that they picket all Chicago Transit Authority bus garages in behalf of striking black bus drivers. He said, "This generation is saying no to racism and joining the blacks by putting ourselves in the same risk situation blacks are in."

Beginning at about 3 p.m., a sound truck drove through the streets of the Lincoln Park area, asking residents to open their homes to Yippies Tuesday night in the event the curfew ordinance was enforced. Some merchants in the area also were donating food to those who had been staying in area churches.

At about 4 p.m., in the park, a team of police was surrounded by a group of persons, shouting, "Pigs! Pigs!" The officers were rescued by three squads of police (30 men) who formed a wedge and pushed their way through the crowd without the use of batons. Another group of citizens was more peaceful. They were gathered just west of the main, north-south knoll, clinking pieces of small tile together to create musical notes. Allen Ginsberg was chanting and the police were not in sight. In still another area, a group of 20 young whites was seen picking up chunks of loose paving from a road.

Calls for Revolution

At approximately 7 p.m., a crowd estimated at 1,500 persons listened to Bobby Seale of the Black Panther Party and Jerry Rubin call for revolution in the United States. The rally occurred on a hill at the south end of the park. Based on notes taken at the time, one witness recalls Seale as stating:

> The message of the Black Panther Party is of developing revolution. . . . We must understand as we go forward that there are pigs: Lyndon Johnson, Hubert Humphrey

and Nixon in this society. . . . We go forward as human beings to remove pigs and hogs that are terrorizing people here and throughout the world.

We, as revolutionaries, will let them know we refuse to accept their decisions. We have our candidate, Eldridge Cleaver, running for President on the Peace and Power ticket.

The ticket, he said, is a combination of the Black Panther Party and the White Peace and Freedom Party of the Oakland, California, area. He lectured on the way to handle police:

If a pig comes up and starts swinging a club, then put it over his head and lay him out on the ground.

It's the same thing for other groups in a similar situation when pigs will attack. If you're getting down to the nitty-gritty, you'll have some functional organization like ours to take care of the pigs in a desired manner.

He said that "black people know what police brutality is and you white people who have been asking whether it's real found out last night." Seale urged blacks to "get your shotguns, get your .357 magnums and get your .45's and everything else you can get." He warned that "large groups are wrong. Get into small groups of three, four, and five. Be armed and spread out so we can 'stuckle' these pigs."

Seale predicted that the leadership of any revolutionary group which might be created from those in the park would be black-led and that blacks would carry the guns. Whites, he said, would battle the nation's political parties and back the black leaders. In closing, he said: "If the pigs treat us unjustly tonight, we'll have to barbecue us some of that pork."

Jerry Rubin followed and stated:

We whites have been suppressed as blacks have for the past 100 years. We're going with the blacks. We'll take the same risks as blacks take. If they try to keep us out of the park, then we'll go to the streets. They bring out the pigs to protect the pigs they nominate.

He characterized what was happening as a "new white revolution." He said, "If the pigs try to get us out of Old Town, then we'll go downtown." Rubin finished the meeting with a call for demonstrations at the nearby CTA bus garage at Schubert and Orchard.

At 7 p.m., the Lincoln Park Emergency Citizens Committee rallied on the steps of the Chicago Academy of Sciences Building, 2000 North Clark, just south of the police headquarters. They said they were there to protest police action on Monday night. They informed newsmen of their meeting with the police commander and the requests they had made of him. They also reiterated their plan to participate in the after-hour prayer vigil in the park.

At approximately 7:35 p.m., the group of 25 citizens and clergy, representing the Lincoln Park Emergency Citizens Committee, arrived to meet with a police commander. As they walked north from the Academy of Sciences Building, however, they were met by a line of police. A messenger had to be sent to headquarters to explain that the group was outside. Then, only six persons were admitted into headquarters.

Once inside, the delegation learned that the commander was gone, but that the deputy chief of police was available. Newsmen and photographers were not allowed into the meeting. The deputy chief was unwilling to negotiate the policy of expelling persons from the park. He said this was his order. He was willing, however, to discuss methods of expulsion.

He said that the curfew ordinance would be enforced that night with no unnecessary violence. He admitted that there might have been misbehavior on the part of some policemen the previous night.

Between 7:30 and 8 p.m. a group of 500 to 1,000 marched south on Clark Street chanting "Hell no, we won't go!" Some of the marchers had reached the corner of Clark and Burton Streets when a police car pulled up—apparently to disperse them. Several marchers began pounding on the car, and the police retaliated by macing three of them.

More police arrived, accompanied by a helmeted man in a sports coat who took a position in the middle of Burton and began trying to direct the crowd. Suddenly he pulled out a pistol and fired at least three times. The marchers, screaming, quickly began to disperse. As they fled, about 20 policemen pursued them with nightsticks swinging. There were no reported injuries or arrests.

At about the same time, a newspaper photographer was threatened, he states, by six uniformed policemen at 1848 North Wells. The photographer who was assigned to cover events at the park Tuesday night said an unidentified policeman told him: "You take my picture tonight and I'm going to get you." Moments later he was approached by six policemen, one of whom said: "We're going to get you tonight, no matter what." Hc said he couldn't identify the officers, and some were not wearing name tags. This was one of the photographers struck by police Sunday night on the Michigan Avenue bridge.

March to the Bus Barn

At 8:10 p.m., the Chicago Police Department broadcast a report of 2,500 demonstrators moving from Lincoln Park to the Loop. The report was erroneous. There were, in fact, demonstrators leaving the park, but only 200 and they were heading north. This march was a gesture of sympathy for the black bus drivers who were striking to protest alleged discrimination in the Chicago Transit Workers' Union. Their destination was the CTA bus barn at Clark and Schubert.

Almost immediately after that group was out of the park, a second group—200 to 300 strong—left the park to join up with the march.

At 8:25 p.m., the first group moving north on Clark was approaching Armitage. While the purpose of the march was an expression of solidarity, it was not entirely peaceful. When a bus going north on Clark Street stopped for a light at Armitage, some demonstrators began hitting the windows with bats, trying to force their way into the crowded bus. One passenger describes the atmosphere inside as one of "general panic." None got into the bus, however, and when the light changed, the bus moved on.

A summer intern in the city's legal office, acting as an *ad hoc* marshal, says that the authorities knew nothing of the march and were unprepared for it. A city legal aide, who also accompanied the march, says that the marchers kept to the sidewalks and police were able to keep it under control. The pace was fast, traffic signals were obeyed, and neither witness recalls any incidents, other than occasional shouts of "Scab!" as city buses passed.

At 8:45 p.m., another erroneous Police Department report

described 2,500 demonstrators at North and Clark headed for the bus barn. At 8:46 the first group was at 2500 north on Clark Street. Ten minutes later they arrived at the bus barns at Clark and Schubert Streets. The second group soon caught up with them. At 9 p.m. police told demonstrators they could march around the bus barn, but would not be allowed to enter. As they were being directed around the barn, a bus with several passengers aboard came north on Clark. In the view of a *Newsweek* reporter, the driver intended to drive into the crowd. The crowd thought so, too, and scattered. Policemen stopped the bus, but in the process it grazed a police sergeant, who suffered contusions on his arm. The driver was arrested and the crowd, none of whom was injured, cheered.

There were few extremes of dress or behavior during this demonstration. The marchers were mostly young people, including college students, some clergymen and numerous blacks. A few carried picket signs—"Free Black Political Prisoners," "Get U.S. Troops out of Vietnam," "Free Huey," "Youth against War and Fascism"—and some yelled "pig" at police officers. The marchers stood about three deep on both sides of the street for about two blocks. Police kept them moving down one side of the street, across the street, and back down the other side and across to form a rectangle. Officers were instructed to keep batons below their waist at all times and to hold them in both hands. A captain led the group about the block on Schubert to keep them from slowing down at the bus barns and obstructing traffic. After circling the block twice, the marchers headed south. At 10:45 p.m. the first of the marchers were at Drummond and Clark Streets on their way back to the park. A few minutes later, according to police, some were throwing rocks.

A little after 11 p.m. about 20 of the returning marchers tried to stop a slow-moving bus on Stockton Drive. They yelled "Scab!" at the driver, and some threw bottles and rocks. As the bus sped away one threw a cherry bomb through a rear window.

Earlier, another march had started spontaneously from Lincoln Park and headed south. A 50-year-old executive says it consisted of several hundred people, most of them young, walking south on Clark, followed by an unmarked squad car with six plainclothes men. A few more police followed the procession on foot, as the demonstrators continued on Clark and turned east on Huron to Wabash and then south on

Wabash. In a few blocks they turned east again on Ohio. They proceeded to Michigan Avenue and crossed, chanting "Hell no, we won't go," and the police cars continued to follow.

By this time the 200 marchers were followed by four or five police cars and an NBC truck. The group crossed the Michigan Avenue Bridge and continued south. As they approached Lake Street, a car drove onto the sidewalk and four plainclothes men, all wearing helmets, got out. The driver, taking off his coat, said to the others: "This is the time to break it up and send them home. It's gone far enough." He took a club from the car, and the four started across the street. A light green sedan pulled up alongside the car, a white-shirted police officer got out, caught up with the other four, grabbed the leader and said, "Get back in that car. Go up and cover Lake Street." The executive says the officer had to yell the command again before the plainclothes men drove off. The march, with police following, continued to Grant Park.

While the CTA sympathy marchers were demonstrating at the bus barn and the Michigan Avenue group was approaching Adams Street, another group left Lincoln Park and headed west on Eugenie Street. A Near North Side resident described them as 200 to 300 "hippie types" going east at 10:30 p.m. on Goethe from LaSalle, throwing rocks at cars and windows, and breaking a window in her apartment. A police car arrived and dispersed the crowd with tear gas, some of which seeped into her apartment. The gas drifted into the nearby Pump Room and Ambassador East Hotel as well. As the dispersed marchers headed back to the park some of them went north on State Street, where they tried to tip over a car. A police car came and the demonstrators left the Corvair.

A final group of marchers left Lincoln Park at this same time. At 10:25 p.m. approximately 1,000 persons moved out of the park, heading south on LaSalle for Grant Park. It was an orderly march, followed closely by the police. At 10:35 they had reached Division and LaSalle; at 11:17 p.m. they were at State and Wacker; and by 11:30 they were at Michigan and Monroe. There were no reported incidents or arrests.

A Vigil

While these marches were proceeding, the clergymen gathered at the Church of the Three Crosses to plan the vigil in

Lincoln Park, began walking south on Clark Street toward Lincoln Park. They were wearing armbands and at the head of their single line of marchers was a large wooden cross, 12-feet high. They cut across Clark Street at the intersection with Wisconsin and headed into that area of the park near the site of Monday night's barricade. The picnic tables and trash baskets had been taken away. The clergy formed a small circle. They prayed, gave short sermons, began singing various hymns and folk songs and soon a crowd of some 1,500 persons gathered around them in a half circle. Some 50 yards northeast another, smaller apparently more militant, group also gathered.

At the South Pond, according to the school teacher involved in a scuffle with police Sunday night in the park, he was back again, searching for twigs and paper to build a small fire. He was putting these things into a small, brown paper bag. He intended to return to another area of the park to pop popcorn and roast wieners with his girlfriend. Suddenly, eight policemen came out of the bushes and one said: "What do you have in that bag." Somewhat nervously, he replied: "Sticks and paper." An officer said: "Oh, it's a fire bomb."

"No," said the teacher, "it's sticks and paper for hotdogs and a wiener roast we're having." The officers pushed the teacher against a tree and searched his clothing. Then they took him by the arms, half carrying and half dragging him, and shoved him into the pond.

As 11 p.m. approached, newsmen querying police about the clearance plans were told that orders to clear the park stood, despite the presence of the clergymen. Newsmen were told, however, that they would be given protection behind the police skirmish lines. The curfew announcement, similar to the one used on Sunday night, was prepared. Officials then circulated through the park in an attempt to get newsmen to move behind the police lines. About 14 newsmen agreed.

At the vigil site, clergymen and those gathered about them were singing "The Battle Hymn of the Republic."

A brief debate flared between those who wanted to resist police violently and those advocating nonviolent civil disobedience. One of about a half-dozen blacks in this first group asserted that blacks had "undergone police brutality, now you whites are experiencing it." There were conflicting shouts like "Kill the pigs!" and "No, man, let's make love!"

The majority was opposed to calls for violent resistance. When anyone from the more militant group addressed the clergymen's group, someone—usually a clergyman—refuted him. The militants were also booed. In response, at one point, a militant called the clergy "mother fuckers."

Author and radio personality, Louis (Studs) Terkel said he was at the vigil to "see what life is like and life is here. Therefore, I'm not at the Amphitheatre where life is not." The crowd applauded.

A representative of the striking CTA bus drivers asked the crowd to assist in picketing additional bus garages that evening, but his appeal was generally rejected. The sentiment of the moment was that Lincoln Park was "their thing."

By 11:30 p.m., police slowly began massing at the foot of Cannon Drive, directly opposite the crowd, and also to the north along the bridle path leading to the Grant statue. A sound truck moved into the area and an announcement boomed that the park was closed. An accompanying fire department light truck lit up the site.

Uncertain about how the anticipated dispersal would be handled, a group of six clergymen proceeded north to meet the district commander at the command post, but the commander was out. Outside, a contingent of 100 officers disembarked from a bus and moved past the clergymen, singing: "Hi, ho. Hi, ho. It's off to work we go." As the men crossed the bridge over the South Pond, they whistled the march from "The Bridge On The River Kwai."

Finally, the clergymen located the commander, who said again that police would clear the park, but with restraint. The clergy returned to advise the crowd.

One of the clergymen who participated in the service held in Lincoln Park on Tuesday evening describes the situation just before the clearing operation:

> At the same time, we entered into dialogue with some of the most radical . . . persons in the group. These people were calling for going into the street to confront the police, but they were also shouted down a number of times. Others would ask for more moderate or more nonviolent approaches. No one wants to say that the people we had in the park were all nonviolent. But I think we ought to understand that a large spectrum of people were there and that most of the people there were not terrorists.

Just before midnight, the deputy chief and the district commander joined 80 Task Force officers along an initial skirmish line, facing the crowd. Behind the Task Force were 160 policemen from the 18th, 19th and 20th Districts.

A Chicago Sanitation Department dump truck was positioned in the center of the Task Force line. A mechanism for spraying tear gas was mounted on the bed, with a nozzle extending over the top of the cab. Both the mechanism and the gas had been requisitioned from the U.S. Army. Two police officers standing on the bed of the truck manned the nozzle.

As the police readied themselves, a news photographer moved to the top of the knoll leading to the Garibaldi statue, to get a picture of the impending dispersal. Suddenly, six policemen surrounded him and despite his protests that he was a newsman, forced him out of the area. In the process, they smashed one of his cameras, tore his shirt and tried to trip him to the ground.

At approximately 12:15 a.m., police announced that if newsmen still with the crowd wanted protection, they ought to move behind police lines.

Clergymen, meanwhile, were also busy advising people. Their advice was "Sit or split." Those who didn't want to be "hit, jailed or gassed" were told to leave the park. Those who intended to stay were told to sit down, lock arms, and remain calm. Many readied handkerchiefs and surgical masks, dampened with baking soda or vaseline as protection against tear gas.

Some prayed, and the crowd sang "Onward Christian Soldiers." About 150 to 200 people moved between the crowd and the police lines to set up a small barricade of picnic tables.

Back at the police skirmish line, a Chicago attorney was listening to the conversation of the officers. He says that he had been "roaming" in the park since 11 p.m., and:

> Wearing my suit and having an all-American crew cut, I was wholly accepted behind the police lines in their staging area prior to their movement on the groups in the park. Other strangers, not so attired, were ordered away. I believe I may have been taken as some official.
>
> For approximately one and one-half hours I stood next to various groups of policemen who were waiting for their orders and listened to their many unguarded and extemporaneous discussions. There seemed to be almost without exception, an attitude or mentality of impatience about

"getting started" and it was the normal thing for policemen to talk about how anxious they were to crack some heads. As I wandered from group to group, those who were saying anything seemed obsessed with getting a "Commie" or "Hippies" and what they would do to them. I am sure that there were many policemen who did not feel this way, but they were not talking or protesting what their fellow officers were saying. What I am trying to say is that there was almost a circus air about the hoped-for opportunities to show the protesters what they thought of them.

Important in assessing the police mood, however, is the fact that they had again received intelligence reports indicating that the crowd was armed with sharpened spears and at least one shotgun, and that people had strung piano wire at neck height to hinder the advancing officers.

Three members of the crowd carried the wooden cross from the vigil site to a point about six feet from the police line, next to the re-established barricade, and planted it there. Several youths volunteered to guard it.

Police sent a squad car across the grass between them and the crowd, and told people to leave. The crowd responded by stoning the car. When another car drove toward the crowd, it, too, was stoned. An Assistant U.S. Attorney was walking among those doing the stone throwing. He said none were Yippies or hippies. "All appeared to be in their late teens, but had relatively short hair and wore clothes similar to that any other teenager might wear."

The attorney said that this group tossed 40 to 50 missiles at policemen in the skirmish lines. Police responded with a blast of tear gas at the cross, and the youth guarding it fled to the main group. The crowd, now numbering 300 to 500 persons, began singing "America The Beautiful."

Three or four times, the police announced that the park was closed, but the people refused to leave. Task Force officers lobbed several canisters of tear gas, one of which exploded near the foot of a minister. The police lines moved at a walk, accompanied by more bursts of tear gas in large white billows from the sanitation truck nozzle. The truck was pelted with rocks, bricks and bottles.

A Task Force officer was riding the running board relaying messages from the driver to those operating the nozzle. When he was struck in the left leg by a hard object, he opened the door of the vehicle slightly and stepped part way in.

A barrage of rocks and bricks hit the door. A rock smashed the vent window of the truck. Still another rock, or brick, flew into the cab, ricocheting about and finally striking the officer's helmet. When the officer saw that the helmet had been cracked, he climbed completely inside the vehicle and slammed the door. Another Task Force officer was hit with a brick in the chest, as he advanced with the first police line. It knocked the wind out of him.

Demonstrator Violence

One policeman said he saw people throwing sharpened stakes taken from the snow fence, and a cork ball with nails driven into it. Later, police found a knife, an ice pick, a cork ball with nails driven into it and six or seven "pungi sticks"—sticks planted in the ground with sharpened edges turned upward—near the barricade. No officers, however, had been injured by any of these items.

As the crowd retreated, one group carried the cross, and, walking backward, thrust it between themselves and the oncoming police. The fire truck lights revealed a police officer dragging a man by the hair along the ground, all the while hitting him about the head and shoulders with a baton. The officer then kicked the man in the head. The crowd responded by calling police: "Fascist pigs." Several persons tore branches from a tree, as if to use them as clubs. No such clubs were seen in use, however.

As the police lines advanced, a wave of gas blew back toward them, forcing a detour to the north, toward the South Pond. The crowd would run a short distance, then stop. The police kept advancing, and shot more tear gas. The crowd poured into the Eugenie and Old Town Triangles, angry and hostile, and throwing anything they could lay their hands on.

At the Eugenie Triangle, two squad cars were trapped and the windows of both were shattered. Two Assistant U.S. Attorneys witnessed the action. As the first squad car came from the north and stopped at the Triangle, someone picked up a metal waste basket and threw it against the rear window, shattering it. About 15 persons then stoned the car with bottles and rocks, breaking every window.

The police tried to avoid the missiles by lying on the seat of the car. During a momentary break in traffic, the driver sped the car down the street to safety. Seconds later, another squad car drove down from the south on Clark and, it too, was stoned. After all the windows had been broken and the car was stalled, the crowd moved alongside the car and threw stones and bottles with all their might through the shattered windows at the officers.

Suddenly, the driver's partner dashed from the car to a passageway between two buildings, where he was stoned and pinned against a wall. Then, the driver also jumped from the car and, with his gun drawn, raced to his partner's rescue. The driver did not fire any shots, but the people dispersed.

A woman who observed the incident said that she felt the people were angry and had pelted the second squad car because they believed that the first car had been trying to run them down at high speed.

When a police car entered the intersection of Lincoln and Clark, it met a barrage of bottles. The driver stopped, got out and drew his revolver. But he neither pointed the gun at the bottle throwers, nor fired it. They dropped their bottles and ran.

At about this time, a CTA bus passed the intersection, headed south on Clark. Its windows were smashed. This appears to have been the same bus that had been assaulted at 12:30 a.m. near the intersection of Lincoln and Clark. A photographer who witnessed the assault said that a group of young men, half of them wearing helmets, surrounded the bus, which had stopped, and two of them smashed in windows with their helmets. He said that those who smashed the windows were not Yippies or hippies. They were wearing white T-shirts and their hair was not long. As he attempted to photograph the attack, five or six of the men jostled him and ordered him not to take the photographs. He complied. The bus driver finally drove off and the group moved northwest on Lincoln Avenue.

Meanwhile the police lines had reached the east side of Clark Street. They had stopped several times in the park during the dispersal and, according to the deputy chief, there had been no incidents. But when the line reached Clark Street just before 1 a.m., he noticed that five or six cars, most of them with "flower-power" stickers on them, were parked in Clark Street near Lincoln and Wells in what he called a "haphazard way." He felt they were contributing substantially to the massive jam-up and had been parked there deliberately.

Although tow trucks were available, the deputy chief decided that he had to move the cars immediately. He ordered a contingent of policemen to smash the windows, release the handbrakes and push the vehicles along the curb of Clark.

Two reporters watched the window smashing from the 12th floor of the Lincoln Hotel, located immediately across the street. They believed that the police were sabotaging the vehicles deliberately. They noticed that the cars were marked with stickers supporting Senator Eugene McCarthy for president.

They say that the smashing occurred just after the crowd and a cameraman had been chased from the intersection. They also say that later on officers at the scene informed them that the damage had been done by "hippies."

As people streamed into and west of Clark Street, the sanitation truck carrying a gas sprayer crossed Stockton Drive and moved almost to Clark, directly opposite Menomonee. From there, the spraying device discharged a burst of tear gas into a crowd of people on the west side of the street.

The gas sent the people scurrying, and floated into the apartments above the street. One young man in the crowd below said the discharge "shocked the hell out of me. I didn't think I would get tear gas. I was out of the park." He ran west on Menomonee. Others running alongside stopped long enough to push a parked Volkswagen into the street to block further movement of the truck. Another segment of the crowd disapproved, however, and pushed the Volkswagen back to its parking place.

Dispersal by Gas

A stiff west wind blew another cloud of tear gas onto busy Lake Shore Drive, gassing motorists. Within minutes, some 50 cars were halted and their drivers were out on the pavement, their eyes tearing. Poet Allen Ginsberg led a group of about 100 persons into the lobby of the Lincoln Hotel, southwest corner of Lincoln and Clark, to escape the billowing gas. Several sprawled on a luggage rack, but there was no vomiting. Most left after about 20 minutes.

The district police line, which had no gas masks, followed

well behind the Task Force officers of the first skirmish line until the gas cleared. They ended up on the east side of Clark Street with their southern flank at the Lincoln Hotel. Several hundred people jammed the triangle at the intersection of Lincoln, Wells, and Clark, shouting obscenities and throwing rocks, bottles and any other missiles they could find. None of the men was hit—they were out of range—but several squad cars were badly damaged by the barrage.

The police commander, receiving orders for further dispersal, used eight to ten squads of ten men each to break up the crowd. Two squads went down Wells to the south and six or seven headed north on Lincoln Avenue, occasionally shuttling off to various side streets. They worked their way several blocks north to the corner of Lincoln and Ogden. At this point the streets intersect in a wide open area and the crowd was easily dispersed. The few remaining officers proceeded northeast through Ogden Park to Armitage and crossed Clark to the command post headquarters on North Lincoln Park West.

The police line moved toward the center of the crowd in Clark Street and split into groups, driving people north and south. During these dispersal movements, an unmarked police car carrying riot-helmeted plainclothes men was assaulted by rock-throwing youths standing on both sides of the street.

A police officer standing on the back of a police van, headed south on Clark, gave the "V" sign to people with his fingers. As he passed, however, someone in the crowd threw a brick at him. It missed.

To complete the dispersal, police lobbed several more canisters of tear gas. Officers at the Eugenie Triangle complained that press photographers and other newsmen refused to clear and that the photographers deliberately directed strobe and TV floodlights into the eyes of policemen. The officers were pelted with rocks and bottles.

Prior to the clearing, four squads, consisting of 40 men and four sergeants, had been added to the Old Town forces as a precautionary measure.

An Assistant U.S. Attorney, walking with the police in the Old Town area after they had crossed Clark, noted that many residents were hanging out of windows observing the action. Police "yelled profanities at them, taunting them to come down where the police would beat them up." The witness says the police stopped a number of people on the street, demanding identification and "verbally abused each pedestrian, and pushed one or two without hurting them."

The police then returned to Clark Street, where they stopped suspected protesters and ordered them out of the area in what the witness calls "a very abusive way." One protester was kneed in the groin by a policeman walking towards him. As the boy fell to the ground, he swore at the policeman who picked him up and threw him down again.

The Assistant U.S. Attorney also relates: "A derelict who appeared to be very intoxicated walked up to a policeman and mumbled something incoherent. The policeman pulled from his belt a tin container and sprayed its contents into the eyes of the derelict, who stumbled around and fell on his face."

At 1:12 a.m., General Dunn asked the deputy superintendent if assistance from the National Guard was needed in the 18th District. The reply was negative.

A crowd in the Old Town Triangle, near Wisconsin Street, was being moved back toward the intersection of Lincoln and Orleans when a police car came from the east on Wisconsin. As it crossed the intersection, demonstrators began pelting it with beer cans. The car immediately went into reverse, backed up for about 15 yards, then charged forward into the crowd and stopped. One of the officers got out and began hitting any demonstrators he could catch. The other chased two demonstrators towards Orleans and Ogden, drew his revolver and fired two shots in their direction as they fled. Both officers drove away.

Two police officers, near the intersection of North and Wells, eluded by a young man they were chasing, ran after another young man. They caught up with him in a vacant lot on the southwest corner of the intersection and one knocked him down with a blow to the back of the head. According to an observer, both hit the man, who did not resist. He asked them to stop. An AP photographer attempted to take a picture of the beating, and police yelled for him to stop. They propped the victim against the wall for frisking, more police arrived, and the observer was pushed into Wells Street and told to leave.

The scene had attracted a large crowd, and they began shouting "Pig, Pig!" A squad car pulled up near another car already at the intersection. As it parked, a brick went flying through the rear window and the policemen came out with pistols drawn and fired three or four times above the heads of the crowd.

The police report on this arrest indicates that vehicle number 9459 was parked at the southwest corner of North and Wells facing west on south side of North. A patrolman was clearing the lot on the southwest corner of the intersection when he saw a young man with a rock in his hand moving in the direction of the police car. He ordered him to stop and the man threw a rock at him. The patrolman was joined by another, and as they moved to arrest the young man, he turned and attempted to strike the officer with his clenched fist. A group attempted to take him from the police shouting: "Kill the pigs, burn the pigs." The patrolman drew his revolver and the crowd withdrew. He then moved south on Wells with the man while groups continued throwing rocks, bottles and sticks in his direction and at the squad car. Another police car came south on Wells at this time, its rear window broken.

Meanwhile, a group of young people came running west on Armitage dumping trash cans and setting fires in them. They stopped at the northwest corner of Armitage and Lincoln where a police car, containing only the driver, was parked across the street. They threw rocks at the car, breaking one window. The policeman drove away and the rock throwers ran from the scene. Minutes later three patrol cars arrived, and eight to 12 officers got out, brandishing revolvers and shotguns. They took off after the first target they saw, a young man wearing a motorcycle helmet, and chased him into the Augustana parking lot, where they clubbed him to the ground with batons and rifle butts, and kicked him in the groin. A sergeant arrived and ordered them to stop. They stopped the beating and arrested the victim on a charge of mob action.

Near the intersection of Lincoln Park West and Menomonee, a clergyman saw a young man leave the sidewalk and walk onto the grounds of one of the houses. A policeman caught him, dragged him out to the street, knocked him to the ground, and ordered him to start moving south on Lincoln Park West.

A police car on the northeast corner of Clark and LaSalle was stoned in the park between Clark and Stockton. The officer in the car stopped on the east side of Clark, opened the door, using it as a shield, and fired east over the top of the car. A self-acclaimed "peaceful revolutionary" witnessed this incident and also observed the stoning of at least six other squad cars. He said that in each case "the crowd was the aggressor in attacking and the police fired in an effort to prevent the cars from being demolished."

At the corner of Wells and Eugenie two more police cars were stoned by a crowd of about 150 people. One of them, moving quite fast, went out of control, ending up on the sidewalk with the driver fleeing for cover.

After midnight a witness saw a young man throw a rock at a police car, shattering the window and injuring the police sergeant inside (who, however, did not report the injury). This witness and another spectator placed the assailant under citizen's arrest until police arrived to arrest him formally on the charges of criminal damage to property, reckless conduct, and aggravated battery.

About 100 police gathered in the two-block area around the Eugenie Triangle some time after 2 a.m., Wednesday morning. They were subjected to constant, loud, and bitter taunting by the crowd. Occasionally, two or three policemen would charge small groups, grabbing one or two persons, hitting them to the ground with a few blows, and continuing to hit them while they were down. Most victims did not resist, but dropped to their knees, cradling their heads in their arms. No arrests were observed after these charges.

Cars were also stoned at LaSalle and Schiller, Clark and Division, and Lincoln and Clark. Shortly after one stoning, 12 police officers arrived in a van and two squad cars and proceeded to disperse the crowd. A policeman fired his revolver into the air, a dispersal technique prevalent from Tuesday evening through Wednesday morning.

The Theatre, near Wells and Clark, was used as a place where the young people slept and were treated for injuries. There was a medical aid station there, staffed by the Medical Committee for Human Rights.

At about 2:30 a.m., a group of 15 policemen moved north on Wells and Clark passing The Theatre. Words were exchanged and, as they passed, two of the policemen reached over the fence surrounding the courtyard and sprayed the area with mace. A clergyman who was standing in the entrance at the gate says: "There was no reason why the mace should have been sprayed into the courtyard and I cannot understand why it was done. This action—as far as I know—only resulted in some people in the area suffering from irritation of the eyes. The mace was not sprayed directly at anyone, it was sprayed without the policemen knowing who they were spraying. It was almost like spraying flies."

The Hitters and the Pitchers

At Clark and LaSalle, two officers were assaulted by a rock-throwing mob and received lacerations on their arms.

Studs Terkel roamed the area with English journalist James Cameron for several hours. When most of the action had died down, Terkel and Cameron agreed to escort a boy and two girls to their car in return for a ride home. When the five of them reached the car they were confronted by "five cold, hostile policemen." Terkel tells the following story in his statement.

One of the police officers recognized and greeted Terkel, who ignored him. The policeman remarked: "People who are here are soft in the head." "Last night," the policeman said to the young people, "we had the hitters. Tonight we have the pitchers. It was better tonight, wasn't it?" Terkel interprets this as a comparison of Monday's clubs to Tuesday's greater use of tear gas.

At about 3 a.m. Wednesday, eight college students in a third floor apartment on west Armitage heard a car pull up, then footsteps on the stairs. This was followed by pounding on their door and voices, identifying themselves as police, demanding entrance. When the door was opened five policemen, three carrying rifles, entered. The armed officers kept the occupants at gunpoint, while the other two searched the apartment. No search warrant was produced, nor, according to one of the students, were the police wearing either badges or name tags.

While the search went on, the student says, the guards threatened the group saying: "We're tired of demonstrators. In Chicago the police have guns and use them. We can smash your heads in and leave, or take you to the street and let the others finish you off."

After about 15 minutes they left, and the occupants found that a helmet, a pair of goggles, a camera and light meter and 50 dollars in cash were missing. The wallet from which the money had been taken had contained an SDS membership card, which was now lying outside the wallet. Eight rolls of undeveloped film had been exposed. One of the occupants of the apartment, which had been obtained through SDS, had visited the National Guard bivouac at Humboldt Park on Tuesday, attempting to distribute leaflets. He said the police had "purposefully rubbed dog defecation which was on the floor of the apartment" into a sleeping bag and had insulted the one girl present.

As the police emerged from the building, a clergyman saw them approach a Volkswagen sedan which had just pulled up on the south side of Armitage, across the street from his church. The police thrust their guns into the car and ordered the occupants out. The minister recognized them—four young people in their twenties, wearing normal dress. The police officers searched the car, took a letter from the glove compartment, and then ordered them to get back in and move on.

The damage to police vehicles, private property and CTA buses was extensive, but the crowd itself was much smaller than on either Sunday night or Monday night (which was the peak as far as numbers were concerned).

Local youths smashed a liquor store window on North Avenue and stole bottles of liquor. A gang, called "The Ventures," from around Augusta and Wood Streets, broke the window of a Dodge automobile agency at 1640 North LaSalle. Members of the same gang were seen with a shotgun. A clergyman asserts that local youths congregating in the area along the west side of Clark Street had participated in the stoning of the police car at Stockton Drive while the park was being cleared.

Police arrest records show ten persons arrested during the night in the area west of Clark Street. Most were charged with disorderly conduct, a few with mob action and aggravated assault.

Ninety-three arrests were made in the 18th District. Seven police officers were injured. Nine vehicles were damaged. Thus ended Tuesday in Lincoln Park.

Flurry in Grant Park

Tuesday morning passed in relative quiet in the Grant Park area, but after noon on Tuesday a flurry of minor incidents erupted. At 1:50 p.m. after a mule train with 75 marchers from the Poor People's Campaign appeared and circled the hotel in an orderly fashion some 300 demonstrators tried to cross Michigan Avenue from Grant Park but were turned back by police without any difficulty. Five minutes later, an estimated 200 marchers led by Staughton Lynd stepped off from the Hilton en route to the Amphitheatre. Shortly after that, the mule train departed, headed north on Wabash Avenue, and an unreported number of demonstrators remained behind in Grant Park. During this time a group of blacks on the sidewalk in front of the Hilton were addressed by Hosea Williams of the SCLC and by a young boy in African attire.

According to a police lieutenant who was there as an observer, persons in the crowd "shouted obscenities at police such as 'mother fucking pig.' Several times demonstrators shouted these obscenities directly in the faces of police officers." The lieutenant also recalls that one speaker, introduced as a delegate from Colorado, stated: "We do not have to put up with these fascist pigs." He further stated: "Four other individuals introduced as delegates used equally strong language. Any time such language was used, the crowd reacted by throwing some rocks, bottles and cherry bombs at the police."

Another witness relates that on Tuesday afternoon, someone started to give a speech to the crowd in the park across from the Hilton and several policemen grouped together and walked into the crowd. He stated that the police suddenly began swinging their clubs and hitting people, and that when he started to leave with a girl, a policeman told him to move. He says he replied "Yes, sir" and began to move but was shoved with a baton by another policeman who was wearing neither a nameplate or badge. He says the police were yelling things like "beat the fuckers."

Several orderly demonstrations took place during the afternoon in and about the Hilton, most of them in support of, or in opposition to, the various candidates. One in the lobby consisted of "a group of 'Yippie-type' individuals . . . jumping up and down, rapping a tambourine and chanting anti-Vietnam slogans." But at least four arrests were made that afternoon and evening. At midnight Chicago police arrested a man at the Hilton for soliciting funds for Eugene McCarthy. At 2:30 p.m. near the hotel, Chicago police seized a postal worker carrying a can of mace in a paper bag. At 6:30 p.m., Secret Service agents picked up a former mental patient who was creating a disturbance in the Lester Maddox campaign suite. Also, a man known by the Secret Service for attempts to approach prominent political figures was arrested on an upper floor of the Hilton for stealing a suitcase and for not carrying a draft card.

There was evidence of attempted arson in the Hilton that afternoon. A witness says that he saw a "clean-cut looking youth with a beard" try to set fire to a stack of campaign literature at the top of a lobby stairwell. A pile of papers was found there and under it a book of matches into which apparently had been inserted a flaming match or lighted cigarette, which burned itself out before igniting the pack. Despite a search, the arsonist was not found. A mock "plastique" bomb was also discovered in the hotel.

March from Lincoln to Grant

In early evening, the Grant Park protesters were joined by two major groups—one moving down from Lincoln Park to the north and another coming from the "unbirthday party" held at the Coliseum to the south. Along the way the marchers picked up other supporters, including a married couple on the way to their car after dining in a Loop restaurant. Later the husband served as a "crowd marshal."

"The march was orderly," he recalls. "The mood was gay, demonstrators continually giving the V-sign and calling on all spectators to come along. At the corner of Jackson, police buses arrived. The policemen who disembarked forced the marchers toward the building on the west side of Michigan, allowing them less room to march. The atmosphere became very tense. Policemen standing with their billy clubs in front of them caused delays at street corners that hadn't been experienced before. The march proceeded in this fashion to the Hilton, where the marchers passed in front of the TV cameras. The V-signs were given. There was laughing, and at this moment tension seemed to disappear."

After passing the Hilton, the march just seemed to break up and most of the participants headed into Grant Park. As the night wore on, they were joined by more demonstrators. By 10:47 p.m. the Secret Service reported from 1,000 to 1,500 demonstrators congregated across from the Hilton in the park.

As the demonstrators poured in, there were some policemen in the park but there were no established police lines. Blue police sawhorses lined both sides of Michigan Avenue.

The police themselves were concentrated on the west side of Michigan in front of the hotel and knots of officers guarded the various hotel entrances.

Initially there was free passage between the park and the hotel and occasionally small groups went back and forth. There were older people in suits, ties and convention badges and clean-cut young workers for Senator Eugene McCarthy scattered among the roughly dressed, long-haired youths. Some gathered around small bonfires in the park, and the smell of burning paper drifted into the police line. Most of the crowd faced the Hilton and the blue-helmeted police in front of it; some shouted: "Hell, no! We won't go!" "Join us! Join us!" "Fuck you, Mayor Daley!" and "Fuck you, L.B.J.!" The shouts were amplified by a portable public address system.

As the various credentials fights underway at the Amphitheatre were lost by the challengers, the mood of the Grant Park crowd gradually changed. Transistor radios and reports from delegates kept the demonstrators continually apprised of the results of convention activities. As the crowd grew and its mood seemed to harden, the scattered police withdrew from the park and police lines were set up on the east side of Michigan Avenue as well as in front of the hotel.

At this point, the crowd became unruly and began to throw missiles at the police. The police, according to one witness, were bombarded by Pepsi Cola cans filled with urine, beer cans filled with sand, ping pong balls with nails driven through them and pieces of ceramic tile. He also says he saw glass ash trays and plastic bags filled with urine thrown from hotel windows.

At 11:28 p.m. three platoons of additional police, about 147 men, arrived in front of the hotel and marched into line, two abreast.

Also, on Tuesday evening, someone poured a container of foul-smelling liquid onto the Hilton's lobby rug. All through the week, stink bombs had been set off in the Hilton and the neighboring Sheraton-Blackstone, and the air in these hotels was described as smelling "stronger than vomit." It is also reported that butyric acid, a colorless and somewhat harmless acid with an odor of rotten eggs and garbage, was poured on the rugs and furniture in the hotel lobbies.

All this while, a rally was underway at the Coliseum at 15th and Wabash, a block west of Michigan, under the auspices of several pacifist groups.

The rally was organized as an "un-birthday party" to mock President Johnson's 60th birthday. William Chayes, a Chicagoan who said he was approached by Rennie Davis to help promote the rally, recalls that the police, fire inspectors and Coliseum management all were "cooperative" in their relations with the meeting's organizers, "although the Fire Department did inspect the premises four times on Tuesday." Among the scheduled attractions for the evening was an appearance of Pigasus, the pig publicized as the Yippie candidate for president.

In the cavernous building, an estimated 3,000 persons listened to such folk-rock music groups as the "Home Juice" and the "Popular Worm" and to Phil Ochs, Dick Gregory, Allen Ginsberg and Ed Sanders of "The Fugs."

There were also speeches. Dick Gregory drew repeated cheers for sarcastic remarks about Mayor Daley. "If there had been a bunch of young people who challenged Hitler the way you challenged Mayor Daley," he was quoted as shouting to the crowd, "there might be a whole lot of Jews alive today. Now the world knows what kind of city we have here."

"What you're trying to do to this system is worth getting knocked for and stomped on for," he continued. "What you're doing to this system is something we old fools should have been doing years ago. I hope you don't turn around. I hope the more tear gas they pour on you, the more determined you are to break this damn system."

Condemnations of Chicago police were also delivered by authors Jean Genet, William Burroughs and Terry Southern and by poet Allen Ginsberg. David Dellinger announced that probably an attempt would be made to march to the Amphitheatre Wednesday after a rally in Grant Park.

As speeches and singing progressed, the pitch of enthusiasm rose. One observer describes the assembly as "like a revival meeting," and at the line "We ain't gwine to study war no more," it seemed to reach a pitch of enthusiasm and commitment. He said this point was like a "Decision for Christ" commitment.

At about 11 p.m., a singing act was in progress, although the rally had been scheduled to end then. "In the midst of the entertainment," recalls William Chayes, "Sidney Peck asked the crowd to join ranks with those gathering in front of the Hilton. He said their numbers were required." One observer says Peck told the crowd, "They're beating kids in front of the Hilton."

At ten minutes before midnight, about 2,000 persons left the Coliseum, headed toward the hotel seven blocks north. At the same time, more demonstrators left Lincoln Park as it was swept by police and headed for Grant Park. En route to Grant Park, some of them set fire to trash baskets and threw them into streets and through store windows, hurled stones, rocks and bottles through the broken windows of squad cars and stoned police officers.

At midnight there were two police lines, one three deep on the east side of Michigan, facing the park and the other, a single line, on the west side of Michigan. One witness reports that some police were rough and rude and others were courteous. At 12:21 a.m. Wednesday, the Chicago police estimated that 3,000 persons across from the Hilton confronted the police lines. Among the crowd were Tom Hayden and Rennie Davis. The Secret Service radio log also reports that "Ron Karenga of the Black Panthers was present." (Karenga, who is not a Black Panther, was actually in Philadelphia at the time.)

Tension between the police and the crowd mounted as the demonstrators poured in from the Coliseum and Lincoln Park. A reporter walking with a group from the Coliseum recalls a young Negro perched in a tree overlooking the police line. "Beware, beware!" he shouted. "The pigs are on your left. The pigs are on your right." Then to the police: "Paul Revere was a Negro!"

The cry of "Pig! . . . Pig! . . . Pig!" was almost incessant. One demonstrator shouted to the police, "We're fucking your wives and daughters while you guys are protecting your city."

On this night the first reports appear of feces being thrown at the police. A Utah newspaperman describes "paper bags containing feces" and "cans of urine" being thrown into police ranks from the windows of the Hilton.

The crowd included demonstrators with motorcycle helmets and military helmet liners. Some—perhaps "refugees" from Lincoln Park—had smeared their faces with unguents as protection against police spray irritants.

A VISTA worker who had attended the "un-birthday party" and then had walked along to Grant Park says that by the time he arrived, marshals drawn from the ranks of the demonstrators "were on their knees with arms locked facing the cops." There was a line of police on each side of the street for the entire block, their batons out. Draft cards were being burned and some people were hanging from trees. Those in the park, behind the marshals, were yelling at delegates' buses (which were starting to return from the Amphitheatre) and to police, such things as "Peace now! . . . Hell, no! We won't go! . . . Pigs! . . . Fascist Pigs!"

When a police commander, a city legal official and a U.S. government official went into the crowd in an attempt to talk to Davis and other leaders, they state they were surrounded by "hippie types" who kept yelling obscenities at them. According to one official they screamed in his face, "Your wife sucks cock." The officials were not able to talk with anyone, and returned to the street.

The demonstrators then began sitting down in the park, and at 1:19 a.m. the police moved toward the crowd. A city legal aide states that at this time, the crowd was "rowdy, missiles were flying, obscenities and filthy taunts were being hurled at police. A policeman had human excrement thrown at him by a girl. Some police were kicked by members of the crowd."

The police command by this time was indecisive as to how to handle the crowd. At 12.39 a.m., a platoon was moved from the east side of Michigan to the west side, leaving the east side unguarded. At 12:56 a.m. two squads from another platoon crossed from the west side to the east side to keep people from spilling over into the street from the park. At 1:11 a.m., it was announced that all police units would remain on the west side of Michigan.

Finally, at 1:35 a.m., the deputy superintendent of police advised the demonstrators by bullhorn they could stay in the park overnight "as long as they remained . . . on the east side of Michigan Avenue and were peaceful." The crowd responded with a lusty "Yip, yip, hooray!"

By 2 a.m., police messages describe the crowd as "orderly." Estimates of its size had varied all night, but there were certainly several thousand (the highest estimate was 5,000). Some members of the crowd, standing on the shoulders of others, continued to burn what they claimed were draft cards, with cheers from the crowd for every flame. Others, wearing GI jackets with division shoulder patches and other castoff military clothes, lofted and waved handmade banners and signs urging "End the war now." Here and there clergymen were conducting religious services on the grass. All the while, motor traffic moved at sightseeing pace along the street between the Hilton and Grant Park. At 2 a.m. two busloads of police arrived at the Hilton to reinforce the police line which was once again on the side of Michigan Avenue.

The 700 policemen stationed at the Hilton were by now exhausted. They had been assigned 12-hour shifts since Saturday (and in some cases even earlier) and, according to the log, they had been on duty the last 15 hours. Official reports indicate that some officers had worked 17 hours.

"It was clear that the Chicago police had 'had it,'" says a *Washington Post* reporter. "Up to this point they have been fairly calm but now they were showing visible signs of the strain they had been under. The kids knew this full well, and they knew they had made them 'lose their cool.'"

In an effort to ease the tension, two of the folk singing trio of Peter, Paul and Mary appeared at a speaker's stand that had been set up by the demonstrators. Peter Yarrow, sporting a droopy mustache and wire-rimmed glasses, took the microphone. "Please be calm, everyone," he urged. Then, with Mary Traverse, a blond with long, straight hair, he began to sing. The crowd joined in with "Blowin' in the Wind," "If I had a Hammer," "This Land is My Land,"—an incongruous choir of protesters and onlookers, standing in the glare of TV lights and police lamps against a backdrop of the dark park.

Finally, the police sought relief by the National Guard. The formal request was received by the Guard at 2:10 a.m. and, for the first time during the convention week, National Guard troops went into action. The 33rd Military Police Battalion was issued guns, ammunition and gas in preparation for hitting the street. At about 3 a.m., 30 Guard vehicles carrying 600 men in full battle dress rumbled out of the Chicago Avenue armory and went south on Michigan.

No announcement had been made to the demonstrators that the Guard was coming, and when the convoy suddenly appeared through the mist and rolled to a stop in front of the Hilton, tension in the crowd reached its peak. "You see, you see!" one demonstrator screamed. "They did it—not us! It was peaceful until they came!" The Guard stirred uneasiness in the crowd, in the opinion of one observer, because they were an "unknown quantity." No one explained that the Guard was there to relieve the tired police.

"The police seemed happy and relieved to see us," says an assistant squad leader. "The demonstrators were shouting:

'Pigs, pigs, fascist pigs!' As I climbed out of my jeep, a jagged rock was thrown from the direction of the park. It was about five inches in diameter and just barely missed me. I also saw some bottles thrown." In the confusion, he heard someone—"It sounded like Peter, Paul and Mary"—singing "If I Had a Hammer."

Holding M-1 rifles, carbines, and shotguns, and carrying gas masks on their belts, the Guardsmen disembarked and moved into the broad boulevard. They stood in the street while police dropped back, formed into squads and marched away to the demonstrators' cadenced chant, "Oink, oink, oink." Then the Guardsmen fell into a skirmish line on the east side of Michigan, shoulder to shoulder. At ease, they stood facing the crowd, guns pointed skyward, butts on hips. The Guard arrived with fixed bayonets, but these were ordered removed a half-hour later. Two Guard companies took up positions on the east side of Michigan, while a third was held in reserve.

"We had to move the demonstrators back toward the park to establish the skirmish line," the assistant squad leader recalls. "They were jeering and swearing. Things like 'Pigs . . . sons-a-bitches . . . fucking pigs . . . fucking son-of-a-bitching pigs . . .' "

The Guard commander, Brigadier General Dunn, reached the scene in a jeep fitted for combat. It was covered with mesh wire as a shield against flying objects and fronted with a large square frame of barbed wire designed to move crowds. This type of vehicle is so new the Guardsmen did not even have a name for it yet. When the general was informed that some Guardsmen had ammunition magazines in their guns, he passed the word that weapons definitely were not to be loaded and that magazines were to be removed.

The General announced to his men through a bullhorn that they should not interfere with demonstrators "unless they become violent." He then climbed onto the hood of a jeep and tried to address the noisy throng. When he held his hand outward and upward for silence, the response was immediate: "Sieg-HEIL! Sieg-HEIL! Sieg-HEIL!"

The demonstrators turned up their own sound system "full blast" and began singing "This Land is Your Land, This is My Land. . . ." Eventually they asked the General to repeat his message into their microphone, which he did, but only after another attempt by the crowd to drown him out by singing.

At about this time, the police official in command (a deputy superintendent of police) was interviewed by television reporters about the decision not to clear the park of protesters. He stated that it was his own decision and a matter of judgment. He said that the demonstrators were not attempting to sleep as they had been in Lincoln Park and the situation, therefore, was different. Furthermore, he interpreted a previous federal court order denying the demonstrators' petition for a permit to stay in Lincoln Park as not applying to Grant Park. He said it remained to be seen whether they would be allowed to remain in the park all night since they were "technically disturbing the peace." He added that no citizens had complained and said that he thought it would be foolish to remove the protesters since there was no way to effectively communicate the order and because women and children were present. Sometimes, he explained, it is better to ignore a technical law violation than to create a major problem.

During the interview, the deputy superintendent showed a practice golf ball with nails driven into it and said that several had been hurled at police that night.

Meanwhile, a frail-looking line of girls, arms linked, quickly formed in front of the soldiers. Each girl began talking softly to the Guardsman in front of her, urging him to take a stand against the war in Vietnam.

Not all scenes were as poignant, however. A reporter says that "a young Negro Guard lieutenant was approached by a group of kids. They began to taunt him mercilessly by making him appear to be a 'tool' of the 'bad guys.' "

"There was a man walking up and back in front of our line whom I will never forget," says the assistant squad leader. "He wore black slacks, a white shirt and had long, greasy blond hair and a pock-marked face. Walking by the line, he would spit at us, flick cigarette ashes and lighted cigarettes at us. He would pick out the Jewish boys from their nameplates and make anti-Semitic remarks to them. He called me a kike. I turned to a Polish boy standing next to me and asked him who the guy reminded him of. He answered, 'A Nazi storm trooper.' But there was no reaction from the men as far as I could see."

Another Guardsman who was on duty, however, stated that during the tour he saw one of his fellow Guardsmen "threaten a pedestrian" at Michigan and Balbo, telling him "Get your ass out of here or you'll get your head busted." On another occasion, the Guardsman said, several of his fellows "stomped" on two "hippies" who had been fighting in an alley near the intersection.

To the speaker's stand now came a series of antiwar orators. One, introduced (according to the assistant squad leader) as "Mr. Love," referred to the President as "that fucking son-of-a-bitch Johnson"—to the crowd's applause. A priest followed him to the platform, the assistant squad leader says, and continued to denounce the war. "The priest then addressed himself to the delegates in the hotel," the witness remembers. "He told them if they agreed with him, they should flick the lights in their rooms. The lights in about ten or 20 rooms flicked off and on."

The Guard apparently stood its ground without any significant response—physical or verbal—to the demonstrators, despite a level of abuse that one Guard official calls "unbelievable."

As the misty night pushed on toward dawn, the crowd gradually quieted and groups began slowly drifting away. At about 4:30 a.m., Tom Hayden grabbed the microphone briefly and explained that he had "gone underground, to get the pig off my back. Now that the pig is on the collective back of all of us, we are going to find a way to go underground."

He turned for a moment and shouted up at the Hilton. "Invite us in the morning into your rooms, or more particularly your bathrooms, so we can clean up." "Get some sleep," Hayden told the crowd. "If you go somewhere, go in groups." Then he was gone.

By 4:55 a.m., the demonstrators had declined to 200, according to Secret Service estimates, and by 5:42 a.m., to 150. Guardsmen were permitted to leave the line for snacks in an all-night coffee shop. Those demonstrators who stayed on through the chilly predawn hours stripped green twigs and branches from the trees and built small camp fires and bedded down in damp grass or on newspapers. They remained orderly and before daylight, half the National Guard troops were sent away.

WEDNESDAY—THE CULMINATION OF VIOLENCE

Dawn broke over Grant Park Wednesday through a thin mist and ground fog, thickened by smoke from the sputtering fires. Many of the "campers" dozed in sleeping bags or huddled in blankets, some of which had been supplied by sympathetic guests at the Hilton. Here and there small knots of people sat on the grass talking, playing guitars or reading. Some were in trees. As the demonstrators awoke, they washed in the park's fountains, some showering under the water cascading from one level of a fountain to another.

Along Michigan Avenue, the assistant Guard squad leader remembers three boys in "hippie clothes" and a "pretty girl, well-kempt and clean looking" were giving the V-sign to passengers in buses stopped for traffic lights and asking them to return the sign. "When it wasn't returned," the witness says, "the boys would swear at the people and call them 'fucking ass-holes' and 'mother fuckers.' "

A girl who had been among demonstrators in Lincoln Park Tuesday night claims that early Wednesday outside the Hilton a policeman assaulted her "with no provocation." In an account substantiated by a friend who was with her, the girl said the officer walked up to them, called her a "bitch" and struck her in the mouth with his fist.

Morning Clean-Up and Afternoon Speeches

At about 9:30 a.m., so that city work crews could clean the area, about 20 policemen carrying nightsticks entered the park and told everyone there to clear out. "Aside from jeers of 'pigs . . . fascist pigs,' there was no trouble," the Guardsman recalls. "Most people obeyed and the nightsticks were never used." One college student who was present says some of the demonstrators joined in the clean-up, and that street department employees furnished sticks with nails in the end so that the volunteers could pick up papers. These sticks were later identified by some witnesses as part of the weaponry in the hands of the protesters.

At 9:45 a.m., with the sun shining pleasantly, police replaced the Guard on duty in front of the Hilton. Later, at about 1 p.m., a National Guard command post was set up on the roof of the Field Museum, south of Grant Park on the lakefront and overlooking the bandshell area. The 2nd Battalion of the 129th Infantry took up positions in back of the museum on the west side and the 2nd Battalion of the 127th Artillery assembled on the east side of the museum. It has been charged that the Guard units in the Grant Park area "whitened" from Tuesday to Wednesday, meaning that Negro Guardsmen were no longer present. This in fact happened, but there is no evidence that it was done by conscious design. The 33rd MP (on duty Tuesday night) has a number of Negro Guardsmen, while the 2/129th and 2/122nd are essentially white.

In the early afternoon the crowd numbered about 700 persons, the speeches continued. Bobby Seale of the Black Panthers demanded, among other things, the freeing of Huey Newton and the painting of the White House black. He exhorted his listeners to "burn the city" . . . "tear it down." He counseled: "We can lead them on a merry-go-round like you have."

At about 1:30 p.m., a young man using his omnipresent, battery-powered speaker (another carried the sound equipment on his head) began urging the demonstrators to move over to the bandshell in the far southeast corner of the park area, about two blocks due east of the south edge of the Hilton, but separated from the hotel by Michigan Avenue, the railroad cut and Columbus Drive. Some who followed his pleas were equipped with helmets and gas masks. Some sticks, on which signs could be mounted, were also in evidence. Many "revolution" posters were visible in the crowd moving off toward the bandshell.

On the previous night, a permit had been granted by the Chicago Park District to the National Mobilization Committee to hold a rally in the bandshell from 1 to 4 p.m. The bandshell is an old structure, painted light blue, located in the park between Columbus Drive and Lake Shore Drive at a point where 11th Street would be if it entered the park. The site of Chicago's outdoor summer concerts, it is furnished with movable park benches.

The Crowd

By 2:15 p.m. the Secret Service estimated 1,000 persons were in the bandshell area, but before the afternoon was over, the crowd had swelled to an estimated 8,000 to 10,000. The makeup of the crowd was mixed: there were a lot of hippies, but there were also some conventionally dressed persons, young and old, and even some infants. A law student states that he saw "about 100 people scattered throughout the crowd" armed with such weapons as sticks with nails, knives and bags of human waste. Other witnesses saw small pieces of floor tile being handed out "as weapons" and rocks and bottles were in evidence.

Some of the persons present, however, can only be described as curious onlookers. Among them, for example, was a woman who lives in a luxurious lakefront high-rise apartment building and who, after lunching at a downtown hotel with several delegates' wives, led the ladies to the bandshell on the hunch that "it might be interesting to listen to hippie speeches." A number of "Viet Veterans for Peace" hats could be seen in the crowd.

There was another element in the crowd, as well. A witness recalls seeing two "clean-cut looking" men with guns sticking out from under their coats. He took them to be "poorly disguised" police undercover men. A Chicago attorney says he saw "roving bands of plainclothes policemen 'disguised' as hippies. . . . They fooled nobody. . . . They seemed to think that if they put on dark glasses, did not shave that morning, and wore a sport shirt and jacket they would be one of the crowd. What concerned me was their manner of traveling in a pack and constantly barging through groups of protesters,

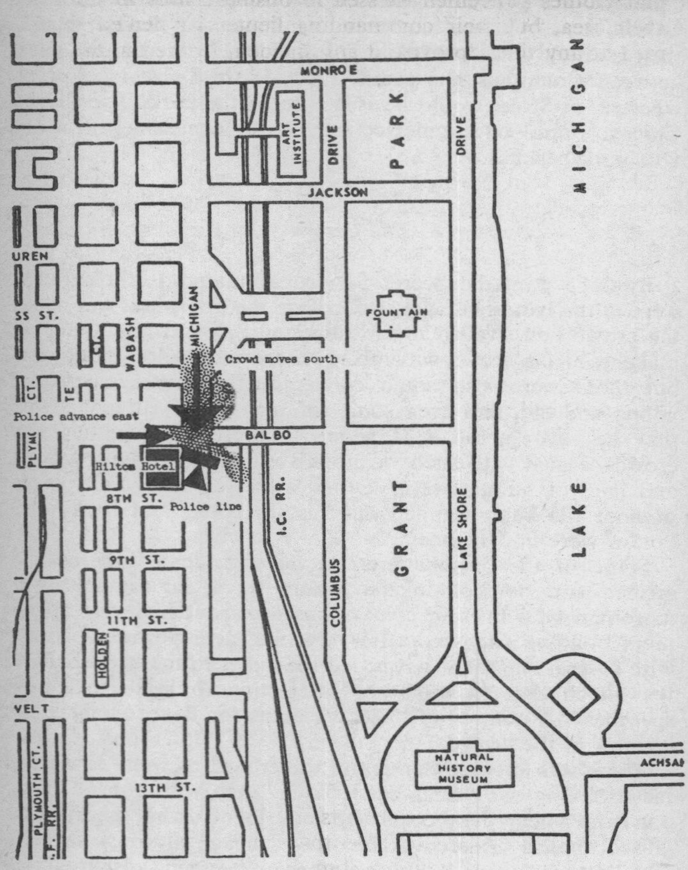
MONROE
ART INSTITUTE
DRIVE
PARK
DRIVE
MICHIGAN
JACKSON
UREN
SS ST.
WABASH
MICHIGAN
FOUNTAIN
Crowd moves south
CT.
TE
Police advance east
BALBO
PLYMO
Hiltom Hotel
8TH ST.
Police line
I.C. RR.
GRANT
LAKE SHORE
LAKE
9TH ST.
COLUMBUS
11TH ST.
HOLDEN
VELT
NATURAL HISTORY MUSEUM
ACHSA
PLYMOUTH CT.
13TH ST.

bumping into them, making cracks and achieving, if nothing else, the escalation of tempers and hostility."

Intelligence reports indicate that there were at least ten plainclothes policemen dressed in business suits in the bandshell area, but their commanding lieutenant denied that his men at any time "provoked any incident." One of the undercover agents said he arrived at the bandshell about 1 p.m. and joined the parade marshal training. He said black armbands were passed out signifying marshals and the unsanctioned march to be held after the rally was discussed. He said Tom Berman, Tom Newman, Eric Weinberg and Rennie Davis, among others, were present at these training sessions.

Two witnesses who had come to the rally from Lincoln Park with a group of about 200 "young, Yippie-type" demonstrators recall that "a lot of literature was passed out among the crowd, urging all varieties of action from passive resistance to violent overthrow." Jutting from the crowd were standards being Viet Cong and red and black flags and protest signs. A Viet Cong flag hung from the loud-speaker stand west of the bandshell.

The Police

Meanwhile, the police set up lines along the west side of Lake Shore Drive, which flanks the east edge of the park; the west (and occasionally the east) side of Columbus Drive, a north-south thoroughfare which divides the park and runs west of the bandshell area; and the north side of the park's southern boundary, Roosevelt Drive. In effect, this boxed the rally in on three sides, while still allowing access to the bandshell area from the north. Reserve groups of police, numbering in total about 100 men, were assembled among a few small, scattered trees north and west behind the bandshell, out of sight to most of the crowd.

A young law student reports that as he and a friend passed near the officers en route to the bandshell, "We were jeered by large groups of police." Some persons, anticipating trouble, brought along wet face cloths in case of tear gas.

More than a dozen police officers kept busy handing out thousands of flyers informing the demonstrators, who sat on the bandshell's open-air benches or on the grass, that the rally was legal and would be "protected" because of the permit. A witness states that many of the officers were Negroes and that they joshed good naturedly with the demonstrators. A minister attending the rally as a medical aide says he thought "the police were working hard to communicate with the crowd."

However, the flyers, which were signed by Chicago's Police Superintendent, warned that no rally would be permitted near the Amphitheatre and that no march or parade outside the park had been sanctioned. "Each and every participant" in any march, the flyers warned, would be arrested. "We earnestly request your cooperation so that rights of dissent and protest will be properly safeguarded as well as the rights of all others including those delegates at the Democratic National Convention," the notice said.

The Speeches

There is no question that the leaders wanted and urged a march on the Amphitheatre, and many persons in the crowd were similarly determined. A Lutheran theology student, who arrived near the start of the rally to observe it for the American Friends Service Committee, recalls overhearing a group of demonstrators discussing a march on the Amphitheatre. "They said they expected violence but were determined to march anyway. They were talking about the fact that medics would be on hand. I also heard [demonstrator] marshals in different areas planning the oncoming march." A march was also endorsed—"whether it is legal or not"—by the rally's various speakers.

Among others appearing during the afternoon were Dick Gregory, William Burroughs ("You are doing something workable about an unworkable system"), Norman Mailer and Vietnam veterans who told of killing civilians and described cooperation of the Vietnamese with the Viet Cong. One young black speaker, a member of the Boston draft resisters group and wearing a red college sweatshirt, burned what he alleged was his draft delinquency notice. To facilitate the rally, says Dellinger's son, David, who was acting as his bodyguard, the park district provided a technician to operate the shell's sound equipment and police stood guard at the rear of the shell to keep unauthorized persons off the stage.

Announcements were made that peanut butter and jelly sandwiches were available and that "Peace" buttons were on sale down front. Ice cream vendors did a brisk business, and occasionally members of the audience with transistor radios would shout out reports on the convention's debate of the Vietnam peace plank. Someone on stage issued a plea for anyone knowing the whereabouts of a teenage girl missing since Monday to contact one of the demonstration marshals. Pigasus, the pig candidate for president, also "spoke"—he was held to the microphone and emitted a stirring "Oink."

Like the rally at the Coliseum, this one featured musical entertainment in addition to the usual antiwar litany. Phil Ochs sang one of the anthems of the war protest movement:

"Call it peace or call it treason,
"Call it love or call it reason,
But I ain't a-marchin' anymore. . . ."

But, on the whole, witnesses agreed, the assembly did not throb with the same fervor as the Coliseum "unbirthday party" of the night before. The matron mentioned earlier insists that there were no speeches of a violent nature and says that the most derogatory remarks consisted of calling the police "pigs."

One witness (a pacifist and a member of CADRE, a group of Chicago draft resisters) recalls that a stubble-faced man in a bright coat and cape repeatedly "interrupted the speeches and called out various phrases, causing confusion." One of the speakers recognized and identified him as a West Side Chicago policeman who, on other occasions, had "tried to appear at meetings as a super-radical." Most of the Grant Park group, the witness said, ignored him.

The crowd was so vast (about 10,000 by this time) that rarely was there a central focus of events. Some people ignored the stage completely to nap or read newspapers. Others huddled in groups, talking among themselves or chanting "Ho, Ho, Ho Chi Minh." Some led small parades or waved the many red, black and Viet Cong flags in the audience. Some on the edge of the crowd are reported by one student witness to have spent their time baiting and spitting upon three young men who appeared costumed as "The Spirit of 1776" to protest the protesters.

Through all this, it appears, the uniformed police remained outside the bandshell area. They gathered in units of strength around the park perimeter; police vans and squad cars lined park roadways; one and possibly two helicopters criss-crossed above the crowd and National Guard troops were clearly visible on the roof of museum buildings at the south end of the park near the Soldier Field post and were stationed, with tear gas, along Roosevelt Drive. Some demonstrators who wandered over to the museums during the rally chanted for the Guardsmen to "Jump, jump!" Others booed the men. The Guardsmen, it was reported, just smiled.

The Flag Lowering

Then at about 3:30 or 4 p.m., the first violence erupted near the bandshell. Because of the enormous size of the crowd and the great confusion that followed, it is difficult now to reconstruct a precise chronology of what happened, but the evidence suggests the following sequence of events.

While a speech opposing the draft was being given, a young man wearing an army helmet shinnied up the base of a slim flagpole to the left of the bandshell stage, climbed onto the pole's braces, from which he could reach the halyard, and began to lower the American flag. A police sergeant says the crowd hollered, "Tear down the flag!" But a young postal worker, in the park as an onlooker and sitting near the pole, says, "People started to yell to lower it to half-mast."

Another witness says that several persons on the bandshell stage shouted to the youth to leave the flag alone, and that one left the stage to tell him personally to get down.

According to a police lieutenant, Dellinger took the microphone and announced to the pole climber that the flag should not be taken down but should be flown at half-mast in honor of the "wounded, loyal demonstrators." Other witnesses say the crowd wanted the boy to leave the flag at half-mast as a symbol that democracy at the Democratic convention was dead.

While the youth was still on the pole, recalls the postal employee, "a white-shirted police officer [on the Chicago force, white shirts denote lieutenants and above] came through the crowd and tried to grab the demonstrator who had climbed the pole." According to one witness, the youth tied the flag at half-mast and began to climb down; he was grabbed by the white-shirted officer and two blue-shirted officers. Two plainclothes men then came up to help. A police lieutenant present at the rally states that the youth was not mistreated "in any manner, shape or form" and that no excessive force was used in making the arrest. But another witness asserts, "They began clubbing the hippie with their nightsticks all over his body. . . ."

A roar of protest rose from the audience: "Pigs! . . . Pigs!" The police sergeant quoted earlier heard the shout, "Kill the pigs!" A marshal at the rally states that while the arrest was being made, another young demonstrator attempted to incite the crowd with "Look at what they are doing to your brother; are you going to let those lousy pigs do that to your brother?"

People in the crowd began throwing things at the retreating police. A demonstration marshal claims that the crowd threw "balloons, paper and flowers at the police." Other witnesses remember it differently. One states: "They were tossing anything they could lay their hands on—heavy chunks of concrete, sticks, cans, bags of what looked like paint." The sergeant recalls, "I was hit in the stomach with a large brick and also on the ankle and back of the head with thrown objects. I suffered a large bruise on my right side from a thrown brick." The lieutenant quoted above was struck by a brick on his leg and a chunk of concrete, ripping his trousers and inflicting a painful injury that caused him to limp for three days. Among the objects he saw flying through the air at police were asbestos, metal and clay floor tiles; placards and placard sticks; balloons filled both with paint and urine; bricks; concrete chunks; tree branches; "all types of stones"; eggs; tomatoes and "many other items." After the officer placed the flag-lowering youth in the squad car, he returned to the police line and was hit by a 5″ by 4″ piece of concrete. Other officers state they were hit with sticks, rocks, soda cans, tomatoes, tiles and pieces of park bench.

A *Denver Post* reporter relates that someone on the stage yelled into the microphone, "Stop throwing things! This is worthless! You're hitting your own people! Stop throwing things." The chant, "Sit down, sit down" was taken by some of the crowd. One youth heaved a large piece of concrete shot-put style and the missile fell short, crumpling a demonstrator several feet in front of him.

Suddenly, a half dozen burly young men from the crowd gathered around the pole, untied the flag rope and lowered the flag to the base. As they removed it, one witness remembers, "a few older ladies in the crowd started crying." A Catholic priest who was there on the east side of the bandshell adds: "The feeling of the crowd, especially around me, was nonapproval. Most people felt lowering the flag to half-mast was symbolic, a form of protesting the actions in and outside of the convention. But to take the flag down was not acceptable." Quickly the youths at the flagpole tied an object to the rope and hoisted it to full height. Just what this object was is not known, despite published accounts that describe it variously as "a black flag of anarchy," "a red flag of anarchy," "a red flag of revolution," and a "Viet Cong flag." Some witnesses contend it was a knotted pair of red long underwear, others a red arm band or rag. But on films of the incident, it appears more likely to have been a knotted red cloth or a girl's bright red slip.

Some of those present claim that the actual flag lowering was the work of police undercover agents. The *Chicago Tribune* reported that Robert L. Pierson, who as "Big Bob" Lavin served in an undercover capacity as Jerry Rubin's bodyguard, was "in the group which lowered an American flag in Grant Park." Pierson has said, however, that he had no part in lowering the flag.

At this point six or eight policemen from the group assembled among the trees north and west of the bandshell charged the flagpole area. "I thought it was insane to send eight men into a group of 15,000," a *New York Times* reporter who had been on the scene said in his statement. "If the crowd had meant business, it would have killed these men."

On their heels now came perhaps 15 others, pushing into the flagpole area in an effort to nab the youth who had raised the red cloth. As they came, Rennie Davis shouted over the loudspeaker, "Here come the blue bonnets." The blue-helmeted police were surrounded by demonstrators who attempted to prevent or interfere with the arrests. Chants of "Fuck the pigs" and "Dirty pigs" drowned out exhortations from the speaker's stand to "Sit down." One demonstrator waved a placard at the police. It pictured a young man burning his draft card and was captioned, "Fuck the draft." The officers swung their batons freely. The officers also were hit with all kinds of material. Someone tried to grab an officer's gun as he fell. Another officer was struck with a liquid which burned a hole in his pants.

"Many people around me panicked and ran," says a law student. "A girl trying to get away was severely beaten over the head and back by the police. She cried hysterically. At this time I noticed that the shell was surrounded by police."

According to some witnesses, Rennie Davis went into the flagpole crowd in an effort to quiet the demonstrators. "The police yelled 'Get Davis!' " recalls one reporter. "They hit him a couple of times." A few minutes later, another witness says Davis appeared on the bandshell platform "with blood all over his face and shirt."

Eventually officers in the flagpole area extricated at least some of the so-called "flag" raisers from the crowd. Then they pulled down the red object but never restored the American flag. The crowd around the flagpole began to pelt them with stones, bricks, planks, chunks of concrete, cans, bottles and some smoking and flaming objects that may have been rags and firecrackers. A second demonstrator was also taken into custody. Several demonstrators crowded around and as the prisoners were being led away to a squad car, a witness relates, "Two girls—one black, and one white, casually dressed—tackled the police officer with the white shirt to try to free the hippie in his custody. They knocked the officer down and then began to run back toward their seats. Several policemen followed them into the seats and held them down. They clubbed them on their stomachs, backs and legs. Then they dragged them away." Later under arrest in a squad car, the Negro girl is alleged to have bitten a policeman on the neck. (The police lieutenant mentions nothing about these girls in his statement and believes the arrest of the lone demonstrator to have been entirely peaceful.) A police officer shouted to news photographers, "Take a picture of those bastards. Show people what they're doing." An Assistant U. S. Attorney was hit with one plastic bag containing urine, another indelible ink.

The Police Reaction

Police in the area fell back for cover. A line of approximately 50 policemen formed facing the crowd, and the rain of missiles continued with such intensity that the police again had to fall back. Sticks, firecrackers, shoes, clods of earth, empty fruit juice cans, bottles, flaming rags and other objects, including a plastic "baggie" filled with what appeared to be a bloody sanitary napkin, showered the lawmen.

A short while earlier, an unmarked police car had pulled into a position between the flagpole and the trees where most of the officers were assembled; and some demonstrators started to pelt the car with, the sergeant recalls, "red paint or dye and cellophane bags of human excrement."

Police huddled inside the unmarked car fled the vehicle, and demonstrators swarmed around it, smashing the windows, pounding on the roof and hood and screaming, "Rock it! Rock it!" One policeman, disregarding the shouted warnings of his fellow officers, ran back to the edge of the mob to get the car and drove it in reverse out of the area under a barrage of missiles.

On stage, Dellinger, the afternoon's master of ceremonies, was trying futilely to quiet the crowd. Many in the audience had climbed onto the benches or were trying to join the unruly mob around the flagpole. "Sit down!" people present remember Dellinger shouting through a microphone. "There's much more of the program to come. Be calm! Don't be violent!"

Around a refreshment stand south of the main crowd, however, two witnesses claim they noticed several persons filling Coke bottles with gravel and breaking benches for "sticks to use as clubs." One boy, they say, had a four-foot piece of inch-square wood with a switch-blade knife taped to one end. Films taken at the rally show another youth armed with a stick to which a can opener had been nailed, and some demonstrators testing strong branches against a park bench.

Someone shouted, "We have two more days to burn Chicago!"

By now it was clear that the demonstration marshals were seeking to regain control over their demonstrators. Leaders linked hands to push their own people back. The priest quoted earlier says Dellinger ordered the marshals to line up between the flagpole demonstrators and those still in the bandshell's bench area, apparently in an effort to segregate the flagpole incident.

A minister's wife entering the area about this time with her husband and several college students noticed a policeman out of range of the crowd nervously rubbing his nightstick. As she passed him, she says, he called to her: "This one's for you, baby!" A young McCarthy worker walking into the park with his girlfriend was urged by a man with a walkie talkie (he thinks possibly a plainclothes man) to turn back because the police were "putting on helmets and gas masks, and you might get hurt." The matron quoted earlier "being a cautious person," hurried up to a policeman near the bandshell and "inquired if they expected any difficulty." One responded, "If I were you, I'd get the hell out of here before we bash their heads in!"

A representative of the police has said that profanity and spitting did not have the same effect on the police that incidents involving the flag did. He feels that abuse or misuse of the flag deeply affected the police.

"At precisely that moment," the McCarthy worker remembers, "I saw tear gas exploding in the center of the crowd." Witnesses were uncertain as to exactly what was exploding. They described it variously as a smoke grenade, a stink bomb, a canister of nausea gas, and "a black object about the size and shape of a softball" that released tear gas. A few believed the object was thrown first from the crowd and hurled back by the police.

Subsequent police statements, however, reveal that the sergeant quoted earlier felt himself jeopardized by the ensuing crowd assaults and took a smoke bomb from a squad car and hurled it into the mass of missile throwers in an attempt to disperse them.

A teenager wearing heat-resistant gloves snatched up the smoking grenade and lobbed it back among the police, who by now were forming in a double line west of the bandshell. The police, who were not wearing gas masks, scattered as the bomb landed in their midst. The crowd applauded. An officer threw it back. Then the police quickly regrouped and several more smoke bombs were hurled. Their front rank stood with nightsticks held at the standard horizontal position. An attorney in the park overheard a plainclothes man say to another, "Let's teach them a lesson."

"Marshals to the point! Everyone else sit down!" came a voice over the loudspeaker.

The police paused for a moment, adjusting helmets and visors and taking test swipes with their clubs, as a chorus of shouts began rising from those in the crowd nearest them. "You're provoking this," someone shouted over the microphone at the police. "Don't turn your back on the fuckers," someone else bellowed.

The marshals, at least one of whom was a girl, were still struggling with the crowd and had locked arms and were facing the police who stood about 50 feet away. One of the marshals, asked later how he imagined the police might have viewed this marshal line, said, "They probably thought we were going to charge," and said they were "wrestling to keep the crowd from moving on the police." In fact, the films show it was the police who rushed forward. While this is not entirely clear, it is possible to conclude from the films that, with the exception of occasional missile throwing, the crowd had now disengaged from the police and that relative calm prevailed in the bandshell area. It is also possible that the police who now advanced into the bandshell were not the same officers who had taken down the red "flag."

They came first in a relatively straight line. Then as the line of marshals broke in the face of the police advance, the officers waded into the crowd individually.

"At first," according to the statement given by a correspondent from the St. Louis paper, "the police stepped forward in unison, jabbing in an upward motion with their nightsticks with each step and [looking] like a well-drilled marching unit. . . . Suddenly they stopped the unison and began flailing with their clubs in all directions. . . . People scattered. . . . Some went down, screaming and cursing and moaning. I saw a number of women . . . literally run over. In the wink of an eye, the police appeared to have lost all control." As the police moved into the crowd, benches were piled in front of and behind them. The demonstrators hurled pieces of concrete at them and one officer had his radio taken from him. Three demonstrators tried to hurl a park bench at the police line.

Another observer (not a demonstrator) states: "Persons who had done no more than listen to speakers were beaten by clubs or shoved backward in chairs." The matron quoted earlier reports "indiscriminate beating of large numbers of people." A woman who was on the stage claims "some medics were hit even though they were plainly marked in white coats and red armbands." Some demonstrators, she says, piled benches in a barricade in an effort to escape the police. "The police," says a young attorney who was standing at the rear of the bandshell area, "hit and shoved whoever was in their path—men, women, clergymen, newsmen. . . . Some were beaten and clubbed while on the ground."

"A number of people fell in the stampede to escape," says the young law student quoted earlier. "One young boy just two rows in front of me had fallen over a bench and was being slugged and kicked in his back by a policeman." In a crowd of more than 10,000, "it was very hard to move fast enough," recalls a girl who was trying desperately to avoid the swinging clubs. "People were stepping on one another. I looked behind me and caught a glimpse of the face of one of the policemen. I became terrified. The expression was like he wanted to kill."

A young seminary student reports police shoving and clubbing a young man of 19 or 20, four of five times in the shoulders. The boy was dressed in a sport coat and had short blond hair. An officer, on being shown a picture published in *The Chicago Daily Defender* showing several police "beating" a prone demonstrator stated that, in fact, the demonstrator had refused to come with the police and had to be carried away. The officer said the picture actually showed the police trying to pick him up.

As police broke ranks and carried out individual actions, one began hitting an older lady. A marshall jumped on his back and was "clubbed off by another policeman." Demonstrators made barricades with the benches and a marshal threw papers under it and lighted them. Other demonstrators put the fires out. The marshal then prepared newspaper torches (with alcohol supplied by the medic teams) and prepared to throw them if the police entered the crowd again.

All this, from the first sighting of the boy on the flagpole to the end of the melee, took place in less than 20 minutes—the longer estimate made by those who state that the film shows that the crowd had become calm before the final police entry. By the time the police had made their way to the center of the seating area, the crowd had scrambled out and the officers stood alone among the jumbled benches, a few bleeding demonstrators moaning on the ground around them, while the dust settled from the air. Medics hurried up to treat head wounds; someone called an ambulance; and crowd marshals darted among the demonstrators urging "Sit, sit! Save your rocks!" and passed out vaseline, instructing demonstrators to smear it on their faces as protection against mace or gas burns; the police walked back to the grove of trees north and west of the bandshell. Cries of "Fuck the pigs!" . . . "Death to the pigs!" and "Fascist bastards!" followed them. Someone on the speaker's platform proclaimed: "We won it, baby!"

A total of 30 policemen were injured at the bandshell incident, according to police reports. Injuries included cuts and contusions on the body as well as head wounds. There is no available count of the demonstrators injured.

After the crowd quieted down, bearded poet Allen Ginsberg, claiming that a sore throat handicapped his appearance, led the throng in a humming of "om-om-om-om," his crowd-calming sound.

The Rally Resumes

As the rally resumed, missiles occasionally were hurled from the crowd toward police; but the officers made no further forays. Witnesses say that by now most of the middle-aged people in the audience had left.

The first speaker was Oglesby, who referred to the "coffin makers at the Amphitheatre." The most biting speech in this section of the rally appears to have been that of Dick Gregory who referred to Mayor Daley as a "fat, red-faced hoodlum."

Also, one witness remembers: "Gregory urged the kids to carry their message to other cities. He talked of revolution, but not of violent revolution. He said the Democratic Party must go and the American political system must be changed in revolutionary degree, but he spoke in terms of doing this through the use of nonviolent means. He never said to burn anything down. He didn't encourage black riots, but said there would surely be more because of the racist oppression so prevalent. He called for radical action, but never spoke of destruction by violence as a means." Gregory, dressed in a jump suit with a turned down sailor cap, also said, "I would rather see the police whip demonstrators than drop napalm on Viet Cong villages." "The cops are the new niggers," he said. "The cops aren't responsible. The real blame goes to Daley and the crooks downtown. Mayor Daley is a prick and a snake and, worst of all, he ain't got no soul."

The Attempted March to the Amphitheatre

The Speeches

At about 4:30 p.m., Dellinger took the microphone and announced that there was going to be an attempt to march nonviolently to the Amphitheatre. A secretary who had come to the rally from her Loop office remembers: "He stressed that 'If you are looking for trouble, don't come with us. We don't want violence.' He then went on to suggest that a second group, primarily the people with families and children, should disperse [or, some witnesses say, "remain in silent vigil at the bandshell"]. He indicated there would be three groups in all:

the group that wanted to march, the one that would disperse and one that was 'going to the streets.' He said Tom Newman would lead this third group."

The sound films reveal a speaker telling those who want violence, or who will at least not abide by the nonviolent principle of the march, to "break up into small groups and do your own thing in the Loop."

A UPI correspondent who was on the scene says that Dellinger "was interrupted while speaking, and asked the crowd to wait a minute." There was then a short conference with the man who had interrupted him, after which Dellinger said, "I am told by some that there is a group which intends to break out of the park and that will be violent. Anyone who wishes to go with that group may, but the group I'm leading will be nonviolent." A young medical student remembers hearing "repeated messages" concerning the march to the effect, "If you want to do violence, that's your thing; but get away from this group."

"Newman got up," says the secretary, "and indicated that he felt his place in society had been taken away and that he was ready to go to the streets to get it back. He was obviously trying to arouse the crowd. After this speech, Dellinger told the crowd to break up and told those who intended to march with him to the Amphitheatre to meet around a statue of Columbus near the bandshell. I walked to the vicinity of the statue with I would estimate about 2,000 people." (Other witnesses put the figure higher; all agreed that this group became the largest assembly in the park.)

Many of the more normally dressed persons drifted off or remained in their seats, returning eventually to their cars or walking north out of the area. The crowd at the bandshell had, on the whole, been made up of young people. Those who joined the line of march were almost all young.

At the Columbus statue, continues the secretary, "Dellinger had a bullhorn and kept saying over and over again that this would be a nonviolent march. He said this at least 12 times. He added that if anyone was looking for trouble, he should leave the area now."

Although the speakers had made no reference to the fact that a city permit had not been issued for the Amphitheatre march, as the police flyers had noted, Dellinger now announced it. "We will try to negotiate for a permit when we get out into the street," the secretary remembers him saying. "Anyone afraid," he added, "should leave before any possible confrontation, because there is a chance there might be trouble."

Another witness, a young McCarthy worker from New York, saw demonstrators putting on helmets and bullet-proof vests. A college student remembers the crowd being told to abandon placards on sticks, for fear the sticks might be provocative. Some of the marchers had broken boards from park benches and were waving them in the air.

The March Negotiations

"We began to assemble into a marching formation," the secretary says. "They told us to line up in lines of eight, boys on the outside, girls on the inside. I was in the middle of one of these lines fairly close to the front."

National Guardsmen were stationed along the south end of the park at 12th Street and at a footbridge leading west from the park to 11th Street; the heavy traffic of Lake Shore Drive swept along the east edge; and police were to the west. The marchers moved north.

A young female college student recalls: "There was a tremendous feeling that what we were doing was right, and there was a great feeling of being close to the people around you even though you didn't know them. People were tearing up cloth and wetting it to use in case of tear gas. Other people were passing out vaseline to use in case of mace."

"We marched up the Columbus Drive sidewalk," says the secretary, "where we met a column of police. Consequently, we stopped."

The marchers, 5,000 to 6,000 strong by Secret Service estimate, had come to a line of about 40 police who blocked their path at the intersection of Columbus and Balbo Drive. The senior police officer told Dellinger: "On orders of the Chicago Police Department, there will be no march today."

When the marchers sat down on the sidewalk to await developments, the police commander on the scene announced that they were in violation of the law. No arrests were made, however. The commander explains that he held off any arrests pending the completion of the negotiations or orders from his superiors.

Discussions were opened between the marchers and the police. The conferees were a deputy superintendent of police (the police commander on the scene), a city legal aid and

Sidney Peck of the National Mobilization Committee. Dellinger had appointed Peck as a conferee when police asked to meet with a responsible member of his group. The bulk of the negotiations were held in a shanty and in a Park District building near 9th Street, with Peck running back now and then to confer with Dellinger.

Peck essentially restated Dellinger's position: He intended to hold a brief rally in a parking lot a mile from the Amphitheatre, and march back to the Loop.

At about 4:30 p.m., the police made announcements from a squad car equipped with a loudspeaker that all those remaining on the east side of Columbus were in violation of the law and that anyone not wanting to be arrested should move to the west side of Columbus. The police estimate that about 2,000 people then crossed Columbus, seeking a way to get out of the park and over to Michigan Avenue. A sound car also warned photographers and newsmen to leave the park. After this announcement, a line of police moved east across Balbo and severed the line of march into several parts.

A police commander states that one of the march leaders said: "Don't create any trouble here, we're in their ball park. Break up into groups of ten and 20, and go into stores, theaters and the like and create trouble." He also states that at this point the southernmost end of the line of march crossed Columbus and moved diagonally across the park's ball fields towards the Balbo bridge and Michigan Avenue.

At about 5 p.m. during the negotiations between police and marchers, a convoy of Guardsmen of the 2/129th Infantry moved south from the staging area near the Field Museum to the intersection and took up positions blocking passage north across Balbo. They then formed a perimeter at the intersection of Balbo and Columbus.

During this period a witness in front of the Hilton saw numerous things dropped from the hotel falling in the middle of the street. A bag of urine landed on a policeman's helmet.

The demonstrators at Columbus and Balbo did little but sit and wait. Allen Ginsberg provided some diversion by wandering through the crowd clutching a bouquet of daisies and leading another "om" experience. Sometimes the crowd chanted: "More pay for cops!" and "Let the people pass." The UPI correspondent says that some persons were smoking marijuana, although this was mentioned by no other witness.

"Periodically," says a woman in the crowd, "one or two

guys would run through the crowd telling everyone to get up and take to the streets. Many people were getting restless, but the crowd did not react to these few would-be inciters. On the other hand, many people sitting on the sidewalk told these guys to sit down. Most of the people around me totally ignored them. During this lull we could see that more police and various news media people were being moved in."

At one point in the waiting, a squad car equipped with a loud-speaker drove backwards on Columbus advising the marchers again that the march was illegal, that they were subject to arrest if they attempted to leave the park as a group and that anyone who did not want to face arrest should pass over to the west side of the drive. Few people in the line of march accepted this offer. Persons in the crowd with loud-speakers, meanwhile, continued to exhort their marchers to "keep your cool."

A crowd marshal states that at one point he took a megaphone, announced that plainclothes men were in the crowd and urged the group not to try to confront them. One of the detectives pointed to him, the marshal claims, and said to his companions, "Don't bring him out walking." But no arrest or assault was actually attempted.

While the negotiators were in session, a Chicago police beat reporter strolled back to the bandshell area. There, he says, he saw a group of demonstrators driving nails into the end of snow fence stakes. On the ground were three or four sticks with four-inch spikes in the end. These, he learned, had been taken from Park District employees whose job it was to pick up litter. While they were fashioning their weapons, the reporter recounts, the demonstrators threatened, "We'll get those fucking pigs with these."

In the negotiations, which dragged on for about an hour, the deputy superintendent of police held firm. He later said he "clearly explained" to Peck that since no permit to march had been given, the demonstrators would not be permitted to march. He said they could move as individuals but that any effort to act in concert would meet with arrest.

When Peck asked what alternatives the group had, the deputy said he named three: One was to stay in Grant Park all night if they wished to demonstrate there; the second was to go to Lincoln Park and demonstrate, and the third was to go to the area of Grant Park east of the Conrad Hilton where the crowd had been on Tuesday night.

Confrontation at the Conrad Hilton

The U.S. Attorney's report says about 2,000 persons, "mostly normally dressed," had already assembled at the Hilton. Many of these were demonstrators who had tired of waiting out the negotiations and had broken off from the marchers and made their way to the hotel. It appears that police already were having some difficulty keeping order at that location. Says the U.S. Attorney's report: "A large crowd had assembled behind the police line along the east wall of the Hilton. This crowd was heavily infiltrated with 'Yippie' types and was spitting and screaming obscene insults at the police."

A policeman on duty in front of the hotel later said that it seemed to him that the obscene abuses shouted by "women hippies" outnumbered those called out by male demonstrators "four to one." A common epithet shouted by the females, he said, was "Fuck you, pig." Others included references to policemen as "cock suckers" and "mother fuckers."

During this time, he said, the officers did and said nothing in retaliation. At one point, he recalled, a policeman made a retort to a "hippie" and "was immediately told to remain silent." All the while, he said, the policemen were "constantly being photographed by hippies with cameras."

According to his statement, "an Assistant U.S. Attorney and a policeman were sprayed in the face with oven cleaner. . . ." The police reporter mentioned earlier recalls that persons in the crowd were chanting, "Hump sucks" and "Daley sucks Hump."

A short time later the reporter noticed a lot of debris being hurled from one of the upper floors of the Hilton. He climbed into a police squad car parked in the area and with the aid of police binoculars saw that rolls of toilet paper were coming from the 15th floor, a location he pinpointed by counting down from the top of the building. He then went to the 15th floor and found that the section the paper was coming from was rented by Senator McCarthy campaigners. He was not admitted to the suite.

If Dellinger's marchers now moved to the Hilton area, an additional 5,000 demonstrators would be added to the number the police there would have to control.

The alternatives presented by the deputy superintendent were not acceptable to Dellinger, who said that the group was going to march. During this conversation, the deputy superintendent said, "individuals kept running up to Dellinger and were making reports that they had broken through the police and National Guard lines and were regrouping for a march on Michigan Avenue."

He added that the orders to the police and Guard were to allow individuals through their lines but not to allow any groups of marchers through. How the men were to distinguish during the dissolution of a crowd of several thousand between individuals and groups was not explained, but the police log shows orders being given to pass groups of two and three through the police lines.

The Crossing

At about 6 or 6:30 p.m., one of the march leaders announced by loudspeaker that the demonstrators would not be allowed to march to the Amphitheatre. He told the crowd to disperse and to re-group in front of the Conrad Hilton Hotel in Grant Park. He cautioned the demonstrators to be careful because many of the bridges over the Illinois Central Railroad tracks (which cut a chasm through the park and lay between the marchers and the hotel) had been closed by National Guard troops.

In a subsequent report to the Superintendent of Police, a police commander on the scene stated that the marchers were also urged to "break up into small groups and go into the Loop and penetrate the hotels, stores and theaters where the police could not get at them, and there disrupt activity. They were also ordered to block street traffic if possible."

The crowd did disperse, apparently with the march negotiators still trying to persuade city officials to permit a march, and people began seeking a way out of the area. A police commander gave his opinion that the march "dissolved" when the TV camera trucks left the intersection to cover developments at the Balbo bridge.

Some of the crowd headed southeast for the Soldier Field parking lot. They found the east side of the park blocked by police and a footbridge exit at 11th Street at the south end of the park blocked by National Guardsmen of the 1st Company of the 2/129th Infantry. Other demonstrators, probably a majority, cut through the tennis courts and playing fields at the southeast corner of the Columbus-Balbo intersection and headed west for the Balbo Drive bridge across the tracks, the most direct route to Michigan Avenue. This exit from the park was shut off by both police and the Guard, and the Guard for awhile refused to let even newsmen through. Guardsmen on the bridge were backed up by two tripod-mounted 30 calibre machine guns. The 2/122nd Artillery then withdrew from the intersection of Balbo and Columbus and moved to 22nd Street and Lake Shore Drive to block any attempt to move south on that thoroughfare by the crowd.

Disorganized and bottled up—"we had a feeling of being trapped by cops," one marcher says—the crowd began to drift north. The demonstrators headed generally toward Congress Plaza, the divided thoroughfare that cuts east through the park from Columbus, at a distance of about five blocks north of the bandshell and about two blocks north of Balbo.

A volunteer medic, who was walking parallel to the exodus, indicated that there was no real semblance of a march anymore. He said groups were walking towards the bridges in total disorganization, looking for a way out of the park.

Police in the area were in a far from cheerful mood. A neatly dressed sociology student from Minnesota says he stepped off the sidewalk onto the grass and two policemen pulled their billy clubs back as though ready to swing. One of them said, "You'd better get your fucking ass off that grass or I'll put a beautiful god dam crease in your fucking queer head." The student overheard another policeman say to a "hippie-looking girl of 14 or 15, 'You better get your fucking dirty cunt out of here.' " Another witness recalls that while he was seeking an exit from the park, a young policeman "walked up to me and just looked at me and said, 'Fuck you, you son-of-a-bitch!' " The witness was getting scared and moved rapidly on. The growing feeling of entrapment was intensified and some witnesses noticed that police were letting people into the park but not out. The marshals referred to the situation as a "trap."

As the crowd moved north, an Assistant U.S. Attorney saw one demonstrator with long sideburns and hippie garb pause to break up a large piece of concrete, wrapping the pieces in a striped T-shirt.

Before the march formally disbanded, an early contingent of demonstrators, numbering about 30 to 50, arrived at the spot where Congress Plaza bridges the IC tracks at approximately the same time as a squad of 40 National Guardsmen. The

Guard hurriedly spread out about three feet apart across Congress with rifles at the ready, gas masks on, bayonets fixed.

Now as the bulk of the disappointed marchers sought a way out of the park, the crowd began to build up in front of the Guard. Occasionally some managed to sneak through when Guard ranks parted to let cars pass. Others jumped on the passing cars or hitched rides with "straights" and the noise of the crowd was joined by the klaxon sound of car horns. "I saw one woman driving a new red late-model car approach the bridge," a news correspondent says: "Two demonstrators, apparently badly gassed, jumped into the back seat and hoped to get through the Guard lines. Guardsmen refused to permit the car through, going so far as to threaten to bayonet her tires and the hood of her car if she did not turn around. One Guardsman fired tear gas point blank beside the car."

Before long, says a college history professor who was present, the crowd wanting to leave the park via the Congress Plaza bridge included not only marchers and demonstrators "but many others, including ball players still wearing their softball uniforms, vacationers and picnickers with their families."

There was a lot of heckling. Some demonstrators tapped Guardsmen's helmets, urging the Guard to join them.

A medic who was in the Guard line says that several "leaders" assembled at the northeast edge of the bridge and with bullhorns "attempted to incite the crowd to break through the line." He says they addressed the crowd with such comments as, "They're more afraid of you than you are of them" and "They're one of us," implying, he felt, that the Guardsmen were draft dodgers.

The crowd's basic strategy, he recalls, was "to mass a sizeable group at one end of the line," as if preparing to charge. Then, when Guardsmen shifted to protect that area, a comparatively small group of demonstrators would push through the weak end of the line. The physical violence included "grabbing the Guard's weapons, punching and kicking." Once the small group had penetrated the line, the medic says, members would "come up behind the Guardsmen and taunt them, as well as push and shove them from the rear." A Guard official said later that his men were attacked with oven cleaner and containers filled with excrement.

When a group of demonstrators dashed between the Guardsmen, one was hit on the head by a rifle butt. The Guardsman turned his back, and the demonstrator came running up behind him and smashed him with a brick, knocking him to his knees. The young man scampered off across the bridge while the dazed Guardsman tried to find his helmet."

The medic recalls that he tried to render medical aid to another youth who was "hit across the forehead by a rifle butt while attempting to grab it away from its owner. The downed man was lying just inside the south edge of the line. I went over. I was surrounded, pushed, punched and kicked by a group of demonstrators." The attack did not cease until the Guardsman finally identified himself as a medic.

As the crowd swelled, it surged periodically towards the Guard line, sometimes yelling, "Freedom, freedom." On one of these surges a Guardsman hurled two tear gas canisters. Later a National Guard official Brigadier General John Phipps exclaimed that the commander of the 40-man platoon on the bridge had a few more people on the scene than he could control and used "a little tear gas" to push them back. Guard reinforcements arrived, and gas was freely dispensed from CA-3 back-pack sprayers (converted flame throwers). One witness says: "A Guardsman stepped in front [of the Guard line] and walked the width of the bridge laying down a stream of tear gas. . . . As cars came up, the ranks of troops closed and the man sprayed more gas." The wind was then from the northeast and the gas was generally blown back into the Guard lines and southwest towards the Hilton and the Blackstone.

Some of the tear gas was fired directly into the faces of demonstrators. "We came across a guy really badly gassed," a college coed says. "We were choking, but we could still see. But this guy we saw was standing there helpless with mucous-type stuff on his face, obviously in pain. There was a medic near us with water and we washed this guy's eyes out and helped him along until he could see."

An Assistant U.S. Attorney says he saw "hundreds of people running, crying, coughing, vomiting, screaming." Some women ran blindly to Buckingham Fountain and leaped into the water to bathe their faces. The Guard medic quoted earlier says he was again assaulted by demonstrators when he went into the crowd to treat a man felled by "a particularly heavy dose of tear gas."

On a stiff breeze off Lake Michigan, the gas swept west through the Guard line, over the blockaded bridge and into Michigan Avenue. Startled businessmen, office workers, late shoppers on the street held their faces and ran into stores and buildings to get away from the stinging fumes. Because of the wind, says one onlooker, the demonstrators in the park on the whole got less gas than "the Michigan Avenue crowd, the conventioneers, strollers, hotel residents, what I call the coat-and-tie-set. They were the hardest hit."

By 7 p.m., the gas was reported "heavy" at Congress and Michigan, two blocks north of the Hilton. A little later when the observer entered the Hilton, he noticed vomit stains on the lobby carpet "from persons who could not hold their gas." A rotten stench pervaded the hotel. There is a good chance that what the reporter smelled was not, in fact, vomit. Throughout the convention week, a putrid odor permeated the Hilton and other hotels where convention visitors were staying. On Friday, police arrested three young women from New Jersey who had allegedly dropped "stench bombs" (made of acid-soaked tissues) on carpets and furniture in several hotels. Vials of the acid were found in the women's purses, police said, and a gallon jug of the acid was found in a locker of a Loop bus station. One of the women had a key to the locker. The three were charged with criminal damage to property.

At the McCarthy headquarters on the 15th floor, young campaign workers were administering first aid treatment to persons who had been gassed. Another first aid station was set up in the Pick-Congress Hotel further north on Michigan.

"In Grant Park, the gassed crowd was angered . . . more aggressive," says the history professor. Shortly after the gassing, says the Guard medic quoted earlier, "two forces of police arrived, one from the Michigan Avenue side of the bridge and one from the south on the east side of the bridge. They immediately waded into the crowd with clubs swinging indiscriminately, driving them off the bridge and away from the area." Once more, the Guardsman said, he was assaulted by demonstrators—this time when he tried "to treat an individual who received a severe head injury from the police."

One of the demonstration marshals says that the "primary motivation" of the crowd was to "get out of the park before dark because there was fear of being beaten out of view of the cameras if it got dark before we reached Michigan Avenue."

Surging north from Congress Plaza to a footbridge leading from the park, the crowd encountered more Guardsmen. More tear gas was dispensed. Surging north from the site of the gassings, the crowd found the Jackson Boulevard bridge unguarded. Word was quickly passed back by loud-speaker "Two blocks north, there's an open bridge; no gas." As dusk was settling, hundreds poured from the park into Michigan Avenue.

The Crowd on Michigan Avenue

At 7:14 p.m., as the first groups of demonstrators crossed the bridge toward Michigan Avenue, they noticed that the mule train of the Poor People's Campaign was just entering the intersection of Michigan and Jackson, headed south. The train consisted of three wagons, each drawn by two mules, and was accompanied by a number of SCLC blacks in fieldwork attire. The wagons were painted, "Jobs & Food for All." The train had a permit to parade within the Loop and south on Michigan Avenue.

The train was accompanied by 24 policemen on foot, five on three-wheelers, and four in two squadrols. A police official was in front with the caravan's leaders. The sight of the train seemed to galvanize the disorganized Grant Park crowd and those streaming over the bridge broke into cheers and shouts. "Peace now!" bellowed the demonstrators. "Dump the Hump!" This unexpected enthusiastic horde in turn stimulated the mule train marchers. Drivers of the wagons stood and waved to the crowd, shouting: "Join us! Join us!" To a young man watching from the 23rd floor of the Hilton Hotel, "the caravan seemed like a magnet to demonstrators leaving the park."

A medic accompanying the march reports that "at this time it appeared that the marshals had lost control and the group was moving more or less under mob psychology."

At this the exodus from Grant Park swelled to a torrent and Michigan rapidly filled out with now revitalized, shouting demonstrators. The two squadrols, driving at the rear of the train, were unable to move to the front because of the crush of the crowd.

Led by Viet Cong red and black flags, and the loud-speaker, and constantly joined by more people escaping from Grant Park, all came slowly south on Michigan with the mule train in the middle of this sea of people. The crowd, estimated at "several thousand" by a police official, filled out an entire city block and chanted "We want peace." As the demonstrators marched, says an Assistant U.S. Attorney, "four or five policemen ran into the crowd swinging nightsticks. I saw a couple of policemen strike some of the individuals." Few policemen were, however, present on the street.

The Balbo-Michigan Crowd Builds Up

When the crowd's first rank reached the intersection of Balbo and Michigan, the northeast corner of the Hilton, it was close to the approximately 2,000 to 3,000 demonstrators and spectators massed east of a police line along the two blocks of Grant Park opposite the Hilton and 500 others contained between another police line and the hotel's east face.

An additional single line of police was formed diagonally across Michigan at the south line of Balbo to divert the new oncoming crowd off the street and into Grant Park. A portion of the crowd had spilled west on Balbo toward Wabash, a block west of Michigan, where there was another police line across Balbo.

The police were armed with riot helmets, batons, mace, an aerosol tear gas can and their service revolvers (which they always carry).

Behind the police lines, parked in front of the Hilton, was a fire department high pressure pumper truck hooked up to a hydrant. Pairs of uniformed firemen were also in the vicinity.

The growing crowds, according to the U.S. Attorney's report, were a blend of "young and old, hippies, Yippies, straights, newsmen and cameramen," even two mobile TV units. TV cameras also were situated on an entrance canopy jutting out from the north side of the Hilton. The smell of tear gas from the Congress bridge encounter still hung heavy in the air.

When the line of march reached the police line across Michigan, it stopped and the crowd began to bunch up in the intersection. It quickly overflowed into all available adjacent areas. All traffic was immobilized, both on Michigan and the cross streets. The forces that would clash at 7:57 p.m. in the unreal glow of TV lights were in final deployment.

Some in the crowd were equipped with helmets and gas masks and armed with rocks, sticks, bottles and other weapons.

Volunteer "medic" teams were on hand among the demonstrators.

While the crowd was not organized in any traditional sense, it had leaders—some self-appointed, some the marshals. Dellinger and other demonstration leaders had disappeared after the dispersal of the line of march at Balbo and Columbus. Among other things, these "leaders" had exhorted the marchers by loudspeaker, while the crowd was pushing south on Michigan with the mule train, to sit down on the pavement if the police tried to prevent their eventual passage to the Amphitheatre.

Facing this vast, virtually encircling congregation of 4,000 to 4,500 people were about 300 police. One demonstrator says that when three policemen on three-wheel motorcycles tried to get through the crowd, the throng surrounded them and covered the cycles with Yippie posters, such as "Vote the Pig Vote." The officers finally were let through when they said they were off duty and on their way home.

A police officer recalls that shortly after 7 p.m. he attempted to clear the intersection by saying, "Get up on the curb, please" and "Clear the streets, please." Initially, he said, "there was compliance with this request" until a tall, slender youth, about 20 years old, "appeared on the scene and told the people to disregard the police request and come back into the street." They obeyed.

The police officer approached the youth and asked him to cooperate with the police. According to the officer, the young man pushed him with both hands. Quickly the two were "surrounded by a large group." Two of them knocked the officer to the ground. In his opinion, he was in danger of being "stomped." Other officers quickly rescued him, but his ankle was badly injured in the scuffle.

From within the crowd were rising the usual shouts from some of the demonstrators: "Hell no, we won't go!" . . . "Fuck these Nazis!" . . . "Fuck you, L.B.J.!" . . . "No more war!" . . . "Pigs, pigs, pigs." . . . "The streets belong to the people!" . . . "Let's go to the Amphitheatre!" . . . "Move on, Move on!" . . . "You can't stop us." . . . "From the hotel," recalls a student, "people who sympathized were throwing confetti and pieces of paper out of the windows and they were blinking their room lights."

The history professor quoted earlier, standing on the northwest corner of the Balbo-Michigan intersection, said: "The police would move periodically north on Michigan, forcing the crowd back, or move east on Balbo, or would split the group north and south." But then they would return to their positions and "the crowd would flow back."

Isolated Incidents

Occasionally during the early evening, groups of demonstrators would flank the police lines or find a soft spot and punch through, heading off on their own for the Amphitheatre. On the periphery of the Hilton and on thoroughfares and side streets further southwest, a series of brief but sometimes violent encounters occurred.

For example, says the manager of a private club on Michigan Avenue, "a large band of long-haired demonstrators . . . tore down the American flag" overhanging the entrance to the club "and took it into Michigan Avenue attempting to tear it." A veteran who happened by, grabbed the flag and returned it to the club. He reports that they tried to strike him.

At about 7 p.m. from the window of a motel room in the 1100 block of South Michigan, a senator's driver noticed a group of demonstrators walking south, chanting: "Hell no, we won't go!" and "Fuck the draft." They were hurling insults at passing pedestrians and when one answered back, the witness says, "five demonstrators charged out of Michigan Avenue onto the sidewalk, knocked the pedestrian down, formed a circle around his fallen body, locked their arms together and commenced kicking him in a vicious manner. When they had finished kicking their victim, they unlocked their arms and immediately melted back into the crowd. . . ."

Within six minutes this action was repeated against four other pedestrians, the witness says. One of them was smashed with a city trash basket "as he lay prostrate on the sidewalk after being knocked down and kicked."

At another Michigan Avenue motel, demonstrators objecting to a "Young Citizens for Humphrey" display in the lobby hurled unidentified objects at the front of the building, breaking a large plate glass window, according to the manager.

A few blocks away, at Wabash and Roosevelt, a university student observed what he describes as "an orderly march" down Wabash. He said that a police squad car drove into the crowd in an effort to break up the march. He states that "a

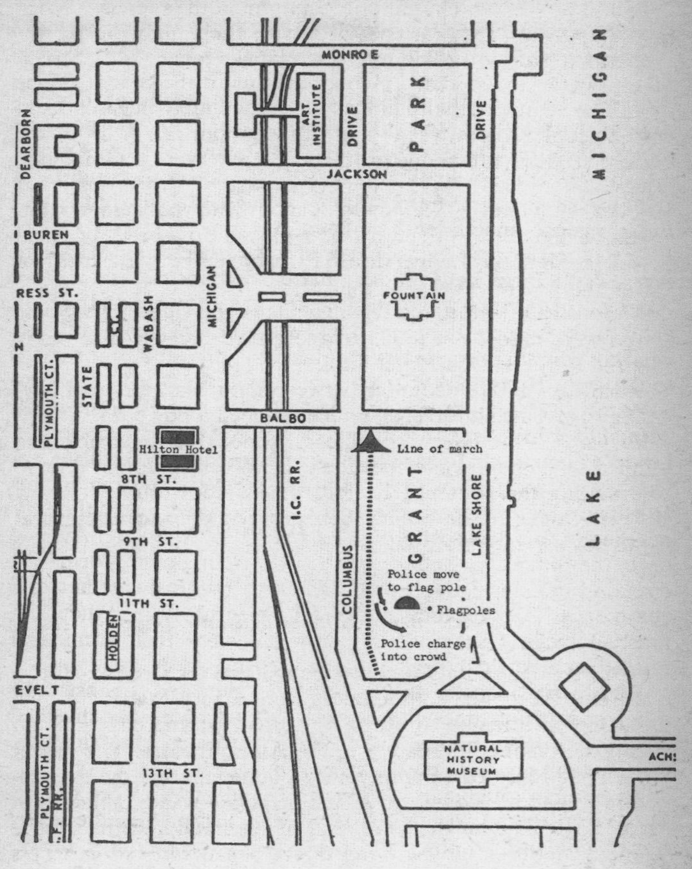
MONROE
ART INSTITUTE
DRIVE
PARK
DRIVE
MICHIGAN
DEARBORN
JACKSON
BUREN
RESS ST.
MICHIGAN
WABASH
FOUNTAIN
PLYMOUTH CT.
STATE
BALBO
Hilton Hotel
Line of march
8TH ST.
I.C. RR.
GRANT
LAKE SHORE
LAKE
9TH ST.
COLUMBUS
Police move to flag pole
Flagpoles
11TH ST.
HOLDEN
Police charge into crowd
EVELT
NATURAL HISTORY MUSEUM
13TH ST.
PLYMOUTH CT.

police bus followed the car through the crowd and, when it reached the outer periphery of the crowd, the bus stopped and unloaded the police. The police then began chasing the marchers."

Several policemen chased one young man, he recalls. "When they caught him, they all beat him with their nightsticks."

A running fray broke out on Wabash near 14th Street. There, says a law student, plainclothes men piled from police cars. "They came out with clubs and immediately began attacking the people. There wasn't any provocation. . . . A lot of the policemen were attacking girls, since they were running the slowest."

Police cars and CTA buses loaded with policemen converged on the area. A demonstrator picked up a brick or rock, the law student says and "threw it through the windshield of one of the police cars."

Demonstrators scattered through alleys and sidestreets. Some arrests were made, but much of the crowd escaped and many returned to the Hilton Hotel area.

During a similar encounter between demonstrators and lawmen, a magazine editor says, police grabbed a boy with a knapsack over his shoulder. An officer opened the knapsack and dumped its contents onto the sidewalk. When he found a brassiere among the contents, he told the demonstrator, "I knew you were a fag." The police then proceeded to arrest several of the boy's companions.

Back at the Conrad Hilton

Vice President Humphrey was now inside the Conrad Hilton Hotel and the police commanders were afraid that the crowd might either attempt to storm the hotel or march south on Michigan Avenue, ultimately to the Amphitheatre. The Secret Service had received an anonymous phone call that the Amphitheatre was to be blown up. A line of police was established at 8th and Michigan at the south end of the hotel and the squads of police stationed at the hotel doors began restricting access to those who could display room keys. Some hotel guests, including delegates and Senator McCarthy's wife, were turned away.

By 7:30 p.m., the SCLC people, too, were growing apprehensive. They were becoming concerned for the mule train because of the press of demonstrators and the crowd's escalating emotionalism. Also a rumor was passing around that the Blackstone Rangers and the East Side Disciples, two of Chicago's most troublesome street gangs, were on their way to the scene. (This was later proven to be untrue; neither of these South Side gangs was present in any numbers in either Lincoln Park or Grant Park.)

At this point, a Negro male was led through the police line by a police officer. He spoke to the police officer, a city official and a deputy superintendent of police. He told them that he was in charge of the mule train and that his people wanted no part of this mob. He said he had 80 people with him, that they included old people and children, and he wanted to get them out of the mob. The police officer later stated the group wanted to go past the Hilton, circle it, and return to the front of the hotel where Reverend Ralph Abernathy could address the crowd.

At this time, says the police sergeant who had thrown the smoke bomb into the bandshell crowd, and who now was on duty at the Hilton, people were screaming foul language of every type at the police and shouting, "Who's your wife with now?" . . . "Where's your wife tonight?" Some were spitting on the officers and daring them to come and hit them. "The obscenities," says an attorney who was present, "were frequently returned in kind by the police."

In response to the mule train leader's plea, the deputy superintendent of police ordered a police escort to lead the wagons through the crowd. Flying wedges of officers pushed back the resisting crowd and the train was let through the police skirmish line at Balbo. It then moved up in front of the hotel.

In a few minutes, Reverend Ralph Abernathy appeared and, according to the police officer's statement, "said he wanted to be taken out of the area as he feared for the safety of his group." The police officer directed that the train be moved south on Michigan to 11th Street and then, through a series of turns through the Loop, to the West Side.

Before the train moved out, a leader of the mule train addressed the crowd with a bullhorn provided by police. He said: "We have nothing against you joining our demonstration, and we have nothing against joining your demonstration . . . I think it was very violent for the police to tear gas you."

The demonstrators did not pay much attention to him but, instead, seemed bent on making their march to the Amphitheatre. Obscenities and vulgar epithets were shouted at the police. There were also chants of "One, two, three, four; stop this damn war"; "Dump the Hump"; "Daley must go"; "Ho, Ho, Ho Chi Minh"; "The streets belong to the people"; and "Prague, Prague, Prague!"

A policeman on Michigan later said that at about this time a "female hippie" came up to him, pulled up her skirt and said, "You haven't had a piece in a long time."

A policeman standing in front of the Hilton remembers seeing a blond female who was dressed in a short red minidress make lewd, sexual motions in front of a police line. Whenever this happened, he says, the policemen moved back to prevent any incident. The crowd, however, egged her on, the patrolman says. He thought that "she and the crowd wanted an arrest to create a riot." Earlier in the same general area a male youth had stripped bare and walked around carrying his clothes on a stick.

An attorney who was present at the intersection, a member of the ACLU, later said that "perhaps ten people were on lampposts and shoulders of other people, waving at the cameras. . . . The noise was very loud. . . . I felt this was a violent crowd that came to fight and was looking for trouble."

The intersection at Balbo and Michigan was in total chaos at this point. The street was filled with people. Darkness had fallen but the scene was lit by both police and television lights. As the mule train left, part of the group tried to follow the wagons through the police line and were stopped. According to the deputy superintendent of police, there was much pushing back and forth between the policemen and the demonstrators. He said that this is where real physical contact began. An old car bearing a sign announcing a draft card burning rally edged up to the police lines.

Continual announcements were made at this time over a police amplifier for the crowd to "clear the street and go up on the sidewalk or into the park area for their demonstrations." The broadcast said "Please gather in the park on the east side of the street. You may have your peaceful demonstration and speechmaking there." The demonstrators were also advised that if they did not heed these orders they would face arrest. The response from many in the crowd, according to a police observer, was to scream and shout obscenities. A Chicago attorney who was watching the scene recalls that when the announcements were broadcast, "No one moved."

"There was roughly a ten-yard distance between the police line and the demonstrators," recalls an Assistant U.S. attorney. "Two policemen periodically walked across the gap, took hold of a demonstrator and walked him to a paddy wagon behind the police line. They arrested approximately ten protesters this way. We saw them hit a few with their nightsticks as they were pushing them into the paddy wagon but it appeared that none of the protesters was injured."

A police observer recalls that the deputy superintendent then made another announcement: "Will any nondemonstrators, anyone who is not a part of this group, any newsmen, please leave the group." Despite the crowd noise, the loud-speaker announcements were "loud and plainly heard," according to this officer. Police state that the messages to clear the street were repeated—officers "walked to the front of the crowd and repeated these messages to individuals all along the line, all the while pointing over to the east side of the street where we wanted them to go."

Presently, a police officer states, he glanced back and noticed that part of the crowd had moved forward and had "completely surrounded" the police car from which the announcements were being broadcast. Police rushed to the car and helped clear a path so that it could be driven slowly north through the crowd. Before it reached the north side of Balbo, according to the officer, its windshield, side windows and headlights had been pasted with McCarthy stickers. "When we finally got into the car and it began to move," said the officer, "it became apparent that the right rear tire was almost flat." The valve had been loosened. The car limped away in search of a filling station.

The deputy superintendent of police states that at this point demonstrators staged "massive sit-downs" in Michigan Avenue. While some sit-downs occurred, the films and still photographs do not show any that were "massive." But this was a tactic that had been discussed earlier among the crowd, should the march to the Amphitheatre ultimately be thwarted. The sitters, according to the deputy, were hampering the orderly movements of his police. "People in the streets were having face-to-face confrontations with the police officers, telling them that they did not have to move and that they were not going to move," he says. As police announcements were made to leave the street, demonstrators with loud-speakers of their own shouted to the crowd, "You don't have to go. Hell no, don't go!"

The crowd was becoming increasingly ugly. The deputy superintendent states that demonstrators were pushing police lines back, spitting in officers' faces and pelting them with rocks, bottles, shoes, glass and other objects.

While this was happening on Michigan Avenue, a separate police line had begun to move east toward the crowd from the block of Balbo that lies between Michigan and Wabash along the north side of the Hilton.

About 7:45 p.m., the police radio had crackled with "10-1," the emergency code for "police officer needs help." A police captain was reporting imminent danger in front of the Hilton and, in response to his call, a reserve platoon had been ordered to the northwest corner of the hotel on Balbo. Shortly after that, all available vans in the vicinity were ordered to converge on the Hilton.

The reserve platoon, numbering some 40 policemen, had arrived by special CTA bus at Wabash and Balbo, one block west of Michigan, at 7:55 p.m., under the command of a deputy chief of police. The men came from a skirmish with demonstrators at 14th and Wabash, several blocks southwest of the Hilton, where they had arrived after another unit had broken up an attempted march on the Amphitheatre and had rounded up a group of demonstrators. Some had also been on duty at Columbus and Balbo in Grant Park that afternoon.

As the bus unloaded, the unit formed up building-to-building across Balbo in four ranks of ten led by a deputy chief and a lieutenant.

At the same time, Sidney Peck with his bullhorn was urging people to follow him west on Balbo in an effort to flee the Michigan intersection. "We saw the police approaching," Peck states. He says he called people back and urged the police "not to move against them." Over the loud-speaking equipment, Peck shouted, "Sit down and no violence will happen. Don't use any violence."

The deputy chief states, on the other hand, that he saw marchers coming toward his men. He felt that "a disorderly mob surging west on Balbo from Michigan, taking up the whole street and sidewalks, shouting and screaming slogans and insults [was] taking over the Blackstone and Hilton Hotel entrances with the intention of taking over these hotels."

The police unit moved east on Balbo toward Michigan

Avenue at a fast walk. As they did so, the throng on Balbo backed east toward the intersection or crowded onto the sidewalk. By the time the officers reached the west edge of Michigan, they slowed to a determined walk.

A 19-year-old boy, working as a chauffeur for Senator McGovern's staff, relates: "An officer was counting off 'Hut, two, three, four,' and several of the men were chanting along with him. . . . The policemen were walking slowly with their nightsticks extended, held in both hands. I did not see anything thrown from the demonstrators at the police at this time or any charge by the demonstrators at the police."

As a response to seeing the police phalanx, however, says a law student who was standing near the front of the mob, the chant, "Pigs . . . pigs . . . pigs" went up.

Policemen in the line of march claim that they suffered more than verbal abuse. One officer states that in the vicinity of the Haymarket, a cocktail lounge in the Hilton's northeast corner with an entrance on Balbo, a bottle shattered about 18 inches behind him. He thought it was dropped from a hotel window. When the line reached Michigan, he said, he heard someone say, "Mother fucker, I'm going to kill you." He saw a man, about 33 years old, bearded and wearing a helmet, standing with a wine bottle in his hand, . . . "ready to swing at me. I knocked the bottle out of his hand at that point, someone behind me hit me with some heavy object in the back, and I fell to one knee." While he was down, he said, the crowd surrounded him, cutting him off from other police. "People were pushing and shoving as well as throwing bottles, shoes and eggs," he said. "I was hit with an egg." He used his baton, he said, "in order to shove the crowd aside."

Another officer states that "many rocks and bottles were being thrown at [us]. . . . A house brick struck me on the side of my head after glancing off my helmet." He lost his balance and fell to the pavement. The films fail to show any barrage of missiles at this time, atlhough some may have been thrown.

Just as the police in front of the Hilton were confronted with some sit-downs on the south side of the intersection of Balbo and Michigan, the police unit coming into the intersection on Balbo met the sitting demonstrators. What happened then is subject to dispute between the police and some other witnesses.

The Balbo police unit commander asserts that he informed

the sit-downs and surrounding demonstrators that if they did not leave, they would be arrested. He repeated the order and was met with a chant of "Hell no, we won't go." Quickly a police van swung into the intersection immediately behind the police line, the officers opened the door at the rear of the wagon. The deputy chief "ordered the arrest process to start."

"Immediately upon giving this order," the deputy chief later informed his superiors, "we were pelted with rocks, bottles, cans filled with unknown liquids and other debris, which forced the officers to defend themselves from injury. . . . My communications officer was slugged from behind by one of these persons, receiving injuries to his right eye and cheekbone." That officer states: "All this debris came instantaneously, as if it was waiting for the signal of the first arrest."

A sergeant who was on the scene later said that "the hippies behind those sitting down appeared to be the ones doing most of the throwing. . . . Police officers were constantly being hit . . . and were obviously becoming anxious to do something."

A patrolman who was in the skirmish line states that "the order was given to remain in position." But then, he says, one of his fellow officers "ran into the crowd, he was surrounded and I lost sight of him." At this point, the patrolman and other officers in the line "broke into the crowd," using their batons to "push away people who had gathered around" their fellow officer.

He claims they then returned to the line. But another patrolman states that "several police officers were being knocked down by the crowd and several policemen broke formation" to help them "because groups of rioters were attempting to kick and pummel them." At this point, he said, "everything went up for grabs."

The many films and video tapes of this time period present a picture which does not correspond completely with the police view described above. First, the films do not show a mob moving west on Balbo; they show the street as rather clean of the demonstrators and bystanders, although the sidewalks themselves on both sides of the street are crowded. Second, they show the police walking east on Balbo, stopping in formation, awaiting the arrival of the van and starting to make arrests on order. A total of 25 seconds elapses between their coming to a halt and the first arrests.

Also, a St. Louis reporter who was watching from inside

the Haymarket lounge agrees that the police began making arrests "in formation," apparently as "the result of an order to clear the intersection." Then, the reporter adds, "from this apparently controlled beginning the police began beating people indiscriminately. They grabbed and beat anyone they could get hold of."

To many other witnesses, it seemed that the police swept down Balbo and charged, with clubs swinging, into the crowd without the slightest pause. What these witnesses may, in fact, have seen was a second sweep of the officers, moving east on Balbo after the first arrest. Once this second action started, the officers did run across the intersection.

"There was just enough time for a few people to sit down before the cops charged," says the law student, quoted earlier. "The guys who sat down got grabbed, and the cops really hit hard. I saw a pair of glasses busted by a billy club go flying through the air."

"The crowd tried to reverse gears," a reporter for a St. Louis paper says. "People began falling over each other. I was in the first rank between police and the crowd and was caught in the first surge. I went down as I tried to retreat. I covered my head, tried to protect my glasses which had fallen partially off, and hoped that I would not be clubbed. I tried to dig into the humanity that had fallen with me. You could hear shouting and screaming. As soon as I could, I scrambled to my feet and tried to move away from the police. I saw a youth running by me also trying to flee. A policeman clubbed him as he passed, but he kept running.

"The cops were saying, 'Move! I said, move, god dammit! Move, you bastards!' " A representative of the ACLU who was positioned among the demonstrators says the police "were cussing a lot" and were shouting, "Kill, kill, kill, kill, kill!" A reporter for the *Chicago Daily News* said after the melee that he, too, heard this cry. A demonstrator remembers the police swinging their clubs and screaming, "Get the hell out of here." . . . "Get the fuck out of here." . . . "Move your fucking ass!"

"People were trying to move but were clubbed as they did" the reporter for the St. Louis paper continued. "I fell to my knees, stumbling over somebody. . . ."

Adds the ACLU representative: "The police kept coming in. . . . The crowd kept trying to get away, but it was so thick that there were many people who seemed . . . to be stuck in the middle and unable to do anything about it. There was a great deal of screaming and yelling. A lot of people were crying and shouting for help. . . ."

The crowd frantically eddied in a halfmoon shape in an effort to escape the officers coming in from the west. A UPI reporter who was on the southern edge of the crowd on Michigan Avenue, said that the advancing police "began pushing the crowd south." A cherry bomb burst overhead. The demonstrators strained against the deputy superintendent of police's line south of the Balbo-Michigan intersection. "When I reached that line," says the UPI reporter, "I heard a voice from behind it say, 'Push them back, move them back!' I was then prodded and shoved with nightsticks back in a northerly direction, toward the still advancing line of police."

"Police were marching this way and that," a correspondent from a St. Louis paper says. "They obviously had instructions to clear the street, but apparently contradicting one another in the directions the crowd was supposed to be sent."

"At first," says the McGovern worker, "the police just pushed the demonstrators with their nightsticks. The demonstrators [nearest the police] tried to move, but couldn't because of the press of the crowd. There was no place for them to go."

The deputy superintendent of police recalls that he ordered his men to "hold your line there" . . . "stand fast" . . . "Lieutenant, hold your men steady there!" These orders, he said, were not obeyed by all.

"Two or three policemen broke formation and began swinging at everyone in sight," the McGovern worker says. The deputy superintendent states that police disregarded his order to return to the police lines—the beginning of what he says was the only instance in which he personally saw police discipline collapse. He estimates that ten to 15 officers moved off on individual forays against demonstrators. But the McGovern worker says "this became sort of spontaneous. Every few seconds more policemen would break formation and began swinging until . . . all the policemen from the original line at Balbo were just swinging through the crowd."

"I turned toward the north and was immediately struck on the back of the head from behind," says the UPI reporter. "I fell to the ground. . . ."

Thus, at 7:57 p.m., with two groups of club-wielding police converging simultaneously and independently, the battle was joined. The portions of the throng out of the immediate area of conflict largely stayed put and took up the chant, "The whole world is watching," but the intersection fragmented into a collage of violence.

Re-creating the precise chronology of the next few moments is impossible. But there is no question that a violent street battle ensued.

People ran for cover and were struck by police as they passed. Clubs were swung indiscriminately.

Two Assistant U.S. Attorneys who were on the scene characterized the police as "hostile and aggressive." Some witnesses cited particularly dramatic personal stories.

"I saw squadrols of policemen coming from everywhere," a secretary quoted earlier said. "The crowd around me suddenly began to run. Some of us, including myself, were pushed back onto the sidewalk and then all the way up against . . . the Blackstone Hotel along Michigan Avenue. I thought the crowd had panicked."

"Fearing that I would be crushed against the wall of the building . . . I somehow managed to work my way . . . to the edge of the street . . . and saw police everywhere.

"As I looked up I was hit for the first time on the head from behind by what must have been a billy club. I was then knocked down and while on my hands and knees, I was hit around the shoulders. I got up again, stumbling and was hit again. As I was falling, I heard words to the effect of 'move, move' and the horrible sound of cracking billy clubs."

"After my second fall, I remember being kicked in the back, and I looked up and noticed that many policemen around me had no badges on. The police kept hitting me on the head."

Eventually she made her way to an alley behind the Blackstone and finally, "bleeding badly from my head wound," was driven by a friend to a hospital emergency room. Her treatment included the placing of 12 stitches.

Another young woman, who had been among those who sat down in the intersection, ran south on Michigan, a "Yippie flag" in her hand, when she saw the police. "I fell in the center of the intersection," she says. "Two policemen ran up on me, stopped and hit me on the shoulder, arm and leg about five or six times, severely. They were swearing and one of them broke my flag over his knee." By fleeing into Grant Park, she managed eventually to escape.

Another witness said: "To my left, the police caught a man, beat him to the ground and smashed their clubs on the back of his unprotected head. I stopped to help him. He was elderly, somewhere in his mid-50's. He was kneeling and holding his bleeding head. As I stopped to help him, the police turned on me. "Get that cock sucker out of here!" This command was accompanied by four blows from clubs—one on the middle of my back, one on the bottom of my back, one on my left buttock, and one on the back of my leg. No attempt was made to arrest me or anybody else in the vicinity. All the blows that I saw inflicted by the police were on the backs of heads, arms, legs, etc. It was the most slow and confused, and the least experienced people who got caught and beaten.

"The police were angry. Their anger was neither disinterested nor instrumental. It was deep, expressive and personal. 'Get out of here you cock suckers' seemed to be their most common cry.

"To my right, four policemen beat a young man as he lay on the ground. They beat him and at the same time told him to 'get up and get the hell out of here.' Meanwhile, I struggled with the injured man whom I had stopped to help. . . ."

One demonstrator said that several policemen were coming toward a group in which he was standing when one of the officers yelled, "Hey, there's a nigger over there we can get." They then are said to have veered off and grabbed a middle-aged Negro man, whom they beat.

A lawyer says that he was in a group of demonstrators in the park just south of Balbo when he heard a police officer shout, "Let's get 'em!" Three policemen ran up, "singled out one girl and as she was running away from them, beat her on the back of the head. As she fell to the ground, she was struck by the nightsticks of these officers." A male friend of hers then came up yelling at the police. The witness said, "He was arrested. The girl was left in the area lying on the ground."

The beating of two other girls was witnessed from a hotel window. The witness says, he saw one girl "trying to shield a demonstrator who had been beaten to the ground," whereupon a policeman came up "hitting her with a billy club." The officer also kicked the girl in the shoulder, the witness said.

A *Milwaukee Journal* reporter says in his statement, "when

the police managed to break up groups of protesters they pursued individuals and beat them with clubs. Some police pursued individual demonstrators as far as a block . . . and beat them. . . . In many cases it appeared to me that when police had finished beating the protesters they were pursuing, they then attacked, indiscriminately, any civilian who happened to be standing nearby. Many of these were not involved in the demonstrations."

In balance, there is no doubt that police discipline broke during the melee. The deputy superintendent of police states that—although this was the only time he saw discipline collapse—when he ordered his men to stand fast, some did not respond and began to sally through the crowd, clubbing people they came upon. An inspector-observer from the Los Angeles Police Department, stated that during this week, "The restraint of the police both as individual members and as an organization, was beyond reason." However, he said that on this occasion:

> There is no question but that many officers acted without restraint and exerted force beyond that necessary under the circumstances. The leadership at the point of conflict did little to prevent such conduct and the direct control of officers by first-line supervisors was virtually non-existent.

The deputy superintendent of police has been described by several observers as being very upset by individual policemen who beat demonstrators. He pulled his men off the demonstrators, shouting "Stop, damn it, stop. For Christ's sake, stop it."

"It seemed to me," an observer says, "that only a saint could have swallowed the vile remarks to the officers. However, they went to extremes in clubbing the Yippies. I saw them move into the park, swatting away with clubs at girls and boys lying in the grass. More than once I witnessed two officers pulling at the arms of a Yippie until the arms almost left their sockets, then, as the officers put the Yippie in a police van, a third jabbed a riot stick into the groin of the youth being arrested. It was evident that the Yippie was not resisting arrest."

A witness adds: "I witnessed four or five instances of several officers beating demonstrators when it appeared the demonstrators could have been easily transported and confined to police vans waiting nearby."

"Anyone who was in the way of some of the policemen was struck," a UPI correspondent concludes in his statement, "Police continued to hit people in the back who were running away as fast as possible. I saw one man knocked to the street. . . . A policeman continued to poke his stick at the man's groin and kidney area. Several newsmen were struck. Individual incidents of violence were going on over the entire area at once, in any direction you might look.

"In one incident, a young man, who apparently had been maced, staggered across Michigan . . . helped by a companion. The man collapsed. . . . Medical people from the volunteer medical organization rushed out to help him. A police officer (a sergeant, I think) came rushing forward, followed by the two other nightstick-brandishing policemen and yelled, 'Get him out of here; this ain't a hospital.' The medical people fled, half dragging and half carrying the young man with them. . . .

"Another incident I vividly recall is two policemen dragging one protester by one leg, with his shoulders and possibly his head dragging on the pavement as they ran toward a paddy wagon. So much violence was going on at one time. . . ."

A university student who was watching the melee from a hotel window says she saw one young man attempting to flee the police. "Two or three grabbed him and beat him until he fell to the ground." Then, she says, "two or three more policemen were attracted to him and continued to beat him until he was dragged into a paddy wagon."

At another moment, the girl says, she saw another youth "felled by two or three policemen." A medic "dressed all in white and wearing a white helmet" came to aid him. When police saw him giving aid to the downed boy, "they came upon the medic and began to beat him."

"I saw a well-dressed man carrying a well-dressed woman screaming in his arms," said a *Chicago Daily News* reporter. "He tried to carry her to the Hilton Hotel front door and get in. It was secured, so it certainly would have been safe to permit them in. But the police stopped him, and he then carried her back into the crowd. She was hysterical, and I can see no reason for the police treatment of this injured woman." Also during the melee, the reporter says, he saw policemen using sawhorses as "battering rams" against the crowd.

The history professor quoted earlier says, "A number of

motorcycle police drove up over the curb on the east side of Michigan and into the crowd." Police also charged demonstrators and onlookers gathered around the old car with the antidraft rally sign which earlier had been taken up to the police line in front of the Hilton.

A series of arrests were made around the antidraft car, some peaceful and some with considerable force. During the course of these arrests, one girl in this group lost her skirt. Although there have been unverified reports of police ripping the clothes from female demonstrators, this is the only incident on news film of any woman being disrobed in the course of arrest.

While violence was exploding in the street, the crowd wedged, behind the police sawhorses along the northeast edge of the Hilton, was experiencing a terror all its own. Early in the evening, this group had consisted in large part of curious bystanders. But following the police surges into the demonstrators clogging the intersection, protesters had crowded the ranks behind the horses in their flight from the police.

From force of numbers, this sidewalk crowd of 150 to 200 persons was pushing down toward the Hilton's front entrance. Policemen whose orders were to keep the entrance clear were pushing with sawhorses. Other police and fleeing demonstrators were pushing from the north in the effort to clear the intersection. Thus, the crowd was wedged against the hotel, with the hotel itself on the west, sawhorses on the southeast and police on the northeast.

Films show that one policeman elbowed his way to where he could rescue a girl of about ten years of age from the vise-like press of the crowd. He cradled her in his arms and carried her to a point of relative safety 20 feet away. The crowd itself "passed up" an elderly woman to a low ledge. But many who remained were subjected to what they and witnesses considered deliberate brutality by the police.

"I was crowded in with the group of screaming, frightened people," an onlooker states, "We jammed against each other, trying to press into the brick wall of the hotel. As we stood there breathing hard . . . a policeman calmly walked the length of the barricade with a can of chemical spray [evidently mace] in his hand. Unbelievably, he was spraying at us." Photos reveal several policemen using mace against the crowd.

Another witness, a graduate student, said she was on the periphery of the crowd and could see that "police sprayed mace randomly along the first line of people along the curb."

A reporter who was present said a woman cried, "Oh no, not mace!" He said a youth moaned, "Stop it! We're not doing anything!" "Others," recalls another witness, "pleaded with the police to tell them where they should move and allow them to move there."

"Some of the police then turned and attacked the crowd," a Chicago reporter says. The student says she could see police clubbing persons pinned at the edge of the crowd and that there was "a great deal of screaming and pushing within the group." A reporter for a Cleveland paper said, "The police indiscriminately beat those on the periphery of the crowd." An Assistant U.S. attorney put it, "The group on the sidewalk was charged by police using nightsticks." A young cook caught in the crowd relates that:

> The police began picking people off. They would pull individuals to the ground and begin beating them. A medic wearing a white coat and an armband with a red cross was grabbed, beaten and knocked to the ground. His whole face was covered with blood.

"The cops just waded into the crowd," says a law student. "There was a great deal of clubbing. People were screaming, 'Help'."

As a result, a part of the crowd was trapped in front of the Conrad Hilton and pressed hard against a big plate glass window of the Haymarket Lounge. A reporter who was sitting inside said, "Frightened men and women banged . . . against the window. A captain of the fire department inside told us to get back from the window, that it might get knocked in. As I backed away a few feet I could see a smudge of blood on the glass outside."

With a sickening crack, the window shattered, and screaming men and women tumbled through, some cut badly by jagged glass. The police came after them.

"I was pushed through by the force of large numbers of people," one victim said. "I got a deep cut on my right leg, diagnosed later by Eugene McCarthy's doctor as a severed artery. . . . I fell to the floor of the bar. There were ten to 20 people who had come through . . . I could not stand on the leg. It was bleeding profusely.

"A squad of policemen burst into the bar, clubbing all those who looked to them like demonstrators, at the same time screaming over and over, 'We've got to clear this area.' The police acted literally like mad dogs looking for objects to attack.

"A patrolman ran up to where I was sitting. I protested that I was injured and could not walk, attempting to show him my leg. He screamed that he would show me I could walk. He grabbed me by the shoulder and literally hurled me through the door of the bar into the lobby. . . .

"I stumbled out into what seemed to be a main lobby. The young lady I was with and I were both immediately set upon by what I can only presume were plainclothes police. . . . We were cursed by these individuals and thrown through another door into an outer lobby." Eventually a McCarthy aide took him to the 15th floor.

In the heat of all this, probably few were aware of the Haymarket's advertising slogan: "A place where good guys take good girls to dine in the lusty, rollicking atmosphere of fabulous Old Chicago. . . ."

During the evening, at least one other window of the Hilton was also broken by crushing crowds.

There is little doubt that during this whole period, beginning at 7:57 p.m. and lasting for nearly 20 minutes, the preponderance of violence came from the police. It was not entirely a one-way battle, however.

Firecrackers were thrown at police. Trash baskets were set on fire and rolled and thrown at them. In one case, a gun was taken from a policeman by a demonstrator.

"Some hippies," said a patrolman in his statement, "were hit by other hippies who were throwing rocks at the police." Films reveal that when police were chasing demonstrators into Grant Park, one young man upended a sawhorse and heaved it at advancing officers. At one point the deputy superintendent of police was knocked down by a thrown sawhorse. At least one police three-wheeler was tipped over. One of the demonstrators says that "people in the park were prying up cobblestones and breaking them. One person piled up cobblestones in his arms and headed toward the police." Witnesses reported that people were throwing "anything they could lay their hands on. From the windows of the Hilton and Blackstone hotels, toilet paper, wet towels, even ash trays came raining down." A police lieutenant stated that he saw policemen bombarded with "rocks, cherry bombs, jars of vaseline, jars of mayonnaise and pieces of wood torn from the yellow barricades falling in the street." He, too, noticed debris falling from the hotel windows.

A patrolman on duty during the melee states that among the objects he saw thrown at police officers were "rocks, bottles, shoes, a telephone and a garbage can cover. Rolls of toilet paper were thrown from hotel windows. I saw a number of plastic practice golf balls, studded with nails, on the street as well as plastic bags filled with what appeared to be human excrement." He said he saw two policemen, one of them wearing a soft hat, get hit with bricks.

A sergeant states that during the fracas, two men under his command had their plastic faceguards (which they pay for themselves) shattered by bricks or rocks.

A number of police officers were injured, either by flying missiles or in personal attacks. One, for example, was helping a fellow officer "pick up a hippie when another hippie gave [me] a heavy kick, aiming for my groin." The blow struck the officer partly on the leg and partly in the testicles. He went down, and the "hippie" who kicked him escaped.

An attorney who was present also told of seeing demonstrators kick policemen in the groin.

In another instance, a Chicago police reporter said in his statement, "a police officer reached down and grabbed a person who dove forward and bit the officer on the leg. . . . Three or four fellow policemen came to his aid. They had to club the demonstrator to make him break his clamp on the officer's leg." In another case, the witness saw a demonstrator "with a big mop of hair hit a police officer with an old British Army type metal helmet." The reporter said he also heard "hissing sounds from the demonstrators as if they were spraying the police." Later he found empty lacquer spray and hair spray cans on the street. Also he heard policemen cry out, "They're kicking us with knives in their shoes." Later, he said, he found that demonstrators "had actually inserted razor blades in their shoes."

Another type of police difficulty was described by a police captain and mentioned by several other officers in their statements. The captain said that when news cameramen equipped with portable flood lights turned them toward the police, this "caused temporary blindness" and reduced the police effectiveness.

Against the demonstrators' missile throwing and otherwise,

police tended to move in groups of eight or ten, regrouping now and then in the street.

Squadrols continually drove into the intersection. "The police kept pulling as many people as they were able to get and taking them into the paddy wagons," say the ACLU representative quoted earlier. The manner in which this was done ranged from restraint to deliberate brutality. In one case, for example, a heavy woman in a muu-muu insisted on using the step at the back of the squadrol as a platform from which to address the crowd. The police repeatedly attempted to move her, but she continued to speak. Finally, a large policeman grabbed her under both arms and lifted her up and into the squadrol.

By contrast, police dragged some persons up the squadrol step, throwing them bodily inside and then hitting them. In one arrest, captured on film, a male demonstrator used his hand to trip one of two policemen carrying him to a paddy wagon. After picking himself up from the pavement, the officer severely beat the demonstrator on the head and chest with his baton. Another policeman joined in, repeatedly jabbing the youth in the groin with his baton.

A man who served as a medical liaison to the demonstration marshals states that he saw the police beat a boy incessantly before putting him into a paddy wagon. He said that the boy looked as if he were already unconscious, but the police continued beating him. According to the university student, quoted earlier about her view from the hotel window, "When an individual was brought to the paddy wagon, two or three policemen stationed at the door would grab the person and continue to beat him."

An Assistant U.S. Attorney who was at the battle reported later: "The arresting officers frequently used their clubs to hit the arrested person in the stomach and kidneys, even though the arrested persons were not in any way resisting arrest or struggling with the police officers." On the other hand, both police officers and a city observer who watched the loading of the paddy wagons state that no excessive force was used in placing nonresisting prisoners in the vans.

Meanwhile, more CTA buses with police reinforcements were pouring into the area. Blue police buses by now were bringing reinforcements into the area. A Chicago attorney who was near the Hilton watched one contingent unload. He says they "gave the finger" to subdued demonstrators in the vicinity and also made obscene remarks, like "Hippies eat shit." Moving quickly through the Balbo-Michigan intersection, they hurried to join their fellow officers pushing north on Michigan.

Says an ACLU representative: "The buses would discharge at the corner of Wabash and Balbo and then the men would form into a line and march down Balbo with their night sticks, chanting, "Kill, kill."

With each new police attack and flurry of arrests, the crowd dispersed farther into the park and east on Balbo.

Peck wound up on the east side of Michigan Avenue. From that vantage point, he said, he thought he saw the deputy superintendent of police and a person in civilian clothes, who he thought was a city official, coming across the avenue in his direction. In a similar situation during the Pentagon confrontation when federal marshals moved in against demonstrators, Peck says, he had been able to obtain a loudspeaker, address himself to commanding authority, calm the crowd and prevent further assaults. With this in mind, he said he went out to "resume negotiations" with the deputy superintendent and the other man. Peck admits he was "probably pretty emotional" at this point, but says he had his senses about him.

Using his hand to emphasize his words, he addressed the deputy: "Why did you have your police move against us when I said we were not violent? Isn't there any way we can get our people to safety?"

At this, Peck insists, they both lunged at him. Peck said he tightened up in "a defensive posture" to break their hold and then ran. Other police came after him. He again assumed the defensive posture and, he claims, was beaten brutally by the officers. Then, Peck says, he was dragged some 200 feet to a police van. Later several stitches were taken on his head, his back and sides were bruised and his genitals were swollen.

A witness to this incident, the Chicago police reporter quoted earlier, says that Peck initiated the trouble by shouting at the deputy: "You're the cause of all this." Then, the witness states, Peck slugged the deputy in the right eye with his fist, knocking his glasses to the street. A police sergeant went after Peck, but was "grabbed by a group of demonstrators who beat the daylights out of him." Finally, another officer made a flying tackle of Peck as he was "trying to escape through the crowd." As Peck was arrested, "the demonstrators broke up a yellow wooden [saw] horse approximately ten or 12 feet long . . . and began throwing [the pieces] at the police." The deputy superintendent, the reporter said, was hit again. The sergeant was rescued from the mob only after several policemen used their batons against the demonstrators. The deputy's version of the incident agrees essentially with this account.

Wild in the Streets

By 8:15 p.m., the intersection was in police control. One group of police proceeded east on Balbo, clearing the street and splitting the crowd into two. Because National Guard lines still barred passage over the Balbo Street bridge, most of the demonstrators fled into Grant Park. A Guardsman estimates that 5,000 remained in the park across from the Hilton. Some clubbing by police occurred; a demonstrator says he saw a brick hurled at police; but few arrests were made.

Now, with police lines beginning to re-form, the deputy superintendent directed the police units to advance north on Michigan. He says announcements were again made to clear the area and warnings given that those refusing to do so would be arrested. To this, according to a patrolman who was present, "The hippie group yelled 'fuck you' in unison."

A police officer remembers the deputy superintendent saying, "I want this street kept completely clear. I don't want anyone except people in uniform out in the street. The objective is to get the street clean, open it to traffic and hold it."

Police units formed up. National Guard intelligence officers on the site called for Guard assistance. At 8:30 the Secret Service reported trucks full of Guard troops from Soldier Field moving north on Michigan Avenue to the Conrad Hilton and additional units arrived about 20 minutes later. The troops included the same units that had seen action earlier in the day after the bandshell rally and had later been moved to 22nd Street.

By 8:55 p.m., the Guard had taken up positions in a U-shaped formation, blocking Balbo at Michigan and paralleling the Hilton and Grant Park—a position that was kept until 4 a.m. Thursday. Although bayonets were affixed when the troops first hit the street, they were quickly removed. Explains a Guardsman who was there: "The bayonets had gotten in our way when we were on the Congress Street bridge."

"The crowd that remained behind in the park was very noisy and restless," he remembers. "People were milling around on the sidewalk. Police said that these people who were walking on the sidewalk could be subject to arrest. The parade marshals kept them away from the sidewalk."

At one point, however, a demonstrator tried to "take the muzzle off" one of the Guardsmen's rifle. "All the time the demonstrators were trying to talk to us. They said 'join us' or 'fuck the draft.' We were told not to talk to anyone in the crowd."

Meanwhile, having left about 50 of their number behind with the Guard in front of the Hilton, the police pushed the demonstrators north on Michigan, the crowd chanting "The streets are for the people," and "Pigs eat shit." At times, they sang "America" and "We Shall Overcome."

One Guard unit followed behind the police as a backup group.

With the police and Guard at its rear, the crowd fractured in several directions as it moved away from Balbo and Michigan. Many continued on up Michigan to the vicinity of the Art Institute. Some went east on side streets back into Grant Park, eventually working their way back in front of the Hilton. Others raced west on cross streets into the Loop.

One large group in particular ran west on Jackson Boulevard, chased by the police almost to State Street where, the U.S. Attorney reported, the police re-formed and went back toward Michigan. When the crowd reached State, two blocks west of Michigan, it again broke in three parts. One segment kept going west to a store front Lutheran Church across the street from the Federal Building which had been prepared as an emergency casualty center. Another moved south on State Street, some members taking the subway or the elevated to escape the Loop and others filtering south on State and Wabash to 8th, 9th and 11th streets, where they swung east to Grant Park and the Hilton area. Some made their way deeper into the Loop where they broke into the Civic Center and painted on the floors "Property of Pigs." The largest portion moved north on State toward the Palmer House, another of the principal convention hotels.

Strong police guards had been set up at the Palmer House entrances and the guard at the State Street entrance tensed as the remnants of the crowd surged up the sidewalks. But the crowd passed this entrance without incident and turned east on Monroe Street at the north side of the hotel. It continued east back to Michigan, where it joined up with those who had moved directly north on Michigan.

Near Michigan and Monroe another casualty center had been set up in the headquarters of the Church Federation of Greater Chicago. This, plus the melding of the crowds north-bound on Michigan and east-bound on Monroe, brought about 1,000 persons to the west side of Michigan between Adams and Monroe, facing the Art Institute. There were few demonstrators on the east side of Michigan.

At 9:25 p.m., the police commander ordered a sweep of Michigan Avenue south from Monroe. At about this same time the police still had lines on both the west and east sides of Michigan in front of the Hilton and additional National Guard troops had arrived at 8th Street.

At 9:57 p.m., the demonstrators still on Michigan Avenue, prodded along by the southward sweep of the police, began marching back to Grant Park, chanting "Back to the park." By 10:10 p.m., an estimated 800 to 1,000 demonstrators had gathered in front of the Hilton.

By then, two city street sweeping trucks had rumbled up and down the street in front of the hotel, cleaning up the residue of violence—shoes, bottles, rocks, tear gas handkerchiefs. A police captain said the debris included: "Bases and pieces of broken bottles, a piece of board (1″ x 4″ x 14″), an 18-inch length of metal pipe, a 24-inch stick with a protruding sharpened nail, a 12-inch length of ½-inch diameter pipe, pieces of building bricks, an 18-inch stick with a razor blade protruding . . . several plastic balls somewhat smaller than tennis balls containing approximately 15 to 20 sharpened nails driven into the ball from various angles." When the delegates returned to the Hilton, they saw none of the litter of the battle.

As the crowd had dispersed from the Hilton in the pattern just described, the big war of Michigan and Balbo was, of course, over. But for those in the streets, as the rivulets of the crowd forked through the areas north of the hotel, there were still battles to be fought. Police violence and police baiting were some time in abating. Indeed, some of the most vicious incidents occurred in this "post-war" period.

Individual encounters are too numerous to catalogue *in toto*, but accounts from a series of witnesses will suffice in showing the tone of the two-hour period following the Michigan-Balbo battle. These accounts from both police and nonpolice witnesses are summarized in the following pages.

The U.S. Attorney states that as the crowd moved north on Michigan Avenue, "they pelted the police with missiles of all sorts, rocks, bottles, firecrackers. When a policeman was struck, the crowd would cheer. The policemen in the line were dodging and jumping to avoid being hit." A police sergeant told the FBI that even a telephone was hurled from the crowd at the police.

A member of the volunteer medical committee walking on the west side of Michigan said that he noticed "bags filled with liquid" being thrown from windows of one of the hotels. "Also liquid was poured out of cups down into the street and onto the crowd," the doctor said. His impression was that the crowd "became rather irritated" by this.

"Individuals in the middle of Michigan Avenue were setting fires on the street and in garbage cans on the street," a police lieutenant stated later. "Some attempted to roll the burning garbage cans into the skirmish line. . . ."

In the first block north of the Hilton, recalls a man who was standing outside a Michigan Avenue restaurant, demonstrators "menaced limousines, calling the occupants 'scum,' telling them they didn't belong in Chicago and to go home."

As the police skirmish line moved north, the police lieutenant said he "saw people standing on the hoods and trunks of two marked police cars and one unmarked police car about 150 feet north of the skirmish line." He said he could hear windows being smashed and the crowd shouting its approval." (A college coed says a demonstrator first tried to kick in a squad car's back window and failing that, smashed it with a trash basket.) The lieutenant said he was approached by two young police officers, apparently refugees from one of the squad cars, who said they "were not supposed to be in that area and did not know what to do or where to go." They told the lieutenant they had been among the squads accompanying the mule train on its parade south on Michigan earlier, but had been cut off by the crowd. The lieutenant told them to report to their headquarters.

As the skirmish line drew nearer to the squad cars, the lieutenant said, he saw several persons shoving paper through the cars' broken windows—in his opinion, a prelude to setting the cars on fire. A theology student who was in the crowd states that "a demonstrator took a fire extinguisher and sprayed inside the car. Then he put paper on the ground under the gas tank. . . . People shouted at him to stop." To break up the crowd, the lieutenant said, he squirted tear gas from an aerosol container and forced the demonstrators back.

"The crowd [was] unruly," reported an Assistant U.S. Attorney. "Some people had climbed on top of traffic signals, others started a fire in a trash basket, and someone had commandeered a giant spotlight which was operating on Michigan Avenue to promote some event.

"The police approached the crowd from both ends. . . ."

* * *

"Two or three policemen, one with a white shirt, advanced on the crowd," one witness said. "The white-shirted one squirted mace in arcs back and forth before him."

A cameraman for the *Chicago Daily News* photographed a woman cowering after she had been sprayed with mace. A *News* representative states that the officer administering the mace, whom the photographers identified as a police lieutenant, then turned and directed the spray at the cameraman. The cameraman shot a photograph of this as he ducked. The police lieutenant involved states that he does not remember this incident.

"The white-shirted officer, after pushing the crowd back about 20 feet, looked across the line, sometimes for a full minute, then suddenly arresting just one demonstrator," another witness states. "This procedure was repeated about ten times, each time with a single unresisted arrest, with no apparent provocation on the part of the individual demonstrators. Two or three demonstrators, moving about well behind the front line, harassed the police by throwing cherry bombs. This was the only weapon I saw."

* * *

A priest who was in the crowd says he saw a "boy, about 14 or 15, white, standing on top of an automobile yelling something which was unidentifiable. Suddenly a policeman forced him down from the car and beat him to the ground by striking him three or four times with a nightstick. Other police joined in . . . and they eventually shoved him to a police van."

A well-dressed woman saw this incident and spoke angrily to a nearby police captain. As she spoke, another policeman came up from behind her and sprayed something in her face with an aerosol can. He then clubbed her to the ground. He and two other policemen then dragged her along the ground to the same paddy wagon and threw her in.

"We were moving ahead of the police up from Balbo, in the park," says a law student. "Suddenly about ten cops charged down from a cross street just to the north, swinging clubs and yelling to get out of the way. I saw one kid who fell while running to get away from them. He was being beaten badly by three or four cops using their clubs."

"We moved north on Michigan Avenue again. . . There are metal posts about three feet high bolted to the sidewalk along one section. One kid had torn one post loose and was carrying it as if it were a weapon. "Next cop that hits me, I'll lay his head open," he yelled.

A UPI reporter said in his statement that in this area he saw "bottles or pebbles thrown five or six times. However, some of the leaders, medics and others in front of the crowd, were picking up bottles and breaking them in order to prevent them from being thrown. I saw four demonstrators seize a bottle from another as he was about to throw it."

"At the corner of Harrison and Michigan where police had difficulty clearing the mob from the intersection," a deputy chief of police states that the National Guard "gassed the unruly mob and drove them north. . . . This mob blocked traffic at Congress and also Van Buren before they were driven north."

* * *

"At the corner of Congress Plaza and Michigan," states a doctor, "was gathered a group of people, number between 30 and 40. They were trapped against a railing [along a ramp leading down from Michigan Avenue to an underground parking garage] by several policemen on motorcycles. The police charged the people on motorcycles and struck about a dozen of them, knocking several of them down. About 20 standing there jumped over the railing. On the other side of the railing was a three-to-four-foot drop. None of the people who were struck by the motorcycles appeared to be seriously injured. However, several of them were limping as if they had been run over on their feet."

A UPI reporter witnessed these attacks, too. He relates in his statement that one officer, "with a smile on his face and a fanatical look in his eyes, was standing on a three-wheel cycle, shouting, 'Wahoo, wahoo,' and trying to run down people on the sidewalk." The reporter says he was chased 30 feet by the cycle.

A few seconds later he "turned around and saw a policeman with a raised billy stick." As he swung around, the police stick grazed his head and struck his shoulders. As he was on his knees, he says someone stepped on his back.

A Negro policeman helped him to his feet, the reporter says. The policeman told him, "You know, man I didn't do this. One of the white cops did it." Then, the reporter quotes the officer as saying, "You know what? After this is all over, I'm quitting the force."

An instant later, the shouting officer on the motorcycle swung by again, and the reporter dove into a doorway for safety.

Near this same intersection, a Democratic delegate from Oklahoma was surrounded in front of his hotel by about ten persons, two of them with long hair and beards. He states that they encircled him for several minutes and subjected him to verbal abuse because they felt he "represented the establishment" and was "somewhat responsible for the alleged police brutality." The delegate stood mute and was eventually rescued by a policeman.

At Van Buren, a college girl states, "demonstrators were throwing things at passing police cars, and I saw one policeman hit in the face with a rock. A small paddy wagon drove up with only one policeman in it, and the crowd began rocking the wagon. The cop fell out and was surrounded by the crowd, but no effort was made to hurt him."

At one point, three or four three-wheel motorcycles came into the area and dispersed demonstrators who were in the street, forcing them to run to the curb. An Assistant U.S. Attorney observed one cyclist hit one demonstrator and narrowly miss others. He pointed out, however, that the demonstrator who was hit did not fall and did not appear to have been injured.

"Around the intersection, two or three police tricycles began driving fast at people, doing dry skids and tipping on two wheels to avoid hitting people," another witness says.

"The motorcycles, three-wheelers, raced around the street, running people down," says the graduate student. Near the intersection, he says, several persons were sitting on guard railings that flank a ramp leading down to an underground parking garage. These persons included "some children, ten to

12 years old. Several were knocked off backwards down onto the concrete ramp, as the cycles raced along the railing. Others were beaten in front of the structure as police closed in on them. Finally a tear gas canister was thrown in after the people who had fallen over backwards."

At Jackson, says the graduate student quoted earlier, "People got into the street on their knees and prayed, including several ministers who were dressed in clerical garb. These people, eight or ten of them, were arrested. This started a new wave of dissent among the demonstrators, who got angry. Many went forward to be arrested voluntarily; others were taken forcibly and some were beaten. . . . Objects were being thrown directly at police, including cans, bottles and paper."

"I was in the street," a witness who was near the intersection states, "when a fire in a trash basket appeared. . . . In a few minutes, two fire engines passed south through the crowd, turned west on Van Buren and stopped. They were followed by two police wagons which stopped in the middle of the block. As I walked north past the smaller of the two wagons, it began to rock." (The wagon also was being pelted by missiles, the U.S. Attorney states, and "PIGS" was painted on its sides.)

"I retreated onto the east sidewalk," the witness continued. "The two policemen jumped out of the smaller wagon and one was knocked down by a few demonstrators, while other demonstrators tried to get these demonstrators away. The two policemen got back to the wagon, the crowd having drawn well back around them." The U.S. Attorney's report states that one of the policemen was "stomped" by a small group of the mob.

A young woman who was there and who had attended the bandshell rally earlier in the afternoon states that the crowd rocked the wagon for some time, while its officers stayed inside. "Then," she says, "the driver came out wildly swinging his club and shouting. About ten people jumped on him. He was kicked pretty severely and was downed. When he got up he was missing his club and his hat."

A police commander says that at about this moment he received "an urgent radio message" from an officer inside the van. He radioed that "demonstrators were standing on the hood of his wagon . . . and were preparing to smash the windshield with a baseball bat," the commander recalled. The officer also told him that the demonstrators were attempting to overturn the squadrol and that the driver "was hanging on the door in a state of shock." The commander told the officer that assistance was on the way.

"I heard a '10-1' call on either my radio or one of the other hand sets being carried by other men with me," the U.S. Attorney states, "and then heard, 'Car 100-sweep!' [Car 100 was assigned to the police commander.] With a roar of motors, squads, vans and three-wheelers came from east, west and north into the block north of Jackson."

"Almost immediately a CTA bus filled with police came over the Jackson Drive bridge and the police formed a line in the middle of the street," says a witness. "I heard shouts that the police had rifles and that they had cocked and pumped them. Demonstrators began to run."

"With riot helmets and clubs raised, the police quickly cleared the street," an observer from the Chicago Legal Defense Committee states. "As one area was cleared, another contingent of police arrived with rifles raised and pointed at the people massed on the sidewalk. They pointed guns at the crowd, which responded with catcalls and slogans 'Pigs' . . . 'Fascists' . . . 'Shoot, go on, shoot.'

"I ran north of Jackson . . . just as police were clearing the intersection and forming a line across Michigan," says the witness quoted above. "The police who had formed a line facing east in the middle of Michigan charged, yelling and clubbing into the crowd, running at individuals and groups who did not run before them."

* * *

A political science student, who was a driver for one of the convention delegations, states: "A man about 30 or 40 approached a policeman on the corner with tears in his eyes and asked him why they were beating [the people]. The policeman responded by beating him on the side of the head. The man's glasses fell off, and as he bent to retrieve them he was beaten on the back and head until he lay huddled on the ground.

"When he tried to get up, a Green Beret of about 25 to 30, in uniform, came out of the crowd and started beating the man. The original cop was about to intervene when another cop yelled, 'Leave him alone. He just got back from Vietnam.' [It was later discovered that the man was not a Green Beret but, in fact, a deserter from the Army.]

"They left him alone and a group of officers pushed us away from the scene by advancing in a line. I saw the beaten man being arrested. I tried to get the badge numbers of the cops, but neither had them on.

"They pushed us down the street. Suddenly we saw the Green Beret across the street. A man in front of me yelled 'mother fucker' at him. Immediately he ran across the street with two police following and protecting him. He started hitting everyone around him with the police protecting him. He did this for a minute or so and crossed the street again. Some people were lying on the ground bleeding and moaning.

"As soon as he left, the police line on our side of the street rushed us, yelling. The crowd had nowhere to run. The masses of the people stopped us. People fell. People were trampled. Two of us tried to hide in a building. Three officers came after us. I looked around as I ran out of the doorway and was sprayed in the face and eyes with gas. The fellow with me was clubbed. . . . I could see only slightly. Policemen and people were running everywhere. I passed a priest leaning against a wall holding his rib cage. I tried to help him. The police rushed at me and I ran. I saw them hit the priest and he fell to the ground. I ran down a side street and got away. My face was on fire. . . ."

Another witness states: "One straggler of a demonstrator told the cops to get back. The police started clubbing the kid, saying 'Get out of here, mother fucker!'

"A Green Beret in uniform came from the other side of the street, and helped the 12 policemen who were beating the kid. The police formed a circle around the kid and the Green Beret, who continued to fight. Several kids tried to get at the Green Beret, but the police told them to get away."

"As the fray intensified around the intersection of Michigan and Jackson, a big group ran west on Jackson, with a group of blue-shirted policemen in pursuit, beating at them with clubs," says the U.S. Attorney's report. "Some of the crowd would jump into doorways, and the police would rout them out. The action was very tough and, in my judgment, unnecessarily so. The police were hitting with a vengeance and quite obviously with relish because of what had happened to the men in the van. Some of the crowd ran up the alleys; some north on Wabash; and some west on Jackson to State with the police in pursuit."

"I ran west on Jackson," a witness states. "West of Wabash,

a line of police stretching across both sidewalks and the street charged after the small group I was in. Many people were clubbed and maced as they ran. Some weren't demonstrators at all, but were just pedestrians who didn't know how to react to the charging officers yelling 'Police!' "

"A wave of police charged down Jackson," another witness relates. "Fleeing demonstrators were beaten indiscriminately and a temporary, makeshift first aid station was set up on the corner of State and Jackson. Two men lay in pools of blood, their heads severely cut by clubs. A minister moved amongst the crowd, quieting them, brushing aside curious onlookers, and finally asked a policeman to call an ambulance, which he agreed to do. . . ."

An Assistant U.S. Attorney later reported that "the demonstrators were running as fast as they could but were unable to get out of the way because of the crowds in front of them. I observed the police striking numerous individuals, perhaps 20 or 30. I saw three fall down and then overrun by the police. I observed two demonstrators who had multiple cuts on their heads. We assisted one who was in shock into a passer-by's car.

"A TV mobile truck appeared . . . and the police became noticeably more restrained, holding their clubs at waist level rather than in the air," a witness relates. "As the truck disappeared . . . the head-clubbing tactics were resumed."

Reported an Assistant U.S. Attorney: "We saw police arrest one boy who claimed he was walking to make a telephone call. At no time did I see any arresting officer write down the name of the person he was arresting or make any notes assisting him in remembering the identity of the individual.

"They were hitting the demonstrators who were running on the sidewalks on both the north and south sides of the street. . . . As the policemen came to the end of the block, an officer yelled for them to stop. Finally after his and our repeated screaming, they stopped and regrouped, leaving four or five fallen demonstrators.

"We found one 'hippie type' at the northeast corner of Jackson and State with a bad head cut and stopped a private car to take him to Michael Reese Hospital," the U.S. Attorney recalled. "There was another hippie type injured less seriously at the northeast corner of State and Jackson and an apparent clergyman with a reddish beard in the doorway of the drug store at the southeast corner of Jackson and State. He was rather badly injured, and we stopped a private ambulance and asked them to help him."

One demonstrator states that he ran off Michigan Avenue on to Jackson. He says he and his wife ran down Jackson and were admitted, hesitantly, into a restaurant. They seated themselves at a table by the window facing onto Jackson and, while sitting at the table, observed a group of people running down Jackson with policemen following them and striking generally at the crowd with their batons. At one instance, he saw a policeman strike a priest in the head with a baton. He said he saw the policeman strike the priest only once and then go on. The clergyman also moved on.

At the intersection of Jackson and Wabash, says the student whose wife was beaten in the race from Michigan, "the police came from all four directions and attacked the crowd. Demonstrators were beaten and run to the paddy wagons. I saw a black policeman go berserk. He charged blindly at the group of demonstrators and made two circles through the crowd, swinging wildly at anything."

* * *

An Assistant U.S. Attorney watching the action on various side streets reported, "I observed police officers clearing people westward . . . using their clubs to strike people on the back of the head and body on several occasions. Once a policeman ran alongside a young girl. He held her by the shoulder of her jacket and struck at her a few times as they were both running down the sidewalk.

"I saw one young man lying on the sidewalk. . . . He was cut and bleeding from a head wound. I gave him my card and flagged a passing motorist . . . to take him to a hospital."

A traffic policeman on duty on Michigan Avenue says that the demonstrators who had continued north often surrounded cars and buses attempting to move south along Michigan Avenue. Many males in the crowd, he says, exposed their penises to passers-by and other members of the crowd. At times, they would run up to cars clogged by the crowd and show their private parts to the passengers.

To men, the officer says, they shouted such questions as, "How would you like me to fuck your wife?" and "How would you like to fuck a man?" Many of the demonstrators also rocked the automobiles in an effort to tip them over.

At the intersection of State and Monroe, at the northwest

corner of the Palmer House, a traffic officer looked at the on-coming crowd and said, "You're not marching down my street." "With this," a reporter states, "The crowd separated to each side of the officer and continued on."

A housewife who had come downtown as a demonstrator states that she had stood on this corner about five minutes when "a squad car pulled up and two or three policemen got out. They immediately went into the crowd and started swinging their nightsticks. The six policemen who had been directing traffic joined in." The woman fled east on Monroe, back toward Michigan. As she turned, she says, she was struck from behind in the buttocks by a policeman.

A witness who was leaving a building where a temporary medical center was set up on Michigan says he "noticed two policemen taking a prisoner south. . . . They were beating his legs in cadence as he walked. His legs became flimsy. He kept crying, 'I'm going, I'm going, stop hitting me.' "

A policeman states that bags of feces and urine were dropped on the police from the building.

The policeman also said "people would arrive without any visible injury and subsequently leave, heavily bandaged and smeared with blood." Also "groups would arrive at the headquarters in clerical garb and then strip their collars off, saying, 'Well, we sure fooled the police again tonight.' "

* * *

As the crowd moved south again on Michigan, a traffic policeman, who was in the vicinity of Adams Street, recalls, "They first took control of the lions in front of the Art Institute. They climbed them and shouted things like, "Let's fuck" and "Fuck, fuck, fuck!"

A young attorney standing in front of the Institute said that he "could clearly see four or five policemen chase a young man down Michigan. The man was about 20, white, and dressed in blue denim pants and a plaid cloth jacket. He was wearing rather long hair.

"When the police caught him, they grabbed him and started to strike him all over with their knees. This incensed the people nearby and they yelled at the police to stop.

"A few yards away, there was a policeman walking alone on Michigan. The crowd had gathered somewhat by this time and it appeared that the policeman might have been in trouble.

"At this, a group of youths formed a semi-circle around the

cop. It was formed toward the sidewalk, leaving the cop a free access to the street.

"As the cop was standing there, he was struck in the back of his helmet with a half-brick. The people who had formed the semi-circle turned and berated the youth who had thrown the brick. The cop was apparently unharmed."

Another witness said that at about this same location he saw five policemen chase a man in his late teens or early twenties. "When they caught him, they began to beat him with their nightsticks until he fell to the pavement. They continued to beat him briefly after he fell. Then they dragged him about 30 feet to a paddy wagon."

At this same intersection, an officer rescued two Loop secretaries from being molested by demonstrators. He asked them, "What are you doing here?" They replied, "We wanted to see what the hippies were like." His response: "How do you like what you saw?"

* * *

An assistant U.S. Attorney standing on the east side of Michigan near Van Buren, reported that the street was "almost completely clear of people, including demonstrators. There were isolated persons walking in groups of one or two at widely spaced intervals.

"On one occasion a young man was walking . . . out of Grant Park towards the intersection. . . . [His] path crossed the path of approximately six policemen walking north on the east side of Michigan. . . . I did not initially observe any physical contact between the police officers and the youth. I did hear a grunt, and I turned and saw the youth fall to his knees and clutch his stomach. He was in the midst of the group of policemen. . . . A policeman said, 'Arrest him.' The youth was then arrested and walked away by two police officers.

"In the same general area . . . at approximately the same time, I saw police officers arrest two other young people who were walking along Michigan. . . . The arrests were made without any provocation by the young people, who were walking alone and who did not attack the police either physically or verbally.

"There appeared to be absolutely no consistent pattern to standards for arrest. On other occasions, I observed other small groups of police officers who were simply directing individuals to clear the area and not to loiter about whenever they encountered one or two people walking along Michigan Avenue."

Old Town: The Mixture as Before

While all that was going on in and around Grant Park, Lincoln Park on Wednesday was quiet and uncrowded; but there was sporadic violence in Old Town again that night. Two University of Minnesota students who wandered through the park in the morning say they heard small groups of demonstrators saying things like "Fuck the pigs," and "Kill them all," but by this time that was not unusual. They also heard a black man addressing a group of demonstrators. He outlined plans for the afternoon, and discussed techniques for forming skirmish lines, disarming police officers, and self defense.

Also during the morning Abbie Hoffman was arrested at the Lincoln Hotel Coffee Shop, 1800 North Clark, and charged with resisting arrest and disorderly conduct. According to Hoffman's wife, Anita, she and her husband and a friend were eating breakfast when three policemen entered the coffee shop and told Hoffman they had received three complaints about an obscene word written on Hoffman's forehead. The word was "Fuck." Hoffman says he printed the word on his forehead to keep cameramen from taking his picture.

At 11:30 a.m., the North Side Cooperative Ministry again met, this time at St. Paul's Church and a number of ministers again expressed their determination to remain in the park Wednesday evening after the curfew hour.

Early Wednesday evening, at about 7:30 p.m., another delegation of citizens and ministers from the Lincoln Park Emergency Citizens Committee met with the District Commander in the police command post in Lincoln Park. The delegation demanded citizen participation in the police dispersal lines Wednesday and the police agreed.

Most of the violence against police, from all reports, was the work of gang-type youths called "greasers." They dismantled police barricades to lure squad cars down Stockton Drive, where one observer says "punks engaged in some of the most savage attacks on police that had been seen." Ministers and hippies in the area were directing traffic around the barricades and keeping people from wandering into the danger area. Two ministers in particular were trying to "keep the cool." Some youngsters also bombarded police cars passing through the Eugenie Triangle between 10:30 and 11 p.m. One officer got out of his car and chased the youths. They threw more rocks, prompting him to draw out his revolver. He fired three shots into the air. Some of those throwing missiles were also in hippie dress. Others were wearing black leather jackets.

Two National Guard jeeps were also stoned in the Eugenie Triangle. When another police car was assaulted with missiles at about 11:15 p.m., its driver halted, and, crouching behind the right side of the car, shot four or five times in the air. Two cars which had been stoned where abandoned at Lincoln and Clark.

Fight on Wells Street

A woman who lives in the neighborhood relates:

> It was about 12:00 Wednesday evening, I walked out to Clark Street. Just as I got there a police car stopped on Clark right in front of the courtyard in my apartment building, where a lot of people were throwing bricks at police cars. The police rushed in and the people ran into the courtyard to get out the back. I was too terrified to run so I just stood there and hid behind a bush. I was in the dark and policemen came in and were looking behind bushes and things and they were taking people out to Clark Street sidewalk and making them put their hands on the building, lining them up.
>
> While I was standing there, a policeman went into the courtyard to get a man. He was lying—I think he fell—on the grass in the courtyard. The policeman was standing above him holding him by the shirt in one hand and hitting him with his club with the other and spouting foul words. The man was on the ground, lying on his back and was saying "Don't hit me, I'm not with them, don't hit me." The policeman dragged him out of the courtyard and I assume he lined him up with the other people on Clark Street.

* * *

In the alley on Wells Street between Eugenie and North

Avenue, a girl was shouting at the police from a second story window. The policemen shouted back at her and someone from the crowd warned her to get away from the window. She shouted back at the police, "you bastards." Most of the policemen turned around and looked, but did nothing. One policeman, however, came up beneath the window, looked up quickly and sprayed mace up into the window.

Another woman was on her front porch around midnight when three young persons walked north on North Avenue on her side of the street and crossed to St. Paul. As they came past her, she called out "What's going on on Wells Street?" One of the men replied, "Murder, man."

At this time three police cars, driving north on North Park Avenue, stopped beside her apartment building. Some policemen got out of the cars. One yelled, "What're you kids doing here? You have no business here." Then all the officers converged on them.

The woman says that the police then started hitting the young people with their nightsticks; however, two of them ran and were not badly beaten.

The other young man was hit several times over the head by two policemen and fell to the ground at the corner of the witness' front porch. He gave no resistance whatever and was lying on his side covering his head with his arms and hands. Several more blows with nightsticks were struck while he was down. The officers then got into their cars, but one came back and kicked him several times. The woman says she cried out, "Stop, or I'll report you." The officer who had kicked the man went back to the car and she said again, "Stop, or I'll report you." This officer took a rifle or shotgun from the car and advanced a couple steps and pointed the weapon at her face. She ran into her apartment.

The woman and a neighbor called the police. About 30 minutes later, officers came and were "apologetic" about the actions of the other policemen, who they said were apparently "getting out of hand." But, they explained, they had been provoked with such missiles as balls with nails in them and bottles, and that some policemen had been working 15 hours straight.

She said the three young people were obviously "hippies," with whom she is not generally sympathetic. However, in this instance she believes the beating was without provocation and unnecessarily brutal, since no resistance was offered.

No attempt was made to arrest any of the three young persons.

The young man was taken to Presbyterian-St. Luke's by his friend and treated for skull lacerations. He required two stitches.

At the corner of Eugenie and La Salle, four boys, about 20 years old, had stopped for the traffic light. A policeman came over to them and said through the window, "Hi ya hippies," and sprayed a chemical into the car.

* * *

Meanwhile, back in Lincoln Park, two National Guard companies were utilized in the clearing operation Thursday morning. Four clergymen also joined the police, in accordance with the agreement reached earlier with the district commander.

The clearing began at about 1 a.m. with a Guard skirmish line in the lead followed by the four ministers and then a police line. However, they found practically no one present; the demonstrators were all in Grant Park or elsewhere.

One officer was injured, three squad cars were severely damaged and 56 persons were arrested.

Finally, one observer reports that he spotted a member of the Chicago press riding his bike in the Lincoln Park area "with a banner sticking high up from the back wheel, extending about seven feet high into the air, a little white banner saying 'Press.' "

Back At The Hilton

By 10:30 p.m., most of the action was centered once more in Grant Park across from the Hilton, where several hundred demonstrators and an estimated 1,500 spectators gathered to listen to what one observer describes as "unexciting speeches." There was the usual singing and shouting. Twice during the evening police and Hilton security officers went into the hotel and went to quarters occupied by McCarthy personnel—once to protest the ripping of sheets to bandage persons who had been injured and a second time to try to locate persons said to be lobbing ashtrays out of the windows. But compared to the earlier hours of the evening, the rest of the night was quiet.

In Grant Park, the sullen crowd sat facing the hotel. Someone with a transistor radio was listening to the roll call vote of states on the nomination and broadcasting the count to the rest of the throng over a bullhorn. There were loud cheers for Ted Kennedy, McCarthy, McGovern and Phillips. ("He's a black man," said the youth with the bullhorn.) Boos and cries of "Dump the Hump" arose whenever Humphrey received votes. "When Illinois was called," says the trained observer, "no one could hear totals because of booing and the chant, 'To Hell with Daley.' "

During this time the police line was subject to considerable verbal abuse from within the crowd and a witness says that both black and white agitators at the edge of the crowd tried to kick policemen with razor blades embedded in their shoes. Periodically several policemen would make forays into the crowd, punishing demonstrators they thought were involved.

At about "Louisiana," as the roll call vote moved with quickening pace toward the climax of Humphrey's nomination, the crowd grew restless, recalls a trained observer. About this same time, according to the Log, the police skirmish line began pushing the demonstrators farther east into the park. A report of an officer being struck by a nail ball was received by police. Film taken at about this time shows an officer being hit by a thrown missile, later identified as a chunk of concrete with a steel reinforcement rod in it. The blow knocked him down and, as he fell, the crowd cheered and yelled, "More!" The chant, "Kill the pigs," filled the air.

"At 'Oklahoma,' " recalls an observer, "the Yippie on the bullhorn said, 'Marshals ready. Don't move. Stay seated.' "

"The front line rose [facing the police] and locked arms, and the others stayed seated. Humphrey was over the top with Pennsylvania, and someone in the Hilton rang a cow bell at the demonstrators. Boos went up, as did tension. A bus load of police arrived. Others standing in front of the Hilton crossed Michigan and lined up behind those in front of the demonstrators.

"The chant of 'Sit down, sit down' went out. An American flag was raised on a pole upside down. Wandering began among demonstrators and the chant continued.

Shortly before midnight, while Benjamin Ortiz was speaking, National Guard troops of the 2/129 Inf. came west on Balbo to Michigan to replace the police in front of the Hilton. "For the first time," says an observer, "machine guns mounted on trucks were pulled up directly in front of the demonstrators, just behind the police lines. The machine guns, and the Guard's mesh-covered jeeps with barbed wire fronts made the demonstrators angry and nervous. Bayonets were readied. In films of this period the word "pig" can be seen written on the street.

"Ortiz continued, 'Dig this man, just 'cause you see some different pigs coming here, don't get excited. We're going to sleep here, sing here, sex here, live here!' "

As the police moved off, one of the first Guard maneuvers was to clear demonstrators from Michigan's east sidewalk. This was done to allow pedestrian traffic. The crowd reacted somewhat hostilely to the maneuver, but by and large, the demonstrators seemed to view the Guard as helpless men who had been caught up in the events and did not treat them as badly as they had the police. Having secured the sidewalk, the guards shortly retired to the east curb of Michigan Avenue. A line of "marshals" sat down at the edge of the grass at the feet of the guards. Access to the hotel was restored and people began to move from the hotel to the park and vice versa. By now, there were an estimated 4,000 persons assembled across from the Hilton. Most of the crowd sat down in a mass and became more orderly, singing "America" and "God Bless America."

A witness remembers that a chant of "Join us, join us" started. There were shouts of "Take to the streets" and "Take the South Side."

Other demonstrators yelled "Don't go home." . . . "Hell no, we won't go." . . . "Don't be afraid." . . . "Blink your lights." A number of lights blinked on and off. There was some burning of draft cards and induction notices.

McCarthy supporters joined the crowd and were welcomed.

By 12:20 a.m., Thursday, the crowd had declined to 1,500 and was considered under control. By 12:33 a.m., the police department had retired from the streets entirely and the Guard took over the complete responsibility of holding Michigan from Balbo to 8th Street. At 12:47 a.m., another contingent of Guard troops arrived and was posted at the Hilton. At about this time delegates were returning and were being booed and jeered unless they could be identified as McCarthy or McGovern supporters. Those delegates were cheered and asked to join the group.

The crowd grew in number. By 1:07 a.m., the Secret Service

estimated 2,000 persons in the park across from the hotel. Ten minutes later the crowd had grown by another 500. Those in the park were "listening to speeches—orderly" according to the log.

THE POLICE AND THE PRESS

Not only in Chicago, but also throughout the nation there has been a storm of controversy over the fairness of mass media coverage—and particularly television coverage—of the Democratic National Convention. We have not been charged with investigating that aspect of convention week. Our concern here is with instances of violence involving media representatives and police.

We address the following questions, and shall consider media coverage only insofar as it bears on them.

1. Was any news staged and manufactured by demonstrators and newsmen?
2. Were newsmen calculated targets of violence by police?
3. Were any police attacks on newsmen unwarranted and unprovoked?

There is good reason to seek answers to these questions—of about 300 newsmen assigned to cover the parks and streets of Chicago during convention week, more than 65 were involved in incidents resulting in injury to themselves, damage to their equipment, or their arrest.

Background

Welcome, Newsmen! Welcome to Chicago, the City of "The Front Page," with an outstanding tradition of competitive journalism. Another tradition has been the excellent rapport between the Chicago police and newsmen.

> —From a brochure distributed by the Chicago Police Department to members of newspapers, magazines and television networks who covered the Democratic National Convention.

As long as press and police have worked together in this country there have been incidents of conflict and harassment. Bitter words have been exchanged by both sides. Newsmen have been slugged before in Chicago and elsewhere. And more than one photographer has had his equipment smashed or his film confiscated by police. Mostly the friction has resulted from the news media's wish to interpret broadly the First Amendment of the Constitution which guarantees "freedom of the press." For their part, the police have maintained they have the freedom, and also the duty, to use whatever force is necessary to maintain order and reduce the threat of violence or insurrection.

The practical and legal constitutional questions arising from this conflict have never been resolved. Police concede that newsmen have the right to be present at public demonstrations in order to gather and report information. But do they have special rights other than those of the general public? How are their rights affected when demonstration becomes disorder? To what extent may the rights of newsmen, like those of the public, be abridged by the use of police force in order to maintain or achieve order? Since these questions are not adequately answered by existing decisions on constitutional law, neither the press nor the police is certain of its legal position and the controversy continues.

M. L. Stein, chairman of the Journalism Department of New York University, wrote in the *Saturday Review:*

> Through history, editors and writers have been shot, jailed, horsewhipped, caned, spat upon, and reviled. Their offices have been sacked and burned, and attempts have been made to pass laws taking away the press freedom embodied in the First Amendment to the Constitution. George Washington, Thomas Jefferson, and John Quincy Adams were among the many Presidents and politicians who bitterly assailed the press.

In Chicago the press and police have a long history of cooperation. In 1947, discussions were held concerning procedures to be followed when violence, riots or other major calamities occurred in the city. Their purpose was to protect relations between press and police and to assure fair and accurate reporting of events. In 1955 a code for radio and television was devised. The major points provided for checking rumors before broadcasting them and the use of temporary news blackouts until a story could be confirmed. Though the agreements were informal and not binding on either party, neither the police nor the press has had serious cause to complain about them. For the most part their provisions have been followed.

In recent years cities throughout the nation have faced major outbreaks of violence—usually concerning racial problems. In a number of these situations newsmen were injured. Most notable were the civil rights disorders in the South in the 1950's and early 1960's, when police charged that newsmen impeded their work and made the task of controlling mobs more difficult.

After the riots in the Watts area of Los Angeles in August, 1965, a commission appointed by California Governor Edmund G. Brown suggested that members of the media meet to consider voluntary guidelines for reporting civil disorders. Under the guidance of the School of Journalism and the Department of Telecommunications at the University of Southern California, newspaper reporters, radio and television newsmen, programming executives, scholars and professors of journalism, wire service reporters and executives got together to offer suggestions. Many journalists felt no code was necessary, citing the traditional right of newsmen to "get the story."

After much discussion a code was drawn up. Among the provisions pertinent to this study were these:

1. Because inexpert use of cameras, bright lights, or microphones may stir exhibitionism of some people, great care should be exercised by crews at scenes of public disorders. Because, too, of danger of injury and even death to news personnel, their presence should be as unobtrusive as possible. Unmarked vehicles should be used for initial evaluation of events of this nature.

3. All news media should make every effort to assure that only seasoned reporters are sent to the scene of a disaster.
5. Every reporter and technician should be governed by the rules of good taste and common sense. The potential for inciting public disorders demands that competition be secondary to the cause of public safety.

This code was sent to newspapers, radio and television stations throughout the nation with the recommendation that they try to adopt similar procedures in cases of violence. In only a few cities were serious efforts made to implement it.

Police in Chicago and elsewhere have recognized that essential to any responsible and accurate treatment of civil disturbances is reasonable opportunity for newsmen to cover the event. General order number 64-11 issued by the Chicago Police Department states, "It is the policy of the Department to assist newspapers, radio, television and other news media to gather news information." In the Detroit riot of 1967, a prior conceived plan for handling the news media went quickly and efficiently into operation. There were numerous examples of officials taking extra measures to assist newsmen in covering various aspects of the disorders.

However, in Newark, when rioting broke out, newsmen wondered who were the more hostile—rioters or policemen. Charges by the press ranged from outright attack by the police to city indifference to the newsmen's needs in covering the disturbances. A Justice Department report of the Newark riots put out by the Community Relations Division criticized Newark police and city officials for hostility to the press.

The Justice Department report stated:

> The best guarantee for the most responsible handling of disorders by the news media should and must be the utilization by editors and newsmen of the soundest judgment. Each news medium ought to designate specific manpower and plan in advance for handling these situations. Moreover, each news manager ought to see that his personnel receive as much training as possible in advance. Secondly, the news media in every city should demand from city officials that advance procedures be spelled out for law enforcement and other officials working with the

press in times of civil disorders. The media should know who will be responsible in times of crises and how this responsibility will be carried out.

The National Advisory Commission on Civil Disorders, reacting to racial violence in Newark and Detroit, issued a number of recommendations on how the press should handle itself in such situations. The commission suggested that newspapers improve coordination with the police in reporting riot news. It suggested that discussions be held encompassing all ranks of the police, all levels of media employees and a cross section of city employees.

Despite these recommendations, few cities have established guidelines for media—police relations in riot-type situations. Martin S. Hayden, editor of the *Detroit News,* states that the problem with formal guidelines is "that they are inevitably based on yesterday's riots." He added, "riots vary greatly and our great fear is that we will set up formal guidelines which will prove more harmful by steering us in the wrong direction when we face a new situation."

Even in the absence of formal guidelines, most law enforcement agencies recognize the need for good relations with the media. Thomas Reddin, Los Angeles Chief of Police, said this in a message to his force in November, 1967:

> [The media representatives] are our only avenue for getting our message to the public, and they have served as salesmen, advertisers, defenders of our force. Occasionally, sometimes deservedly so, they serve as critics.
>
> Recent reports from other cities have indicated some conflict with the press at major incidents with comments that news people "were in the way."
>
> Hopefully, such an attitude is not present among members of this Department. The working press has a job to do, just as we have. And their job naturally puts them right beside the police—because that's where the news is being made. Just as we have police traditions of long standing, so does the press. They operate under a tradition that says, "The public has a right to know."
>
> Of all the professions, law enforcement has the greatest desire for the public "to know" what is happening with the world and clientele that we deal with. So the press is our "partner" . . .

Put another way—familiarity has bred cooperation, not contempt—and the press has certainly earned our lasting cooperation in return.

PreConvention Planning

The news media earnestly began planning their coverage of the Democratic National Convention after October 8, 1967, when Chicago was announced as the convention site. Actually the TV networks had begun to work out complex technical details months earlier. Naturally all media preferred that Republican and Democratic conventions be held in the same city, since it would have simplified their planning and reduced their costs. But not since 1952 had this occurred.

Almost from the outset, for reasons described earlier in this report, the press began making plans to cover Chicago as two stories—(1) the convention and (2) the announced demonstrations. To facilitate matters, many decided to assign some reporters and photographers to cover the political story and others to the demonstrations. The latter were frequently assigned to what became known as the "street team." In making their selections, assignment editors often tended to seek younger men who had had previous riot experience and who were "capable of keeping up with the action." Against the possibility that racial disturbances occurred, reportorial teams were integrated as far as possible.

As convention week drew near, the press sensed the increasing drama that was to occur in Chicago and intensified its plans for coverage. At the time, most news gathering organizations were assuming that in addition to the thousands of demonstrators, there could be trouble in Chicago's ghetto areas. The Community Relations Division of the U. S. Department of Justice warned a group of Washington reporters that convention week would be a scene of violence like they had never seen before. The *New York Times* planned to send a staff of 50, more than most state delegations would send to the convention. *Chicago's American* made plans for reporter Dwayne Okelpek to disguise himself as a volunteer and infiltrate first the SDS and later National Mobilization. Other news media planned to send young reporters in advance to establish a communications bridge with the young demonstrators. The *Chicago Tribune* hired off-duty Sheriff's police to guard its reporters and photographers.

In May, *The Washington Post,* based on its experience in the April riots, revised its guide for reporters, photographers and editors covering civil disorders. It was reviewed with all who were sent to Chicago. Some of the pertinent recommendations were:

1. *Press passes.* Every news employee should have both the official pass issued by the Police Press Pass Committee and the laminated orange pass issued by *The Washington Post.* The orange pass should be hung around the neck during coverage of a disorder, or clipped securely to a lapel, so as to ensure immediate identification by authorities. A hand darting into a pocket to pull out a pass may be misunderstood. It is helpful to have the police pass laminated and strung around the neck as additional identification.

7. *Tear Gas Protection.* Reporters traveling in areas that have been heavily gassed have encountered significant problems. Each of the cars is now being equipped (in the trunk) with small containers of oxygen, and with watersoaked cloths. The cloths, enclosed in plastic bags, should be used to sponge out eyes and remove the gas from the skin. The oxygen containers will give the opportunity to refresh the lungs. An additional small supply of oxygen containers will be kept in the radio room cabinet. This style of tear gas protection was decided upon since the Army-type of gas masks would tend to make reporters targets, and are quite uncomfortable to users who are not accustomed to their use.

9. *On-Street demeanor.* Reporters on the street should take great care not to make themselves conspicuous in any way. For instance, during the April rioting, a reporter-photographer team climbed to the roof of a building at one point so they could obtain a better location to watch troops run down a sniper. They realized in time that they themselves looked like snipers, perched on the rooftop. Those driving cars should stay within speed limits, so as not to

appear to be fleeing from an incident. Reporters and photographers should be alert to the possibility of their presence changing the character of a happening and should maintain their roles as far in the background as possible, while still being able to get the story. If they encounter a situation in which they feel their presence may have affected the behavior of participants, they should make sure that their editors are aware of this. Under no circumstances should we ask participants to "act out" situations for our cameras. Similarly special care should be used with flash equipment to avoid triggering a situation.

10. *Safety*. Reporters and photographers should not be heroes. When in danger, withdraw to safety. Your information will be of no value to the newspapers if you are unable to provide it.

16. *Sources of Information*. During a riot, accurate and adequate sources of information are hard to come by. Often, officials are just too busy to give out information they do have. In other times, they have their own reasons for refusing to cooperate with the media.

25. *Our role*. We have a difficult role to play, in normal times, and in time of disorder. There are many who would try to use us, to manipulate us in such a way as to advocate their own views, to the exclusion of others. We must try to be the carriers of the news, to exercise journalistic tenets of balance and fairness, and to make sure that we get the story right.

A memorandum written by Dr. Frank Stanton and distributed to the CBS staff reflects the policies of the networks in similar situations. Among other things, it instructs the staff to obey all police instructions instantly and without question.

More specific planning was also going forward. For example, the Associated Press Chicago Bureau Assistant Joe Dill provided Chicago and out-of-town AP people with specially designed armbands, made of heavy transparent plastic, which carried the words "Official Press." Drill felt this was safer than having reporters reach into their pockets for press credentials. He furnished AP staffers with the names, addresses and phone numbers of all hospitals within a 40-block-radius of the Amphitheatre, information where police planned to take prisoners and where demonstrator leaders were likely to be found. Dill also arranged extra phones reserved in private homes for AP use.

Bill Blair of the *Times* Washington bureau worked for months on advance preparations for his crews. He hired a fleet of cars with chauffeurs to transport the staff and provided a list of doctors. Others made similar plans.

Convention Arrangements

The dispute over convention credentials was the beginning of media irritation with convention arrangements; irritation which later contributed to a feeling of hostility between media representatives and Chicago. This hostility in turn, may have been reflected in the newsmen's attitudes and, again in turn, unquestionably played some part in the tenseness that developed between police and media representatives.

Convention-Pass Problem

The Democratic National Committe was informed initially that 2,000 media work passes would be needed in Chicago. These were for the workrooms only and for messengers, teletype operators and the like. Users would not clutter up the galleries or the floor. When the passes were handed out there were only 375 along with 25 parking stickers—not enough to meet the needs of more than the wire services and a couple of larger papers. A strong protest from the Standing Committee of the Congressional Press Gallery finally resulted in a total of 1,600 workroom passes and 200 parking stickers.

Credentials for the press platforms were equally reduced compared to past years. Many smaller papers just gave up trying. Some managed to get them through other connections.

But the real credentials squeeze was on floor passes. In 1964 the Republicans supplied 150; this year only 100. Four years ago the Democrats allotted 200; this year only 80.

The television networks ran into pass and security restrictions unprecedented for a convention. More than 1,100 reporters from station groups and individual stations had to share 45 floor passes. Bill Roberts of *Time-Life* and chairman of the Freedom of Information Committee of the Radio-TV News

Directors Association, complained formally to Democratic Party Chairman John Bailey, President Lyndon Johnson and Vice President Hubert Humphrey.

The arrangements committee of the convention made an eleventh hour announcement limiting the three major TV networks to one mobile camera each on the floor of the convention and seven floor passes each. Convention Executive Director John Criswell countered news media complaints by saying that the committee had a strong inclination to eliminate floor cameras entirely.

The number of floor passes was also compromised, since Criswell had originally prescribed two TV floor reporters only. This was ostensibly done in the belief that too much floor coverage would add to the congestion of people (delegates, security people and political guests) on the floor. But some newsmen charged that the convention committee wanted coverage to concentrate on the podium—a controlled show. Without floor passes, reporters felt they could not reach delegates to learn the real story of the moment.

Democratic officials tried to get editors to pool the services of reporters and photographers. When this was not agreed to, officials tried to limit representatives of any one publication to 20-minute turns on the convention floor. Finally, the publications that had obtained credentials were allowed one reporter and photographer each on the floor, without time limit. UPI audio was not granted a single pass, although the service is classified as a network.

Independent station reporters, seeking seats in the gallery, found their seats taken by persons other than members of the press. Floor passes for smaller stations were limited to 45 minutes. Some reporters complained of waits of up to 90 minutes for a pass. Others reported no problem. Complaints from both print and broadcast media about access to the floor were registered every day of the convention. TV networks got one break. They were given an additional six floor passes each for messengers. These were used by seasoned reporters—the most expensive "messengers" in the city.

As might be expected, the wire services survived better than anybody else. Both Bill Beale of the AP and H. L. Stevenson of UPI found the squeeze a hindrance but not an obstacle impossible to overcome. Offered at first only one floor pass at Chicago, the AP protested so vigorously it finally got four (compared with eight in 1964), which was hardly adequate for all its reporters and photographers, but enough to make do. Despite the complaints and maneuvering, the press generally was, if not pleased, at least satisfied with the number of credentials they received.

Strike Problems

Basic difficulties in providing coverage began weeks before the convention when a strike by the International Brotherhood of Electrical Workers (IBEW) against Illinois Bell Telephone Company held up most of the advance preparation of the convention hall facilities. The International Amphitheatre was the vital control and origination center for all media. Normally a minimum of ten weeks is required to install the complex cable systems, including microwave relay links for live remote coverage at the key hotels and elsewhere. The impasse almost forced the convention elsewhere.

Microwave antennas, which dotted hotel roofs in Miami Beach for the Republican convention and allowed live television coverage inside and outside of hotels, could not be installed in Chicago. Seemingly endless union jurisdictional disputes on top of the three-month old telephone strike left network news officials apparently convinced that there was virtually no chance of live pickups outside the convention hall and fearful that there might be none inside either.

The alternative in either case was reliance on video tape and film for television and on tape for radio. The procedure, according to network sources, could delay radio-TV transmissions for 20 to 30 minutes to an hour or more. Extent of the delay would depend not only on time needed to develop the film that was used—probably under 30 minutes—but also on transportation to the stations. Finally, a month before the convention was to start, a moratorium on the telephone strike was reached. The moratorium requested by city officials allowed IBEW volunteers to wire the Amphitheatre only. This blocked virtually all live coverage elsewhere.

CBS, ABC and NBC constructed studios and offices from the ground up at the Amphitheatre. CBS moved in with 22 vans and a fleet of trailers. Metromedia set up its own station on the convention floor, manned by two dozen newsmen. Westinghouse Broadcasting planned to bring a trailer complex to the convention hall to support the efforts of its radio and TV film teams. RKO took the trailer facility approach also; theirs would be served by a team of 15 reporters. A significant center that got little domestic notice was the trailer complex of the European Broadcasting Union. It planned and executed live color coverage, via satellite, around the world. The Voice of America provided live international radio coverage operating from a small studio next to the convention hall.

Another labor dispute involving film editors at CBS-owned WBBM-TV in Chicago boiled to the surface on Friday, August 2. The other local network editors supported the WBBM-TV editors. So not only was live coverage jeopardized, but now film coverage as well.

Telephones in the downtown area hotels, where the delegates were housed, were plentiful during pre-convention week. But as more and more delegates and newsmen arrived the situation became acute. Hotel switchboards were constantly overloaded. Incoming calls took as long as 15 minutes to complete during peak periods. It was common to find a bank of six pay telephones with as many as five covered with small signs: "Sorry, temporarily out of order." They were jammed by coins that had not been collected because of the strike. UPI reporters were told in an advance memorandum that a first item of business upon reaching their hotel was to look for "out of the way" pay telephones in corridors or on upper floors. "And keep a supply of dimes at all times," the memorandum said.

Two UPI reporters found two phones with "out of order" signs that actually were working. They completed their calls but police officers quickly stepped in and ordered them away with the explanation they had tagged the phones with the "out of order" sign to keep them available for the "private use of police."

The TV film editors union reached a settlement before the convention, but a taxi strike had started and it continued throughout convention week. AP hired five cars, a small bus, and college students as drivers. CBS rented buses and offered rides to any reporter or photographer in need. Others news media arranged their own transportation to fill the breach of the 30-minute run from downtown to the Amphitheatre. Two other problems were scarce hotel rooms and a wildcat strike by dissident bus drivers. ABC tried to solve the problem of getting from downtown Chicago to the convention hall by renting a pigpen as a landing site for its helicopter. But security precautions at the Amphitheatre prevented its usage.

A number of the major media made it a practice to check in with the Chicago Police Department in advance to get the "lay of the land." Among them were *Time, Life, Newsweek, New York Times, Philadelphia Evening Bulletin, Washington Post*. The meetings were cordial. But in response to a request for police cars to help carry newsmen and film back and forth to the Amphitheatre, as had been done in previous years at conventions, the police demurred, saying that all cars would be utilized during the week for police work.

The press and police meetings had stressed cooperation, with the police promising to assist press coverage, mobility and freedom, and the press reporters agreeing to obey the police. Editors generally told their people, "If the police say move, move!" On Wednesday, August 21, every member of the Chicago police force received the following message from Superintendent Conlisk:

> During the next week the eyes of the nation and the world will be on our city and our Department. . . .
> Within the next few days thousands of delegates, newsmen and visitors, will assemble here. Our responsibility is to assure them a safe and pleasant stay. We know what a magnificent city we have, what great people live here and what capable police officers we have. Largely by our conduct, these facts can be relayed to the rest of the world through the news media. To a substantial degree it will be on our actions that the rest of the world will judge Chicago and to some degree our nation itself. . . .
> We must continue to be constantly mindful of the welfare of others, never act officiously, and never permit personal feelings, prejudices, or animosities to influence our decisions or our actions.

On Thursday prior to the convention Superintendent Conlisk directed the following order which was read at all roll calls for the next three days:

> During and prior to the Democratic National Convention there will be many out-of-town newsmen in the city who will not have Chicago police press cards but will carry

other types of press credentials. These credentials whether issued by the Democratic National Committee News organizations or other police departments will serve to properly identify the bearers as newsmen.

Newsmen who seek to enter the area surrounding the International Amphitheatre bounded by Emerald, Ashland, Pershing and 47th Street, must possess credentials issued by the Democratic National Committee. At locations outside the International Amphitheatre security area, all press credentials issued by police departments, news organizations and the Democratic National Committee will be accepted as bona fide.

It is in the interest of the department and the City of Chicago that there be a harmonious relationship between department personnel and the news media representatives who will report the Democratic National Convention to the world.

But the press and Chicago officials, particularly the police, had disagreements just prior to the convention. The Chicago Fire Department inspected television equipment vans and ordered them re-wired, saying they did not conform to the Chicago code. Police imposed a parking ban on TV camera vans. They ordered TV cameras off sidewalk locations near the convention hotels and threatened, according to one TV technician on the scene, to take the cameras apart "piece by piece" if they weren't moved.

Frank Sullivan, a former Chicago newspaper reporter, and now director of Public Information for the police, denied the parking ban was aimed at stifling television coverage. "It is no device to block TV coverage," he said. "It is simply a matter of priority. The delegates need space to board buses and the delegates take priority over television." He said the police were working to locate nearby lots for television trucks. Some video tape trucks were already parked in a lot behind the Conrad Hilton Hotel. Cables were strung into the hotel to cameras, but no cameras were permitted on the sidewalk in front of the hotel or in open windows overlooking the front entrance. The police said that, because of security problems, cameras would not be allowed to shoot film out of hotel windows. In addition, no cameras would be allowed on the roof of the Amphitheatre.

At a meeting with top representatives of the TV industry

in Mayor Daley's office on Saturday noon a compromise was reached. The Mayor instructed a city street official to give them what they wanted "as long as security measures aren't violated." As it turned out, the TV representatives wanted live cameras in Grant Park across from the Hilton. The Mayor approved, but the Secret Service vetoed the plan.

They also wanted to construct a wooden TV platform at the southwest corner of Balbo Drive and Michigan Avenue in front of the Haymarket Lounge. This was rejected on the grounds that cameras at that location would tie up traffic. Finally it was decided to allow cameras in certain fixed positions.

The mounting list of television network problems led Richard S. Salant, CBS News president, to say that they formed "a pattern well beyond simple labor disputes, logistics and security problems."

Minor friction between police and press continued over the weekend before the convention opened. Overhead camera shots from "cherry picker" units were discouraged. Mobile news vans were told to move along from chosen locations. Between the restrictions created by the IBEW strike and the denial of parking to news vans on the street, live coverage other than at the Amphitheatre and at O'Hare Field (where President Johnson might arrive) had been pretty effectively barred, and newsmen felt more and more "squeezed" by the overwhelming security measures. They speculated among themselves, "Was the Democratic Party trying to minimize coverage of violence in the streets, should it occur?"

The stage was set. Press facilities were operational, and newsmen were ready to cover the many-sided convention story, determined to do so despite whatever problems arose.

By the time the convention began, there were over 6,000 newsmen in Chicago, 4,000 of them from out of town. The TV networks sent, by far, the largest contingents; NBC had over 750 in its Chicago Task Force, CBS about 740 and ABC about 500.

Credentials and Other Problems

> This official identification card is the property of the Chicago Police Department and may be revoked for just cause.

> The holder is entitled to pass Police and Fire Lines, whenever formed, subject to approval orders and directions of Police in charge of lines.
>
> —Official Chicago Press Card

A wide variety of press credentials were in use during the convention week. They took the form of press cards issued by police departments, news gathering organizations or the Democratic National Committee, as well as helmets marked "PRESS," armbands, network jackets, pins and bright pieces of cloth and cardboard worn on clothing. Press cars and trucks were marked in a number of ways. The job the police had in identifying bona fide newsmen was compounded by the fact that some demonstrators wore clothing and insignia with false press identifications. The variety of identification devices apparently confused some police. An Associated Press reporter was stopped Monday night by a policeman, but the officer's superior, noting the AP armband, ordered, "Let him through, he's Air Police!"

In June, Frank Sullivan, director of Public Information for the Chicago Police Department, requested sample copies of Democratic Committee press credentials. He offered to reproduce them in a bulletin for police officers so they might be given proper recognition throughout the city. Copies were never received; consequently the bulletin was never issued.

Some Chicago police involved in controlling demonstrators made five general complaints about the press:

1. That they persisted in using lights which blinded them—making them better targets for missiles thrown by demonstrators;
2. That they refused to obey police orders and requests;
3. That they interfered with police performing their duties;
4. That they staged incidents two ways—by faking stories and by attracting demonstrators by their presence;
5. That their mode of dress made them difficult to distinguish from the demonstrators.

A police officer says that police skirmish lines were frequently blinded by television camera lights. When the lights were on police, he says, the demonstrators threw missiles. The lights, according to him, were almost always trained on policemen. When the press turned their lights on the demonstrators, the patrolman says, the throwing of missiles stopped. Another patrolman commented that camermen disregarded police orders to turn the lights off.

There were police complaints that members of the press disobeyed orders to get behind the police skirmish line and that congregations of press members caused incidents by attracting demonstrators who followed them. Newsmen complained that they were kept behind police lines and that this inhibited their seeing, and getting pictures of, the action. Some Chicago newsmen said police had not followed this practice in other similar situations.

A police sergeant states that newsmen contributed to staged violence by photographing demonstrators who engaged policemen in conversation, then suddenly posed as if being assaulted. He also reports that some demonstrators wore fake bandages wrapped around their heads.

An Assistant U.S. Attorney reported that at 8:30 p.m. Sunday evening at Lincoln Park he saw a young man lying on the ground with two men in white coats kneeling beside him. A three-man TV crew wearing blue armbands and dark helmets filmed the scene. After the crew left, the man on the ground got up and walked away, as did the medics. The witness said the man did not appear to be injured and was wearing no bandages.

Senator Gale McGee of Wyoming tells about walking over to Grant Park with his wife and two grown children to see what was going on. Walking through a gang of hippies, they saw two girls, one playing a flute. Then they saw a TV camera team lead the girls over to a spot by the National Guard troops. When the cameras started to roll one of the girls cried, "Don't beat me! Don't beat me!"

Police-Media Confrontations

As has been documented, there were ample causes before and during the convention week for media-police hostility. The media representatives felt hampered and frustrated by the convention arrangement difficulties and the ever-present precautions. The police are never enthusiastic about the presence of newsmen in large-crowd situations and their irritation during the week grew for the reasons described above. Police emotions were heightened by their impression, as they listened to radio, watched TV and read newspapers, that the media coverage was anti-Chicago, anti-Mayor Daley and anti-Police.

There is further support for the police view. On August 30, 1968, a National Guard Colonel was interviewed by NBC in connection with the actions of the Guard and the Police Department in clearing the McCarthy staff suite in the Hilton. The Colonel spoke of the "great job" done by the Police Department. As he walked away, he heard one of the technicians or cameramen say to the announcer, 'You can't use that.' "

In this emotional climate, with police tempers already shortened by conflicts with demonstrators, it was perhaps inevitable that incidents of police-press violence would occur. They did. We shall only summarize these incidents under the name of the newsman involved. To avoid repetition, there is an "also see" page reference under each name to enable the reader to find the place in the text where the background and context of the incident appears.

(We have deleted from this report accounts of certain incidents involving newsmen because cases involving them are under active consideration by the United States Department of Justice. The incidents are, however, included in the statistics appearing at the end of this chapter.)

Saturday - Sunday

Lawrence Green
(Also see page 139)

The first instance of violence involving a member of the press in connection with the demonstrators took place Saturday night at about 11:45 p.m., at Clark Street opposite Menomonee Street on Chicago's Near North Side. *Chicago Daily News* reporter Lawrence Green came across some youthful demonstrators on the sidewalk who were shouting at police patrolling the street.

According to Green, he and other newsmen at the scene were ordered "in front" of the police lines and the police then charged the crowd on the sidewalk. Green said he was pushed, then stumbled, and another reporter fell on top of him. Green had his press credentials visible around his neck. As he scrambled to his feet, he said he held out his press card and yelled, "Press! Press! Press!" Nonetheless, a policeman came up to him and clubbed him on the back. Another police officer, seeing his credentials, said, "Fuck your press cards."

Late Sunday night, the Chicago police cleared Lincoln Park of demonstrators. The demonstrators left the park and flowed into the Old Town area of Chicago's North Side and later marched down to the Michigan Avenue bridge. In the process, several clashes with the press occurred.

Howard M. Berliant

(Also see page 157)

Free-lance photographer Howard M. Berliant was standing on the porch of an apartment at 1726 North Clark Street near Lincoln Park, at about 11:45 p.m. Berliant, a friend who lives at that address, and several other people were watching the clash of police and demonstrators. Berliant had two cameras but wore no press identification. As police approached the porch of the apartment building, a policeman said, "Get the man with the camera." He also ordered the group to "move on." Some protested that they lived there and retreated into the outer lobby of the apartment building.

Several police followed them into the lobby, and one of them clubbed Berliant on the head. Berliant was pulled into the inner lobby by his friend. When a policeman threatened with gestures to break the door, it was opened. The police entered the inner lobby, ignored Berliant's plea that they call an ambulance for him, turned and left. Berliant was driven to Henrotin Hospital by his friend. According to hospital records, he was treated for a two-inch laceration of the scalp, requiring seven stitches. The entire incident was observed by several residents of the building.

John Culhane

(Also see page 158)

Newsweek reporter John Culhane was on the east side of Clark Street shortly before midnight as police cleared Lincoln Park. He was accompanied by *Newsweek* trainee Monroe

Anderson, III. Culhane asked a policeman where it would be safe to stand and was sent across Clark Street, where he joined a group of reporters in front of the Herman Baptist Church. Police entered the churchyard and called to the reporters, "Walk to us." Culhane shouted, "Press, press." He was wearing a blue helmet, business suit, and press credentials hung around his neck. As the group of reporters left the churchyard, one of the police shouted that the reporters were from *Newsweek,* adding obscene words. The police advanced and Culhane was clubbed on the back of the head. Then, as he moved down the street, he said, another policeman hit him on the right thigh. Several reporters took refuge in a doorway. The police surrounded the doorway, shouting for them to come down. As they did, Culhane was hit again, causing a six-inch bruise on his leg.

James K. Davis and Charles H. Phillips
(Also see page 158)

Life magazine reporter James K. Davis and *Life* photographer Charles H. Phillips covered the clearing of Lincoln Park. At about 12:30 a.m., they became separated in the crowd moving to the west side of Clark Street near the LaSalle Street intersection. Phillips, wearing three cameras and press identification around his neck, says he was told to move onto the sidewalk by a policeman. Phillips replied, "Yes, sir." He started to move without further word when, he says, the policeman hit him a glancing blow on the side of the head with a club. Phillips was moving at the time and was not injured.

Meanwhile, Davis also had crossed Clark Street and stepped between two parked cars to avoid the melee of police and demonstrators. According to Davis, while an officer approached, he pointed to his two press cards on the front of his shirt. The officer, while passing, kicked Davis in the leg and then pulled Davis' legs out from under him. Davis fell, and the officer clubbed him on the shoulder. He crawled toward a space between the parked cars, and two or three other police clubbed him on the back before he retreated into the crowd. He then rejoined Phillips. His injuries—a sore right shoulder, aching back and cut ankle—did not, he felt, require hospital care.

It was about this time that a free-lance photographer was taking pictures of a girl in the same neighborhood who had been hit by a policeman. The police warned him to "Take your fucking camera and get the fuck out of here." Before he could do so, he was knocked to the ground and kicked.

Frederick DeVan
(Also see page 155)

Free-lance photographer Frederick DeVan III was on assignment for *Life* magazine. He reported being in Lincoln Park at about the same time as the above incidents occurred, wearing press passes on his shirt and a helmet marked "LIFE" front and rear. While with Larry Fleetwood of the *Manhattan Tribune* and another photographer, he saw Fleetwood photograph police loading someone into a van. He said about 15 police surrounded the photographers, left an opening at one end of the circle, and yelled to the photographers to run.

DeVan reported he ran along the edge of the park and stood between parked cars, to be out of the way, yet in position to photograph a police line moving a crowd past him. He said he heard someone shout, ". . . get the camera, get the photographer," and a policeman wearing neither badge nor name tag appeared on his right and broke his camera and two viewfinders with the butt of a shotgun.

Claude Lewis
(Also see page 158)

At about 12:40 a.m., Claude Lewis, a political reporter for the *Philadelphia Evening Bulletin,* was walking slowly down the west sidewalk along Clark Street, about one-half block north of the LaSalle Street extension. He said he was wearing convention credentials and a press card about his neck. He had seen police beating a girl and stopped to make notes. According to Lewis, an unidentified patrolman stepped forward from a police line along the curb saying, "Give me that god dam notebook you dirty bastard." Then the policeman grabbed the notebook, tossed it into the gutter, and clubbed Lewis four or five times on the head, knocking him to the ground. Lewis' blood covered his head and clothing. He was taken to Henrotin Hospital by two *New York Times* reporters. He was treated for a contusion and abrasions of the scalp. The next day, complaining of dizziness, he was readmitted into the hospital, where he was held under observation for 36 hours and then released.

James Peipert and Photographer

(Also see page 152)

A confrontation between police and about 300 demonstrators took place at the Michigan Avenue bridge. As the demonstrators and some members of the press moved onto the bridge, the police commander gave an order for everyone to clear the bridge.

An Associated Press reporter, James Peipert, and a photographer were on the bridge. The photographer was clubbed by a policeman on the left jaw and shoulder. His photographic equipment was broken.

Peipert was not displaying his press credentials, which were in his pocket. After the police ordered the clearing of the bridge, an officer who was chasing a demonstrator came up behind Peipert and struck him on the back of the head. He said he felt pressure on his back and then was struck three more times from behind by the policeman. Peipert said he identified himself as a reporter to the police commander, who sent the policeman back to the police lines but refused to let Peipert obtain the officer's name or number. The commander has denied this and Peipert has stated that he could have been mistaken for a demonstrator. (Pictures relating to this incident appear in the photographic section.)

Monday

On Monday, before the convention started, the first reports of beatings of newsmen began circulating, and articles and pictures appeared in the newspapers late Monday.

Police Superintendent James B. Conlisk ordered an investigation of the reports of clubbing of newsmen and photographers, and a general order was issued emphasizing the order of the previous week and calling for complete cooperation with newsmen:

> There have been reports during the past 24 hours of altercations between personnel of this department and repre-

> sentatives of the news media. It is imperative that such conflicts be averted. Visiting and local news media representatives are here to report to the world the events surrounding the Democratic National Convention. Press cards issued by Police Departments, news organizations and the Democratic National Committee will serve to identify the bearers as bona fide newsmen at all locations in the city except for the security area surrounding the International Amphitheatre.
>
> Despite any personal feelings of individuals, department personnel should avoid conflicts with newsmen. It is in the best interest of the department and the City of Chicago that there be a harmonious relationship between the news media representatives and our personnel.
>
> To be read and repeated at all roll calls daily through the Convention.

Despite these precautions, Monday, August 26, was to be one of the most hazardous days for newsmen. On Monday afternoon, a TV reporter was warned by two police detectives, separately, that "the word is being passed to get newsmen" and "be careful—the word is out to get newsmen."

Charles Pharris
(Also see page 160)

In the early afternoon, an ABC-TV crew assigned to cover the hippies and demonstrators went to Lincoln Park. The crew consisted of correspondent James Burns, cameraman Charles Pharris, electrician Jud Marvin and audio-man Walter James. All were neatly dressed, wearing suits, and had clearly visible press badges. They went to the park because Burns had heard a report that there would be self-defense exercises by the National Mobilization Committee To End War in Vietnam. They were the only crew there. Only a few police officers and demonstrators were present. About 2 p.m., the four were sitting on the grass when a squadrol moved into the park. A number of demonstrators gathered around the squadrol. The police jumped out and pulled Tom Hayden out of the crowd. Pharris, who was kneeling on the ground about 35 yards away, started to film the arrest. As he rose, a policeman rushed up behind him and clubbed the zoom lens of his camera, breaking it and knocking it to the ground. Then he struck Marvin on the back with his club, and ran away before any of the four could get a clear look at him.

Don Johnson
(Also see page 166)

Newsweek reporter Don Johnson (a Negro) was in Grant Park witnessing the General Logan statue incident at about 4 p.m. Johnson, like all *Newsweek* representatives, was wearing a blue helmet with a plastic face shield. He had his hotel pass and press credentials hanging around his neck. After a demonstrator was pulled off the statue, the police held their clubs with both hands at neck height and began clearing the hill, starting at the top. In the process, Johnson was pushed to the ground by a policeman. The reporter yelled "Press, press," but as the policeman walked by, he struck Johnson on the left knee with his baton. (A picture relating to this incident appears in the photographic section.)

Art Shay
(Also see page 166)

Art Shay, on assignment for *Time* magazine, was taking pictures of a policeman part way down the hill beating a teenage girl. He says a second policeman came up and also hit the girl, and then went after Shay, swinging a club at his head. Shay backed up, and the club landed on his right hand. Shay yelled, "Press" as the policeman approached. He says he was wearing press credentials around his neck and carried four cameras.

Brian D. Boyer
(Also see page 171)

Later that evening *Chicago Sun-Times* reporter Brian D. Boyer was covering the area of LaSalle and Wells Streets near Lincoln Park. He said that several police threatened him with "Just wait, we'll get you Boyer." (His paper thereafter stopped using his by-line on disturbance stories.) Boyer went to Division and Wells Streets later that evening, showed his press credentials and asked to cross a police line. He said a policeman replied he had never heard of press credentials, told him to "move the hell out" and shoved him with a nightstick. Boyer continued arguing to cross the police line. The policeman said "I'm sick of this shit" and arrested Boyer, who was taken away in a squadrol. He was locked up at the station but not charged. His newspaper obtained his release two hours later.

Jeff Lowenthal and Marv Kupfer

(Also see page 171)

A group of demonstrators left Lincoln Park at about 9 p.m., going to Wells Street, then south to Division Street. At about 9:30 p.m. a line of police moved west on Division Street ordering the demonstrators to turn back. *Newsweek* photographer Jeff Lowenthal took pictures of the action. He said he heard the police say, "Get the cameras" and "Beat the press." He believes his efforts attracted police to him. He was struck on the arms and shoulder while attempting to show police his press identification.

Newsweek reporter Marv Kupfer witnessed the Lowenthal incident. Kupfer was wearing *Newsweek* credentials (blue helmet, hotel and press credentials around his neck), when a policeman grabbed him by his lapels. Kupfer states that the policeman held onto him, saying, "Get out of here or I'll kill you." The policeman ripped his coat, Kupfer says. According to the policeman, he told Kupfer to move to the sidewalk and then began to push him. He states that Kupfer then said, "Don't put your filthy hands on me, you pig. This is a 50-dollar jacket."

Robert Black

(Also see page 171)

At 9:30 p.m., *Sun-Times* photographer Robert Black was also on Division Street, between Clark and LaSalle. He was dressed conservatively, and wore a press armband and a helmet labeled *Sun-Times*. A witness says Black was taking pictures of a demonstrator being beaten by police near a squadrol when a policeman noticed him. The officer walked over to him and struck him twice with his nightstick. He suffered a bruised lip, but did not require medical attention.

Delos Hall
(Also see page 171)

At about 10:30 p.m., CBS-TV cameraman Delos Hall was filming the demonstration on Division Street near Wells and LaSalle, shooting without artificial lights, behind three policemen. Ten or 12 other policemen ran up to Hall from behind as he continued taking pictures of the demonstrators. One officer hit Hall on the head with his club, opening a scalp wound. (It later required seven stitches at Passavant Hospital). Hall fell to one knee, but then got up to continue filming the police as they charged the demonstrators. He was jostled and threatened by policemen, but was not hit again. Hall was wearing no visible press identification but his movie camera was labeled "CBS NEWS" on both sides.

James Stricklin
(Also see page 171)

NBC-TV cameraman James Stricklin was at Wells and Division Streets at 10 p.m. when the police were dispersing demonstrators. He saw CBS cameraman Delos Hall being hit by policemen and filmed the incident. He says one of the participating officers turned and clubbed him in the mouth, chipping a tooth. Stricklin, who was wearing a 2″ x 3″ NBC News badge on his jacket, told the officer he was with NBC. He reports the officer said, "I don't care." While turning to leave he was jabbed in the kidney area with a club. The next day Stricklin entered Passavant Hospital to be checked for possible kidney damage and was there two days.

Paul Slade and Marshall Goldberg
(Also see pages 180-183)

Paris Match photographer Paul Slade saw a newspaper photographer pushed against a car and his camera and strobe light hit by the policeman. Slade rushed to film the incident. The same officer turned and swung at him. Slade dodged and ran back to the sidewalk. At that point, *Manhattan Tribune* photographer Marshall Goldberg appeared. He photographed the policeman involved and then turned and ran. He was clubbed on the back of the head, and his strobe light was also broken.

Fred T. Schnell
(Also see pages 180-183)

Photographer Fred T. Schnell, president of the American Society of Magazine Photographers and a free-lance photographer on assignment for *Time-Life*, was standing near Clark Street in Lincoln Park shortly after midnight. He was photographing a girl being dragged behind a police line toward a squadrol. According to Schnell, one of the police involved turned to him. Schnell held his credentials in his hand and said, "I'm a *Time-Life* photographer." The policeman knocked Schnell's strobe light and his press identification out of his hand. He clubbed Schnell on the back and shoulder and said, "I don't care who the hell you are—get out of the street."

Ken Regan
(Also see pages 180-183)

Ken Regan, a free-lance photographer on assignment for *Time*, went into Lincoln Park shortly after midnight with other newsmen, after hearing some commotion. He was carrying six Nikon cameras around his neck, plus a four-inch wide *Times* magazine press card. He also had pinned to his shirt a white card with red letters stating "Time-Life Convention Staff" and was wearing a blue helmet. Police fired tear gas into the area where Regan was working, and there was much confusion. Then, states Regan, "One policeman chased me out into the street and hit me on the head with his riot stick. I was wearing a helmet, however, and was just stunned."

"For the next hour, the police sporadically chased demonstrators and newsmen . . . away from the park," says Regan. "At one point, I ducked into a doorway. Two policemen found me there and chased me out. As I ran out, both hit me on the back with their sticks."

James Jones
(Also see pages 180-183)

James Jones, Detroit bureau chief of *Newsweek* magazine, was in Lincoln Park with *Newsweek* News Editor Hal Bruno at about 12:30 a.m. as police Task Force Units moved through the area. Jones and Bruno were standing on Clark Street after the park had been cleared. Jones, wearing business suit, blue helmet and press credentials, was crashed into and struck in the ribs by a large policeman. X-rays at Henrotin Hospital show Jones' ribs were not broken.

Later on, while Bruno was standing amidst a melee of police chasing demonstrators, a young hippie came running by and shouted, "Man the pigs have gone wild. They're not after us, they're after you."

P. Michael O'Sullivan

(Also see pages 180-183)

According to an account by *Business Week* staff photographer P. Michael O'Sullivan, he was wearing a press pass and three cameras around his neck while photographing five police beating a young person in Lincoln Park. At about 12:30 a.m., without warning, he was struck from behind by a policeman holding a shotgun, knocking him to the ground. Another policeman joined the first. Together they grabbed him, swore at him and searched his pockets, taking a roll of exposed film. They they started to grab his cameras, threatening to smash them. One policeman was heard to say, "Give us your film or I'll break your head."

O'Sullivan gave them all the film in his cameras. The two officers then pushed him out of the park toward Clark Street and a third policeman grabbed him. One of the first two police said, "That's ok, we've already taken care of him." The third policeman released O'Sullivan. The first two were not wearing identification and refused to give their names to the photographer.

Donald Jonjack

(Also see pages 180-183)

Sun Times reporter Donald Jonjack was at the edge of Lincoln Park near Clark and LaSalle Streets between midnight and 1 a.m. He was dressed in shirt, tie, coat and slacks. The police were making their third sweep of the park when three of them approached Jonjack and ordered him to leave. According to Jonjack, he told them he was a *Sun-Times* reporter and pointed to the press pass pinned to his left lapel.

He was struck or pushed from behind, fell to the ground, and was clubbed several times on the back. He says he suffered bruises and temporary paralysis of his left side. Jonjack was treated at Presbyterian-St. Luke's Hospital.

Stephen Northrup
(Also see pages 180-183)

Washington Post photographer Stephen Northrup was involved in two incidents with the police while taking pictures of action on the North Side early Tuesday morning. On both occasions Northrup was wearing full press identification.

The first incident occurred when police were chasing a group of demonstrators near Wells and Goethe. One of the policemen ran right into Northrup with his baton raised. He did not strike a blow but the force of the collision knocked Northrup to the ground with the officer on top of him. Both Northrup and a witness felt that the attack was deliberate. (See photograph in Monday night picture chronology.)

The second incident occurred shortly thereafter, when Northrup was taking a picture of police hitting a demonstrator on the ground. According to Northrup and a witness, police yelled: "Drop the camera," or "Get him, he's got a camera." Northrup tried to run, but two policemen grabbed him. He was struggling when a third policeman came up from behind and hit him on the head.

Northrup fell to the ground and curled up in an effort to protect his camera from the policemen's blows. As the policemen left, one of them took his strobe light, threw it into the gutter and stamped on it. Northrup was bandaged and taken to Henrotin Hospital by hippie "medics," where he was treated for a scalp laceration requiring five stitches. (Another picture of Northrup appears in the photographic section.)

Wallace W. McNamee
(Also see pages 180-183)

In response to a radio report of a disturbance, *Newsweek* photographer Wallace W. McNamee was at the intersection of Wells and Schiller Streets at 12:30 a.m. McNamee, wearing a business suit and with a camera, lighting equipment and press credentials around his neck, was about to photograph four policemen attacking a demonstrator when another policeman ran toward him with his nightstick raised. McNamee believes he yelled "Press" before the officer struck the flash unit on his camera. As McNamee moved away, he says, the officer hit him a glancing blow on his left forearm. Four steps further a second policeman clubbed the strobe light battery case off McNamee's shoulder.

Frank Hanes
(Also see pages 180-183)

Chicago's American photographer Frank Hanes reports that while he was photographing the incident above, he was hit on his helmet from the rear, then spun around and was maced by a policeman. He identified himself as a reporter with the *American*. The policeman replied, "I don't give a fuck who you are with." Hanes was wearing a press arm band.

Robert Jackson
(Also see pages 180-183)

Chicago's American reporter Robert Jackson was walking with police officer Stanley Robinson of Gang Intelligence at about 12:30 a.m. They were caught between a confrontation of demonstrators and police on Burton Place between LaSalle and Wells Streets. Both ran, Jackson going by himself, northbound, into an alley. Five steps into the alley, Jackson says, he was hit on the head from behind by a policeman's hand. Jackson went down. As he started to get up, he showed his press credentials. Jackson says the policeman replied, "That don't mean a damned thing to me, nigger," and clubbed him on his right shoulder, leg and on his buttocks and back. He quotes the policeman as saying, "Get your black ass out of the alley." No medical attention was required.

John Evans and Dan Morrill
(Also see pages 180-183)

Dan Morrill, a free-lance photographer without press identification, was standing in the front courtyard of his home at 155 West Burton Place at about 1 a.m. when four policemen came by. One of them asked Morrill, "What do you have the camera for?" Morrill said he was a photographer and that he lived there. The officer then maced him in the face.

Morrill went out on the sidewalk and shouted to the policemen that he wanted to take their picture. They turned toward him, and he took a flash photo. At this point, NBC-TV news cameraman John Evans came up. Evans carried tape recording equipment labeled "NBC."

The officers charged Morrill and struck him with their nightsticks. Morrill bent over to protect his camera; his head was bleeding. (The lacerations required 11 stitches.) John Evans came closer and held up his microphone to tape the exchange between Morrill and the police. This is the transcript:

Unidentified Voice:	Give me that.
Dan Morrill:	I'm sorry, I apologize, I apologize, please, I apologize.
Unidentified Voice:	Give me the film.
Dan Morrill:	I won't (?) give you the film.
John Evans:	Why do you want the film, officer?
Unidentified Voice:	None of your business.
John Evans:	You don't have to surrender that film, sir.
Dan Morrill:	No, I'll give it to him.
Unidentified Voice:	Thank you.
Unidentified Voice:	Mind your own business.
Unidentified Voice:	Who are you?
John Evans:	NBC News, who are you?

The taping ends at this point because a policeman ripped Evans' microphone off the recorder. Another clubbed Evans, knocking his helmet off. Police clubbed him again, causing a laceration on the right side of Evans' head, requiring six stitches. (A picture relating to this incident appears in the photographic section.)

Tuesday

At 5 a.m. *Newsweek* News Editor Hal Bruno dispatched the following telegram to Mayor Daley and Superintendent James Conlisk. The telegram was typical of others to follow.

Newsweek Magazine hereby informs you that for the

> second night in a row our reporters and photographers were subject to unprovoked attacks by Chicago policemen. Three of our men were injured and we have evidence that individual policemen are deliberately assaulting newsmen. We can identify men and units and are anxious to cooperate with you so that immediate measures can be taken to safeguard newsmen in the performance of their duty.

CBS News Vice President Bill Leonard demanded an "immediate and full investigation" of the attack on cameraman Delos Hall. Leonard also wanted assurance that "such unwarranted attacks" on CBS personnel would cease. Leonard concluded his telegram, "I understand that Deputy Police Superintendent Rochford will re-emphasize an earlier order calling for police cooperation with newsmen. I would presume in this connection, action will speak louder than words and that there will be no further incidents of this kind."

Elmer Lower, president of ABC News, wired Mayor Daley: "We wish to strongly protest the unprovoked attack on our ABC news cameraman Chuck Pharris and soundman Walter James by a city of Chicago officer. . . . The incident was unprovoked in that they neither disobeyed, nor ignored police instructions or warning. I would appreciate an explanation from your office as to the recent unfortunate incident and your assurance that there will be no recurrences."

Headlines in Chicago's morning newspapers said: "Accuse Cops in Beating of Newsmen" and "Police Continue to Beat Newsmen."

An assistant deputy superintendent of police promised a full investigation of the assaults on newsmen. "This situation is inexcusable," he said. "We must put a stop to this."

The Chicago Newspaper Guild said it would be "unsophisticated" to believe none of the policemen involved conspired with each other to wage planned mayhem on men serving as the public's eyes and ears. The Guild demanded that policemen attacking newsmen without provocation be arrested.

A police officer said, "The police who struck newsmen Monday made a mistake. It won't happen again." Another told his men not to interfere with newsmen performing their jobs. "If you arrest or harass a reporter or photographer, you had better be prepared to back that arrest with solid evidence the newsman had violated the law," he said.

Roy Fisher, editor of the *Chicago Daily News*, demanded a meeting between representatives of news media and police. Emmett Dedmon, editor of the *Chicago Sun-Times*, called Frank Sullivan, police press information officer, and insisted that a meeting be held that afternoon. He said he and ten other news executives wanted to meet with Superintendent Conlisk to discuss additional allegations. Conlisk agreed to meet with the press executives at 3:30 p.m. at police headquarters. Fisher, Dedmon, Lloyd Wendt, editor of the *Chicago's American*, and Thomas W. Moore, managing editor of the *Chicago Tribune*, along with various broadcast, magazine and wire service representatives, met with Conlisk.

Conlisk stated, "People who are involved in the park area have come here with the avowed purpose of disrupting the city and the convention. We are here to preclude the possibility of this happening. We are going to investigate deviations of individual members of the department." Dedmon asserted that the police had aimed their attack at the press. The Superintendent asked for identification of policemen allegedly involved. Hal Bruno, news editor of *Newsweek*, furnished some names and Fisher furnished some photos.

The editors were incensed not only by the beatings of their reporters and photographers but also by the failure of some policemen to display badges and other identification. Fisher observed that newsmen were attacked by policemen properly attired and officially identified, as well as by those who apparently removed badges and nameplates. Fisher further pointed out that it is a violation of the police manual for a policeman to strike any person on the head with a billy club or nightstick. Superintendent Conlisk said he had ordered a full investigation of the incidents.

Following the meeting, Conlisk cautioned commanders that any policeman who removed his badge or nameplate on duty would be disciplined. He also requested that officers of the rank of lieutenant serve as field press officers. The following order was issued by Conlisk:

> To all commanding officers: Information presented to me by my staff has indicated the need for special procedures to reinforce directions given during the past week regarding news media relations. The following procedures are to be promptly implemented:
>
> 1. Any uniformed members of this department who

improperly fail to wear the star or nameplate are subject to disciplinary action.

2. Officers of the rank of Lieutenant will be assigned as press officers in areas of potential disorders where news media representatives are in attendance. Beginning this date, Deputy Chiefs: Merlin J. Nygren, James Riordan, John E. Hartnett and Robert J. Lynskey, and Task Force Commander Richard Lionhood will assign at least one press officer in their area of responsibility.

   The primary function of the press officer will be to assure that the news representatives move freely to accomplish their assignment without interfering with police operations. News media representatives at the same time are not permitted to violate any law. Safeguards should be established and coordinated by the press officer to accomplish both objectives without conflict.

   Names of press officers shall be made readily available by the above-named personnel to representatives of the news media upon request.

3. No member of this department shall call upon any representative of the news media to give up any photographic or recording equipment, including films and tape recordings, without due process of law.

To be read at all roll calls, through Friday, August 30.

Mayor Daley, quoted by the press on the disorders, said: "We ask that newsmen follow the orders of the police too. There is no exception. . . . With all of this running and rushing of photographers, the Police Department deserves cooperation, too.

"These men [police] are working 12 hours a day. If they ask a newsman and a photographer to move, they should move as well as anyone else. How can they [the police] tell the difference [between a demonstrator and a newsman]?"

On Tuesday morning the *Chicago Sun-Times* published pictures (reproduced in the photographic section), depicting the beating by police of *Sun-Times* photographer Duane Hall on the Michigan Avenue Bridge. That night, Hall was told by a policeman: "You take my picture tonight and I'm going to get you." But there were no media injuries on Tuesday night, although there were numerous demonstrations and marches. Superintendent Conlisk's orders were effective.

* * *

Newsmen working the convention floor at the Amphitheatre were having problems of their own. Some delegates and alternates have reported that they were irked by the aggressiveness of TV and radio reporters. Security personnel complained that they had a difficult time clearing the aisles. Newsmen said they were shadowed by security forces, intent on keeping track of their conversations, including control room cue calls. (Security on the floor was under the supervision of the Democratic National Committee.)

Tuesday evening was the first time security forces came into violent conflict with a member of the press. CBS news correspondent Dan Rather was on the floor attempting to find out why a member of the Georgia delegation was being evicted. While he was on the air, TV viewers watched and heard Rather say, "Take your hands off me. Unless you intend to arrest me, don't push me, please. Take your hands off me unless you intend to arrest me." At this point, a security man in a blue suit delivered a short right to Rather's stomach. Rather grimaced and fell (or was pushed) to the floor. (The man who hit Rather was later identified as an employee of the convention's sergeant-at-arms.)

Moments later Rather said on television. "This is the kind of thing going on outside the hall. This is the first time we've had it happen inside the hall. I'm sorry to be out of breath, but somebody belted me in the stomach. . . ." Walter Cronkite replied, "I think we've got a bunch of thugs here, Dan. . . ."

Richard Salant, president of CBS News, promptly protested to the convention program director, demanding that security forces in the convention hall refrain from physically attacking the press. Soon after, the convention director sought out Rather and apologized. This incident and the continued "shadowing" of reporters on the floor and the problems of the streets prompted CBS president Frank Stanton to wire John Bailey, chairman of the Democratic National Committee the next day (Wednesday):

> Public confidence in our basic political processes is wholly dependent on full disclosure of all events surrounding them. Newsmen of all media must be free from threat,

harassment and assault in carrying out their duty to inform the American people. This has not been the case during the Democratic National Convention.

Wednesday

Wednesday morning, Chet Huntley on NBC radio broadcast nationally: "We in the calling of journalism have hesitated to talk about our problems in Chicago . . . but the hostility toward any kind of criticism, and the fear of telling how it is has become too much and it becomes our duty to speak out. . . . The significant part of all this is the undeniable manner in which Chicago police are going out of their way to injure newsmen, and prevent them from filming or gathering information on what is going on. The news profession in this city is now under assault by the Chicago Police."

On Wednesday night the violence broke out again.

Robert Kieckhefer
(Also see page 246)

Wednesday evening UPI reporter Robert Kieckhefer followed the Southern Christian Leadership Conference mule train south on Michigan Avenue to Balbo Drive. He was not wearing any press identification. At about 7:30 p.m. Kieckhefer was near the southernmost part of the crowd of demonstrators on the west side of Michigan Avenue. A police line blocked Michigan Avenue to the south of the demonstrators. Some police moved east on Balbo Drive and then turned south at Michigan, moving Kieckhefer and the crowd ahead of them against the police line. The police line prodded and shoved Kieckhefer and the crowd northward. As he turned to go north, Kieckhefer says, he was clubbed on the head from behind. The laceration required five stitches.

Caleb Orr
(Also see page 260)

As the police emerged from Balbo Drive, sweeping both north and south to break up the crowd, other newsmen were caught in the action. UPI writer Caleb Orr was on Balbo Drive with a group of demonstrators wedged against the

Hilton Hotel. Orr was wearing a large UPI white button, and other press credentials. A policeman walked around the group and sprayed them, including Orr, with mace. Orr states that he does not believe he was singled out.

Ed Kerins
(Also see page 260)

UPI staffman Ed Kerins was in front of the Hilton Hotel just after the police sweep from Balbo Drive. He was dressed in suit and tie, wore a large white UPI pin, a yellow press identification card on his shoulder, and carried a tape recorder labeled UPI. Kerins was in a "no man's land" between police and demonstrators when the police gave an order to move away from the area. He continued to interview a girl and tape her commentary on the conflict. A policeman walked over to him and sprayed mace in his face.

Winston S. Churchill II and James Auchincloss
(Also see page 264)

Winston S. Churchill II, reporting for the *London Evening News,* and James Auchincloss of NBC were standing together in front of the Hilton Hotel, apparently after the first police sweep, when, they report, they saw a plainclothes man catch a girl demonstrator and beat her with a blackjack. Both of them went to help the girl and asked the man to identify himself. They say that Auchincloss was hit twice by the plainclothes man as a result, and Churchill was knocked to the ground. As Churchill rose, a policeman on a three-wheel motorcycle charged them, pinning both of them against the hotel wall for a moment.

David A. Setter
(Also see page 260)

Washington Post reporter David A. Setter was also in the crowd at Balbo Drive and Michigan Avenue at about 8 p.m. He wore a business suit, shirt and tie, and carried press credentials around his neck. He reports that a black car bearing city identification attempted to drive through the intersection. The crowd booed and cried, "Shame, shame." The police pushed the crowd onto the sidewalk. Setter ended up in the front row and subsequently was maced by a policeman spraying into the crowd. Setter does not think the officer knew he was a reporter.

Lesley Sussman
(Also see page 260)

Part-time photographer Lesley Sussman, of the Lerner (Chicago neighborhood) Home Newspapers, was in the Hilton Hotel. He was dressed in a blue shirt and levis; wore very long hair and a heavy mustache. Shortly after 8 p.m., he started to leave the hotel, accompanied by a girlfriend. Seeing the troubled situation outside, they returned to wait in the lobby. Sussman pinned his press card onto his lapel as a precaution. He heard a loud noise (the windows of the Haymarket Lounge, located on the ground floor of the Hilton at the corner of Michigan and Balbo, had broken under the pressure of the crowd backed up against them by the police). Some of the crowd came through the window into the lobby. Sussman then saw five policemen enter from the lobby yelling, "Get 'em the hell out of here." Three of the officers grabbed Sussman, threw him down and began beating him. He went into a crouched position and yelled "Press." The policemen then began kicking him on the back. Sussman tried to crawl away and was finally picked up and taken to a suite by unidentified people from Senator McCarthy's headquarters. Sussman later was treated at Cook County Hospital for a laceration requiring stitches.

Paul Sequeira
(Also see page 274)

Chicago Daily News photographer Paul Sequeira was covering the demonstrations near the Hilton Hotel. After taking a picture of a police lieutenant spraying mace at people, he was himself maced by the same lieutenant. His camera blocked the spray, so he was not affected. (A picture relating to this incident appears in the photographic section.) A short while later Sequeira was following a police line moving north from the Hilton on Michigan Avenue. He wore a helmet marked "PRESS" and carried cameras around his neck. The police line turned west on Jackson Boulevard. As it did, Sequeira came upon the following scene:

A man in an army sergeant's uniform was beating a man

dressed in white (identified as Dr. Richard Scott, intern at Presbyterian-St. Luke's Hospital). Approximately 12 policemen were standing around watching. Sequeira began photographing the incident. At least two policemen approached him saying, "Get out of here." Sequeira showed his press card and shouted "Press." He was hit on the helmet, arm and back by police and forced to his knees. Suddenly his helmet was on the ground. Sequeira tried to use a camera to fend off the blows to his head. Then, he curled up in the street and the police stopped clubbing him. His right hand was broken and he had head injuries. Despite his injuries, Sequeira continued covering the demonstrations. He took another picture of the "sergeant" (later identified as an AWOL soldier, but not a sergeant) about 20 minutes later. When the man demanded the film and tried to kick him, Sequeira stopped a police car. The police took the sergeant into custody. Sequeira was treated for his injuries at Passavant Hospital later that night.

John Burnett

(Also see page 271)

UPI reporter John Burnett was also near the hotel at Harrison Street near Michigan Avenue earlier in the evening. He wore a UPI button, press identification around his neck, and was carrying a tape recorder marked UPI. While following a crowd down Harrison Street, Burnett turned and saw a policeman behind him with a raised nightstick. He called, "Press," but was clubbed to the ground anyway. Burnett says he was lifted to his feet moments later by a Negro policeman who had tears in his eyes. Burnett identified himself as a reporter, and the officer told him, "You know man, I didn't do this. One of the white cops did it. You know what? After this is all over, I'm quitting the force." Burnett is white.

Barton Silverman

(Also see page 264)

New York Times photographer Barton Silverman was arrested at about 9 p.m. near the Blackstone Hotel while photographing policemen arresting demonstrators. He was standing behind the policemen and was wearing and displaying press credentials when arrested. At first he was charged with interference in police actions, but was released at 11 p.m. without formal charge. (A picture related to this incident appears in the photographic section.)

David Nystrom, Jeff Blankfort and Thomas Corpora
(Also see page 264)

Chicago Tribune photographer David Nystrom was arrested at about 9:15 p.m. while standing behind a barricade in the same general area. A police commander had told him it was all right to stand there, out of the way. He showed press credentials at the time of arrest. Nystrom had been photographing an incident involving *Ramparts* magazine photographer Jeff Blankfort, who was on the east side of Michigan Avenue near the Blackstone Hotel photographing demonstrators. (A picture relating to this incident appears in the photographic section.)

At about 9:15 p.m., a police captain and a sergeant approached Blankfort. He took off the gas mask he was wearing and showed the police his press credentials. Both officers began to club him on the head and shoulders. Then they took Blankfort to a police van and two other policemen started to beat him.

Nearby, UPI reporter Thomas Corpora showed a policeman his press card in order to get through a police line. When the officer swore at him, calling him a "Jagoff," Corpora asked the officer for his name. The policeman pushed him with his baton, whereupon Corpora repeated his request. Another policeman ordered the first officer to arrest Corpora.

All three newsmen were taken to the police station at 11th and State Streets and were released at about 11 p.m. without being charged.

These and other incidents prompted more protests. Thursday President Mel Brandt of the American Federation of Television and Radio Artists (AFTRA), sent a wire to Mayor Daley:

> I fully realize the pressures of your office in the matters of law and order at a time like this; however, these disgraceful storm trooper tactics can bring nothing but shame and discredit to the City of Chicago and specifically to your administration's handling of its affairs.

Several of our reporters were witnesses to police forcibly taking tape recordings and film away from television people.

A similar wire went to Vice President Humphrey.

Meanwhile, during the fracas in front of the Hilton, another CBS reporter got into difficulty on the convention floor. The case was to become one of the most widely publicized of the entire convention week.

CBS reporter and commentator Mike Wallace was forcibly removed from the convention floor at 8:30 p.m. by a uniformed policeman and a plainclothes man. Wallace was trying to reach Alex Rosenberg, New York delegate, who was being taken from the floor for a security check. There is disagreement as to exactly what happened, but it appears that in the congestion Wallace encountered a police commander and said, "You can't prevent me from doing my job—the press has a right to cover the story." Wallace shook his finger at the officer, touching his face. The officer punched Wallace on the chin. Wallace was threatened with arrest and taken to the police command post at the Amphitheatre. Both Mayor Daley and CBS News president Richard Salant appeared at the command post shortly thereafter; Wallace and the officer shook hands and agreed to forget the incident.

Thursday

On the *Today* show Thursday morning, Hugh Downs asked his NBC-TV viewers if there was any word to describe Chicago policemen other than "pigs!" One viewer who objected was Frank Sullivan, the beleaguered press officer for the Chicago police. "I was so incensed that I asked Superintendent Conlisk if it would be o.k. for me to hold a press conference," he said.

At 10:30 a.m., speaking extemporaneously before a large and stormy gathering of newsmen, Sullivan described demonstration leaders as communist revolutionaries "bent on the destruction of the United States. They are a pitiful handful. They have almost no support. But, by golly, they get the cooperation of the news media. They are built into something really big. . . . Let's get this thing into perspective." He charged news media with bias and poor judgment in criticizing the Chicago police.

"Gentlemen, the laws of the City of Chicago are going to be upheld. The people all over America . . . know that someday unless somebody holds the line somewhere, these mobs are going to roam through their streets, they're going to come into their town and they [the people] will want their police departments to stand firm and take the same action the Chicago Police Department took yesterday."

Sullivan admitted, "There were some policemen who swung more than they should have," but he again urged, "let's keep it in perspective." He also conceded there had been "officers who removed their stars and nameplates." The conference was called, he emphasized, "to correct much misinformation concerning the Police Department that has been given this past week."

Sullivan denied that there was any pattern of excessive force used by the policemen. "When LBJ said he wouldn't run again, these revolutionaries needed another target," Sullivan said. "This target is the number two politician in the country—Mayor Daley." He continued: "Apparently some media reporters are so fascinated with the trees that they can't see the forest.

"The whole background of the demonstrators' calculated plans to disrupt Chicago have been ignored. The drilling of demonstrators in formations calculated to break police lines, the demonstrators' own medical corps, the threats of demonstration leaders to ignite racial violence, have been duly reported in the press. The same groups who occupied Columbia University and tried to storm the Pentagon are leading this week's Chicago demonstrations. If the Grant Park demonstrators seized the Michigan Avenue hotels and burned and sacked them, what would these same commentators then be saying? Who would they hold responsible then? Could they guarantee that a runaway mob could not become violent and endanger lives and property? Could these critics warrant that some of the demonstrators don't possess credentials capable of such horrible actions?"

Meanwhile, William J. Farson, vice president of the American Newspaper Guild, protested the "unprovoked and brutal assaults upon members of the working press." He said the 35,000 members of the Guild felt that policemen who attacked newsmen should be "promptly identified and disciplined."

Chicago's Mayor Richard J. Daley held a press conference of his own late Thursday morning. He publicly criticized both the media and the protesters. Reading from a prepared statement, and giving no opportunity for questions, Mayor Daley placed much of the blame for the street disorders on the news media. He said the media set the stage for the disruptions by detailing the advance plans of the demonstrators. He also claimed that the efforts of law enforcement agencies were "distorted and twisted" in news accounts. The Mayor further charged that television was a "tool" used in plans for "calculated disruption and rioting."

He said:

> On behalf of the city of Chicago and its people and the Chicago Police Department I would like to issue this statement and I expect that in the sense of fair play that it will be given the same kind of distribution on press, radio and television as the mob of rioters was given yesterday.
>
> For weeks—months—the press, radio and television across the nation have revealed the tactics and strategy that was to be carried on in Chicago during the convention week by groups of terrorists.
>
> In the heat of emotion and riot some policemen may have overreacted but to judge the entire police force by the alleged action of a few, would be just as unfair as to judge our entire younger generation by the actions of this mob.

Also, on Thursday, a federal appellate judge, responding to the appeal of photographers O'Sullivan, Berliant, Morrill and Schnell, issued an injunction. The order restrained police from interfering "by force, violence or intimidation" with the constitutional rights of newsmen to cover public events.

That night, in an appearance with Walter Cronkite on CBS, Mayor Daley challenged the television networks to cover the more positive side of the police-demonstrator story, rather than merely the violent aftermath of each incident. He contended that the cameras never showed the police reasoning with the marchers or showing them where they could move freely or safely. Nor did TV ever tell about the policemen who were hurt, he said.

"I'd like them to show the 51 policemen injured, some of them severely," he said. "I've never seen on television a picture of a wounded policeman lying on the street, seeing them badly hurt. Is this the kind of color of the news we should get?" Mayor Daley also complained that some newsmen looked so much like protesters that the police could not tell them apart. "The police have been given instructions," he said, "but one must realize that in many instances—and we have pictures of them—they (newsmen) never identify themselves. They're in the crowd and many of them are hippies themselves in television and radio and everything else. They are a part of the movement and some of them are revolutionaries and they want these things to happen."

CBS News President Richard Salant said in response to Mayor Daley: "The pictures and sound of the Chicago Police Department in action speak for themselves—louder than any words of ours or any attempts by them to find a scapegoat."

A total of 49 newsmen are described in the above events as having been hit, maced, or arrested, apparently without reason, by the police. Forty-three were hit, three were maced and three were arrested. Of the newsmen involved, 22 were reporters, 23 were photographers and 4 were members of the TV crews.

In ten of these incidents, photographic or recording equipment was deliberately broken; in one, the police intentionally knocked a reporter's notebook out of his hand.

In over 40 instances, the newsman involved was clearly identifiable as such; that is, even aside from photographers carrying the identifying apparatus of their trade, newsmen wore helmets, carried visible press badges or press passes hanging around their necks. In only four situations do the facts indicate that the newsmen were so mixed in with the crowd that the police could have hit them under the mistaken apprehension that they were demonstrators.

Forty-five of the incidents occurred at night, four during the daytime. Fourteen of the newsmen were from Chicago and the balance were from out of town. The average age was about 31 years; 28 were in the 20 to 30 year age bracket; ten were from 31 to 35; seven were over 35. We do not know the ages of the other four.

Ten of the incidents took place on Saturday and Sunday.

The greatest number—25—occurred on Monday. None occurred on Tuesday (except for the Dan Rather incident at the Amphitheatre, which is not represented in the above statistics). On Wednesday, however, the violence resumed: there were 14 incidents.

There is evidence of a number of other instances of police-press violence. In 12 of these incidents, newsmen were struck by police batons; in three, their photographic equipment was damaged by police. There are not reported in this chapter either because they took place when the police were moving large crowds (making it possible that any injury to newsmen was accidental) or because we do not have enough information to warrant their inclusion in this report.

CONFLICT AND COMMUNION

At about midnight on Wednesday, August 28, a battalion of National Guardsmen stood shoulder to shoulder along the east side of Michigan Avenue. At Balbo Drive and 8th Street they closed off the avenue, thus forming a "U" in front of the Conrad Hilton Hotel. Within this cordon, Chicago police protected the hotel's main entrance.

The Guardsmen faced about 1,000 demonstrators gathered in Grant Park. The crowd milled listlessly, occasionally aroused to chanting or applause by speakers repeating demands made earlier in the week and proclaiming their distaste for the nomination of Hubert Humphrey.

Marshals with bullhorns entreated the crowd to "Stay together. Stay in the park. Sit down. We'll march tomorrow." Though some demonstrators taunted the Guardsmen, most gathered in small groups, some huddled around small fires kindled of newspaper, others singing, and still others bedded down in blankets or sleeping rolls. From time to time, a chant would get underway: "Dump the Hump!" or "If you support us, blink your lights." In response to the latter, some windows of the Hilton blinked a visual support. The entry in the police radio log reads: "0044: Conditions around Hilton Hotel—good."

The Candlelight March

Five miles away at the International Amphitheatre, a caucus was in session. More than 500 delegates and alternates, supporters of Senators McCarthy and McGovern, met to discuss their tactics after defeat. Led by Paul O'Dwyer, the New York senatorial candidate, the meeting included representatives from New York, California, Wisconsin, Minnesota and North Dakota. Among those attending were Richard Goodwin, speech writer for John Kennedy and Robert Kennedy and currently an advisor to McCarthy; William Ryan, congressman from New York; George Brown, congressman from California, the Reverend Richard Neuhaus, Episcopal minister from Brooklyn; and Donald Peterson, head of the Wisconsin delegation.

Delegates had seen on TV brief and extremely violent segments of the police-demonstrators melee at Michigan and Balbo, and intruding upon the discussion of political tactics were repeated suggestions that they in some way display their concern. A suggestion to hold a sit-in at the Amphitheatre drew little favor. But a proposal that bail money be collected for those arrested was approved, and approximately $2,500 was contributed by the delegates.

They decided to march past the home of Mayor Daley, on to the Conrad Hilton, and there conduct a silent vigil. After being advised by O'Dwyer "to march quietly and orderly," members of the caucus left the Amphitheatre to reassemble in the parking lot. A city legal aide was present at this time and told some of the delegates that they were planning a very long walk and tried to dissuade the delegates from marching past the Mayor's home. In the parking lot, it was decided to abandon that march and instead to take buses to Randolph Street and Michigan Avenue and from there march to the Conrad Hilton, carrying candles.

While O'Dwyer arranged for buses to take them to the central area, candles were distributed to members of the group. (It is not clear whether the candles were on hand because the vigil had been anticipated or because someone feared that the lights might be turned off.)

It was well past 1 a.m. when the first load of delegates arrived at the Michigan Avenue staging area. Since there were only three buses, two trips were necessary. O'Dwyer and the others who went in the first caravan waited more than an hour for the others to arrive at Randolph Street.

At the hotel, security force activity was routine. The police detail lining the east side of Michigan Avenue was relieved shortly after midnight by the National Guard, but police still controlled hotel entrances. Some demonstrators in the park shouted epithets at the police and Guard. Others tried to engage the troops in discussion about the Vietnam War, suggesting that Gaurdsmen lay down their weapons and join the crowd. Occasionally, the Guard lines which crossed Michigan Avenue at Balbo Drive and 8th Street were opened to allow returning busloads of delegates to disembark in front of the hotel. Some stink bombs had been ignited and their stench was fresh as delegates stepped off the buses.

At about 3:10 a.m., the delegates began their quiet march from Randolph Street south along Michigan Avenue to the Hilton. The march was orderly. At the head of the parade were O'Dwyer, Ryan, Goodwin and Brown. Behind them followed nearly 600 delegates, carrying their lighted candles in Pepsi Cola cups. Folk singer Theodore Bikel, a New York delegate, led them in song, as they paraded two or three abreast along the east sidewalk. Half a block north of Balbo some demonstrators left the park to join the delegates.

At 3:30 they arrived at Balbo Drive, where they were met by a police commander who asked, "Now what is it you want to do, gentlemen?" O'Dwyer replied that they wanted to walk past the demonstrators. The commander said, "We welcome you and hope you can keep it peaceful. We are here to protect lives and property. Keep it orderly and keep moving."

From the park a voice yelled, "The delegates are here." Cheers rang in response. Still in orderly ranks on the sidewalks the paraders crossed Balbo Drive and filed into the corridor formed by the sitting demonstrators and the standing Guardsmen.

From a bullhorn in the park someone declared, "Those candles mark the wake of the Democratic Party." Another called for bail money to free those arrested earlier. While a collection was made of the delegates, the demonstrators were told that the $2,500 already collected was in the hands of a lawyer at police headquarters. Another long and loud cheer rose from the park. Lights blinked in some windows of the hotel as the delegates filtered into the park to join the demonstrators in song: "Ain't Gwine To Study War No More" and "Black and White Together." Folk singer Peter Yarrow sang "Where Have All the Flowers Gone?"

Some delegates and other celebrities addressed the demonstrators. Clarence Jones, Negro alternate delegate from New York, said, "I heard you say, 'Now, not in four years.' But don't put us down. We intend to take the party. In four years those people sitting in the convention will be relics. The party belongs to the people, as the streets belong to the people."

The crowd took up the chant: "The streets belong to the people, the streets belong to the people." For the past hour the troops had stood in formation, ready for anything. Now they were ordered "at ease," and the men were visibly less tense.

Ellen McCarthy, the Senator's daughter, told the demonstrators, "I just came down to let you know I'm not going to give up fighting now. I'm with you. Daddy has been watching from the window up there and wanted me to thank you and the delegates here tonight." The crowd chanted "We want Gene."

Others who spoke to the crowd of demonstrators were Julian Bond, the Negro Georgia delegate; Monique Dzu, daughter of Truong Dinh Dzu, the imprisoned runner-up in the Vietnam presidential election; a soldier on leave from Vietnam; and author Norman Mailer, who asked that at least 200 delegates join in a march later in the day. Some pledged their support, but by this time most had gone back to their hotels.

Thursday Morning in the Park

At dawn on Thursday, the part of Grant Park across from the Hilton was a dreary mess. Where three days before had been grass, a field of litter was now strewn over near barren ground. Beer cans, bottles, sandwich wrappers, newspapers, dirty and rumpled. Here and there, demonstrators slept, singly or in groups, as disheveled as their surroundings.

At 6 a.m., the weary 122nd National Guard infantry unit was relieved from a vigil of its own. The 131st Infantry Battalion took over the "mission" of retaining the demonstrators east of Michigan Avenue. Aside from the National Guard and the police, not many in the area came to life before 9 a.m. The atmosphere has been described as "something like a bad hangover." Small groups of demonstrators hunched over improvised breakfasts. Some delegates and others left the hotel and walked the east sidewalk of Michigan, surveying the scene of Wednesday night's activity. Among them were Pierre Salinger, former senator and now a delegate from California, and members of the McCarthy staff.

Late in the morning, ten to 15 busloads of youths left Chicago to return to New York and California. The National Guard strength stationed along the east curb of Michigan Avenue had been reduced to one company. Other forces remained in nearby staging areas. Early morning traffic flowed on Michigan Avenue. About 175 demonstrators were assembled across from the Hilton, while a larger group collected east of the Illinois Central Railroad tracks, just north of the bandshell where leaders of the Yippies, National Mobilization, SDS and the Progressive Labor Party began regrouping ranks.

Though the overall conditions were described by the police as "pretty good," National Guard intelligence had learned by 10:30 a.m. that "dissidents were planning some kind of demonstration later in the day." Gas protection instruction was given to demonstrators in the park. Shortly after noon, a public address system had been set up across from the hotel and leaders of some of the demonstration groups—Tom Hayden, Rennie Davis, Jerry Rubin and David Dellinger—asked the crowd of about 2,000 to stay in the park and march to the Amphitheatre later in the day. In the street, police escorted a column of 200 people and their "Poor People's Campaign" mule trains past the Hilton. The street and sidewalks were jammed with noon-hour traffic and pedestrians.

By noon, police had set up manned barricades on the west sidewalk in front of the Conrad Hilton Hotel, leaving only a corridor on the outer half of the walk open to pedestrians.

A sociology student from Southern Illinois University acted as master of ceremonies in the park, although he describes most of the crowd as "the stringy, long-haired type I didn't care to be associated with." He goes on to say that "they were saying things like, 'We're going to have a revolution' and talking about Che Guevera; and their prime purpose was to get people who had been beaten the night before to speak."

Tom Hayden told the crowd, "We should be happy we came here, fought and survived. If we can survive here, we can survive in any city in the country." "When they injure us," he said, "we will be warriors. When they gas us, they will gas the rooms in their own hotels. And when they smash blood from our heads there will be blood from a lot of other heads."

Endicott Peabody, a delegate from Massachusetts and [illegible] former governor of that state, had been calling for "equal time." When he got it, Peabody addressed the group on the merits of the two-party system and received some heckl[illegible] but considerable applause. Julian Bond also received a [illegible] response from the crowd, which had grown to about 4,000. There were songs from Peter and Mary of the Peter, Paul and Mary singing group.

Sporadic incidents were reported at noon. A lawyer from Wenatchee, Washington saw a "hippie" spit on a policeman, who did not retaliate. Soon afterwards he saw seven or eight "hippies" open a shopping bag, apply bandages to their heads, and walk up Michigan Avenue shouting "police brutality."

Throughout the morning Guard strength at the Hilton had been one-half to one-third. At 1:30 p.m. the National Guard Action report described the mood of the crowd as "increasingly restless and progressively ugly." Troop strength was renewed to that of the night before. The crowd at this time was somewhat different from Wednesday's. More McCarthy supporters had joined and had brought people who had heard about the violence of Wednesday night or seen it on television.

For the most part, exchanges between the demonstrators and Guardsmen were verbal. One man addressed the troops as "Fucking draft dodgers, too chicken to serve your time in the regular Army." Though such taunts went on for about 20 minutes at a time, no response by the Guard was reported.

Delegates March Again

Early in the afternoon, the Wisconsin delegation caucused in its Bismarck Hotel headquarters and Chairman Donald Peterson discussed "taking a walk" later in the day to "establish whether citizens were free to walk the streets of Chicago."

Another caucus was held by the McCarthy supporters from the New York delegation to decide what course of action the group should take at the convention that evening. The Reverend Richard Neuhaus and Murray Kempton, another delegate and columnist for the *New York Post,* told of the promise, made during the candlelight meeting, to stand with the demonstrators Thursday evening.

By 4 p.m. conditions at the Hilton were becoming volatile. Police intelligence reported that Molotov cocktails were to be dispensed to the demonstrators. (None was seen or used.) Police stationed in front of the hotel had their hands full trying to keep the pedestrians who jammed the sidewalk moving. At the c… of 8th and Michigan, three bus drivers took a black flag … of the demonstrators and beat him up.

As they ran away one said, "Did you get that mother fucker?" Another replied, "I got the son of a bitch. Look at my hand." Police arrested the drivers and returned the flag to the youth.

Also at 4 p.m., the Wisconsin delegation began its "walk" from the Bismarck Hotel. The group, totalling about 500, included 30 members of the delegation, members of the clergy (including nuns) and other "straight" citizens of Chicago.

The "'walk" east on Randolph was peaceful and orderly. A number of sources say there was no solicitation of other delegates or demonstrators, though the After Action Report of the National Guard states: "Dissidents were invited by the Wisconsin delegates to conduct a march to the Amphitheatre, to be joined by delegates to the Democratic National Convention."

Whether invited or not, some demonstrators in Grant Park did learn of the procession, perhaps by radio, and joined the march.

The Wisconsin-led group went east on Randolph Street to State Street, at which point they turned south. Their conduct was mild and silent and they maintained orderly ranks on the sidewalk. At Monroe they turned east to Michigan, south to Adams Street and west to State Street, where they met hundreds of cheering young demonstrators, some of them shouting, "The streets belong to the people." This group, many in hippie attire, joined the end of the column of "suit and tie" walkers. Though they called out "Join us!" to police and groups along the way, they were orderly.

Robert Kritzik, a Wisconsin alternate delegate at large, went to the Conrad Hilton immediately after his state's caucus in the early afternoon, and came out accompanied by about 50 other delegates, all of them headed for the Bismarck. They were walking north on State Street when they met Peterson and his procession at Van Buren Street going south. The Kritzik group joined the main body of walkers, which by now was near 2,000. As the group passed police headquarters at 11th and State, policemen leaning out of the windows were invited to "Join us!"

Approaching 16th and State, the walkers encountered ten policemen who formed a line across the east sidewalk of State Street at a viaduct 100 feet north of the intersection. Donald Peterson asked the police if there was anything wrong with walking on the streets of Chicago. A patrolman answered,

"You can't go on. Those are orders." Four busloads of police arrived.

A discussion ensued over the police contention that the procession was a march and not a walk. Peterson said that he and the other delegates had decided to walk to the Amphitheatre and had not asked anyone to join in what might be construed as a march. He was told that the delegates could proceed to the Amphitheatre but the others would not be allowed to pass. Various avenues of persuasion were explored by Peterson, by the deputy police chiefs and by a city legal aide, but to no avail. Robert Kritzik, who was at the head of the group, says that police were courteous to the delegates at all times.

An Assistant United States Attorney reports overhearing a Negro demonstrator trying to organize a march around the police. When this failed, he said that he and his group would infiltrate the police line, round up the Blackstone Rangers and return. They didn't.

A delegate suggested that the group be allowed to march to White Sox Park or some other park area far from the Amphitheatre, where demonstrators might hold a rally and from which the delegates would continue to the convention site. The city legal aide said his orders were to allow no large group to go south of 16th Street.

Peterson used a police bullhorn to announce that the delegates were returning to the Bismarck Hotel and to ask that the others disperse. Some demonstrators cried out, "Don't leave us. They'll kill us." Others shouted, "No. We want to go on." Peterson said, "There's no reason to be histrionic. We don't want anyone to get hurt. We think we've served our purpose." The march was reversed.

Those at the rear of the procession, having heard that Dick Gregory and Senator McCarthy were speaking in front of the Hilton, began to break up and return to the Grant Park area. Others followed Peterson north on State Street, leaving about 100 of the clergy, laity, demonstrators and delegates facing the police and a company of the National Guard which had arrived.

Arnold Serwer, another Wisconsin delegate, prevailed upon the authorities to let the group advance as close as possible to the convention hall "so they can have something that could be called a victory." It was agreed the group could continue to 39th Street, if it remained orderly and on the sidewalk. This it did without incident, except for heckling from Negroes who lived in the neighborhoods through which the group had passed. The group dwindled as it walked.

Meanwhile Senator McCarthy crossed the cordons of police and Guardsmen in front of the Hilton and addressed a crowd of more than 2,000 persons in Grant Park. Calling the crowd "the government of the people in exile." He said, "I am going to keep the commitment that I made and I pledge that I will stay with the issues as long as I have a constituency, and it looks like I still have one. Work within the political system and you can help seize control of the Democratic Party in 1972."

After McCarthy spoke, approximately 500 people in the park gravitated to the east sidewalk of Michigan Avenue and joined a disorganized march that straggled south, led by a small group carrying a banner identifying them as ex-Peace Corps Volunteers. Abbie Hoffman was with them. At 16th Street, the marchers were met by 50 police officers lined across Michigan Avenue. This cordon was joined by one company of the National Guard 178th Infantry. The 33rd Brigade Commander also arrived on the scene at 5:30 p.m.

Before leaving the Hilton area, "A" Company of the 131st Infantry was ordered to advance on foot to blocking positions at the Illinois Central station at 11th and Michigan. They arrived in time to turn back some of the marchers, but approximately two-thirds of them reached 16th Street, where they faced police and Guardsmen with fixed bayonets. The marshals shouted back to the crowd, "For God's sake, don't push. You're pushing us into their bayonets."

The demonstrators, now led by Abbie Hoffman, were told to return to the park and to stay on the sidewalk, an order enforced by Guardsmen diagonally lined across Michigan at 12th Street. Some Negro demonstrators called the Negro troopers "sellouts." Others called the Guardsmen "killers." The group was back at the park by 6:30 p.m., in time to be invited—along with 3,000 others—to have a glass of beer with Dick Gregory at his home.

The Gregory March to 18th Street

By 6:30, about 3,000 persons were gathered in Grant Park. Included were demonstrators and many others who had decided to join the throng. The crowd around the Logan statue was packed tight, the hill covered with people. Late arrivals stood along the sidewalk at the fringe of the crowd. National Guardsmen formed a cordon along the south edge of the park from Michigan to the Illinois Central tracks, thereby encircling the demonstrators.

As master of ceremonies, Gregory introduced the Deputy Superintendent of Police. When some demonstrators shouted their opposition, Gregory called upon them to respect a man who had come to talk with them directly, which was what they had been asking for. They applauded. "Sometimes the law is not what I'd like," the deputy superintendent said. He then told them that the police would stop a mass march to the Amphitheatre, but that they would not be arrested if they stayed in the park.

In a later statement, he said police feared that the march would go into the ghetto areas and ignite a mass uprising.

An Assistant United States Attorney, having heard Gregory's invitation, passed through the Guard line and suggested that Gregory could keep the risk of violence to a minimum if he made his intentions known to General Dunn of the National Guard. Gregory agreed and the two passed through the Guard line to confer with the General.

Dunn said his orders were to stop any large group of demonstrators from going south of 18th Street and west of State Street, because the Secret Service had determined that a security risk would be present if those boundaries were violated. (The Secret Service denies giving any "orders" and states that the decision to stop the marchers was a joint decision in which police, National Guard and the Secret Service all concurred.) General Dunn recommended that Gregory lead his march south to 18th Street, west to State Street, and then north and back to the park. He added that he would attempt to have Secret Service agents and city officials at 18th Street and Michigan, where this route might be renegotiated. But unless and until such renegotiations took place, he was going to fulfill his orders. Gregory acknowledged that he understood the situation and returned to the crowd of demonstrators. General Dunn then drove to 18th Street to await the marchers. Secret Service and city officials were contacted so that they might have representatives there also.

Gregory told the demonstrators of his meeting with Dunn, but repeated his invitation to accompany him to his home, which lies well beyond the 18th Street boundary. Marshals with bullhorns began lining the people three abreast on the east sidewalk and the group, Gregory in the lead, headed south.

Two companies of the National Guard 131st Infantry accompanied the march in the street, stopping for the same stop lights, keeping the same pace. Along the route, marchers saw paddy wagons parked in side streets and small units of police stationed at regular intervals along Michigan Avenue.

Shortly after this march got underway, the Reverend Richard Neuhaus arrived with 26 fellow delegates and sympathizers. Gregory kept the march to a slow pace until the delegates could attain the lead. With Neuhaus were Murray Kempton, Harris Wofford, president of the State University of New York College at Old Westbury, and a delegate; and Tom Buckley, there as a reporter for the *New York Times*.

Noisy but orderly, the marchers approached 18th Street, where the intersection was blocked by a double line of Guardsmen, a personnel carrier with a 30mm gun atop, jeeps with protective "bird cages" over the cab and 6′ x 6′ barbed wire frames mounted on front. Behind this was a small contingent of police with two squadrols. A lieutenant colonel mounted a jeep and announced that the marchers had to go either west or back north. If they went very far west, however, they would find more troops blocking 18th and Wabash, prepared to turn them north again.

Michigan Avenue between 16th and 18th Streets was completely congested. TV vans, their lights focused on the waning crowd, mixed with the traffic, which had come to a virtual standstill. By 8:30 p.m. police had stopped southbound traffic at Roosevelt Road, and all available police vans were instructed to proceed to 18th and Michigan. Seven responded. A platoon from "C" Company 131st Infantry blocked off the west side of the intersection.

Gregory and Neuhaus advanced to negotiate with police and National Guard officials. The marchers remained fairly orderly along the sidewalk, their ranks extending back to 14th Street. Reverend Neuhaus was told that he and the other delegates were free to pass, one at a time, through the lines and proceed to the Amphitheatre. If they wished, police would provide transportation for them. But no one else could go south of 18th Street. Gregory told the officials that he was only taking some friends home with him.

During this time, Neuhaus was conferring with General

Dunn, who said again that, acting on general instructions of the Secret Service, he could let no one across 18th Street. He said anyone who crossed the line—including delegates—would be arrested. Gregory apprised the marchers of this development, advising those who did not want to be arrested to return to the park, and those who wished to face arrest to proceed into the "zone of arrest."

He was the first to do so, passing through the small space opened by the Guard, and led by police to a waiting van. He was followed by Thomas Frazier, a paraplegic delegate from Oklahoma. Police picked up his wheelchair and carefully put him into the van.

Frazier was followed by Neuhaus and other delegates. As more of the delegates moved forward to be arrested, so did the demonstrators behind them, resulting in a crush against the Guard line. By 9:30, after 79 arrests had been made, the Guard was ordered to close ranks. There were to be no more arrests because there were no more squadrols on hand.

A demonstrator called for a break through the line: "The authorities have broken their promise. They now say anyone who proceeds south to Dick Gregory's house will be arrested. Some have already been arrested. At this rate we'll be here for 20 years. On my signal let's push through and break these lines and go to Dick's house. All right, let's go!"

There was pressure on the Guard lines. Demonstrators in the rear urged those in front to keep moving. Some demanded to be arrested, shouting, "We'll walk to jail!" The troops were ordered to "use your rifle butts and get that crowd back!" Poking, pushing and clubbing with their rifles, the Guardsmen pushed the demonstrators about 50 feet back and were ordered to hold the line there. The demonstrators pressed forward.

A group of 100 came from the west on 18th Street and began pushing the Guards, who were ordered to push them west into an alley. Objects were being thrown from the rooftops and windows of buildings. Bottles were thrown at the Guard lines by demonstrators. Firecrackers were tossed. The glaring lights of the TV vans heightened the tumult. Marchers as far back as 14th Street were now in the street, trying to find out what was happening ahead.

The Guardsmen put on gas masks and CS was hurled into the crowd. The gas was heavy and unavoidable. There seemed to be no place of refuge for two blocks. Guardsmen advanced north, with rifle butts swinging. The demonstrators were running wildly in search of fresh air. Those who ran east or west of Michigan into vacant lots, hoping to reach an alley, were met by police and their nightsticks. Following "A" Company, 131st Infantry, which advanced on foot, came the barbed-wire-encaged jeeps. some of the 178th were left at 18th and Michigan to maintain a blockade. One gas station was overrun by demonstrators washing out their eyes with a water hose. Medics aided the marchers by squirting water from plastic ketchup bottles into their eyes.

At 16th Street, about 200 persons regrouped, sitting in the middle of Michigan Avenue. The Guard continued its sweeping action northward, using gas when necessary to keep the marchers moving. A brick was hurled at the Guardsmen and some persons yelled. They began to yell "Fuck Daley." More gas was fired into their midst. As they proceeded, the Guard fanned out into vacant lots to make sure none of the marchers remained behind their lines.

"C" Company of the 131st had mounted up at 18th and Michigan immediately after the first volley of gas to reinforce the sparse forces which had been left behind in front of the Hilton nearly four hours before. When the sweep reached 12th Street, most of the 178th detoured to advance and set up positions opposite the hotel.

The retreating marchers met a line of troops placed diagonally across 9th Street, funneling them into the park. They responded with curses, jeers, tossed firecrackers and tin cans. More gas was used and the demonstrators ran into the park. Guardsmen were lined five deep on the east side of Michigan Avenue across from the Hilton. A police helicopter flew back and forth along the ten-block route, its spotlight scanning the alleys east and west of the Avenue. By 10:30 nearly 2,000 of the marchers, including many "straight" people, had reassembled in the park. Four or five litter baskets became bonfires. More missiles were thrown at troopers, precipitating more volleys of gas. The crowd dispersed within the park, running mostly toward the Illinois Central tracks to the east. General Phipps spoke to the crowd and told them they could remain in the park overnight as long as they did not attempt to cross Michigan Avenue. Six of the barbed-wire jeeps were brought up and placed between parked cars along the east side of Michigan facing the persons in the park. Mayor Daley was hanged in effigy. Speechmaking was resumed.

Some of the crowd tried to settle down, with the stench of

gas hovering over them. Occasionally someone moved too quickly, stirring up the gas, and he was shouted down. The speakers again asked those in the hotel to show their support by blinking room lights, and some did. Guardmen were confronted by sporadic harassment and occasionally objects were thrown from the crowd. Police and Guardsmen made only one foray into the park, to take a microphone from one of the speakers. Benjamin Ortiz was arrested at Balbo and Michigan and was later indicted for prompting marchers to break the Guard lines.

The Right Reverend Edward Crowther, an Episcopal Bishop, had seen some of Wednesday's action on television in his Santa Barbara, California home. He says he felt that since Chicago looked like a battlefield, a "chaplain" might be useful; and on Thursday he decided to fly to Chicago to conduct a communion service for the demonstrators, the National Guardsmen, and the police. At three in the morning, in full ecclesiastical vestment, the Bishop appeared in the park and celebrated the Eucharist, using dinner rolls and wine obtained from an approving air stewardess on his flight. Between 300 and 500 demonstrators received communion.

Bishop Crowther also offered communion to the line of soldiers and had received the commanding officer's permission to do so. At least two of them wanted to receive it. But in each case as he tried to put the improvised wafer in the Guardsman's mouth, the Bishop was stopped at gunpoint by six men led by a sergeant, with pistol drawn and, at one point cocked. "Don't touch that man," the sergeant ordered.

The night passed quietly and the Final Action of the National Guard reads:

> Item: Actual count of dissident personnel in Grant Park as of 0600 30 Aug revealed that only 33 remained.
> Item: At 0800 hours Police Department requested that all troops be removed from street commitment. Situation under control.

Earlier in the evening there was a report that sharply illustrates some of the week's anxieties. At 9:20 p.m., just before the 18th and Michigan confrontation, the National Guard's duty officer log shows the following message:

> Request of [Brigadier General] Dunn; who ordered L-19's

[Guard observation plane of Piper Cub type] below restricted ceiling around Grant Park. L-19's near-collision with VP Humphrey's helicopter.

The reference to "VP Humphrey's helicopter" could only mean one of the Army helicopters which, as earlier noted, were assigned to the Secret Service. Actually, neither the Vice President nor any of the other candidates who were receiving Secret Service protection rode in any of these helicopters during the week.

The Incident in the McCarthy Suite

Early Friday morning there was a confrontation in the Conrad Hilton involving hotel employees, guests, police and National Guardsmen. The incident, which received nationwide publicity, was itself insignificant as compared to other violent events of the week.

What makes it important is that it happened after almost all other activity had died down, and that many of the persons involved were working members of a presidential candidate's staff.

As the convention week progressed, and their cause did not, many young McCarthy workers had become increasingly sympathetic to the demonstrators outside the Hilton. On Wednesday night they set up emergency first-aid rooms on the 15th floor and distributed torn sheets outside the hotel for use as bandages and emergency gas masks. (But a police officer who had been injured Wednesday by one of the thrown missiles reports that when he applied for first aid on the 15th floor he was turned away.) Their support for and collaboration with protestors were resented by both the hotel officials and the police. Hilton security officers tried to stop the sheet smuggling and police harassed the McCarthy workers as they entered the hotel, even after showing proper identification.

At 4 a.m. Colonel Robert E. Strupp of the Illinois National Guard took charge of operations outside the Hilton, where a number of objects, including ash trays, beer cans, a silver cream pitcher, and—mysteriously—a bag of military chemical irritant and a grenade with pin unpulled, had fallen from the hotel windows to the sidewalk below. Colonel Strupp directed observation teams set up to determine where they were coming from.

Teams were set up in four different positions, and by means of binoculars, rifle scopes and the naked eye they pinpointed a group of windows accurately enough to spot objects a second or two before they struck the pavement. Each of the four teams, reporting separately, described the same set of windows.

Once the windows had been located, the Hilton staff was asked to identify the rooms and, counting up from the clearly demarcated fifth floor, they established the windows as being in suite 1506-A. It occupies the eastern tip of the wing immediately north of the hotel's main entrance, with two windows facing east on Michigan Avenue. Registered in the names of economist John Kenneth Galbraith and two other McCarthy supporters, 1506-A had been used throughout the week as a staff working place and as a meeting and hospitality room for important visitors. (Other candidates had similar space in the Conrad Hilton and other hotels.) Colonel Strupp asked the police department to put an end to the dropping of objects.

The police captain in charge of police security within the hotel consulted with the hotel's night manager, who remembers dispatching the chief hotel security officer to see whether the registered guests were in fact occupying the suite. The hotel security officer does not recall either receiving or obeying the order. The night manager says the security officer returned with the information that the registrants were not in the room and that the hallways and elevator lobby on the 15th floor were crowded, upon which the night manager authorized the police to clear the room and the corridors.

Because of the reported crowd, a police captain decided to take extra police and a small Guard contingent. While he waited for them, a police lieutenant and the hotel security officer went upstairs, accompanied by two or three policemen. When they stepped out into the 15th floor elevator lobby at about 5:10 a.m., they saw about a dozen people, some of them playing bridge and singing. The singing, according to a McCarthy worker, was led by Phil Ochs, arrested previously in the Civic Center when a pig was presented as the "nominee" for President. One of the girls asked what the police were doing there. When they made no reply, she ran ahead of them, exclaiming, they say, "Jiggers—Here they come!"

They followed her through the open door of the room. The windows were open, with blinds all the way up, and draperies spread. A party had been in progress. On a table near the door were 14 liquor bottles, beer cans and mixes; under it a large carton was filled with empty beer cans. People were drinking, and most of the available surfaces held empty highball glasses. Some young women were lying on the couches and on the floor. There was only one ash tray in the room, and the floor was littered with cigarette butts. Hilton officials described the condition of the room as the worst they had ever seen.

The hotel security officer told everyone in the room that, since it was not registered in any of their names, they would all have to leave and the room be locked. Only one of the McCarthy people in the room admits having seen anything dropped from a window. The group protested that the hotel had no right to evict them, but when more police arrived they started to leave. As the last of them left the room the police captain and lieutenant heard shouting from the elevator lobby and they hurried out.

There is general agreement on what the shouting was about, but contradictory accounts of the details. A McCarthy supporter named John Warren was shoved into a card table by a policeman who wanted him to move faster. Warren lifted the table to strike the policeman, who hit him on the head with a nightstick, which split from the impact.

Warren says, and other McCarthy workers testify, that he picked up the table in anger, thought better of it and put it down, then was struck by the nightstick.

The officer maintains that Warren hit him with the table and that he struck in self-defense. A number of witnesses support this. Others maintain that Warren had at least started to swing the table at the officer.

While Warren was or was not swinging, George Yumich, another McCarthy worker, was trying to lead the group to the 23rd floor (where the Senator and key members of his team were staying) rather than to the main lobby as ordered. A hotel employee said they couldn't go up there because "Ninety per cent of these people don't work for McCarthy anyway." When Yumich argued the point, the Hilton employee turned to a policeman and said, "Get 'em out of here." The policeman, holding his baton in both hands, struck a blocking blow at Yumich, who was knocked to the floor and struck on the head and shoulders by two or three policemen, suffering a two-inch gash requiring five stitches.

The 15th floor elevator lobby atmosphere was one of confusion and even hysteria. Girls screamed and cried as police tried to herd them into Down elevators. Although police and hotel personnel had initially been well controlled and even polite, the second wave of policemen had apparently misunderstood their task and began to clear rooms unconnected with suite 1506-A and far back from the street. By about 5:30 a.m., some 40 or 50 people had been removed from 1506-A, the hallway, the elevator lobby and a number of other rooms and taken downstairs. Some left the building, others sat in the lobby.

A McCarthy advisor, Phillip Friedmann, came into the downstairs lobby to see what was going on. When he heard of the 15th floor activity he became enraged, calling the police, "Mother fucking pigs." According to Friedmann, a policeman set upon him and tried to pull him out of the group. Several girls screamed and began grabbing at the policeman. Other police officers intervened, Friedmann was released, and the police left, saying that they were on call if needed.

The officer says that he saw Friedmann reach into his trouser pocket and saw the outline of what he took to be a weapon. When he grabbed Friedmann's wrist, people began grabbing at him and at his revolver until other police came to his assistance and pulled him out.

Soon afterwards, Senator McCarthy arrived, comforted his followers, and suggested that they disperse in small groups and go their rooms, which they did.

Police and National Guard units report that after the closing of Suite 1506-A nothing more was thrown from the Hilton.

Friday—A Day of Departure

On Friday morning, several hundred demonstrators were in the park, and there were more speeches attacking the "establishment." By noon the crowd had grown again to nearly 1,000, many of whom were curious onlookers, including members of the convention assemblage about to leave Chicago. There were long and serious debates, but there was no physical conflict. A detail of police still guarded the Conrad Hilton Hotel. Throughout Thursday night and Friday, the demonstrators were leaving Grant Park to return home. The convention week was over.

SUPPLEMENT

In this supplement, because there has been considerable controversy about them, we have compiled statistical and other information relating to injuries, arrests and weapons.

INJURIES

It is impossible to be precise about the numbers of demonstrators and bystanders who were injured in the various incidents of violence that occurred during convention week. A number of persons did not report their injuries, in some cases because they were slight and, probably in other cases with respect to demonstrators, because they did not want to become involved with the authorities. More complete records are available for police injuries than for demonstrator and bystander injuries.

Police Injuries

According to official police department records, a total of 192 policemen reported injuries in disturbance areas during the Democratic National Convention. Forty-nine policemen were hospitalized.

More than three-fourths of the injuries were sustained on Wednesday, August 28. Many were caused when demonstrators threw objects at policemen. Flying objects caused 122 (63.5%) of the total injuries. Police reported being hit by bricks, rocks, bottles and glass. One policeman says he was injured by a garbage can lid.

Thirteen officers reported burns from unknown chemical substances hurled by demonstrators, 12 were injured making arrests, ten were kicked, and ten were injured attempting crowd control. Most injuries consisted of contusions or abrasions sustained from thrown objects or from skirmishes with demonstrators. Included were injuries ranging from fingernail scratches suffered in a skirmish to a fractured cheekbone sustained from a flying brick.

Of all listed injuries, 99 were reported in or near Grant Park. Fifty-nine policemen were injured near Balbo and Michigan. Thirty injuries were listed at the Grant Park bandshell, and 10 occurred in other areas of the park.

The reported police injuries are recapitulated as follows:

Location of Police Injuries

Location	Injuries	Percentage of Total
Balbo and Michigan	59	30.7%
Grant Park Bandshell	30	15.6%
Lincoln Park	24	12.5%
Michigan Avenue	21	10.9%
Hilton Hotel	19	9.9%
Near North Side	14	7.3%
Grant Park	10	5.2%
Loop	6	3.1%
Convention Hall	1	0.5%
Other	8	4.2%
	192	100%

Date of Police Injuries

Date	Injuries	Percentage of Total
August 25	2	1.0%
August 26	15	7.8%
August 27	13	6.8%
August 28	149	77.8%
August 29	8	4.1%
August 30	5	2.6%
	192	100.0%

Causes of Police Injuries

Injury		
Hit by thrown objects	122	63.5%
Eyes burned by unknown chemicals	13	6.8%
Injured making arrest	12	6.3%
Kicked	10	5.2%
Injured in crowd control	10	5.2%
Struck	6	3.1%
Assaulted by crowd	4	2.1%
Knocked to ground	4	2.1%
Human bites	4	2.1%
Assaulted leaving vehicle	2	1.0%
Eyes gouged	1	0.5%
Thrown in front of police van	1	0.5%
Struck by bus	1	0.5%
Stab wound	1	0.5%
Fingernail scratches	1	0.5%
	192	100.0%

Demonstrator Injuries

It is impossible to recapitulate demonstrator injuries because of the lack of records. We have turned to two sources—hospitals and information by the Medical Committee for Human Rights, a volunteer medical group. The Chicago chapter of MCHR was formed specifically to provide medical assistance to persons involved in civil rights demonstrations.

MCHR set up seven medical centers near Lincoln Park and Grant Park and manned them throughout the convention week. Additionally, mobile medical teams were utilized in the parks. The chapter was formed well in advance of convention week and its purpose and plans were explained to the police and other city officials. All MCHR personnel were identified by credentials, white lab coats and Red Cross arm bands.

It is quite possible that there is overlap between the two sources used for obtaining demonstrator injuries—hospitals and MCHR. Persons treated by the Medical Committee may have been subsequently admitted for hospital care.

The following table shows injuries by location obtained from hospital records. Not included in these figures are injuries such as sprained ankles, which could have been sustained independently of a violent confrontation. Also not included is treatment for after effects of tear gas and mace.

Demonstration Related Injuries
Reported by Chicago Area Hospitals

	Sun.	Mon.	Tues.	Wed.	Thurs.	Unkn.
Lincoln Park ...	9	11	—	5	4	—
Grant Park	—	1	—	28	6	—
18th & Michigan.	—	—	—	—	6	—
Misc. & Unknown	—	—	1	12	5	13
	—	—	—	—	—	—
TOTAL	9	12	1	45	21	13

Of the demonstrators hospitalized, 58 were from the Chicago area and 43 from more distant locations. The age breakdown of those hospitalized is as follows.

Age	Number
16-19	23
20-24	48
25-30	15
31-40	9
41-50	4
51 and over	2

The Medical Committee for Human Rights compiled from its records information on injured civilians. It concluded that about 425 persons were treated at the committee's seven medical facilities. In addition, it estimated that over 200 persons were treated on the spot by mobile medical teams and that over 400 persons were given first aid for tear gas or mace.

POLICE VEHICLES DAMAGED

Chicago Police Department vehicles incurred $15,176.36 in damages during the week of the Democratic National Convention. A total of 81 vehicles were damaged at an average cost of $187.36 per vehicle. Damage costs ranged from $17.53 to $478 with nearly half the vehicles needing between $100 and $199 in repairs.

Twenty-four windshields were broken and 17 cars were dented from stoning. Side windows were also broken, radio aerials snapped and paint splashed on the vehicles. Most of the damage took place near Grant and Lincoln Parks. Thirty cars were damaged in the Grant Park area and 39 in Lincoln Park or the North Side area adjacent to Lincoln Park.

WEAPONS

There have been some published accounts of the extent and variety of weapons used by demonstrators. These accounts report the use of rocks, bricks, sticks, empty and filled cans, bags of urine, feces and paint or ink, golf balls with nails impaled therein, knives, pieces of wood or shoes with imbedded razors, oven cleaner, acid, molotov cocktails and dart guns.

We have found no eyewitness evidence of the use of molotov cocktails or dart guns. We cannot conclude whether these weapons were or were not in the possession of any demonstrators. Nine persons arrested during convention week carried knives and guns. The other weapons listed above were, according to eyewitness accounts, used by some demonstrators.

The statements reviewed show extensive use by the demonstrators of rocks, bricks and sticks and very little use of the bags, golf balls with impaled nails or imbedded razors. There are only a few instances where statements refer to the use of chemicals such as acid or oven cleaner.

Two intelligence sources among the demonstrators advised the government that they did not observe anyone using aerosol spray cans nor did they observe anyone in possession of golf balls fitted with nails during the demonstrations. However, we do know that several of the latter were found on the streets, and there are a few eyewitness accounts of demonstrators using these weapons.

The Intelligence Division of the Chicago Police Department reported as follows on October 3, 1968 (the "he" referred to in the quotation is the Director of the Intelligence Division):

Prior to the Democratic National Convention (DNC), he was advised of rumors circulating that oven cleaner was being purchased for use against law enforcement officers. New $100.00 bills were being used for these purchases.

He had detectives under his supervision conduct a survey of stores selling these items to alert them to the possibility and determine if, in fact, there was any substance to these rumors. The survey did not locate any abnormal sales of caustic materials or oven cleaner and no purchase by new $100.00 bills. As a result of this initial survey, a number of store owners voluntarily removed these items from their shelves.

During the disturbances in connection with the DNC, reports were received that some of the demonstrators had equipped themselves with caustic sprays and golf balls fitted with nails. It was determined that this was not a large-scale arming by the demonstrators.

Another survey was conducted after the DNC in an extensive area which encompassed the districts surrounding Lincoln Park and congregating places of the demonstrators. This survey again did not develop any information to indicate unusual sales of caustic material or oven cleaner. No information was developed which indicated the use of $100.00 bills.

A review was made of all police department reports of arrests related to convention disturbances. None of the reports state that the individual arrested had in his possession caustic sprays, oven cleaner or golf balls fitted with nails.

A charge was also published that black widow spiders were used by demonstrators. The incident which gave rise to this published account is covered in the following federal government investigative report given by a special agent for a railroad. The incident occurred on September 1, 1968 (the Sunday following the close of the convention):

While heading east on Kinzie Street just east of Green Street, driving an unmarked company automobile, I was stopped by an unknown white male.

Upon my stopping, this individual stated that he just wanted to talk to someone and that he had just gotten rid of 25 to 26 "pets." When I asked what kind of pets, he answered "black widow spiders." I then asked him how he got rid of these spiders and he stated he had thrown them two or three at a time into different squad cars in the Grant Park area.

The individual then reached into an inside coat pocket and took out a bottle about three inches high with a perforated lid and threw his bottle into the front seat of my car and said "Here, the others weren't in bottles." The individual then ran off and I haven't seen him since.

I then returned to the depot: a fellow employee advised the spider in the bottle was a black widow. I then called the Police Department at around midnight on September 1, and an officer [of the] Chicago Police Department arrived to pick up the bottle.

The spider was identified by the insect curator of the Field Museum as a black widow spider.

Thereafter, on September 16 and September 26, a police captain advised that he had been unable to develop any information which would indicate that black widow spiders were found in any of the Chicago police squad cars. He said that he had set up contact with police department personnel servicing the cars and that there was no report of any live or dead black widow spiders found in the cars. [The captain] reiterated his previous opinion that the actions of the unknown subject in this case were those of a "nut," and that he did not believe that any black widow spiders were thrown into police cars.

The Police Crime Laboratory reported on September 10 that there were no further developments in the alleged black widow spider throwing incident and that during the course of other investigations conducted by their men they had not heard anyone mention finding black widow spiders.

ARRESTS

Chicago policemen arrested 668 persons in connection with disturbances during the convention week. The majority of those arrested were under 26 years of age, male, residents of Metropolitan Chicago, and had no previous arrest record. Two-thirds of the arrests were made of persons ranging in age from 18 to 25, with those 17 and under comprising 9.6 per cent of the total. Men outnumbered women almost eight to one, accounting for 592 of the arrests.

Although 52.4 per cent of those arrested lived within 40 miles of Chicago, police records listed persons from 36 states, the District of Columbia and five foreign countries. Illinois led the list with 364 followed by New York (84), Michigan (35), New Jersey (17), Wisconsin (16), Ohio (15) and Pennsylvania (10).

Forty-three per cent of the arrested were employed, 32.6 per cent were students, and 19.9 per cent were unemployed. The employed represented a wide range of occupations including teachers, social workers, ministers, factory laborers and journalists. Out of 668 persons arrested, 118 had previous arrest records—39 of these persons were previously arrested solely for misdemeanors arising from "protest-type" activities. More than four-fifths of the previous arrests were for misdemeanors with felonies (11.1%) and narcotics arrests (7.0%) accounting for the rest. Over 40 types of illegal acts were involved in the previous arrests, ranging from "rogue and vagabond" through "vagrant roamer" to counterfeiting and larceny. All traffic offenses, even including driving while intoxicated and reckless driving, were omitted from the arrest data.

Fifty-two persons were in possession of weapons when arrested. The weapons consisted primarily of rocks and bricks, but police also arrested nine demonstrators with knives, two with guns, two with machetes and one with a bayonet.

Age of Persons Arrested

Age	Arrested	Percentage of Total
17 and Under	64	9.6%
18-20	221	33.1%
21-25	221	33.1%
26 and Over	157	23.5%
Not Reported	5	0.8%
	668	100.0%

Occupation of Persons Arrested

Occupation	Arrested	Percentage of Total
Employed	287	43.0%
Student	218	32.6%
Unemployed	133	19.9%
Not Reported	30	4.5%
	668	100.0%

Residence of Persons Arrested

Residence	Arrested	Percentage of Total
Chicago City	276	41.4%
Out of State	291	43.5%
Chicago Suburban	74	11.1%
Other Illinois	14	2.0%
Not Reported	13	1.9%
	668	100.0%

Persons with Previous Arrests

Sex	Age 17 and Under	Age 18-20	Age 21-25	Age 26 and Over	Total
Male	4	26	45	35	110
Female	0	2	4	2	8
	4	28	49	37	118

Nature of Previous Arrests

Charge	Arrests	Percentage of Total
Felony	39	11.5%
Misdemeanor	277	81.5%
Narcotics	24	7.1%
	340	100.0%

MEMBERS OF THE NATIONAL COMMISSION ON THE CAUSES AND PREVENTION OF VIOLENCE

MILTON S. EISENHOWER, Chairman

SENATOR PHILLIP A. HART
Democrat of Michigan

SENATOR ROMAN L. HRUSKA
Republican of Nebraska

REPRESENTATIVE HALE BOGGS OF LOUISIANA
House Democratic whip

REPRESENTATIVE WILLIAM M. MCCULLOCH OF OHIO
ranking Republican on the House Judiciary Committee

THE MOST REVEREND TERRENCE J. COOKE
Archbishop of the Roman Catholic diocese of New York

PATRICIA HARRIS
former Ambassador to Luxembourg,
now a professor of law at Howard University

JUDGE A. LEON HIGGINBOTHAM
a Federal District judge in Philadelphia

ERIC HOFFER
sometimes described as a
"longshoreman-philosopher"

ALBERT E. JENNER JR.
a Chicago lawyer who served on the legal staff
of the Warren Commission

DR. W. WALTER MENNINGER
of the Menninger Clinic

CHIEF JUDGE ERNEST WILLIAM MACFARLAND
of the Arizona Supreme Court

LEON JAWORSKI
senior partner in a Houston law firm

THE STUDY TEAM STAFF

DIRECTOR: Daniel Walker

ASSISTANT DIRECTOR
Victor R. deGrazia

Assistant:

Patricia Oakley

ASSISTANT DIRECTOR
Harvey N. Johnson, Jr.

Assistants:

Elliott W. Anderson
Albert Wright
Kenneth R. Murphy

EDITORIAL DIRECTOR
Ralph Caplan

Assistants:

Dorothy Anderson
Thomas Koerner
Jerry Morton

Subject Matter Teams

Prelude

William R. Carney, *Director*

Gene A. Cimeley
Herman I. Desenhaus
Thomas D. Kitch
John T. Moran, Jr.
Richard J. Troy
B. Raoul Yochim

Assistants:

Muriel H. Altschuler
Edith F. Coleman
Gene R. Davis
Donald L. Gimbel
Gerald G. Golliet
Francis G. Lim, Jr.
Kenneth Mitchell
Joseph P. Mundi
Anne L. Schwab
George C. Stoll
Michael S. Swygert

Security Measures

Verne H. Evans, *Director*

Cameron Carley
Patrick Filter
James G. Speer
Gary Thorsen

Assistants:

Veronica Coyne
Mary Jane Maples
James Norris
Carolyn Wangelin

Lincoln Park

Wesley S. Walton, *Director*

Edward S. Berger
James A. Flanery
Patrick D. Halligan

Assistants:

Michael E. Hawkins
Joel Kaplan
Louis P. Vitullo

Grant Park

Hamilton Smith and
Frank M. Covey, Jr.,
Co-Directors

Theodore A. Breckel
Lawrence M. Freedman
Kenneth E. Marcus
Daniel M. Morris
Charles Remsberg
Rudolf G. Schade, Jr.
Judy A. Underwood

Media

Michael C. Johnson and
John A. Koten, *Co-Directors*

William E. Beringer
Geoffrey Davis
Ronald Grais
Mike Lerner
Edward Small
Robert Storozuk
Sydney Weisman

Assistants:

Joseph Feldman
William Lempke
Nancy Lynn

Isolated Incidents of Violence

James Keffler, *Director*

Robert Berendt
William B. Sawtell
David S. Tatel

Assistants:

Arthur Benson
James F. Devitt
James A. Maland
Marietta Marcin
Walter E. Young

Events of Thursday and Friday

James Barr and
Gary Nelson, *Co-Directors*

Carroll Cihlar
Richard Cochran
Hugh Griffin
John Pendergast

Assistant to the Director

Mary Parrilli

Administrative Assistant

Carla Z. Pierson

Visual Aid Co-ordinators

Paul Levy
Leslie R. Korshak

Interview Co-ordinator

Deborah Long

Typing Co-ordinator

Kathy Raad

Librarian

Judy Pedersen

Staff Assistants

Adrian Foster
Shirley Johnson
J. Vernon Lloyd
Gary Pollack

Accountants

James Raim
Richard Zeder
Julia Odishoo

Organization Consultants

Booz, Allen & Hamilton, Inc.
Maurice J. Walker
Daniel T. Carroll
Lynn F. Chandler

Design Consultants

Latham-Tyler-Jensen Inc.
Charles G. MacMurray
Howard W. Knight

Office Staff

Patricia A. Avants
Beverly J. Berni
Judith K. Kolina
Judith R. Moseley
Lynne M. Wright
Mary Ann Fahrberger

A number of persons provided part time assistance. This included 21 interviewers in Chicago, 35 persons who took statements from witnesses in over 30 cities outside of Chicago and 51 persons who provided part time assistance in the administrative office.